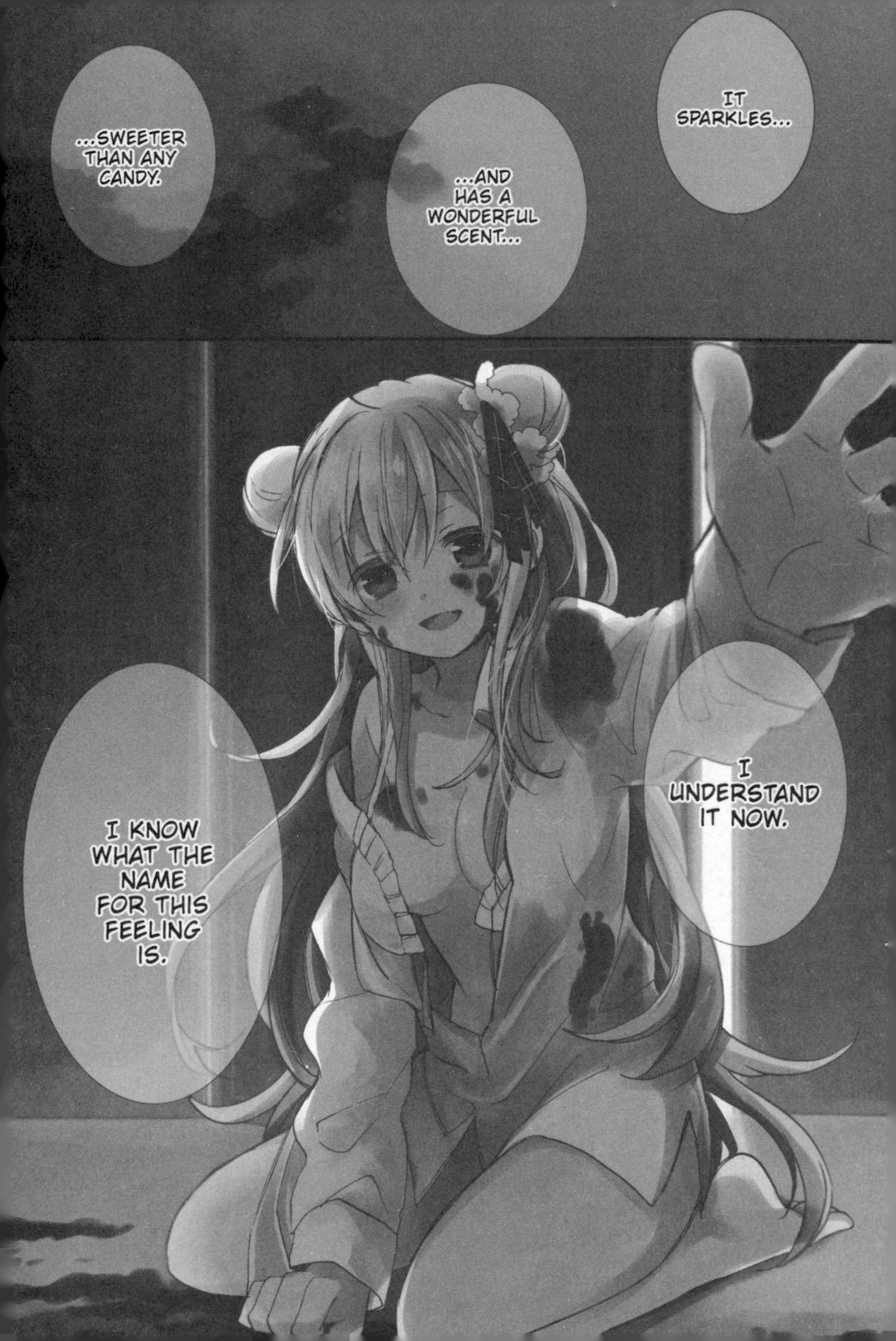
IT SPARKLES...
...AND HAS A WONDERFUL SCENT...
...SWEETER THAN ANY CANDY.
I UNDERSTAND IT NOW.
I KNOW WHAT THE NAME FOR THIS FEELING IS.

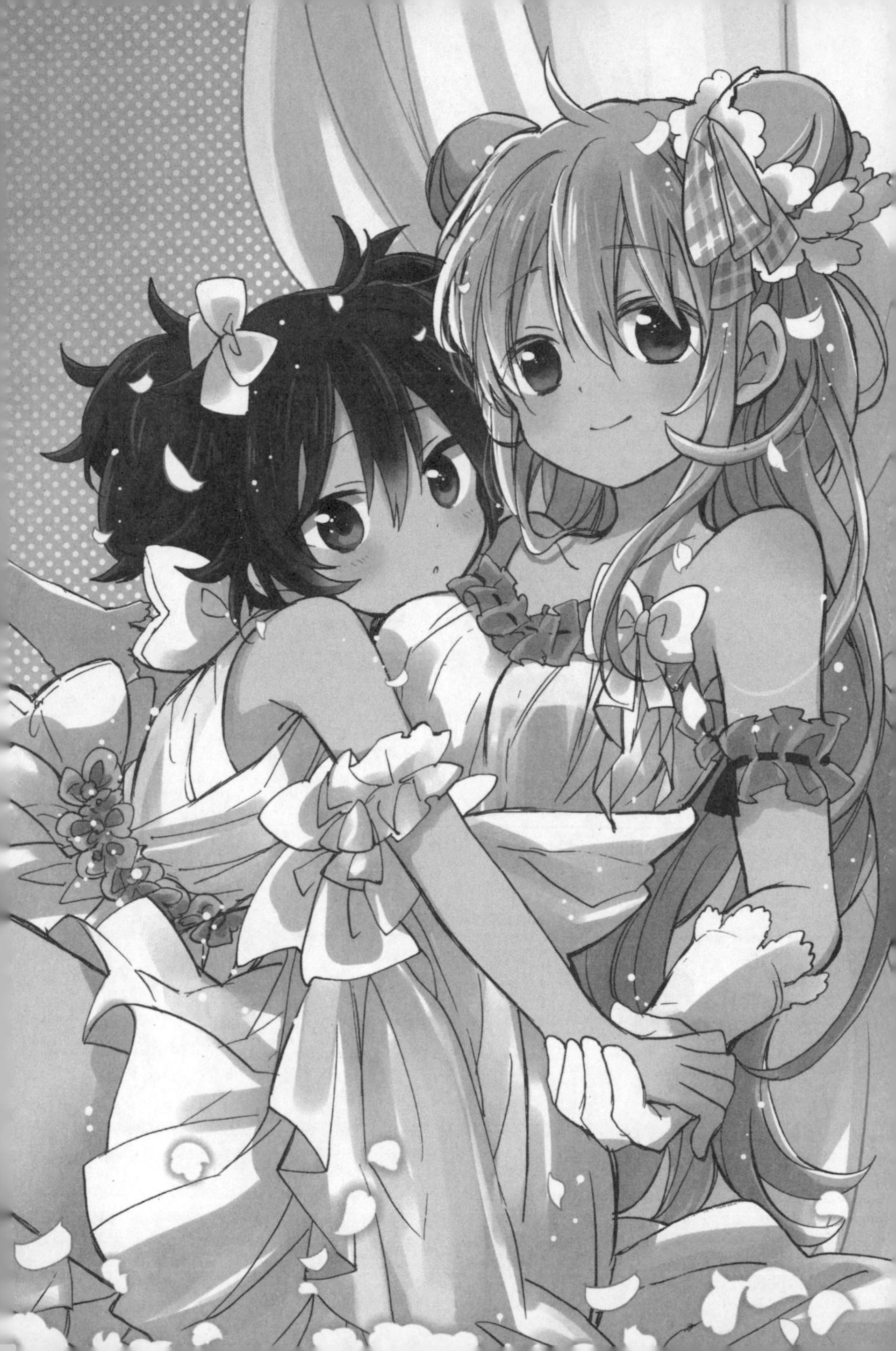

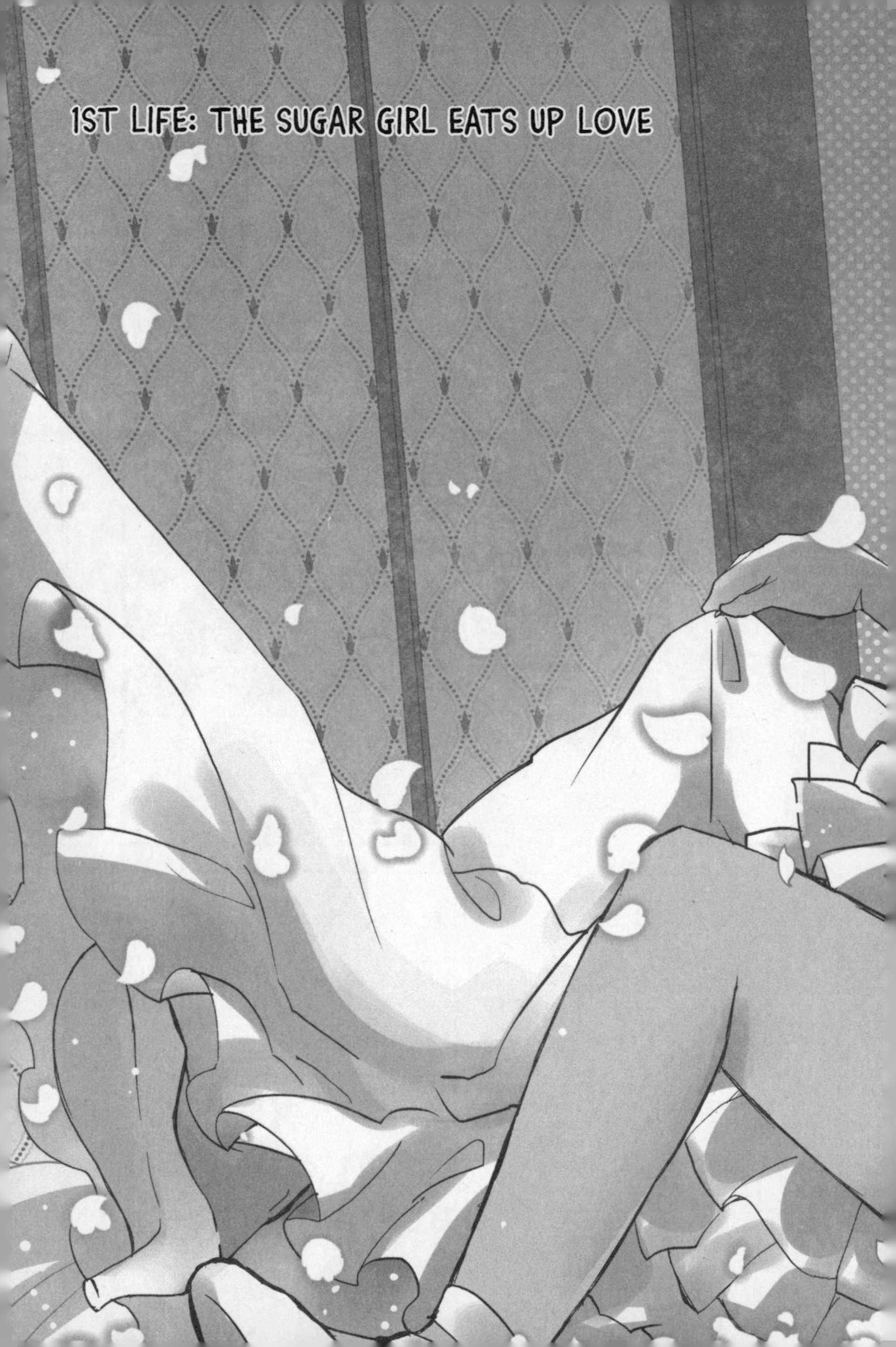
1ST LIFE: THE SUGAR GIRL EATS UP LOVE

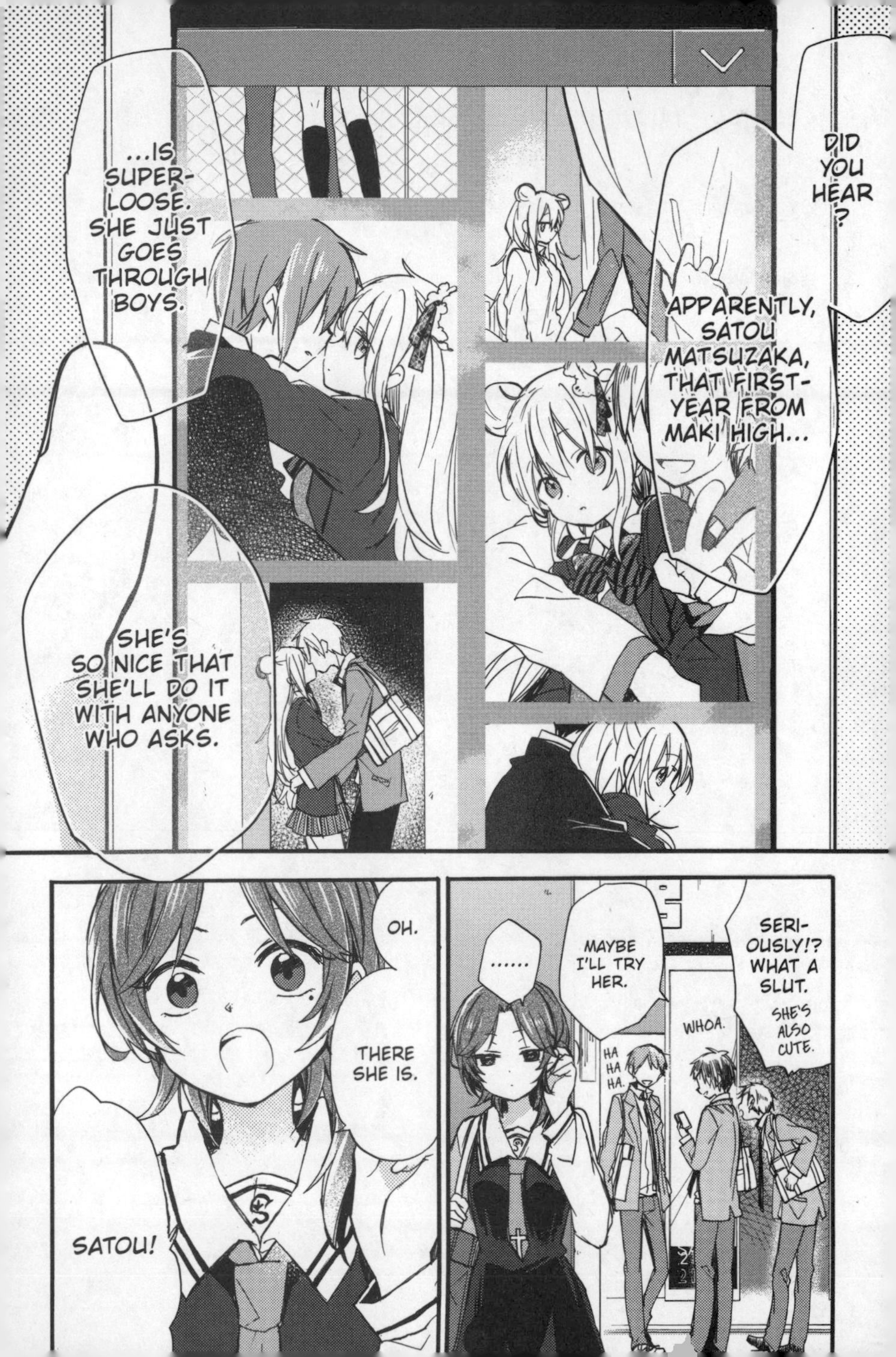

DID YOU HEAR?
APPARENTLY, SATOU MATSUZAKA, THAT FIRST-YEAR FROM MAKI HIGH...
...IS SUPER-LOOSE. SHE JUST GOES THROUGH BOYS.
SHE'S SO NICE THAT SHE'LL DO IT WITH ANYONE WHO ASKS.
SERI-OUSLY!? WHAT A SLUT.
SHE'S ALSO CUTE.
WHOA.
HA HA HA.
MAYBE I'LL TRY HER.
......
OH.
THERE SHE IS.
SATOU!

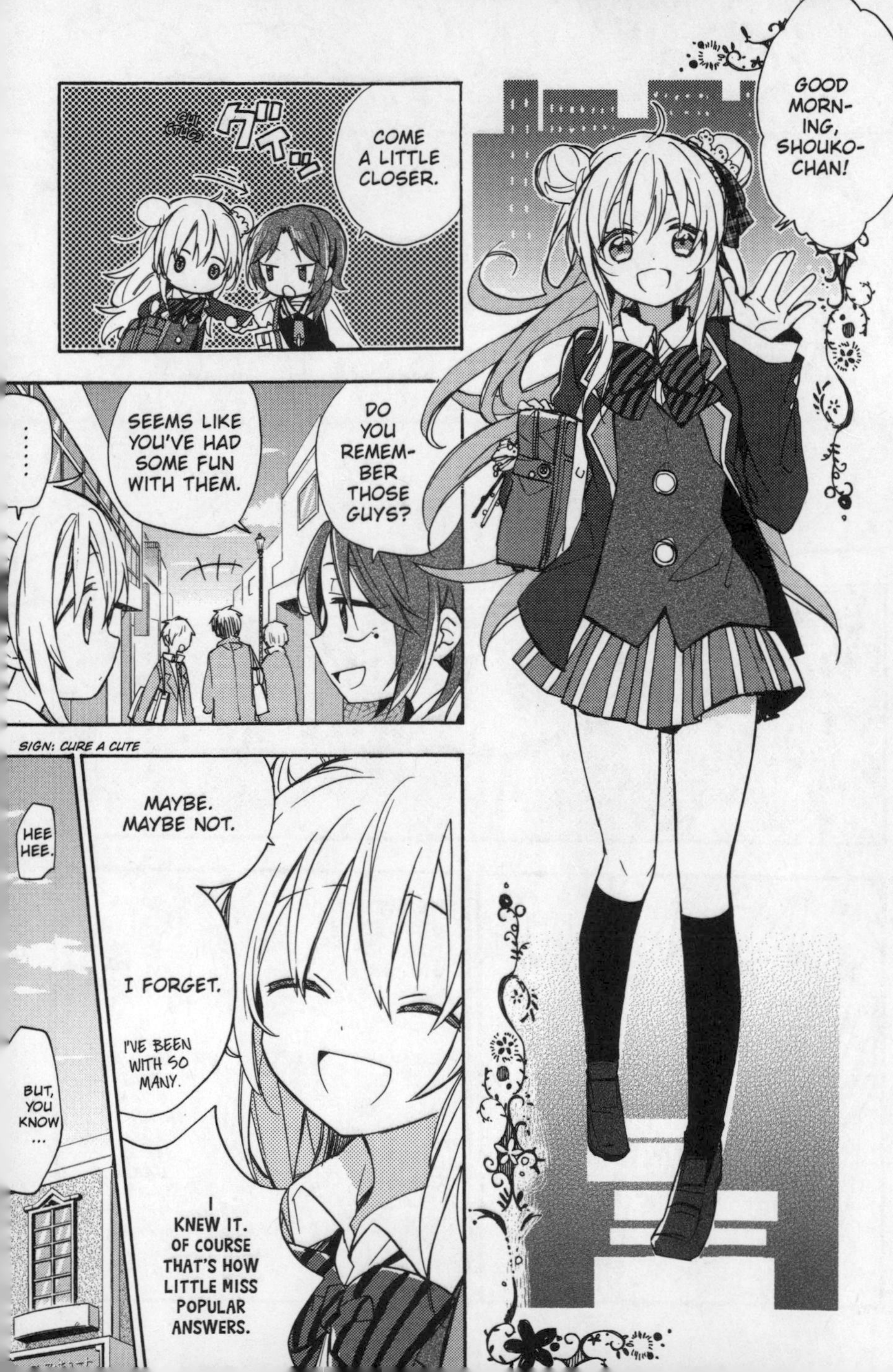
GOOD MORNING-ING, SHOUKO-CHAN!
COME A LITTLE CLOSER.
GUI (TUG)
DO YOU REMEMBER THOSE GUYS?
SEEMS LIKE YOU'VE HAD SOME FUN WITH THEM.
......
SIGN: CURE A CUTE
MAYBE. MAYBE NOT.
HEE HEE.
I FORGET.
I'VE BEEN WITH SO MANY.
BUT, YOU KNOW...
I KNEW IT. OF COURSE THAT'S HOW LITTLE MISS POPULAR ANSWERS.

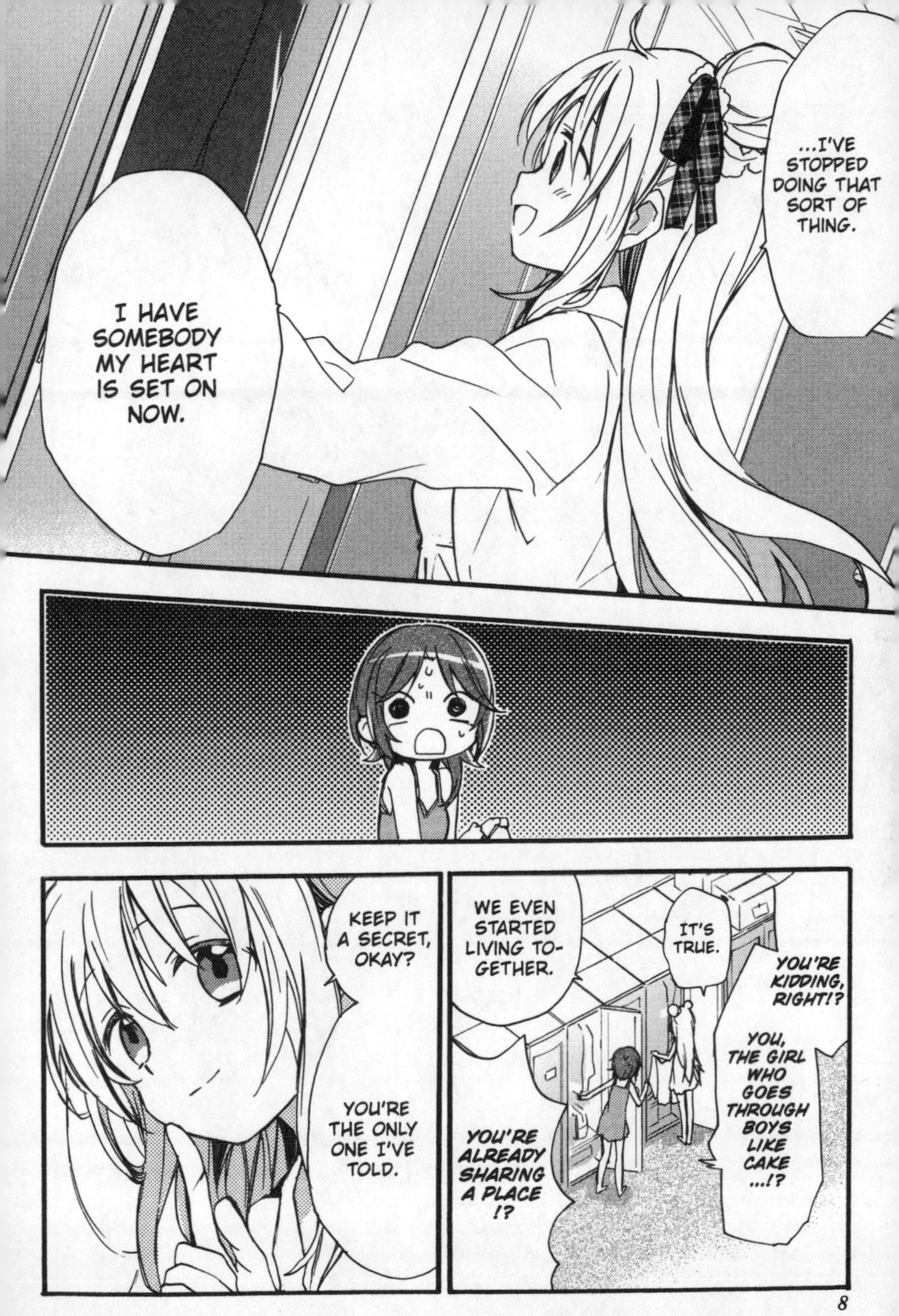
...I'VE STOPPED DOING THAT SORT OF THING.
I HAVE SOMEBODY MY HEART IS SET ON NOW.
IT'S TRUE.
WE EVEN STARTED LIVING TO-GETHER.
YOU'RE KIDDING, RIGHT!?
YOU, THE GIRL WHO GOES THROUGH BOYS LIKE CAKE ...!?
YOU'RE ALREADY SHARING A PLACE !?
KEEP IT A SECRET, OKAY?
YOU'RE THE ONLY ONE I'VE TOLD.

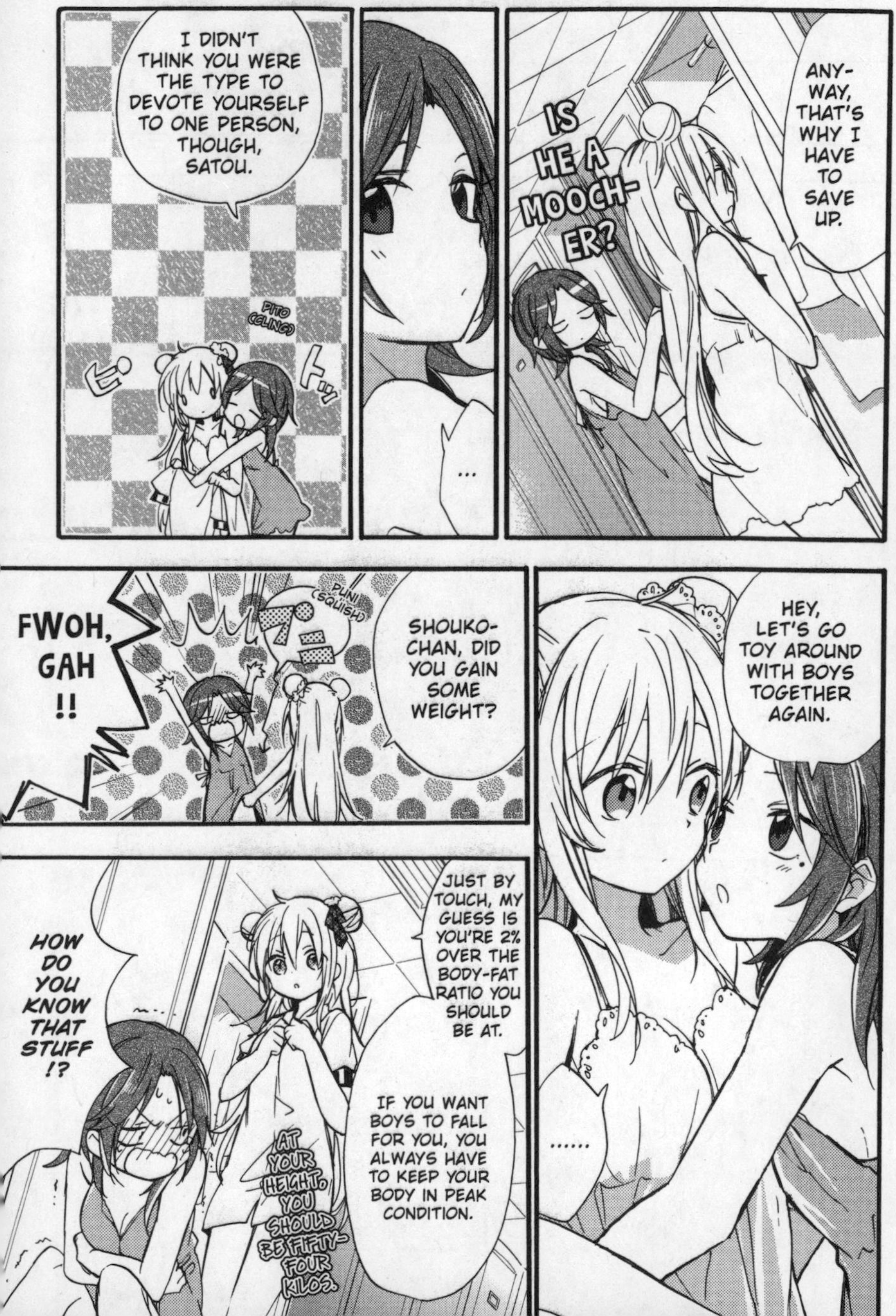
ANY-WAY, THAT'S WHY I HAVE TO SAVE UP.
IS HE A MOOCH-ER?
...
I DIDN'T THINK YOU WERE THE TYPE TO DEVOTE YOURSELF TO ONE PERSON, THOUGH, SATOU.
PITO (CLING)
HEY, LET'S GO TOY AROUND WITH BOYS TOGETHER AGAIN.
......
SHOUKO-CHAN, DID YOU GAIN SOME WEIGHT?
PUNI (SQUISH)
FWOH, GAH !!
JUST BY TOUCH, MY GUESS IS YOU'RE 2% OVER THE BODY-FAT RATIO YOU SHOULD BE AT.
IF YOU WANT BOYS TO FALL FOR YOU, YOU ALWAYS HAVE TO KEEP YOUR BODY IN PEAK CONDITION.
AT YOUR HEIGHT, YOU SHOULD BE FIFTY-FOUR KILOS.
HOW DO YOU KNOW THAT STUFF !?
~...

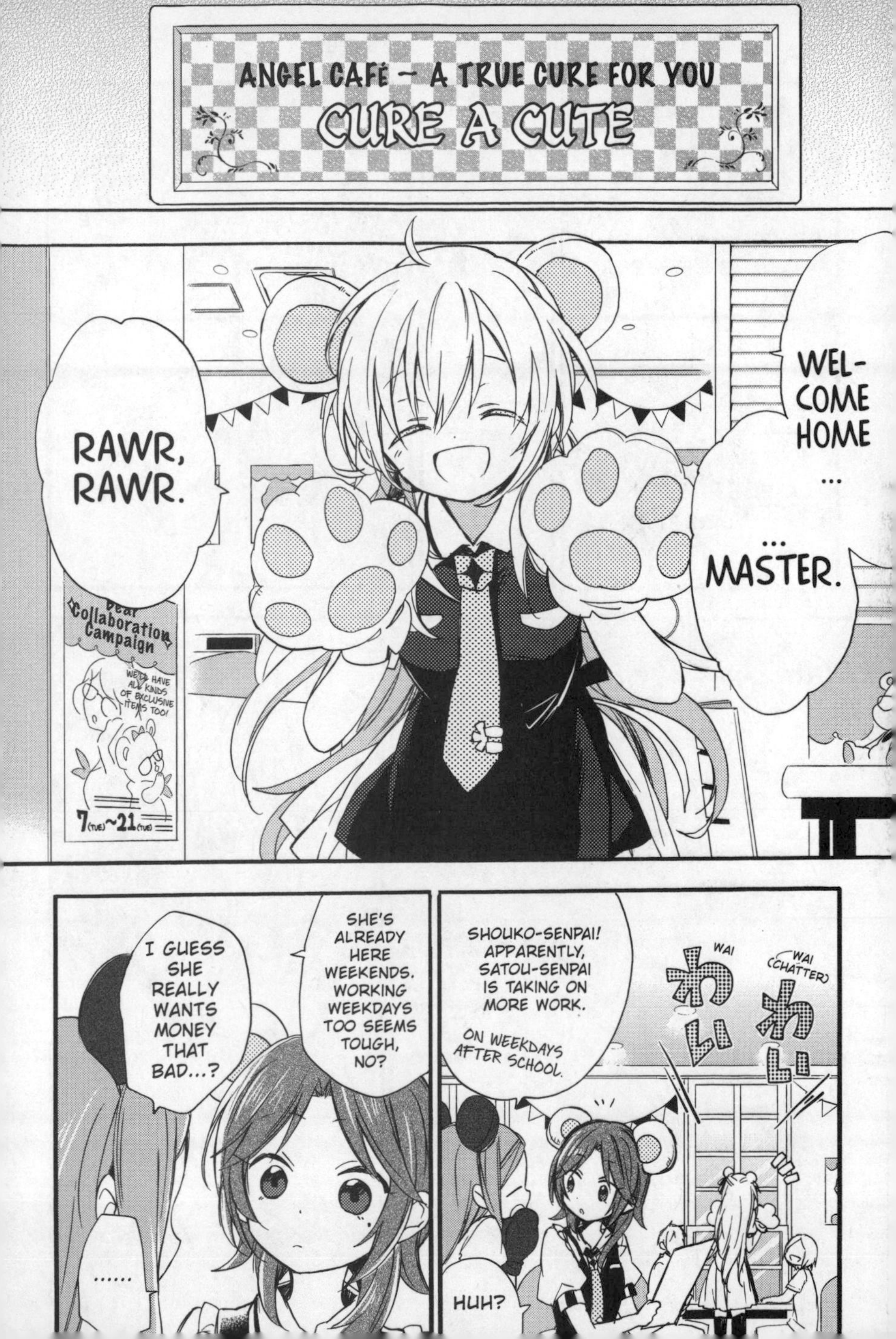
ANGEL CAFÉ – A TRUE CURE FOR YOU
CURE A CUTE
WEL-COME HOME ...
... MASTER.
RAWR, RAWR.
Collaboration Campaign
WE'LL HAVE ALL KINDS OF EXCLUSIVE ITEMS TOO!
7(TUE)~21(TUE)
SHOUKO-SENPAI! APPARENTLY, SATOU-SENPAI IS TAKING ON MORE WORK.
ON WEEKDAYS AFTER SCHOOL.
わい
WAI
わい
WAI (CHATTER)
HUH?
SHE'S ALREADY HERE WEEKENDS. WORKING WEEKDAYS TOO SEEMS TOUGH, NO?
I GUESS SHE REALLY WANTS MONEY THAT BAD...?
......

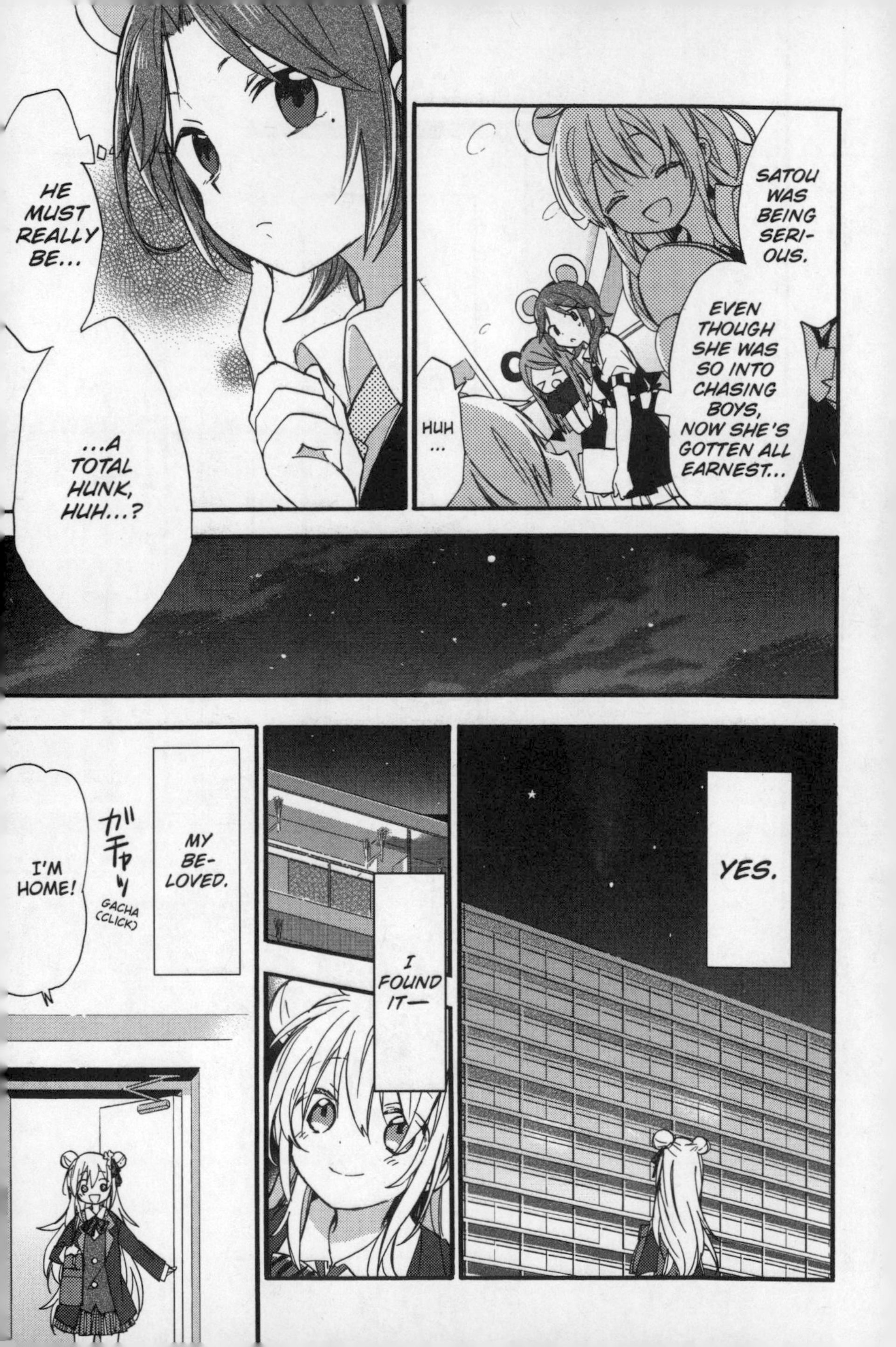
SATOU WAS BEING SERI-OUS.
EVEN THOUGH SHE WAS SO INTO CHASING BOYS, NOW SHE'S GOTTEN ALL EARNEST...
HUH...
HE MUST REALLY BE...
...A TOTAL HUNK, HUH...?
YES.
I FOUND IT—
MY BE-LOVED.
ガチャ
GACHA (CLICK)
I'M HOME!

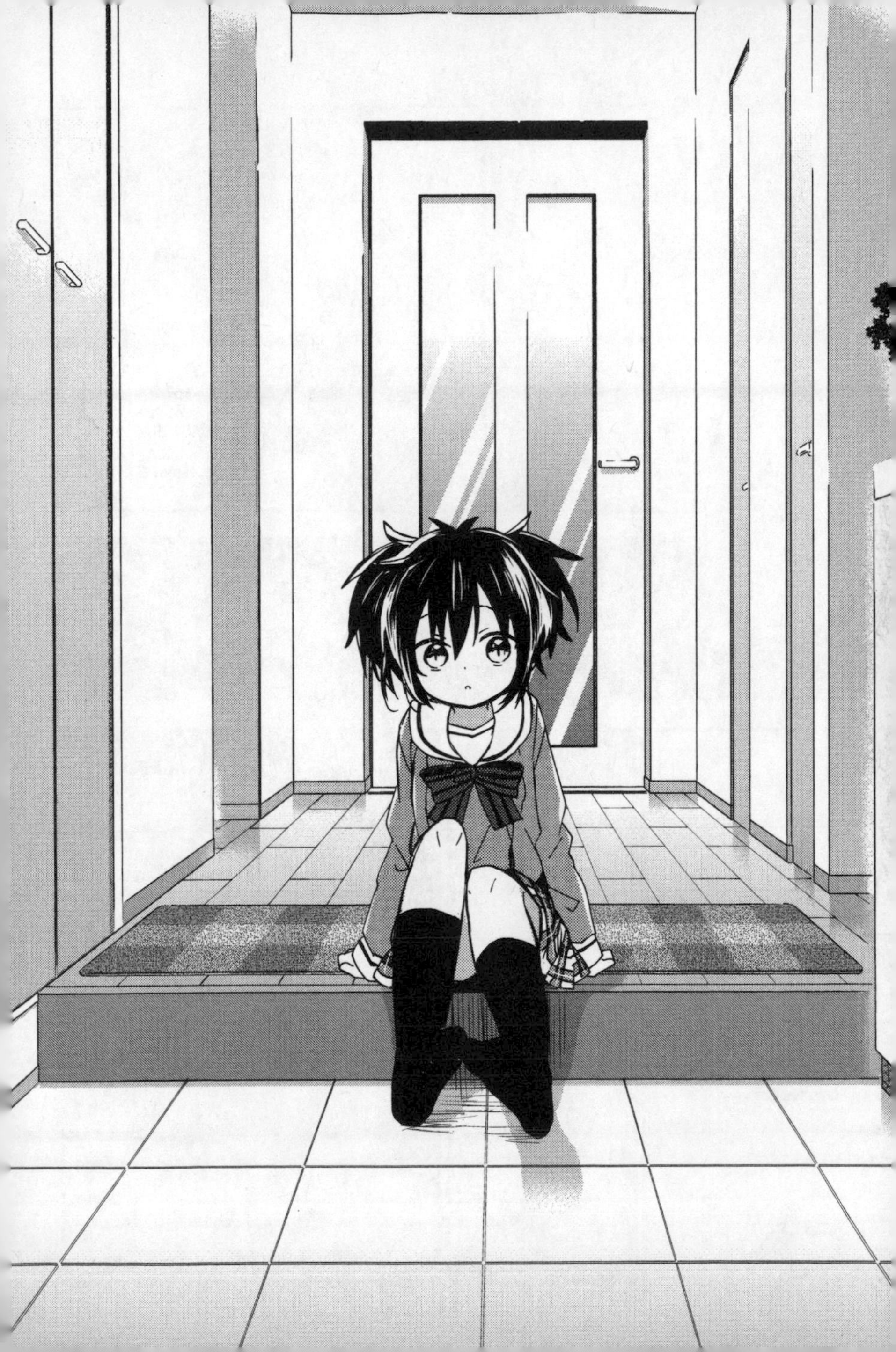

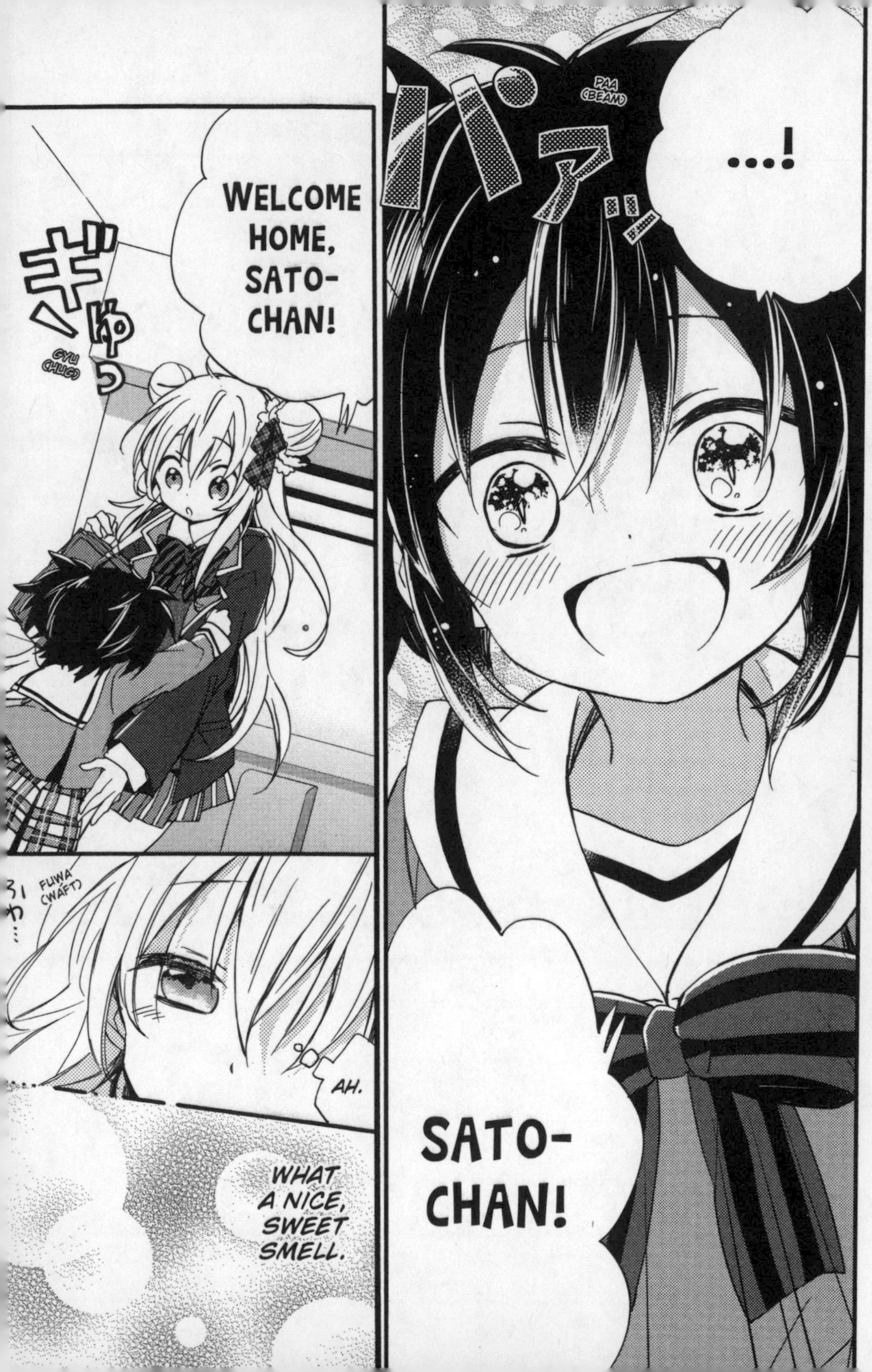
パァ!!
PAA (BEAM)
...!
SATO-CHAN!
WELCOME HOME, SATO-CHAN!
ぎゅっ!
GYU (HUG)
ふわ…
FUWA (WAFT)
AH.
WHAT A NICE, SWEET SMELL.

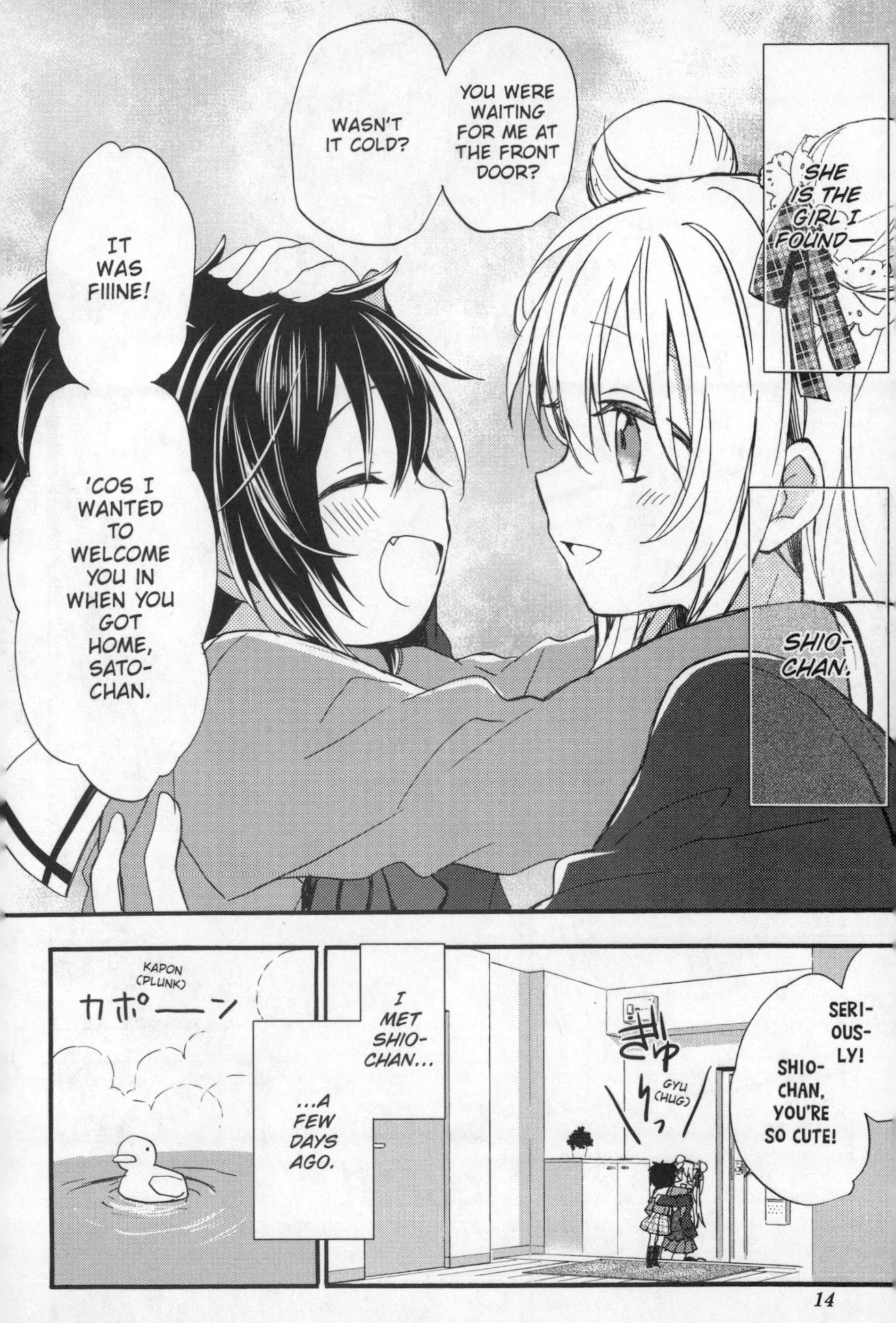
SHE IS THE GIRL I FOUND—
YOU WERE WAITING FOR ME AT THE FRONT DOOR?
WASN'T IT COLD?
SHIO-CHAN.
IT WAS FIIINE!
'COS I WANTED TO WELCOME YOU IN WHEN YOU GOT HOME, SATO-CHAN.
SERI-OUS-LY!
SHIO-CHAN, YOU'RE SO CUTE!
ぎゅっ
GYU (HUG)
I MET SHIO-CHAN...
...A FEW DAYS AGO.
KAPON (PLUNK)
カポーーン

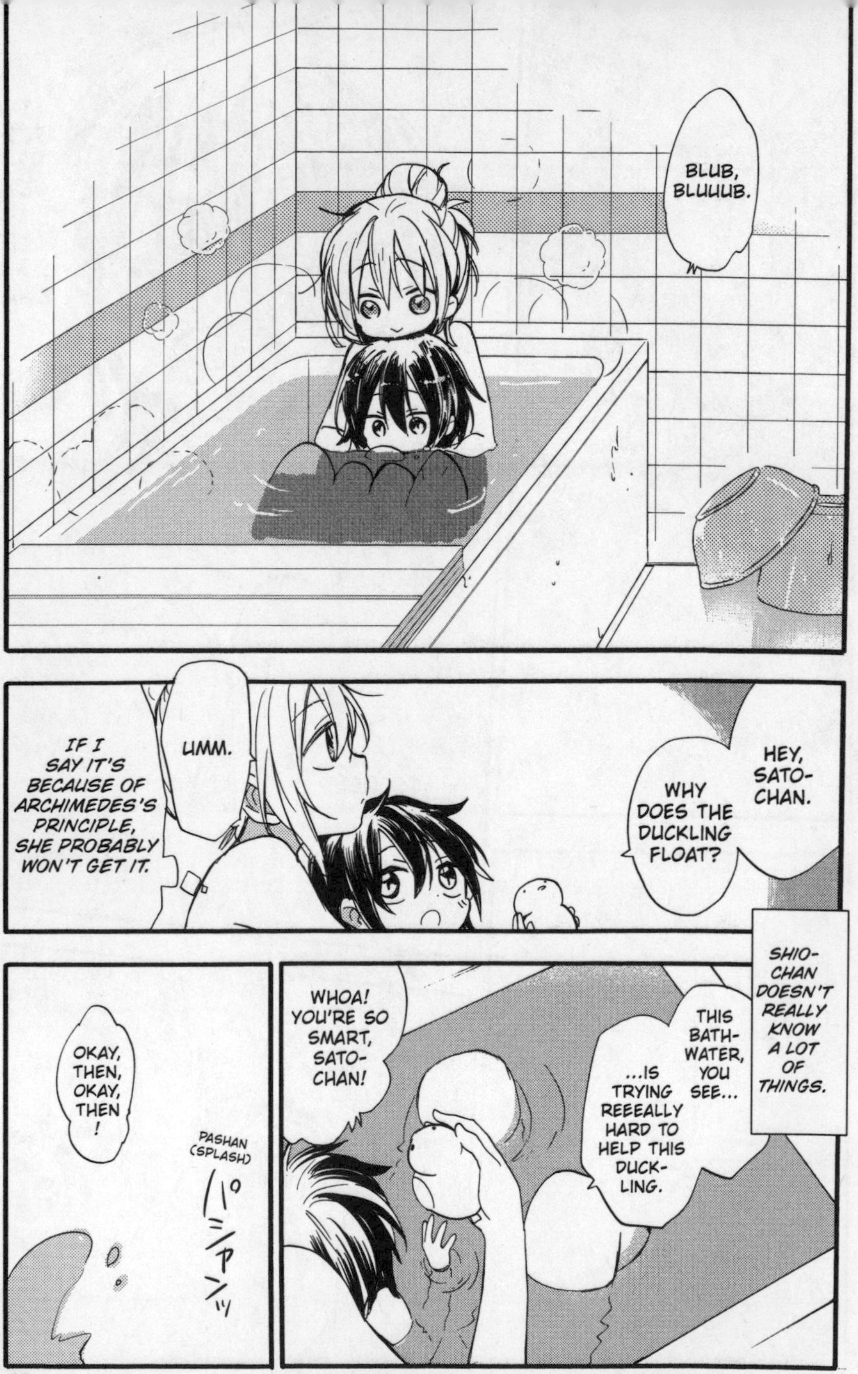
BLUB, BLUUUB.
HEY, SATO-CHAN.
WHY DOES THE DUCKLING FLOAT?
UMM.
IF I SAY IT'S BECAUSE OF ARCHIMEDES'S PRINCIPLE, SHE PROBABLY WON'T GET IT.
SHIO-CHAN DOESN'T REALLY KNOW A LOT OF THINGS.
THIS BATH-WATER, YOU SEE...
...IS TRYING REEEALLY HARD TO HELP THIS DUCK-LING.
WHOA! YOU'RE SO SMART, SATO-CHAN!
OKAY, THEN, OKAY, THEN!
PASHAN (SPLASH)
パシャンッ

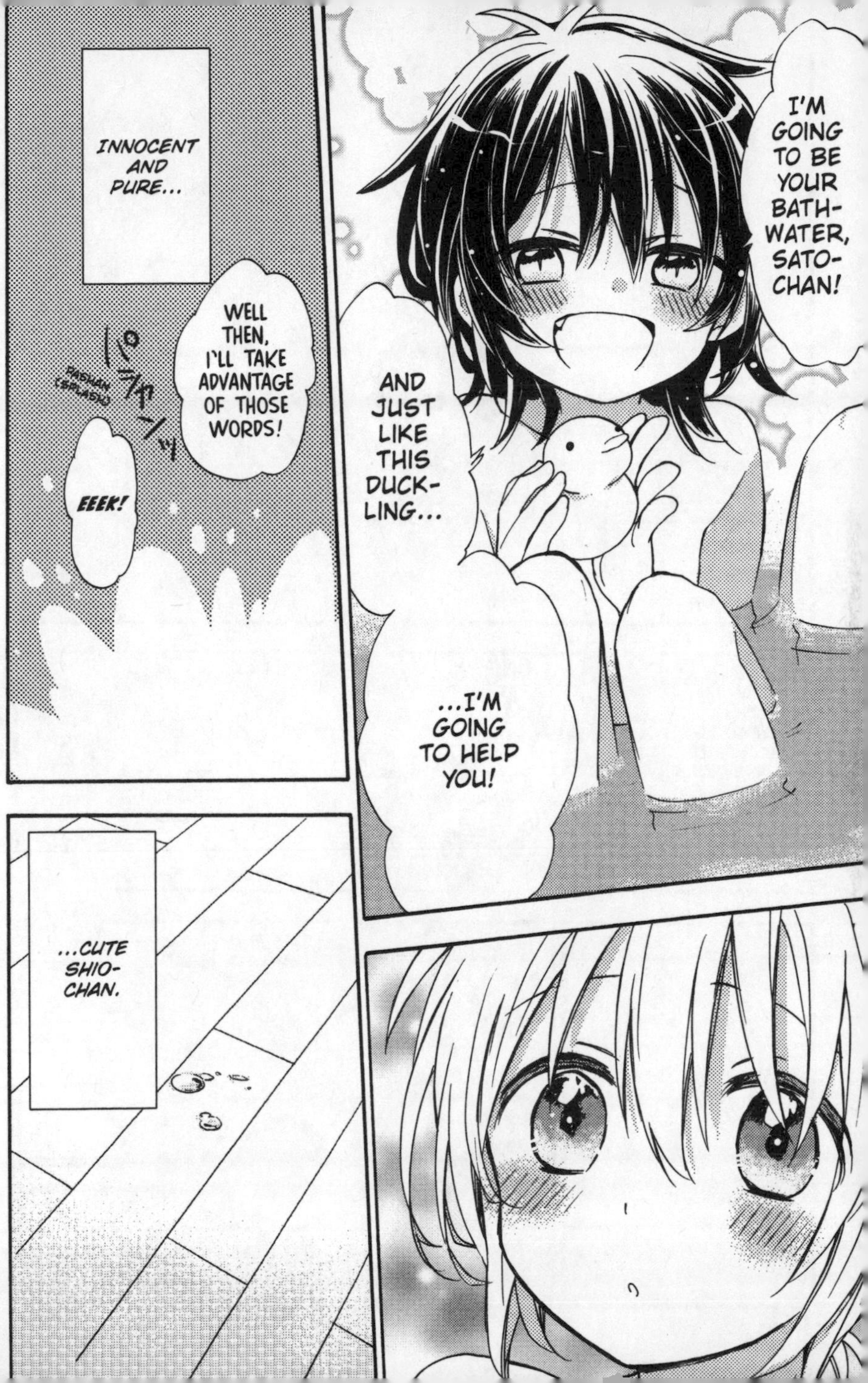
I'M GOING TO BE YOUR BATH-WATER, SATO-CHAN!
AND JUST LIKE THIS DUCKLING...
...I'M GOING TO HELP YOU!
INNOCENT AND PURE...
WELL THEN, I'LL TAKE ADVANTAGE OF THOSE WORDS!
PASHAN (SPLASH)
EEEK!
...CUTE SHIO-CHAN.

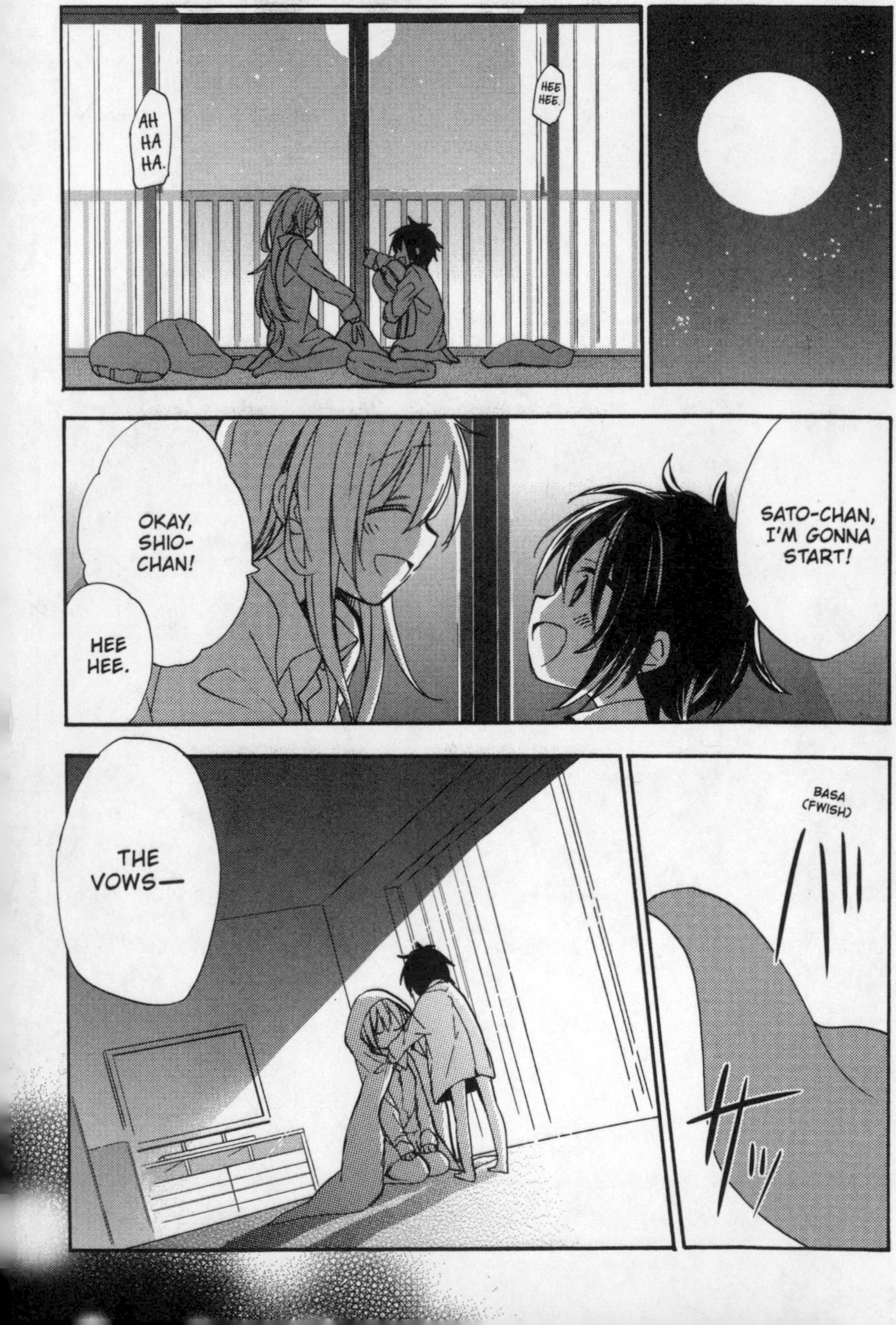
HEE HEE.
AH HA HA.
SATO-CHAN, I'M GONNA START!
OKAY, SHIO-CHAN!
HEE HEE.
BASA (FWISH)
THE VOWS—

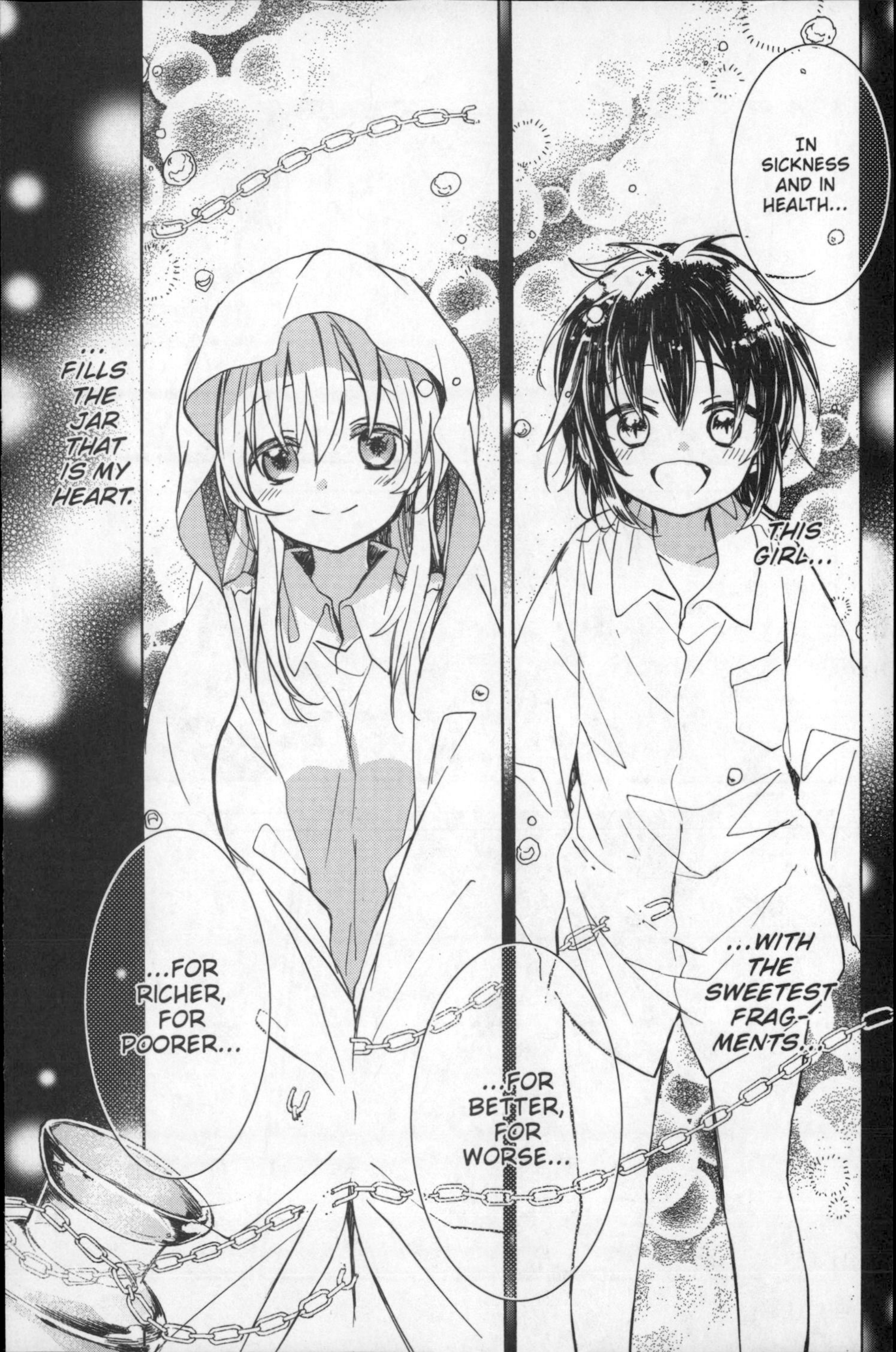
IN SICKNESS AND IN HEALTH...
THIS GIRL...
...WITH THE SWEETEST FRAG-MENTS...
...FOR BETTER, FOR WORSE...
...FILLS THE JAR THAT IS MY HEART.
...FOR RICHER, FOR POORER...

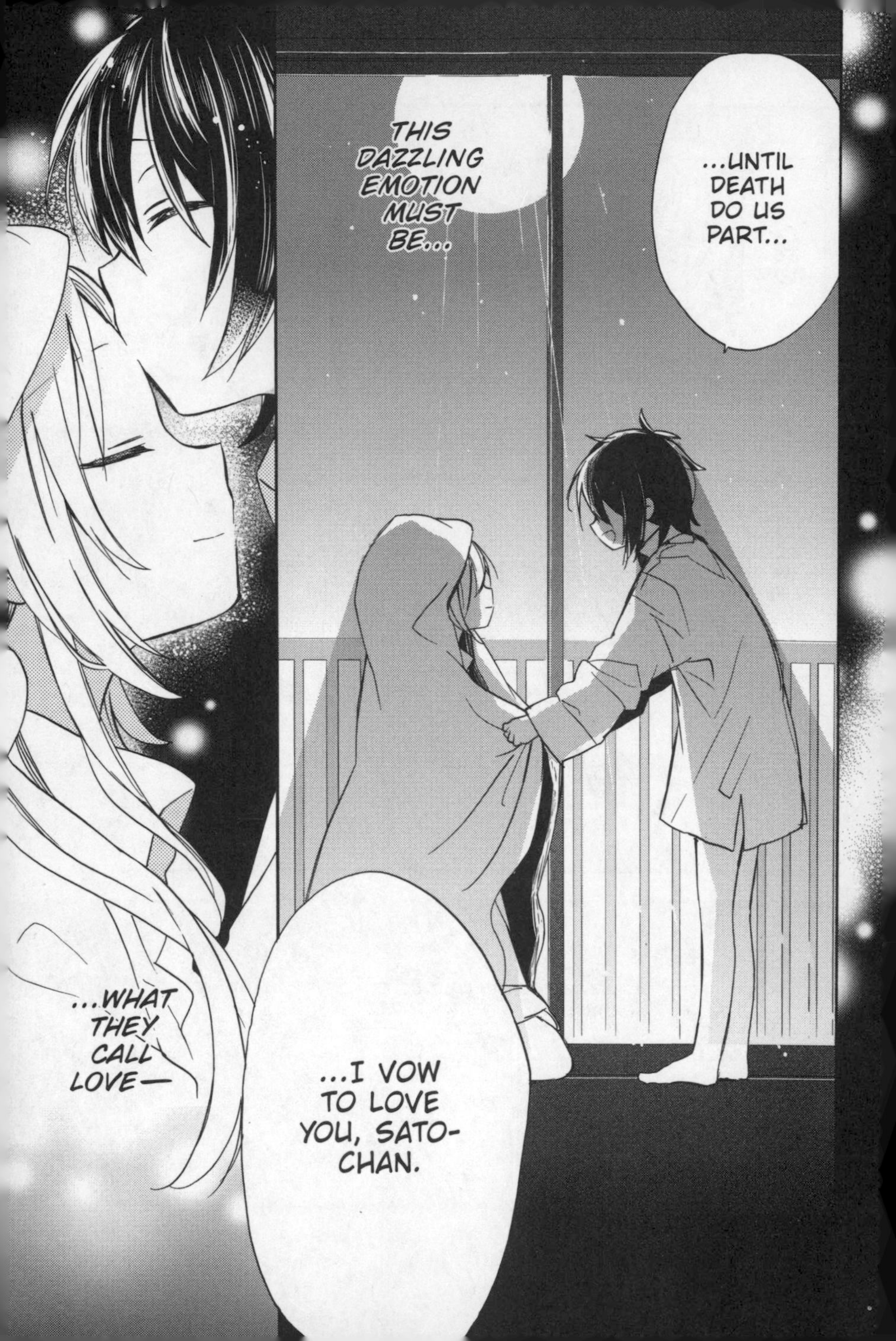
...UNTIL DEATH DO US PART...
THIS DAZZLING EMOTION MUST BE...
...I VOW TO LOVE YOU, SATO-CHAN.
...WHAT THEY CALL LOVE—

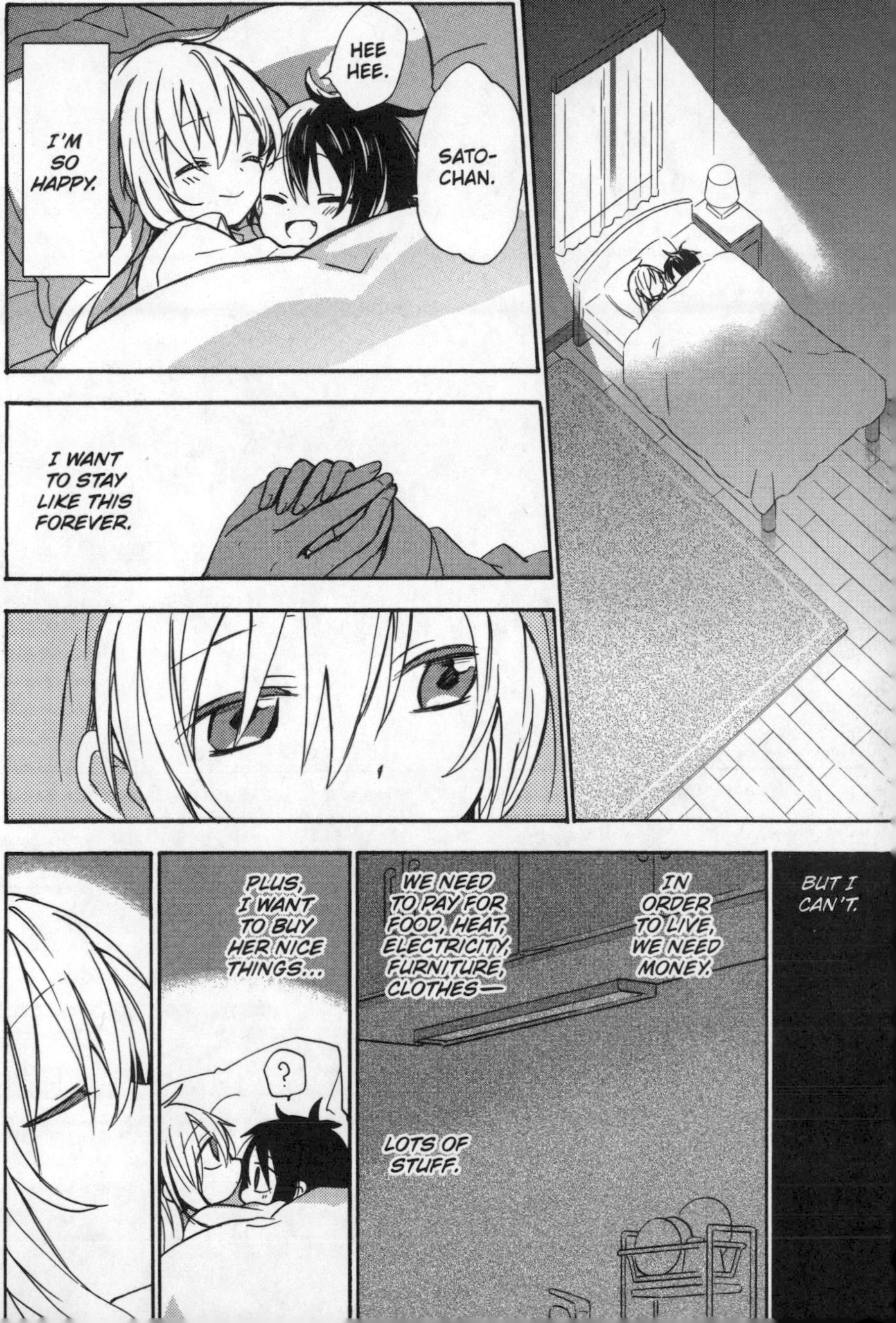
HEE HEE.
SATO-CHAN.
I'M SO HAPPY.
I WANT TO STAY LIKE THIS FOREVER.
BUT I CAN'T.
IN ORDER TO LIVE, WE NEED MONEY.
WE NEED TO PAY FOR FOOD, HEAT, ELECTRICITY, FURNITURE, CLOTHES—
LOTS OF STUFF.
PLUS, I WANT TO BUY HER NICE THINGS...
?

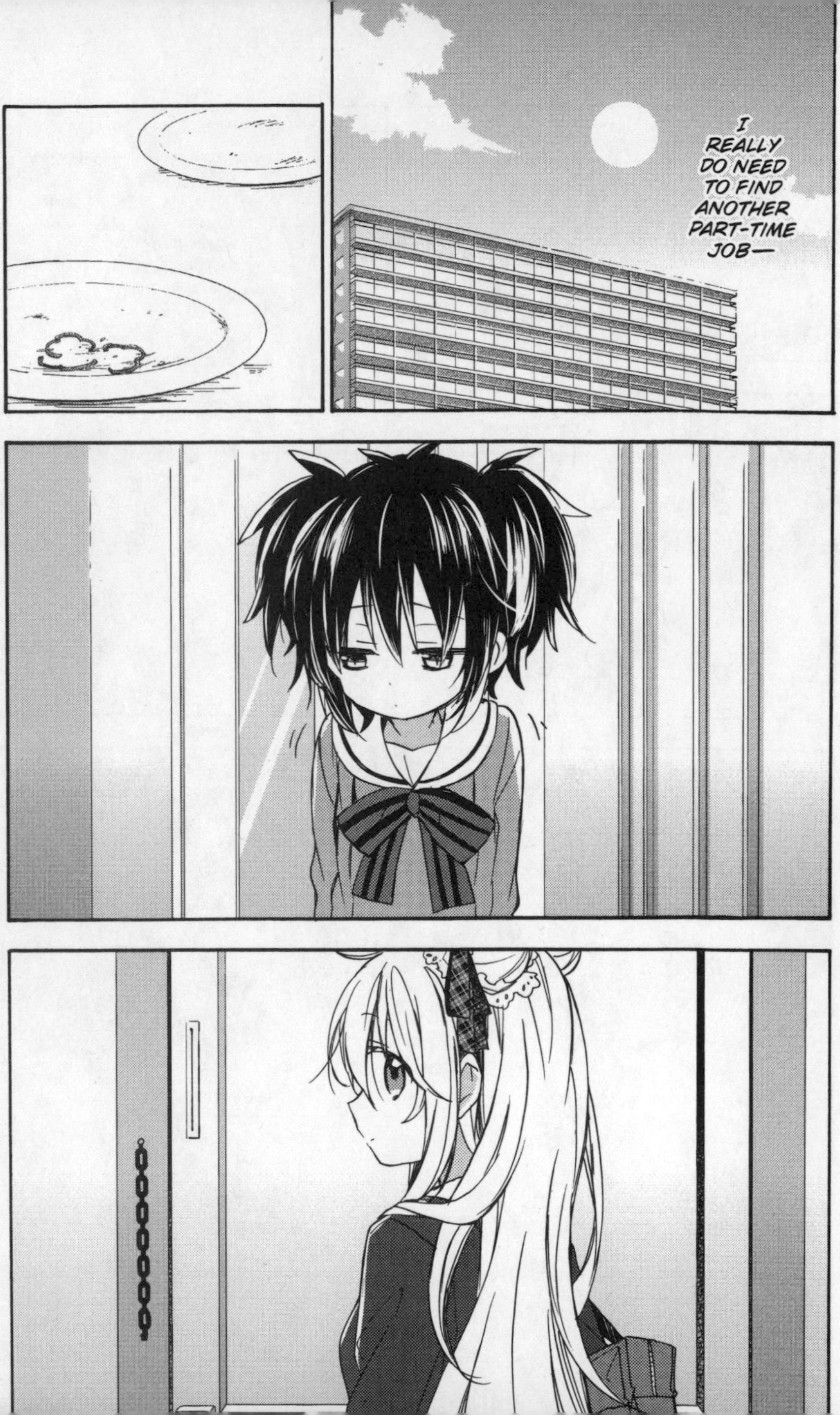
I REALLY DO NEED TO FIND ANOTHER PART-TIME JOB—

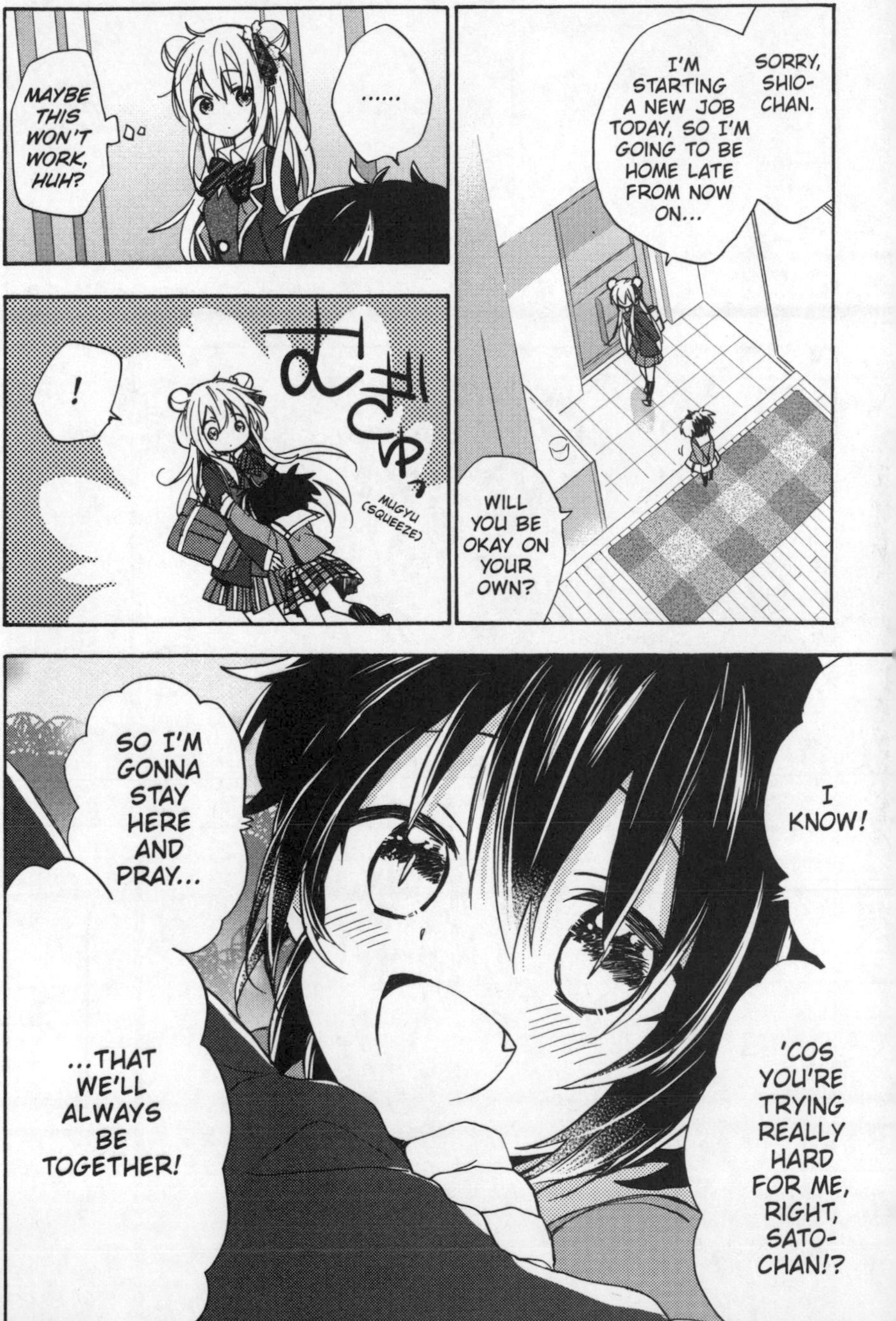
SORRY, SHIO-CHAN.
I'M STARTING A NEW JOB TODAY, SO I'M GOING TO BE HOME LATE FROM NOW ON...
WILL YOU BE OKAY ON YOUR OWN?
......
MAYBE THIS WON'T WORK, HUH?
!
むぎゅ
MUGYU (SQUEEZE)
I KNOW!
'COS YOU'RE TRYING REALLY HARD FOR ME, RIGHT, SATO-CHAN!?
SO I'M GONNA STAY HERE AND PRAY...
...THAT WE'LL ALWAYS BE TOGETHER!

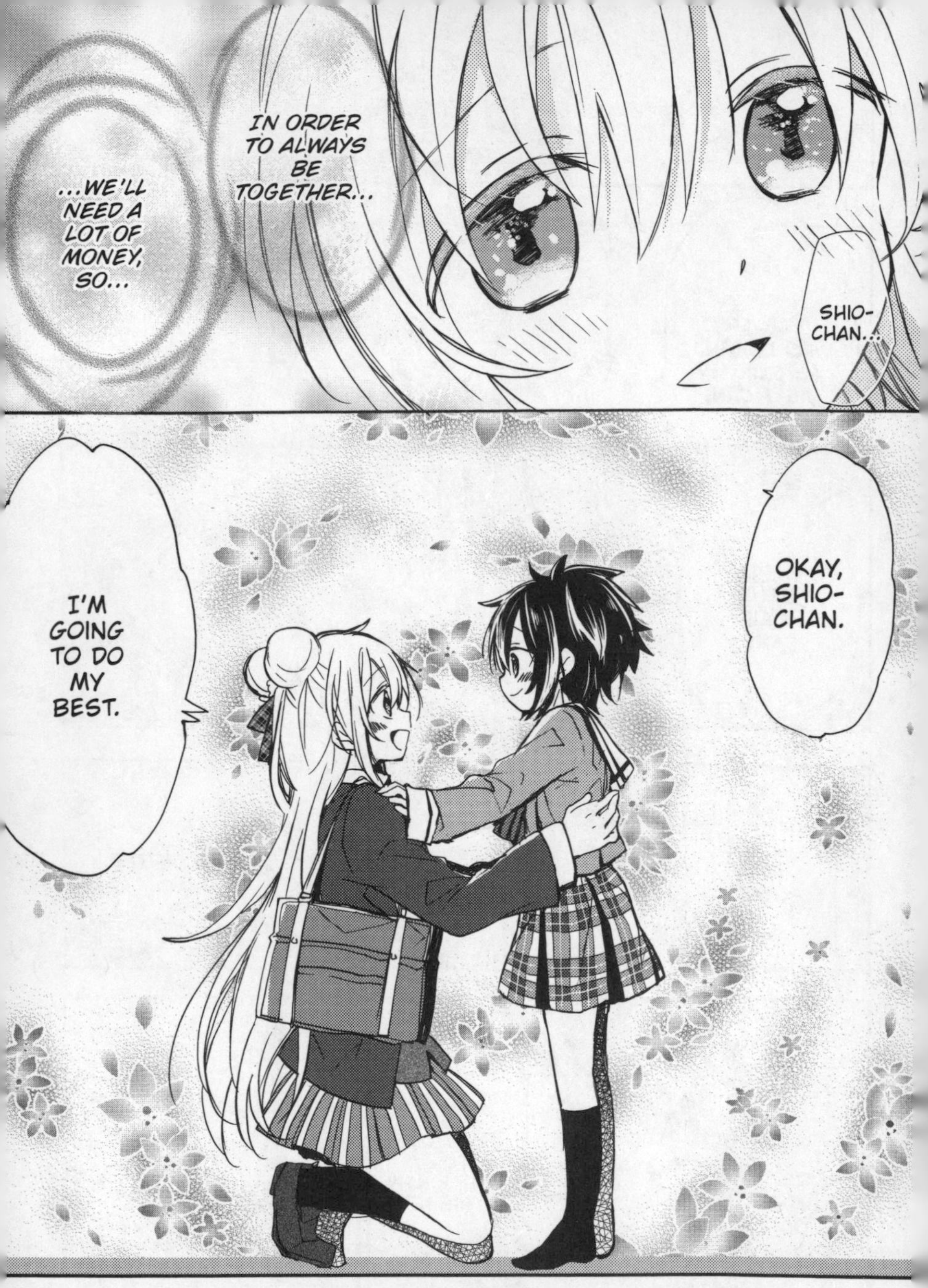
SHIO-CHAN...
IN ORDER TO ALWAYS BE TOGETHER...
...WE'LL NEED A LOT OF MONEY, SO...
OKAY, SHIO-CHAN.
I'M GOING TO DO MY BEST.

I'M GOING TO WORK TODAY TOO!

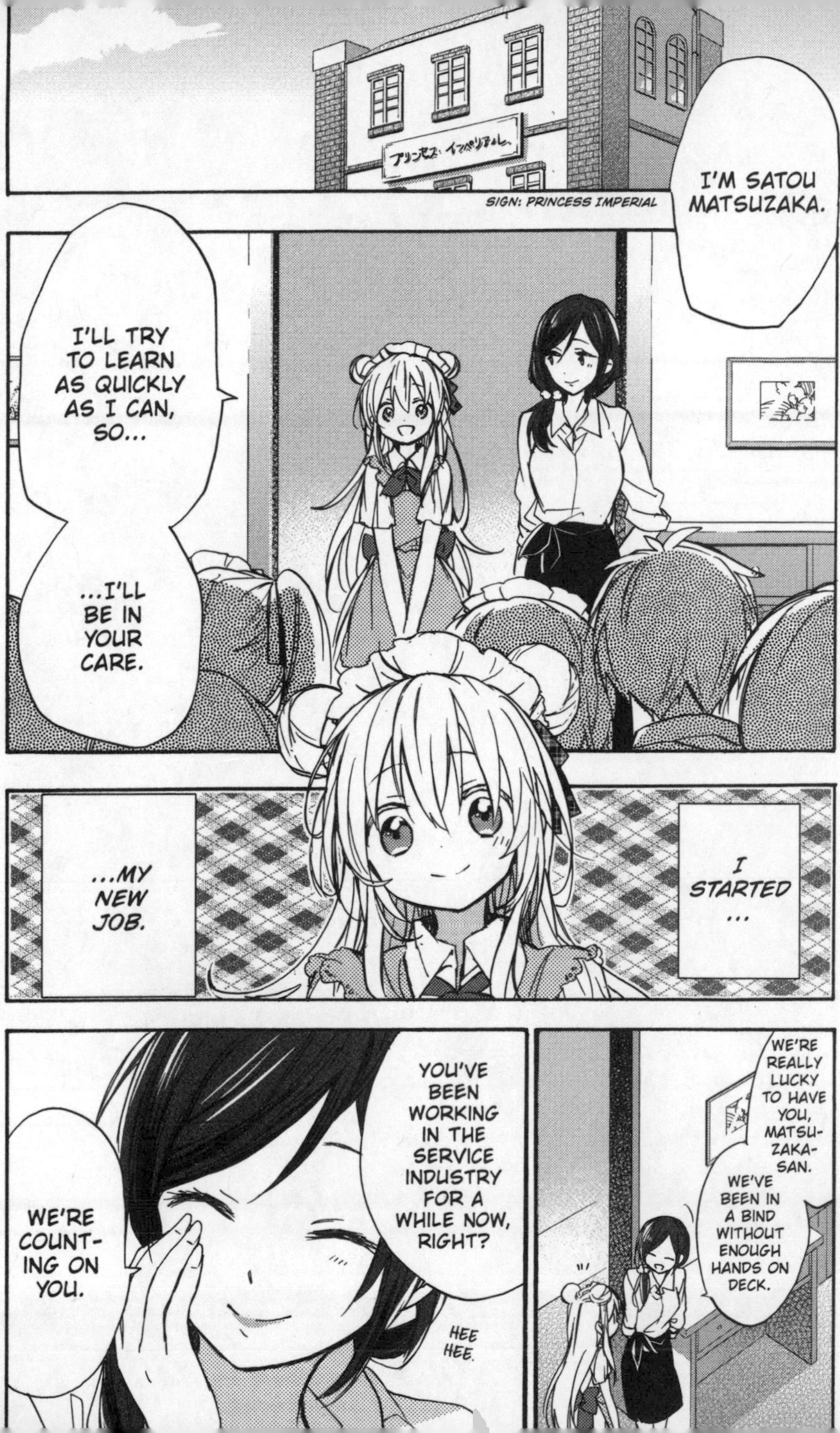
I'M SATOU MATSUZAKA.
SIGN: PRINCESS IMPERIAL
I'LL TRY TO LEARN AS QUICKLY AS I CAN, SO...
...I'LL BE IN YOUR CARE.
I STARTED...
...MY NEW JOB.
WE'RE REALLY LUCKY TO HAVE YOU, MATSUZAKA-SAN.
WE'VE BEEN IN A BIND WITHOUT ENOUGH HANDS ON DECK.
YOU'VE BEEN WORKING IN THE SERVICE INDUSTRY FOR A WHILE NOW, RIGHT?
HEE HEE.
WE'RE COUNTING ON YOU.

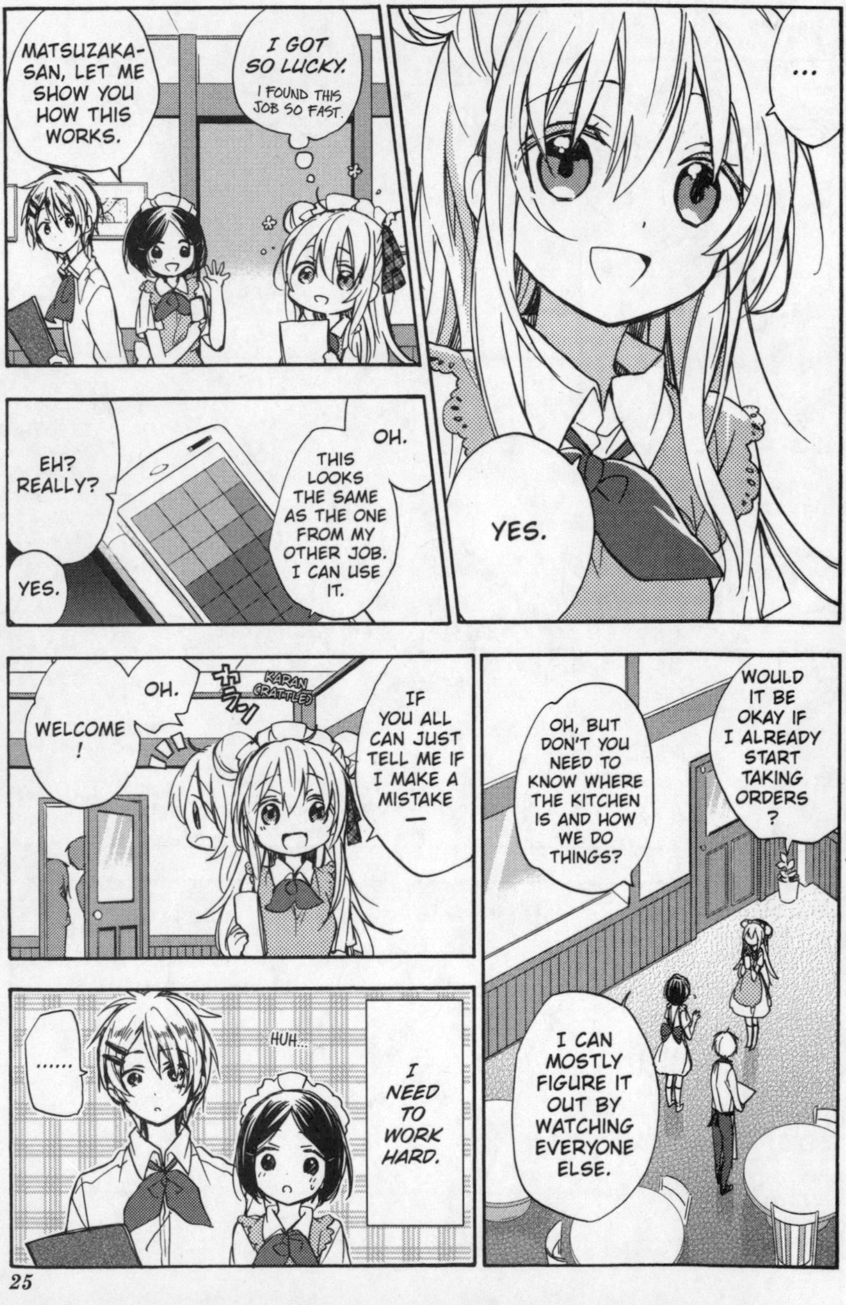
...
YES.
I GOT SO LUCKY.
I FOUND THIS JOB SO FAST.
MATSUZAKA-SAN, LET ME SHOW YOU HOW THIS WORKS.
OH.
THIS LOOKS THE SAME AS THE ONE FROM MY OTHER JOB. I CAN USE IT.
EH? REALLY?
YES.
WOULD IT BE OKAY IF I ALREADY START TAKING ORDERS?
OH, BUT DON'T YOU NEED TO KNOW WHERE THE KITCHEN IS AND HOW WE DO THINGS?
I CAN MOSTLY FIGURE IT OUT BY WATCHING EVERYONE ELSE.
IF YOU ALL CAN JUST TELL ME IF I MAKE A MISTAKE—
KARAN (RATTLED)
OH.
WELCOME!
I NEED TO WORK HARD.
HUH...
......

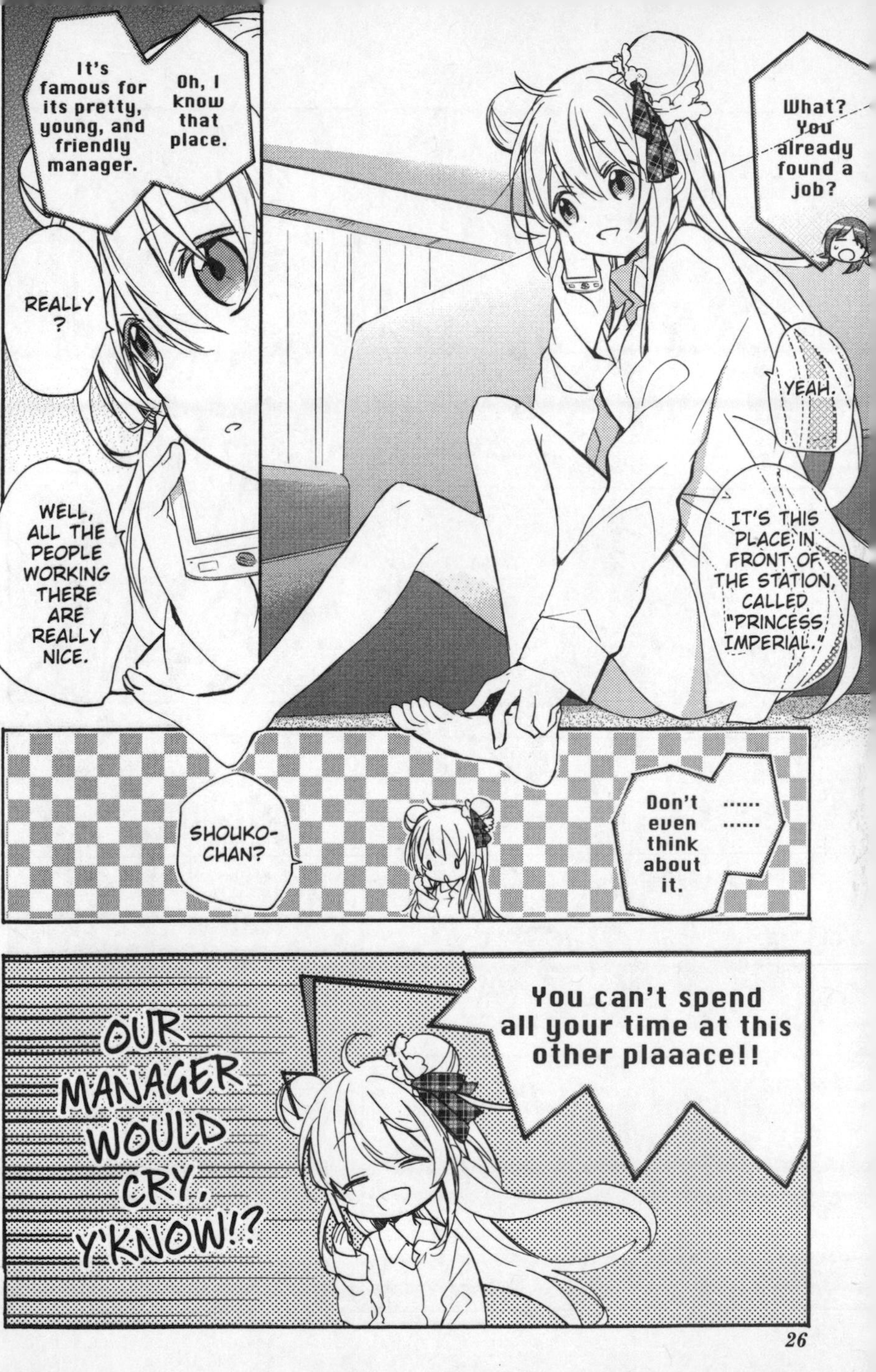
What? You already found a job?
YEAH.
IT'S THIS PLACE IN FRONT OF THE STATION, CALLED "PRINCESS IMPERIAL."
Oh, I know that place.
It's famous for its pretty, young, and friendly manager.
REALLY?
WELL, ALL THE PEOPLE WORKING THERE ARE REALLY NICE.
....
Don't even think about it.
SHOUKO-CHAN?
You can't spend all your time at this other plaaace!!
OUR MANAGER WOULD CRY, Y'KNOW!?

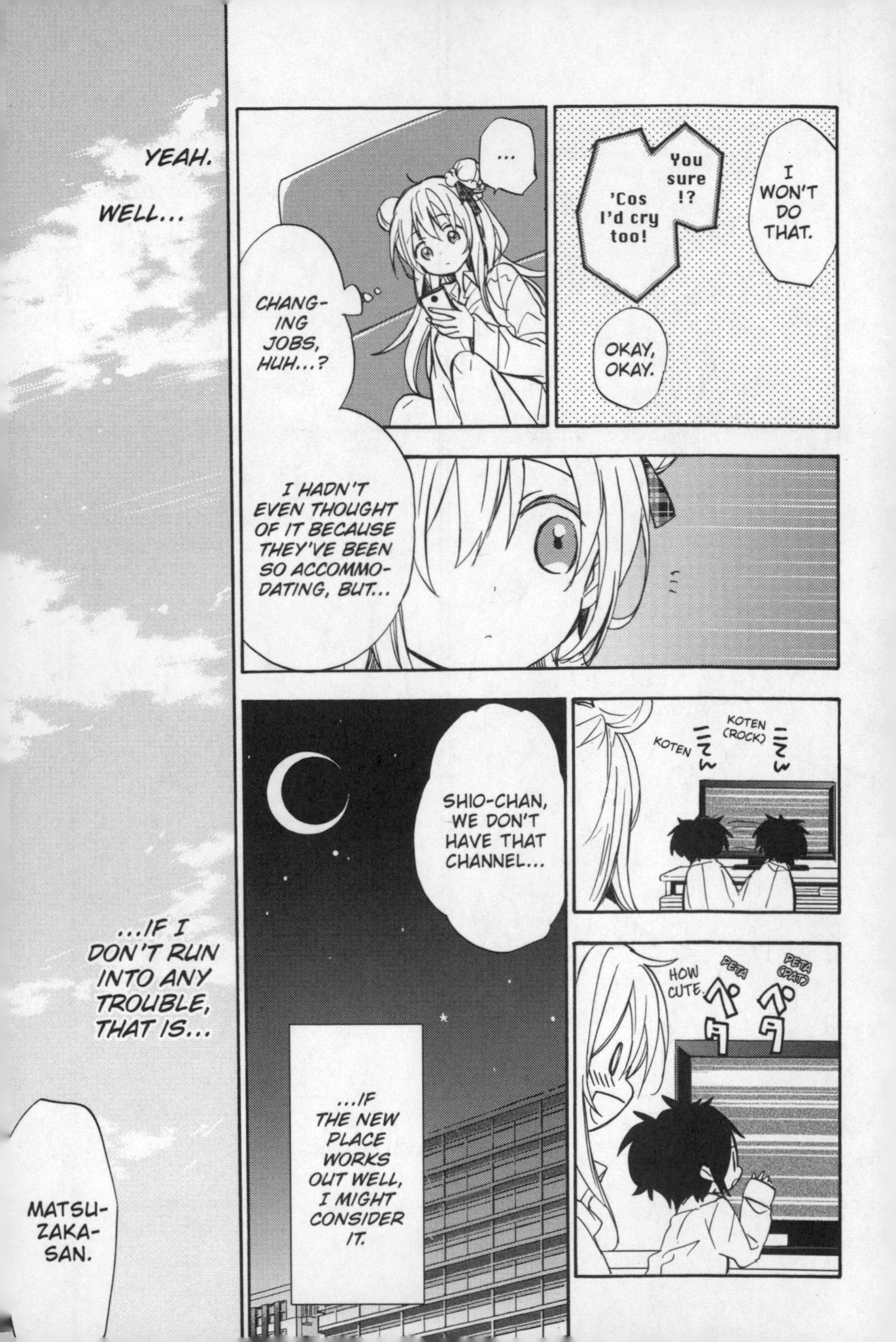
I WON'T DO THAT.
You sure!? 'Cos I'd cry too!
OKAY, OKAY.
...
CHANGING-ING JOBS, HUH...?
I HADN'T EVEN THOUGHT OF IT BECAUSE THEY'VE BEEN SO ACCOMMO-DATING, BUT...
KOTEN (ROCK)
KOTEN
PETA (PAT)
PETA
HOW CUTE.
SHIO-CHAN, WE DON'T HAVE THAT CHANNEL...
...IF THE NEW PLACE WORKS OUT WELL, I MIGHT CONSIDER IT.
YEAH.
WELL...
...IF I DON'T RUN INTO ANY TROUBLE, THAT IS...
MATSU-ZAKA-SAN.

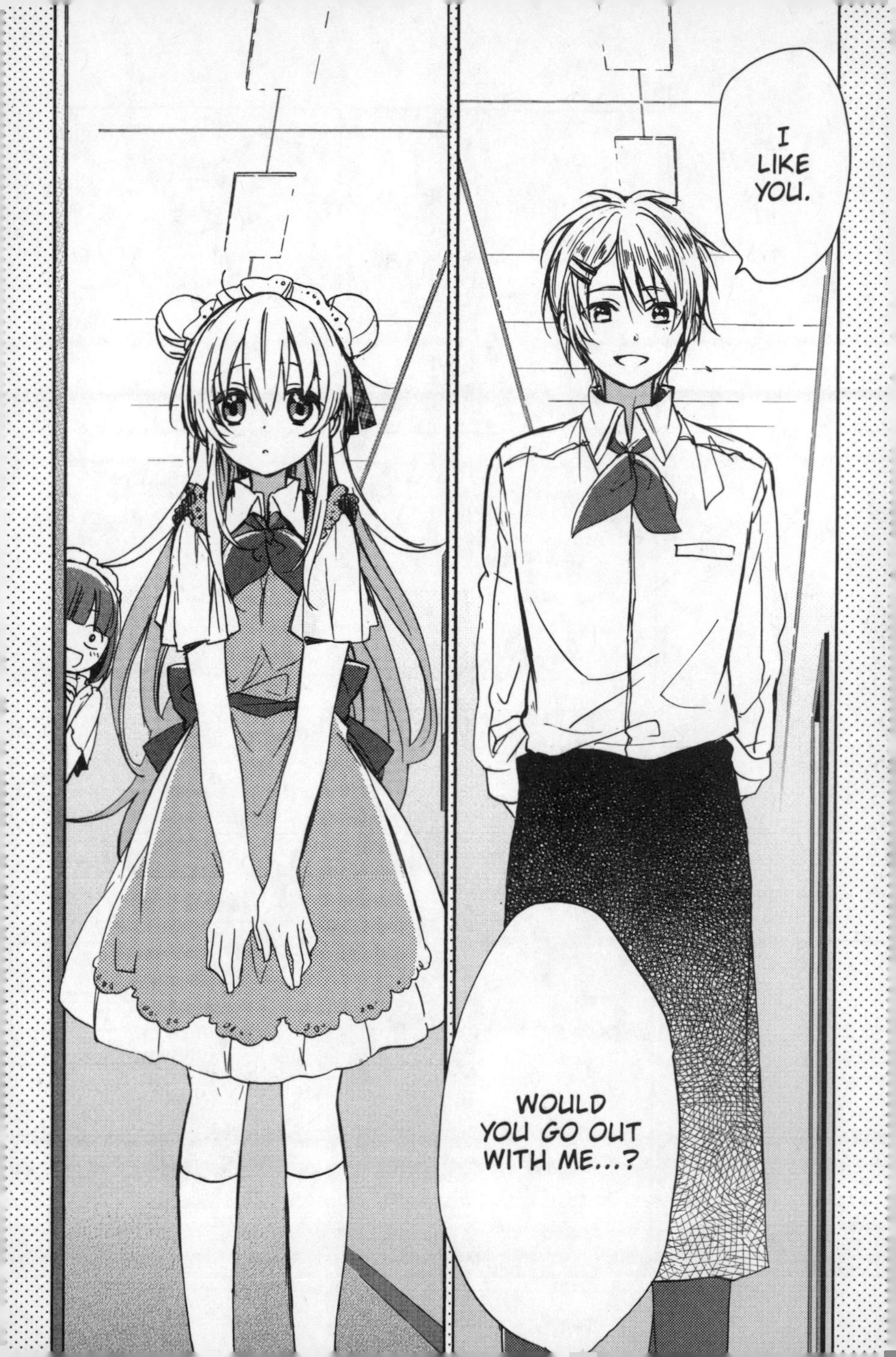
I LIKE YOU.
WOULD YOU GO OUT WITH ME...?

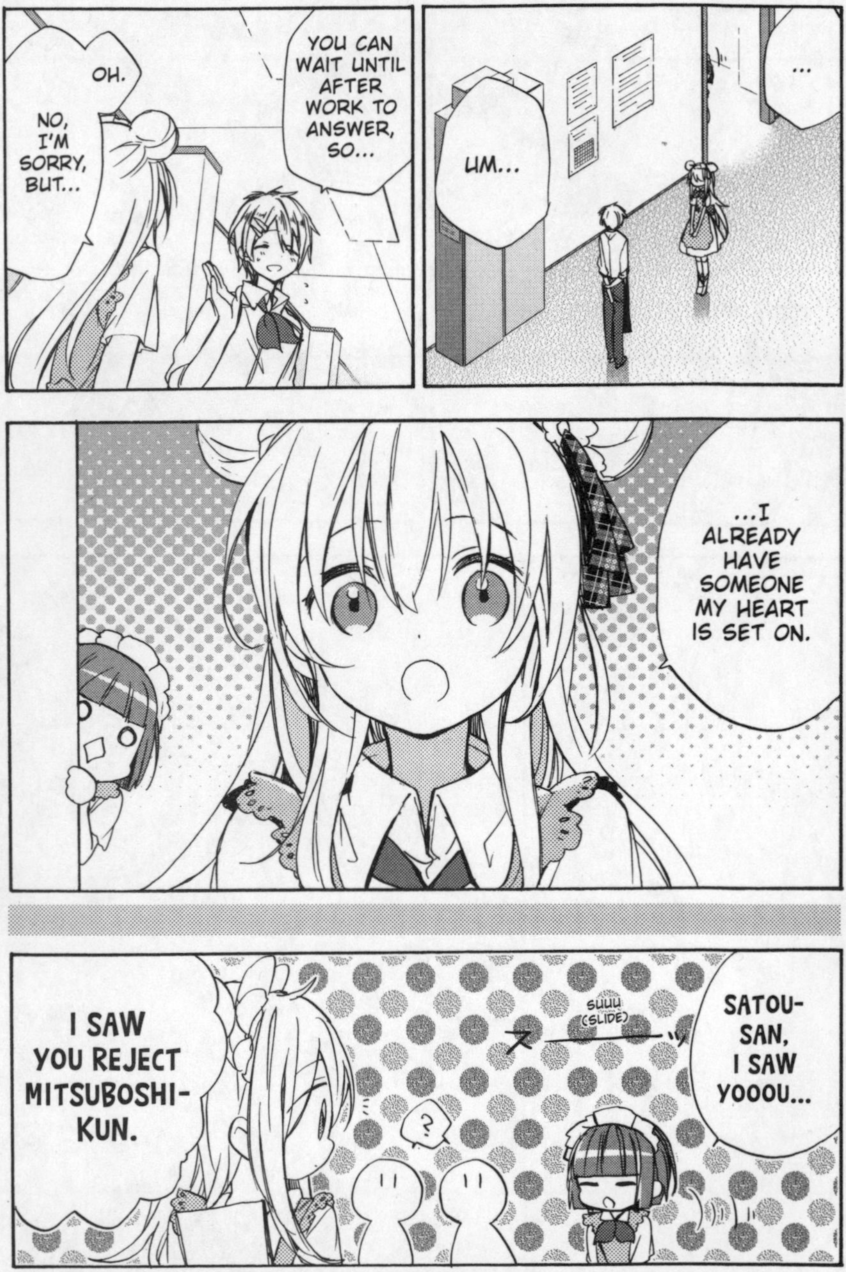
...
UM...
YOU CAN WAIT UNTIL AFTER WORK TO ANSWER, SO...
OH.
NO, I'M SORRY, BUT...
...I ALREADY HAVE SOMEONE MY HEART IS SET ON.
SATOU-SAN, I SAW YOOOU...
SUUU (SLIDE)
I SAW YOU REJECT MITSUBOSHI-KUN.

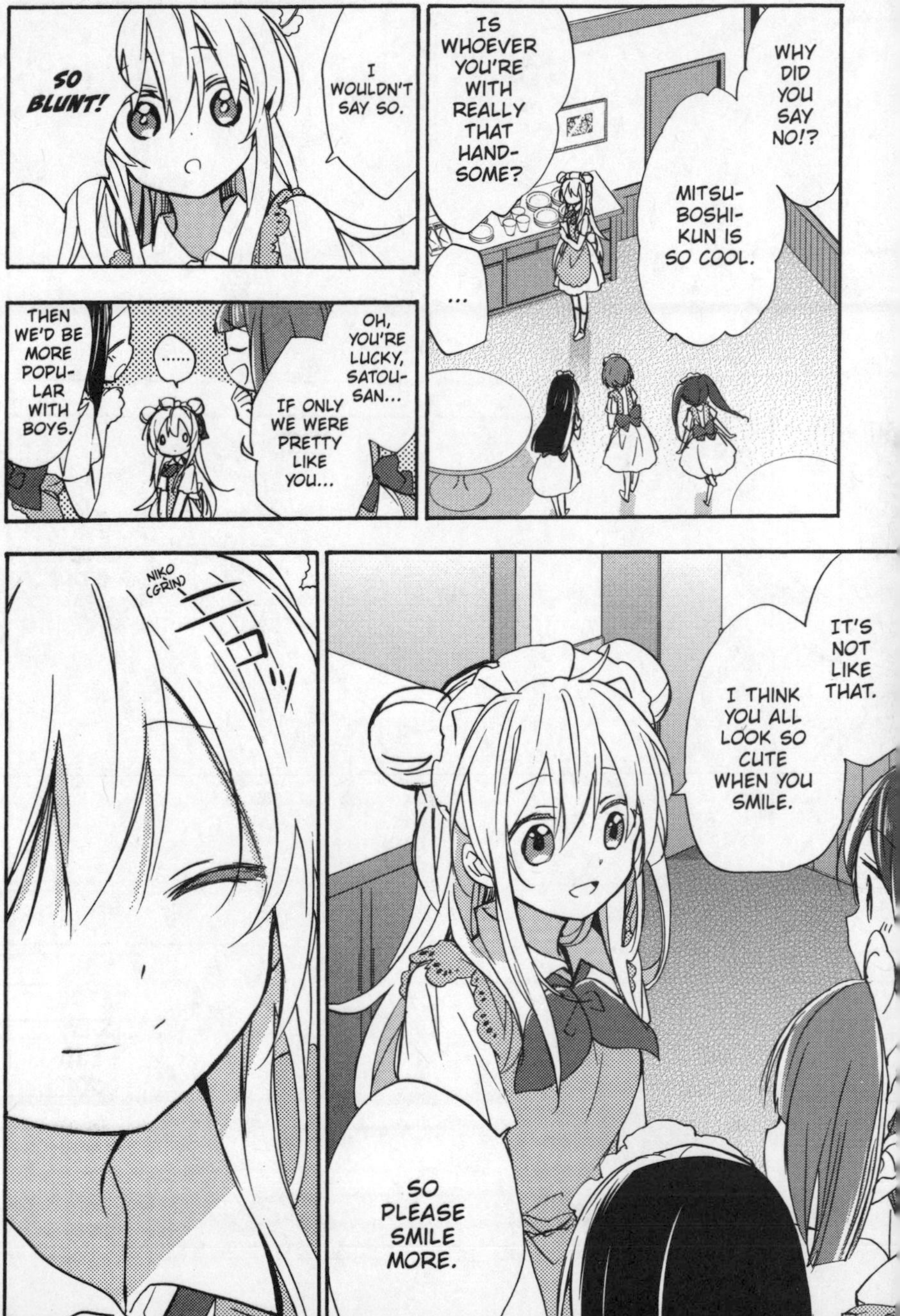
WHY DID YOU SAY NO!?
MITSUBOSHI-KUN IS SO COOL.
IS WHOEVER YOU'RE WITH REALLY THAT HANDSOME?
...
I WOULDN'T SAY SO.
SO BLUNT!
OH, YOU'RE LUCKY, SATOU-SAN...
IF ONLY WE WERE PRETTY LIKE YOU...
......
THEN WE'D BE MORE POPULAR WITH BOYS.
IT'S NOT LIKE THAT.
I THINK YOU ALL LOOK SO CUTE WHEN YOU SMILE.
SO PLEASE SMILE MORE.
NIKO (GRIN)

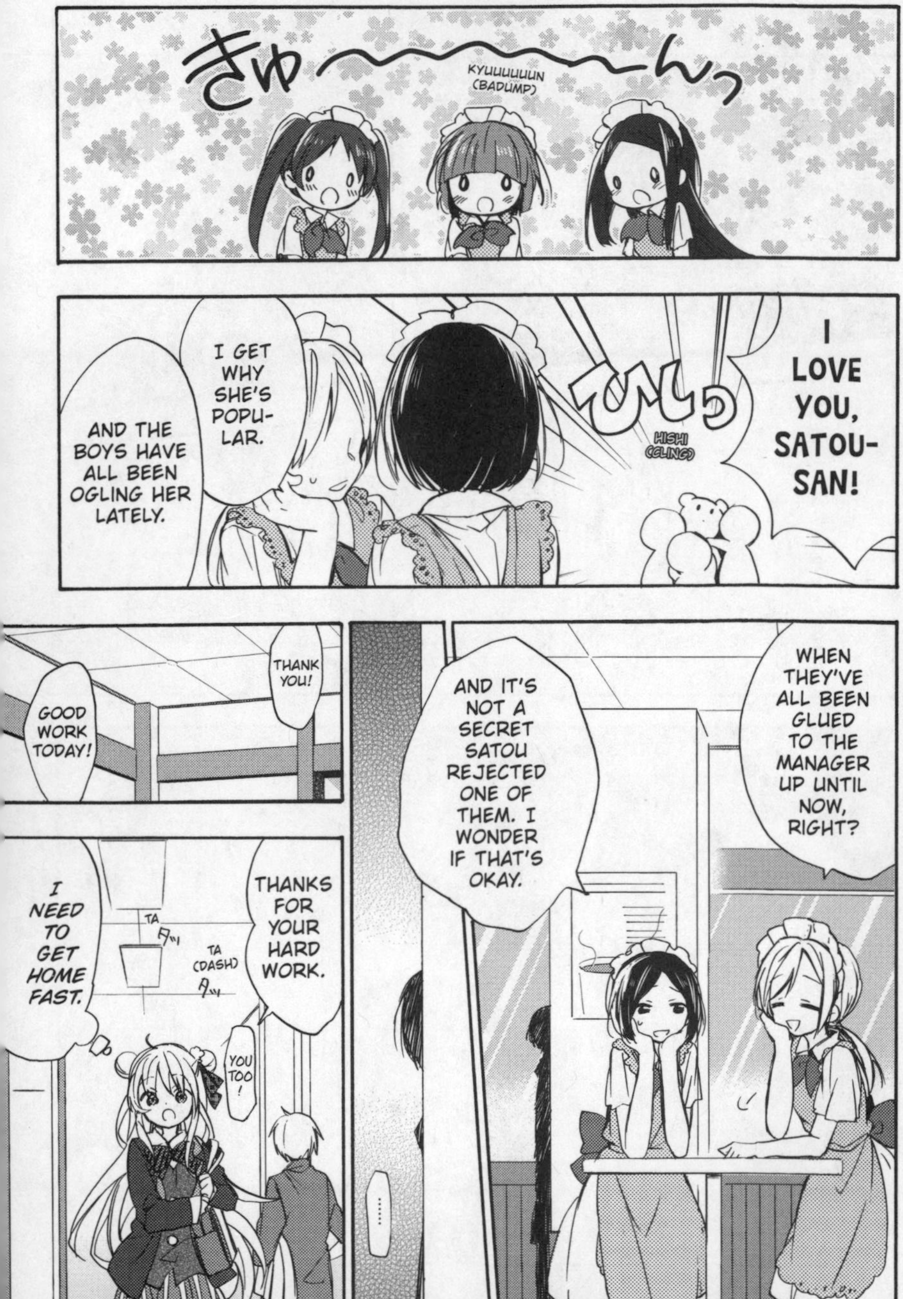

きゅ〜〜〜〜んっ
KYUUUUUUUN (BADUMP)
ひしっ
HISHI (CLING)
I LOVE YOU, SATOU-SAN!
I GET WHY SHE'S POPU-LAR.
AND THE BOYS HAVE ALL BEEN OGLING HER LATELY.
WHEN THEY'VE ALL BEEN GLUED TO THE MANAGER UP UNTIL NOW, RIGHT?
AND IT'S NOT A SECRET SATOU REJECTED ONE OF THEM. I WONDER IF THAT'S OKAY.
......
THANK YOU!
GOOD WORK TODAY!
THANKS FOR YOUR HARD WORK.
TA
タッ
TA (DASH)
タッ
YOU TOO!
I NEED TO GET HOME FAST.

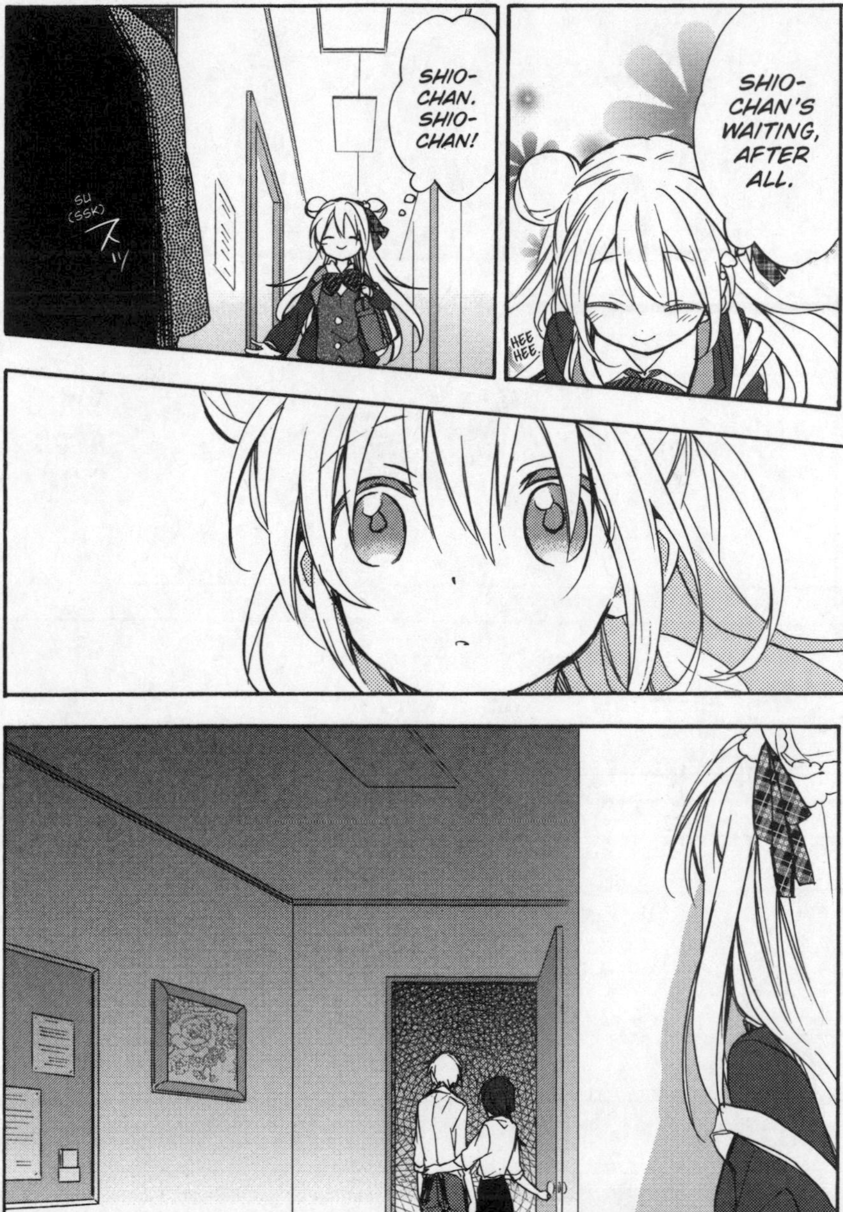
SHIO-CHAN'S WAITING, AFTER ALL.
HEE HEE.
SHIO-CHAN. SHIO-CHAN!
SU (SSK)
スッ

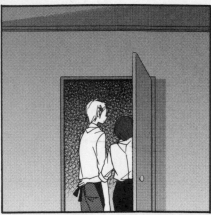

PATAN
(THUMP)

パタ一ン

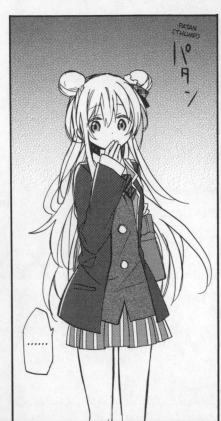

......

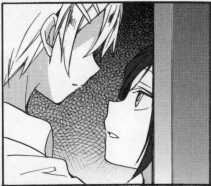

THE
NEXT DAY,
MITSUBOSHI-
KUN STOPPED
COMING TO
WORK.

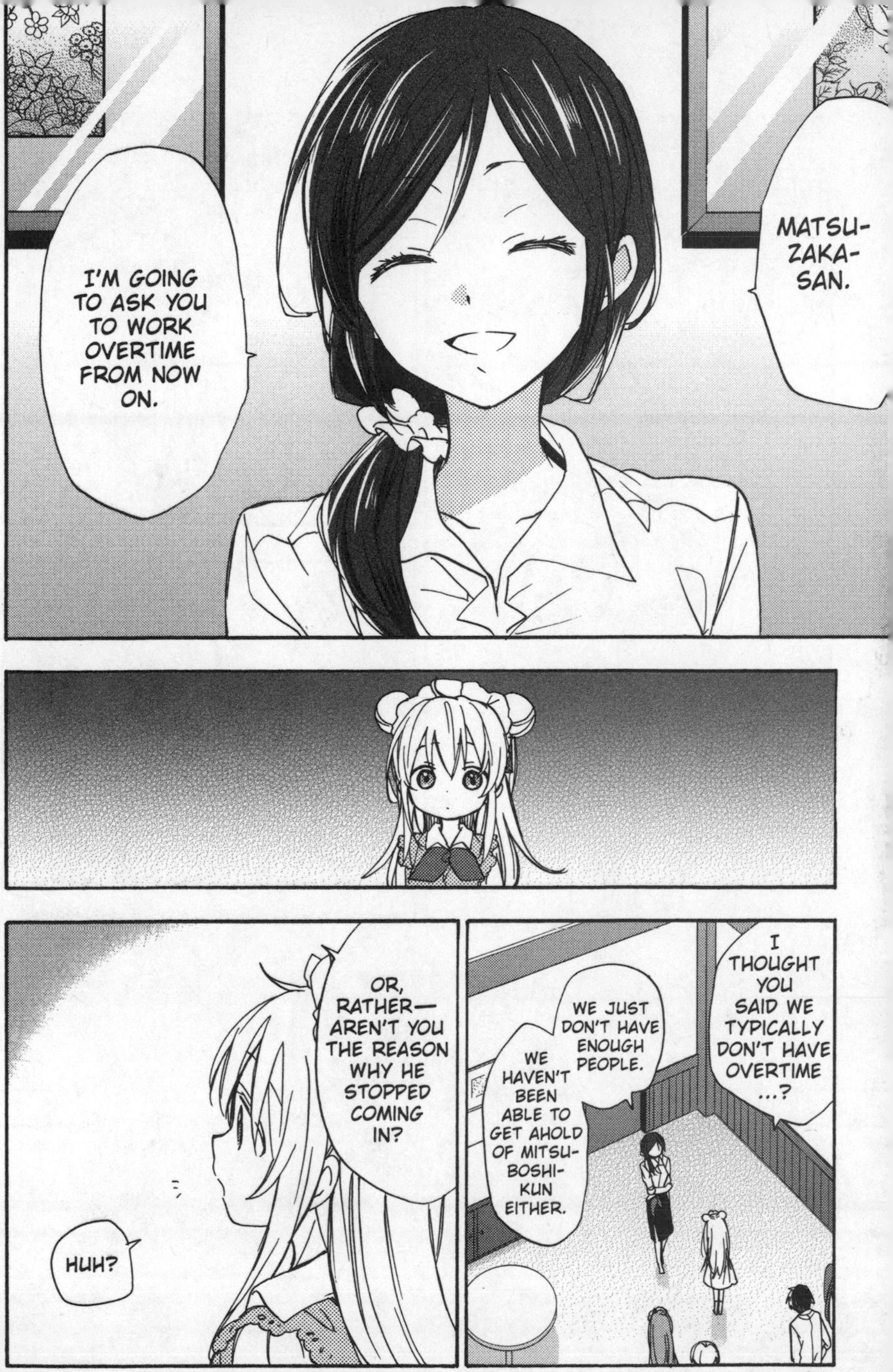
MATSU-ZAKA-SAN.
I'M GOING TO ASK YOU TO WORK OVERTIME FROM NOW ON.
I THOUGHT YOU SAID WE TYPICALLY DON'T HAVE OVERTIME ...?
WE JUST DON'T HAVE ENOUGH PEOPLE.
WE HAVEN'T BEEN ABLE TO GET AHOLD OF MITSU-BOSHI-KUN EITHER.
OR, RATHER— AREN'T YOU THE REASON WHY HE STOPPED COMING IN?
HUH?

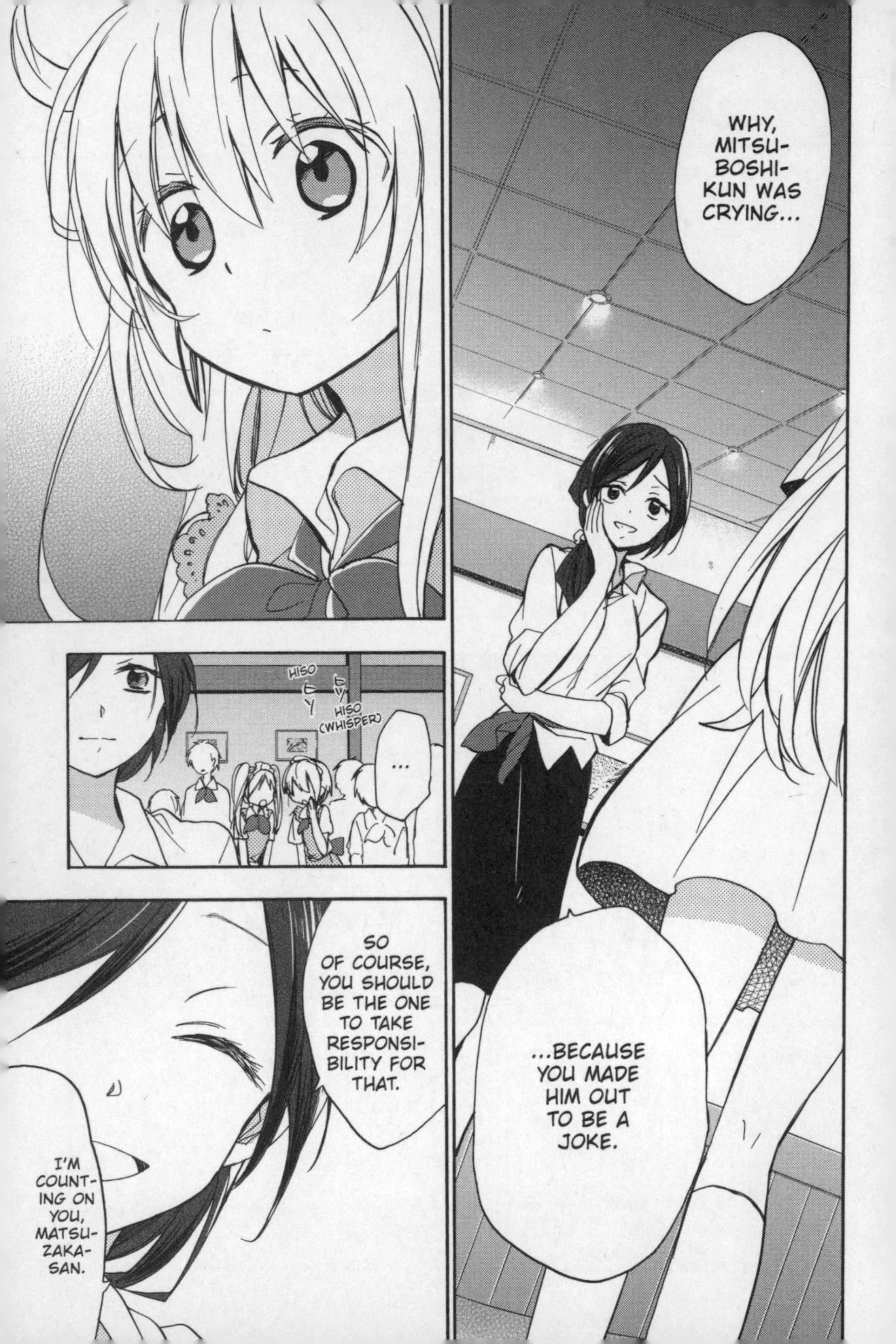
WHY, MITSUBOSHI-KUN WAS CRYING...
...BECAUSE YOU MADE HIM OUT TO BE A JOKE.
HISO HISO (WHISPER)
...
SO OF COURSE, YOU SHOULD BE THE ONE TO TAKE RESPONSIBILITY FOR THAT.
I'M COUNTING ON YOU, MATSUZAKA-SAN.

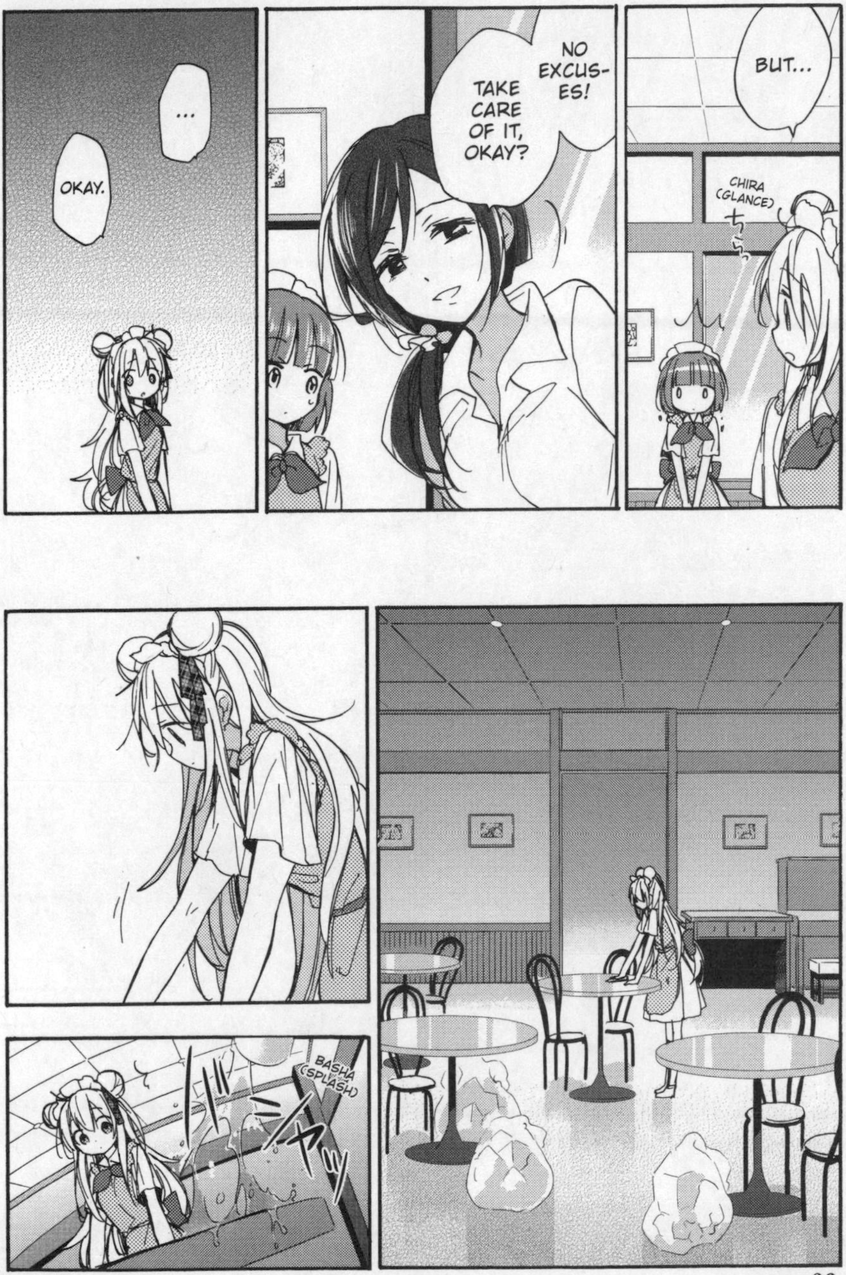
BUT...
CHIRA (GLANCE)
NO EXCUSES!
TAKE CARE OF IT, OKAY?
...
OKAY.
BASHA (SPLASH)

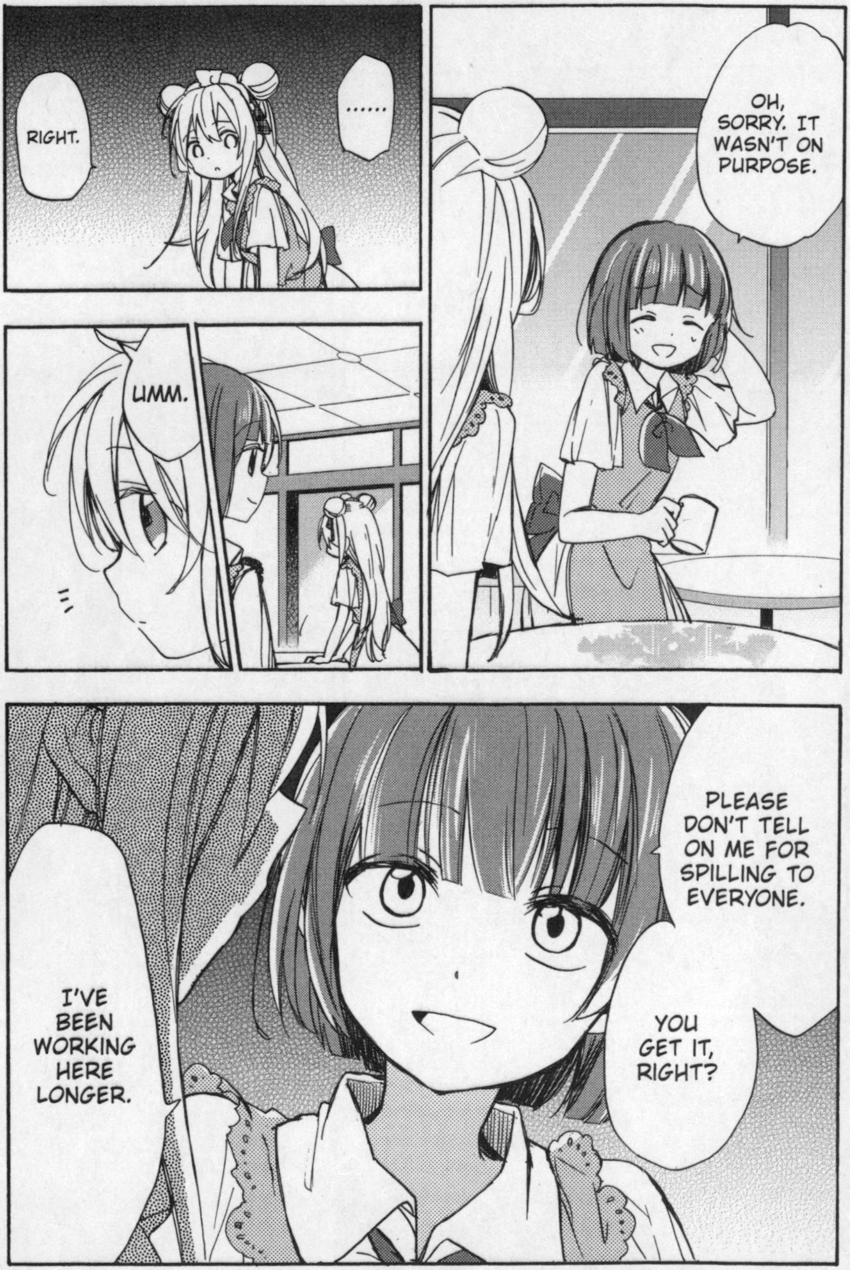
OH, SORRY. IT WASN'T ON PURPOSE.
......
RIGHT.
UMM.
PLEASE DON'T TELL ON ME FOR SPILLING TO EVERYONE.
YOU GET IT, RIGHT?
I'VE BEEN WORKING HERE LONGER.

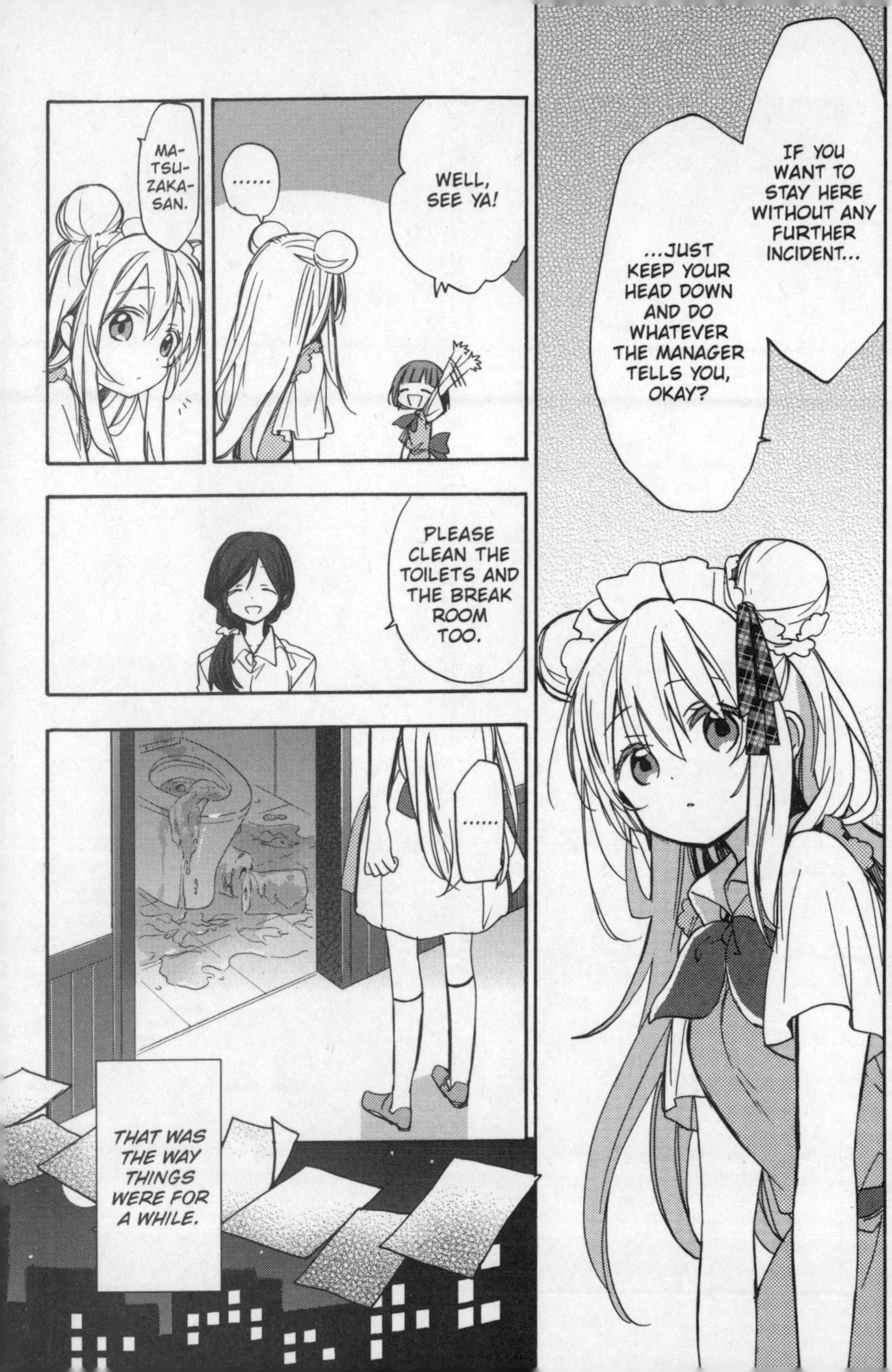
IF YOU WANT TO STAY HERE WITHOUT ANY FURTHER INCIDENT...
...JUST KEEP YOUR HEAD DOWN AND DO WHATEVER THE MANAGER TELLS YOU, OKAY?
WELL, SEE YA!
......
MA-TSU-ZAKA-SAN.
PLEASE CLEAN THE TOILETS AND THE BREAK ROOM TOO.
......
THAT WAS THE WAY THINGS WERE FOR A WHILE.

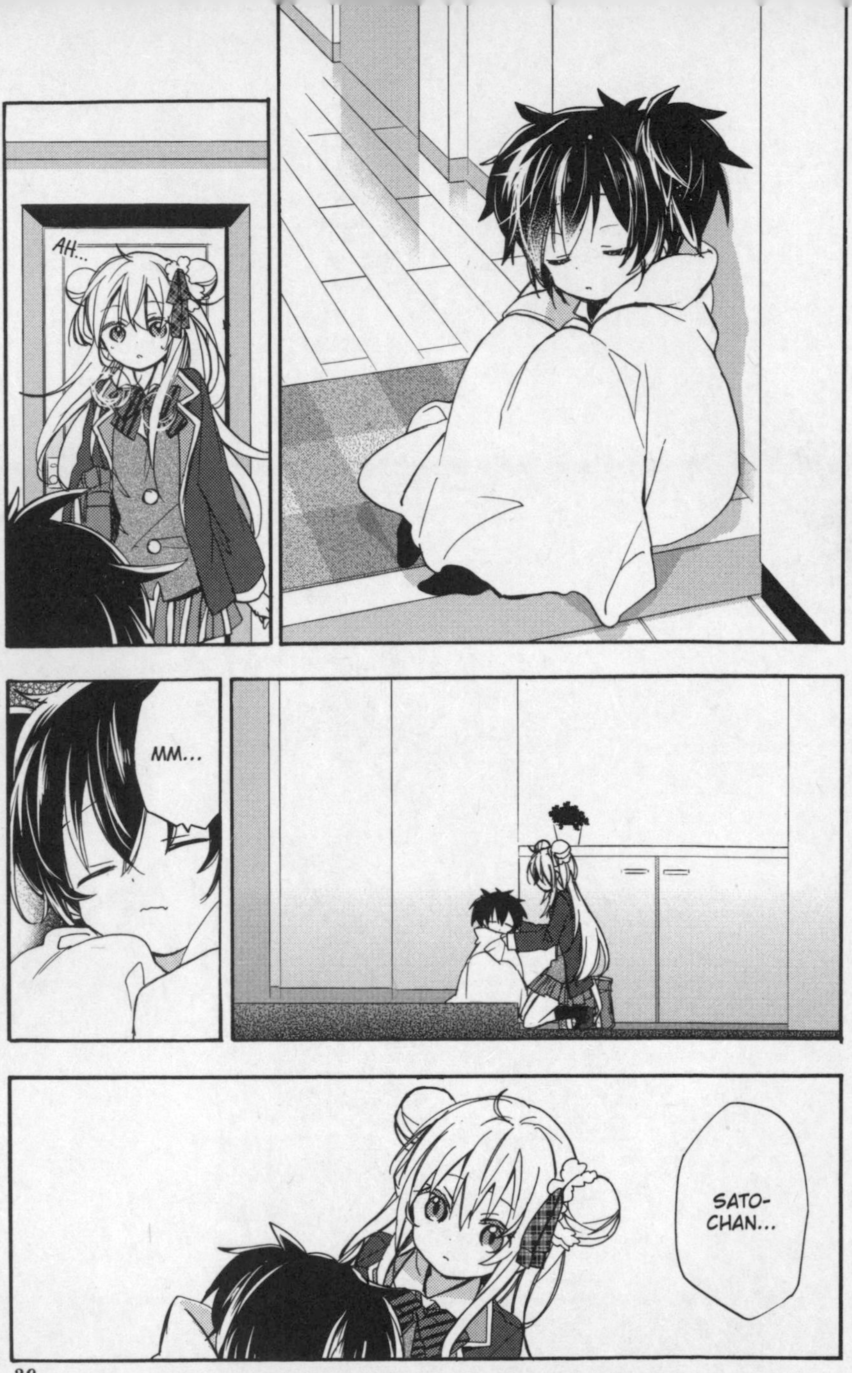
AH...
MM...
SATO-
CHAN...

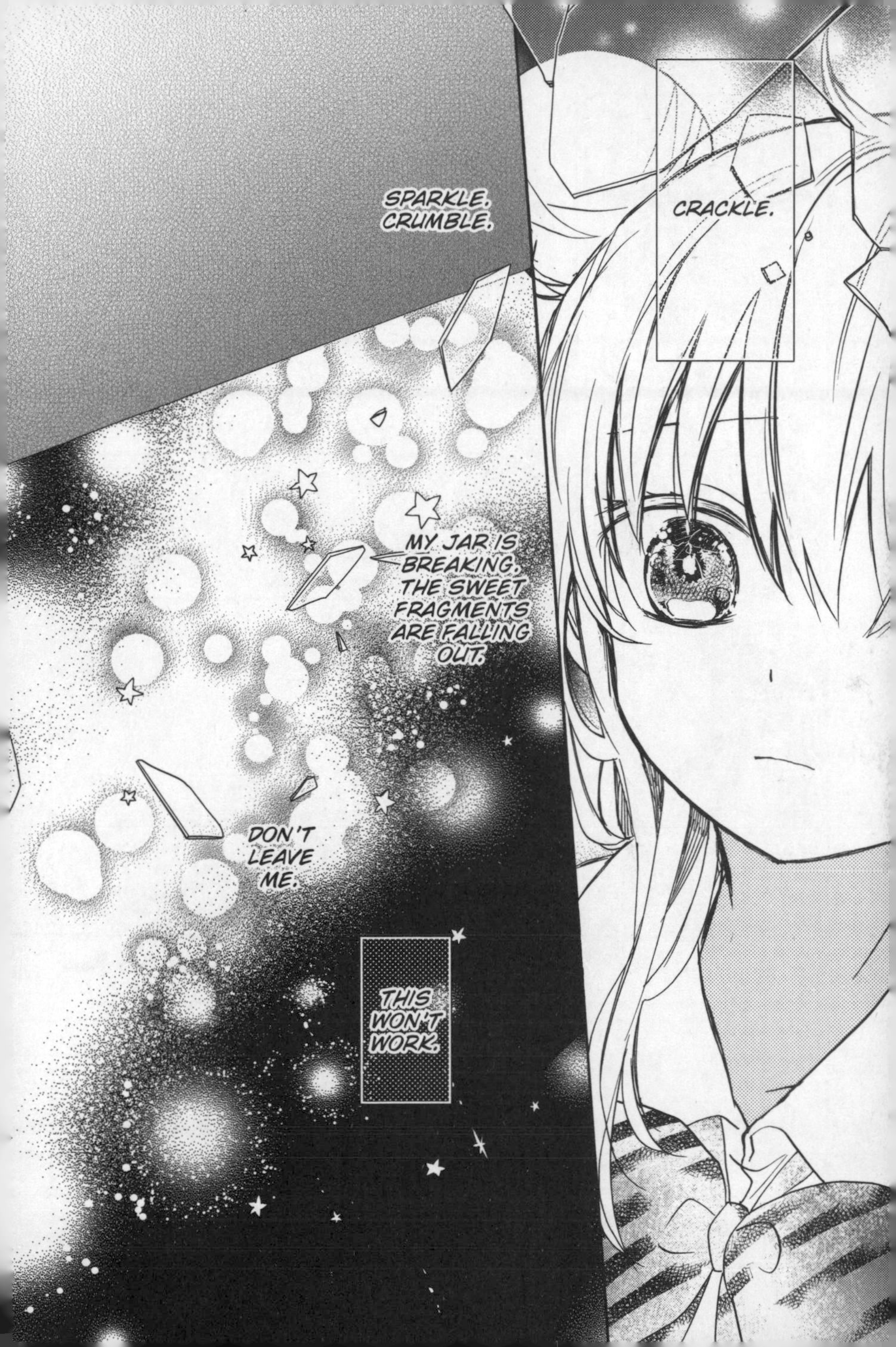
CRACKLE.
SPARKLE. CRUMBLE.
MY JAR IS BREAKING. THE SWEET FRAGMENTS ARE FALLING OUT.
DON'T LEAVE ME.
THIS WON'T WORK.

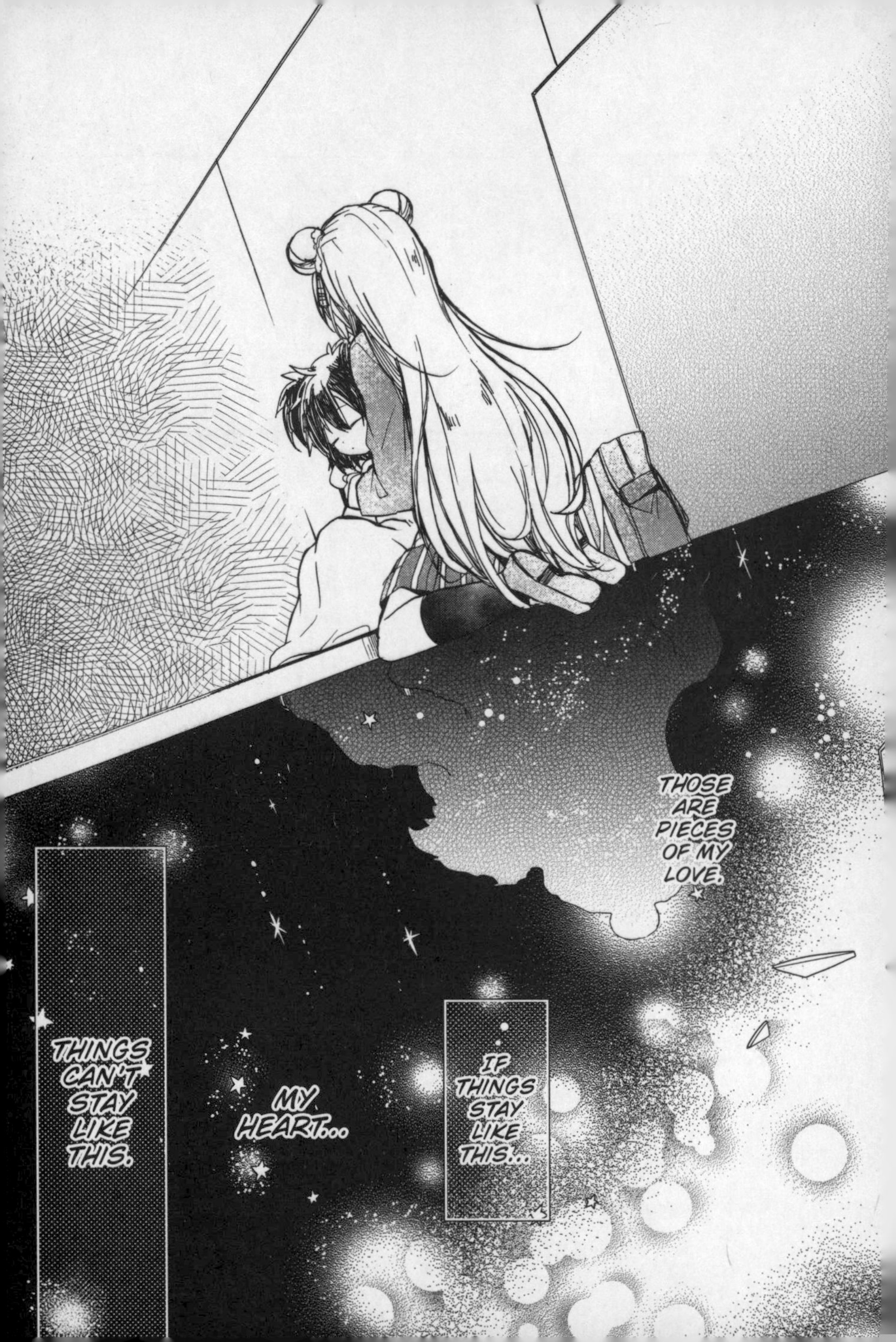
THOSE ARE PIECES OF MY LOVE.
IF THINGS STAY LIKE THIS...
MY HEART...
THINGS CAN'T STAY LIKE THIS.

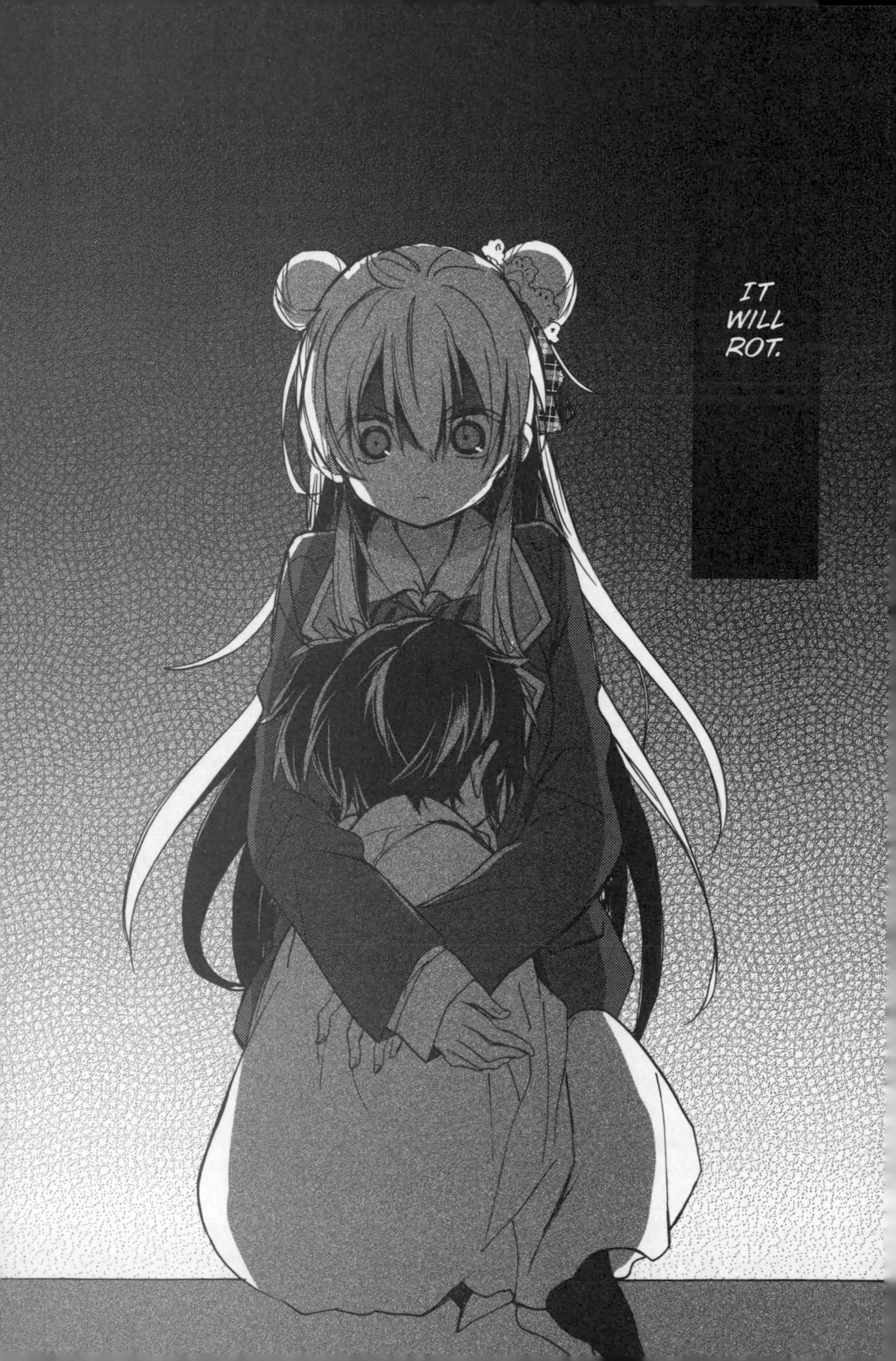
IT WILL ROT.

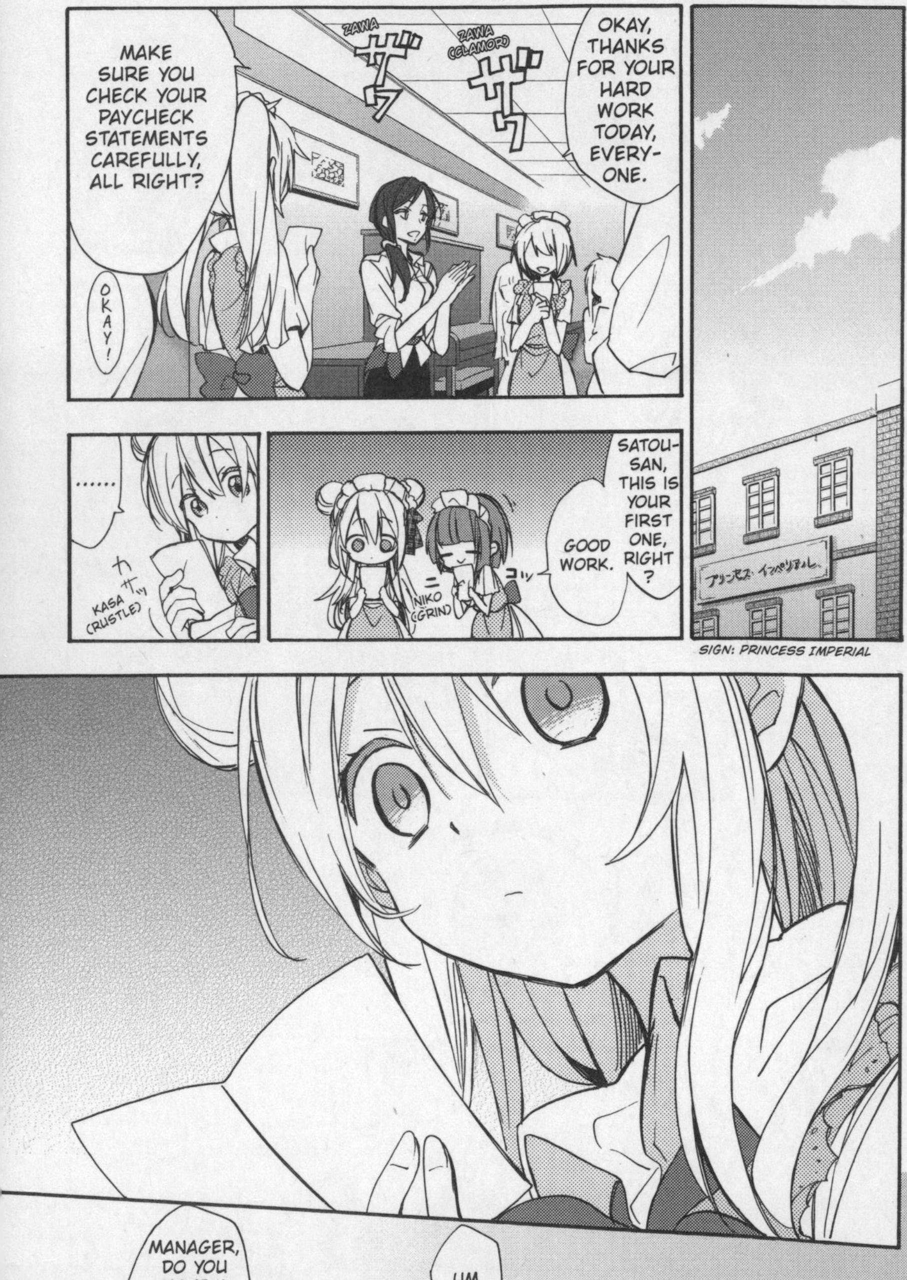
SIGN: PRINCESS IMPERIAL
OKAY, THANKS FOR YOUR HARD WORK TODAY, EVERY-ONE.
ZAWA (CLAMOR)
ZAWA
MAKE SURE YOU CHECK YOUR PAYCHECK STATEMENTS CAREFULLY, ALL RIGHT?
OKAY!
SATOU-SAN, THIS IS YOUR FIRST ONE, RIGHT?
GOOD WORK.
NIKO (GRIN)
......
KASA (RUSTLE)
UM.
MANAGER, DO YOU HAVE A MINUTE?

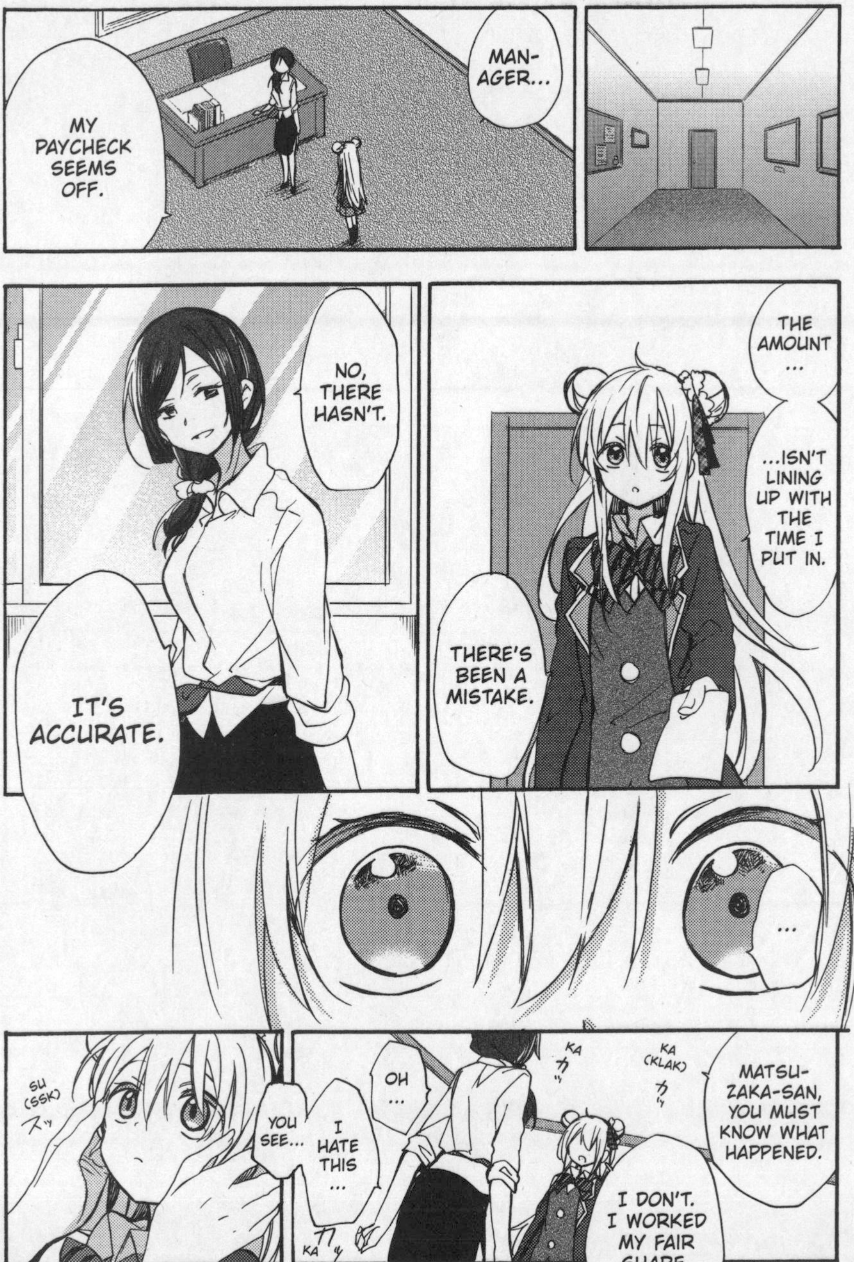
MAN-AGER...
MY PAYCHECK SEEMS OFF.
THE AMOUNT ...
...ISN'T LINING UP WITH THE TIME I PUT IN.
THERE'S BEEN A MISTAKE.
NO, THERE HASN'T.
IT'S ACCURATE.
...
MATSU-ZAKA-SAN, YOU MUST KNOW WHAT HAPPENED.
KA (KLAK) カッ
KA カッ
I DON'T. I WORKED MY FAIR SHARE.
OH ...
I HATE THIS ...
YOU SEE...
KA カッ
SU (SSK) スッ

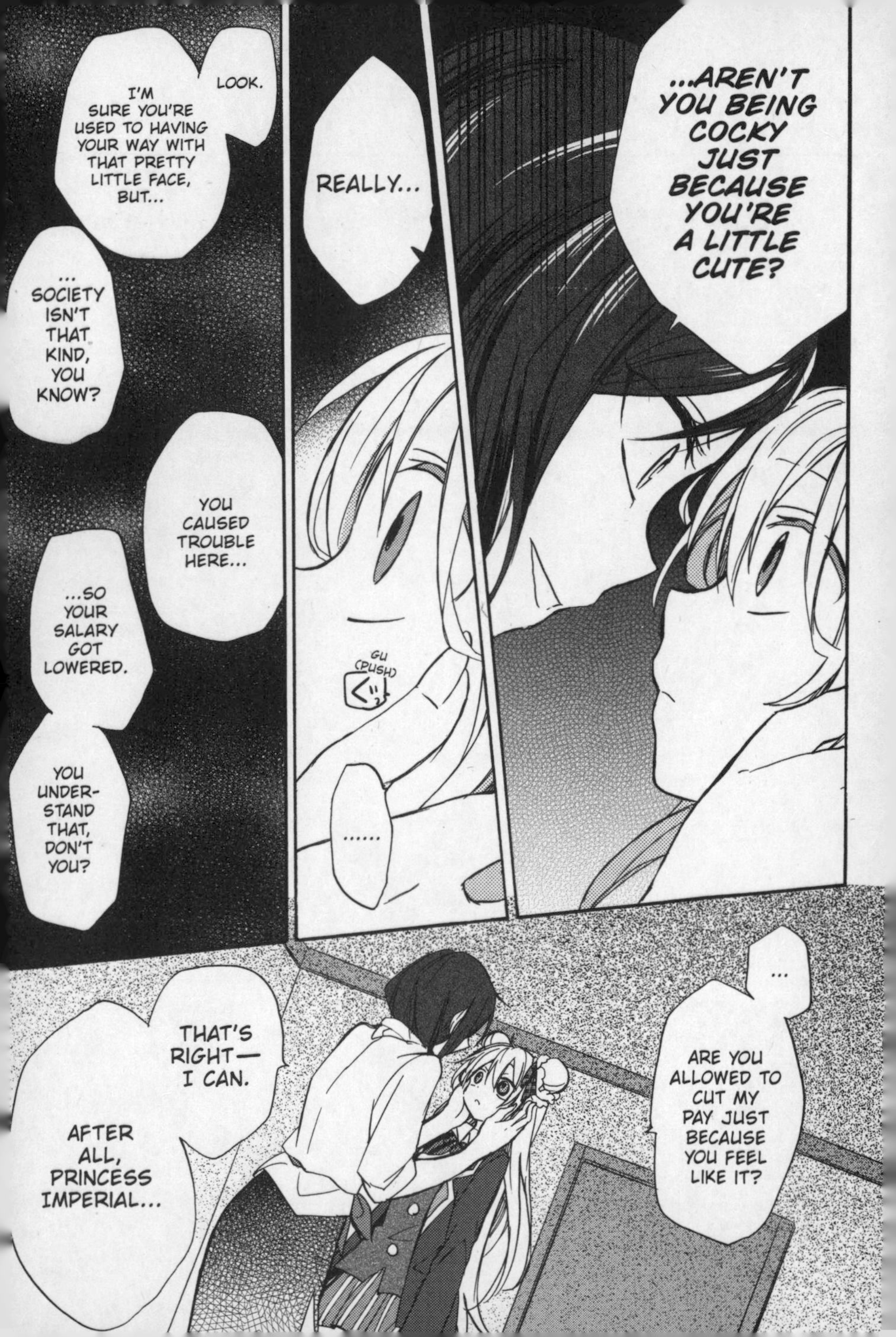
...AREN'T YOU BEING COCKY JUST BECAUSE YOU'RE A LITTLE CUTE?
REALLY...
GU (PUSH)
......
LOOK.
I'M SURE YOU'RE USED TO HAVING YOUR WAY WITH THAT PRETTY LITTLE FACE, BUT...
...SOCIETY ISN'T THAT KIND, YOU KNOW?
YOU CAUSED TROUBLE HERE...
...SO YOUR SALARY GOT LOWERED.
YOU UNDER-STAND THAT, DON'T YOU?
...
ARE YOU ALLOWED TO CUT MY PAY JUST BECAUSE YOU FEEL LIKE IT?
THAT'S RIGHT— I CAN.
AFTER ALL, PRINCESS IMPERIAL...

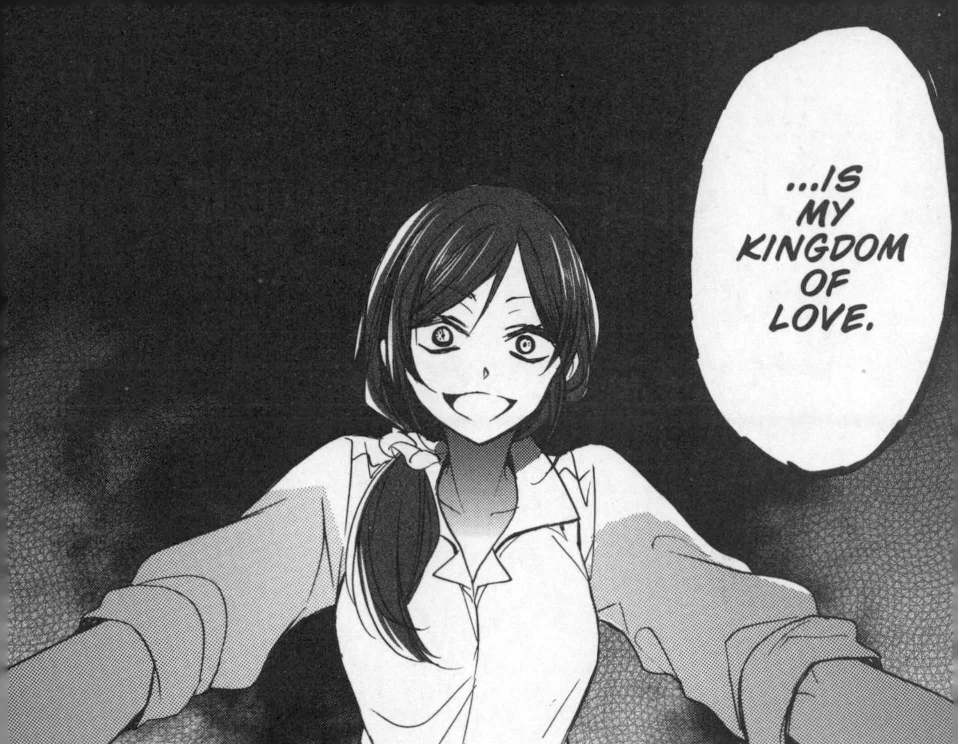
...IS MY KINGDOM OF LOVE.
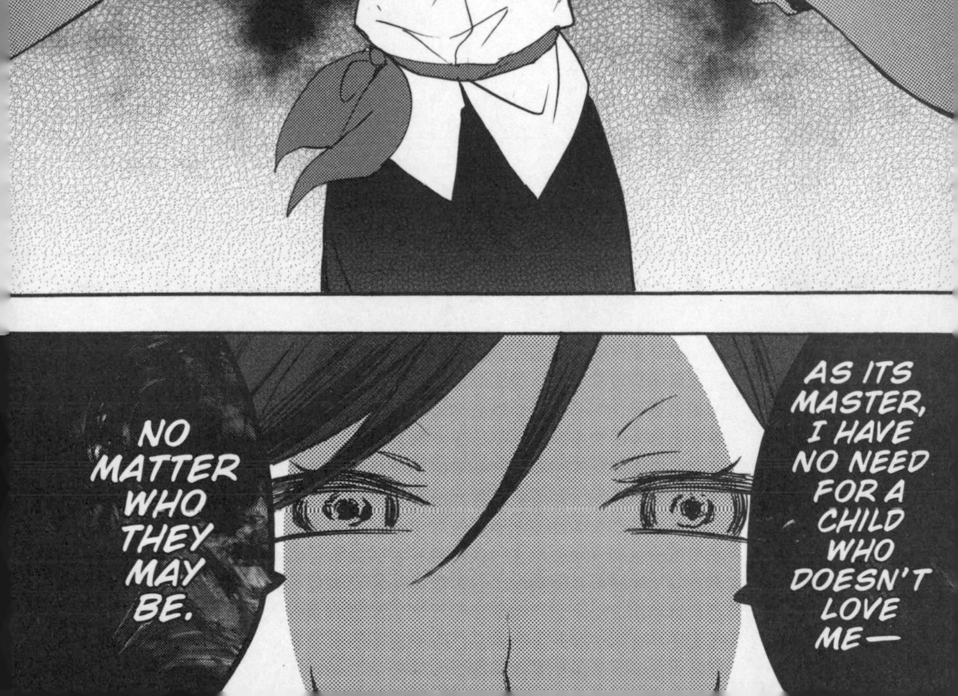
AS ITS MASTER, I HAVE NO NEED FOR A CHILD WHO DOESN'T LOVE ME—
NO MATTER WHO THEY MAY BE.

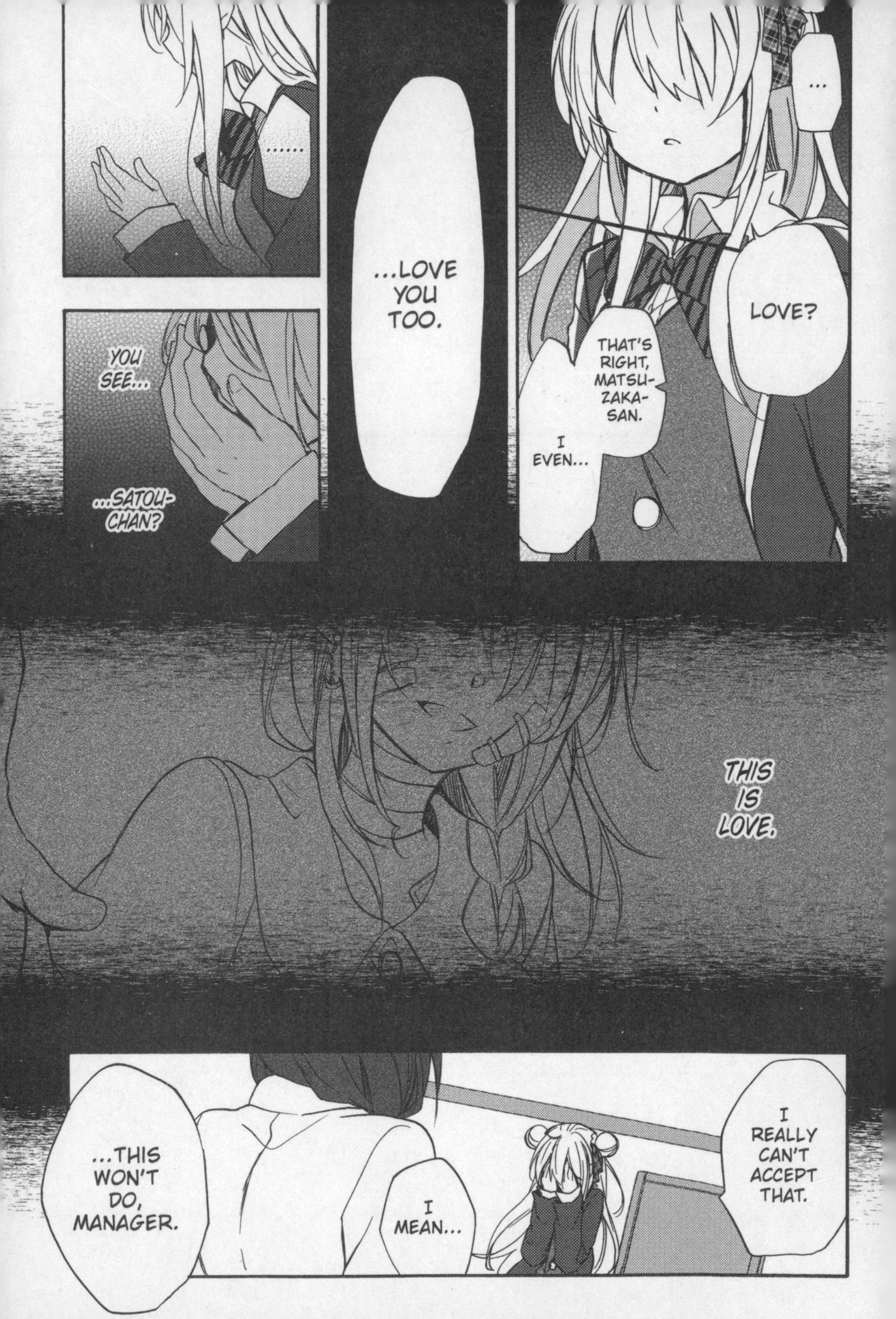
...
LOVE?
THAT'S RIGHT, MATSUZAKA-SAN.
I EVEN...
...LOVE YOU TOO.
......
YOU SEE...
...SATOU-CHAN?
THIS IS LOVE.
I REALLY CAN'T ACCEPT THAT.
I MEAN...
...THIS WON'T DO, MANAGER.

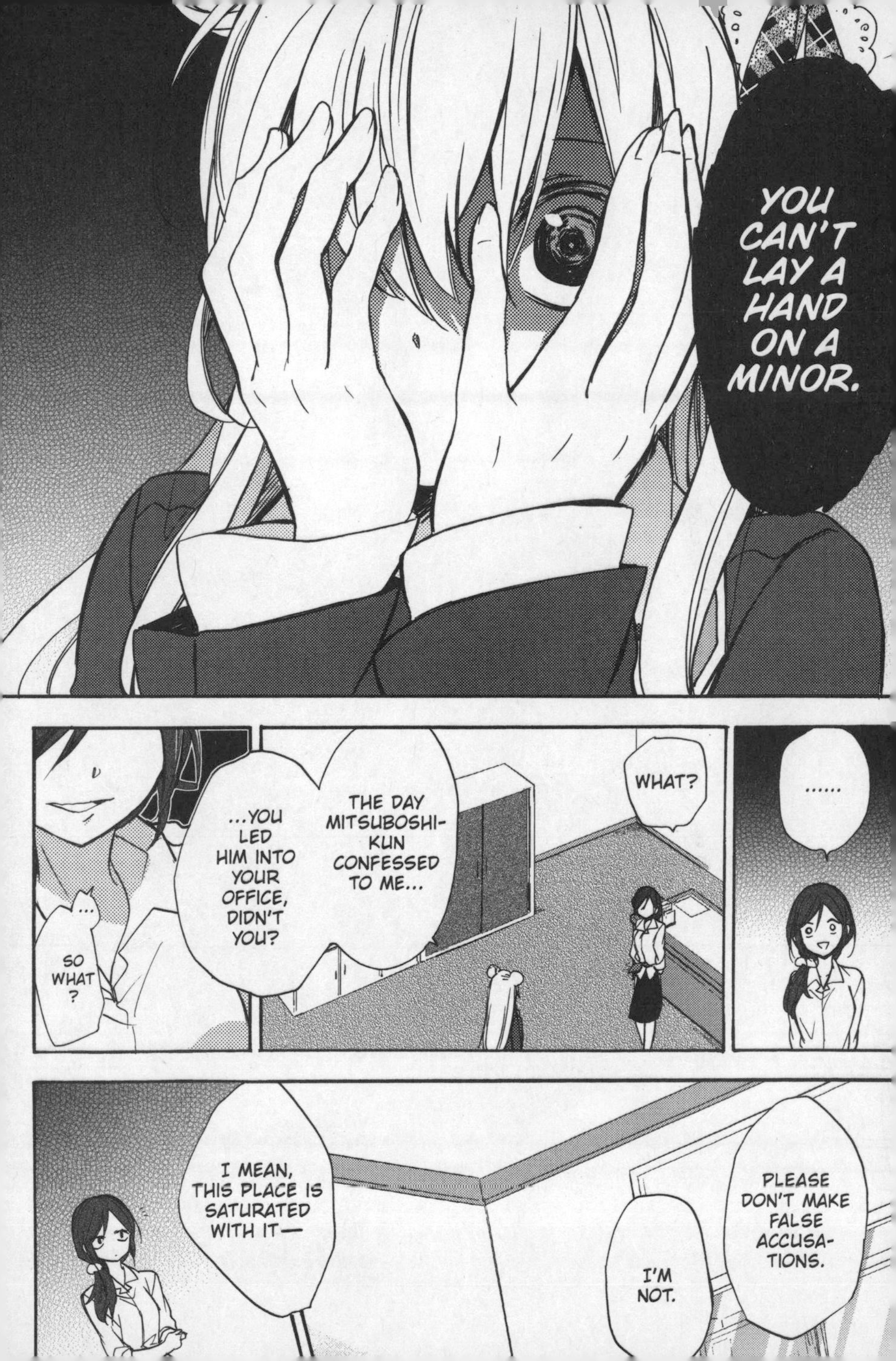
YOU CAN'T LAY A HAND ON A MINOR.
......
WHAT?
THE DAY MITSUBOSHI-KUN CONFESSED TO ME...
...YOU LED HIM INTO YOUR OFFICE, DIDN'T YOU?
...
SO WHAT?
PLEASE DON'T MAKE FALSE ACCUSA-TIONS.
I'M NOT.
I MEAN, THIS PLACE IS SATURATED WITH IT—

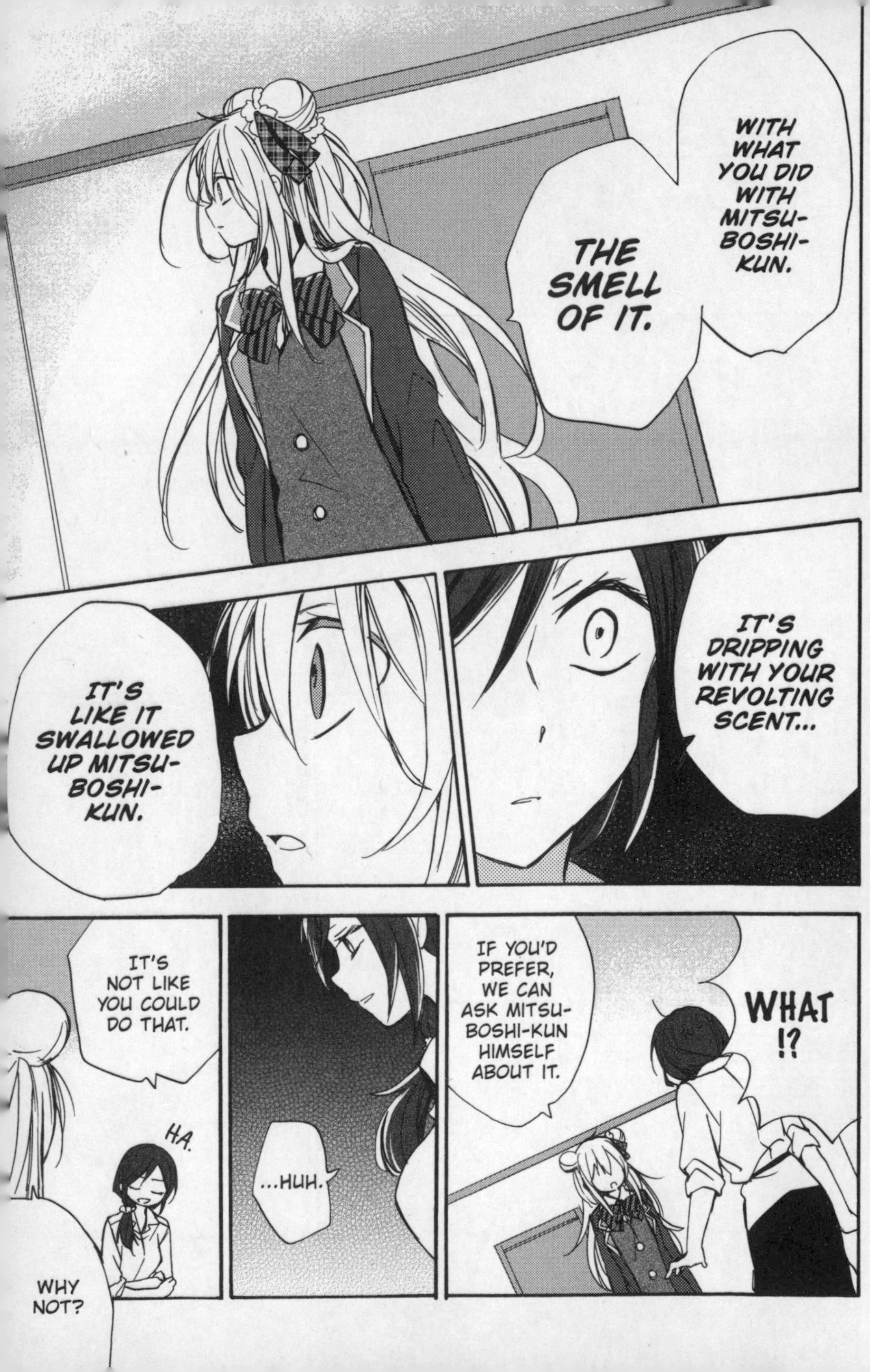

WITH WHAT YOU DID WITH MITSU-BOSHI-KUN.
THE SMELL OF IT.
IT'S DRIPPING WITH YOUR REVOLTING SCENT...
IT'S LIKE IT SWALLOWED UP MITSU-BOSHI-KUN.
WHAT!?
IF YOU'D PREFER, WE CAN ASK MITSU-BOSHI-KUN HIMSELF ABOUT IT.
...HUH.
IT'S NOT LIKE YOU COULD DO THAT.
HA.
WHY NOT?

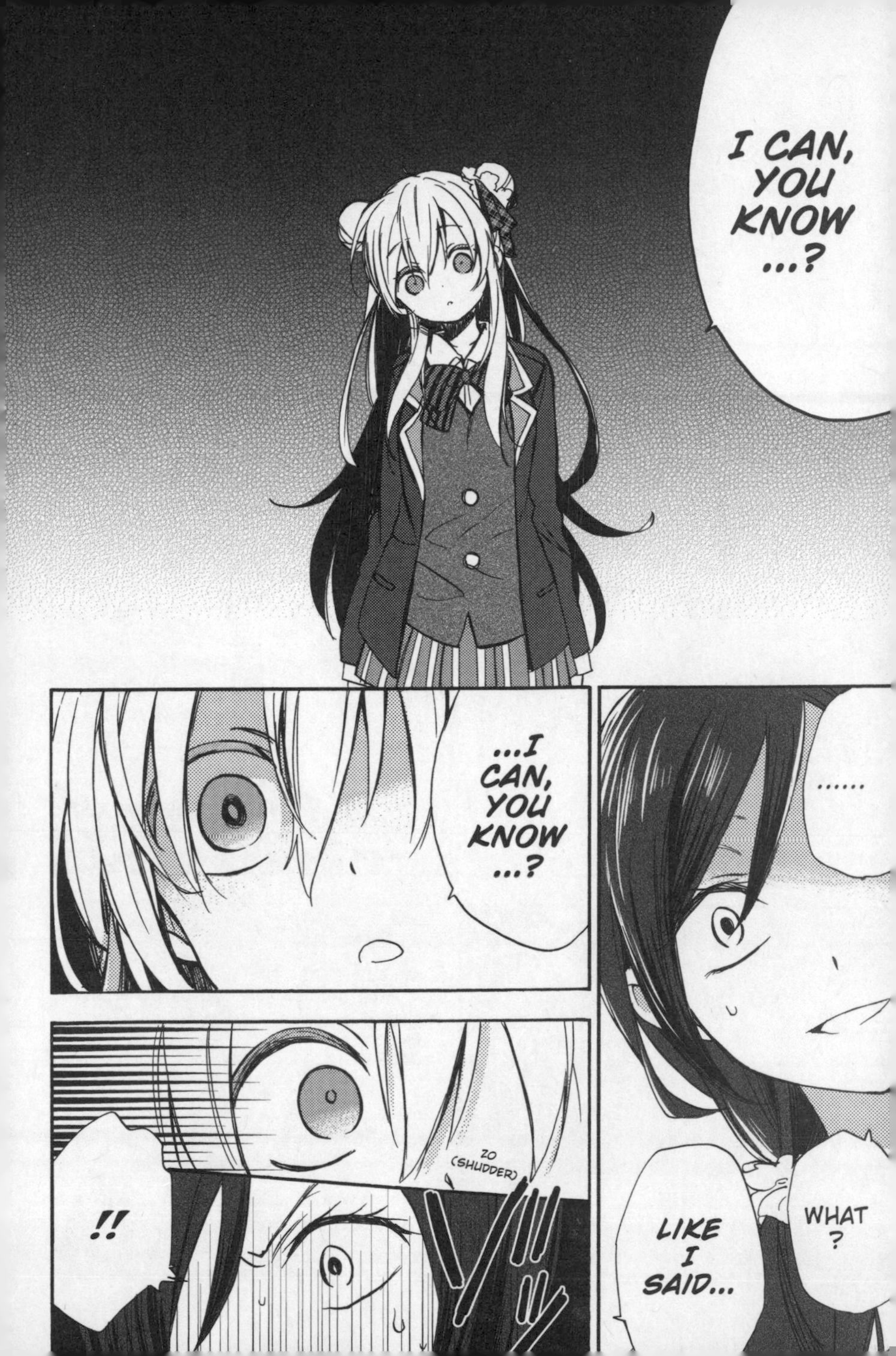
I CAN, YOU KNOW ...?
......
WHAT?
LIKE I SAID...
...I CAN, YOU KNOW ...?
ZO (SHUDDER)
!!

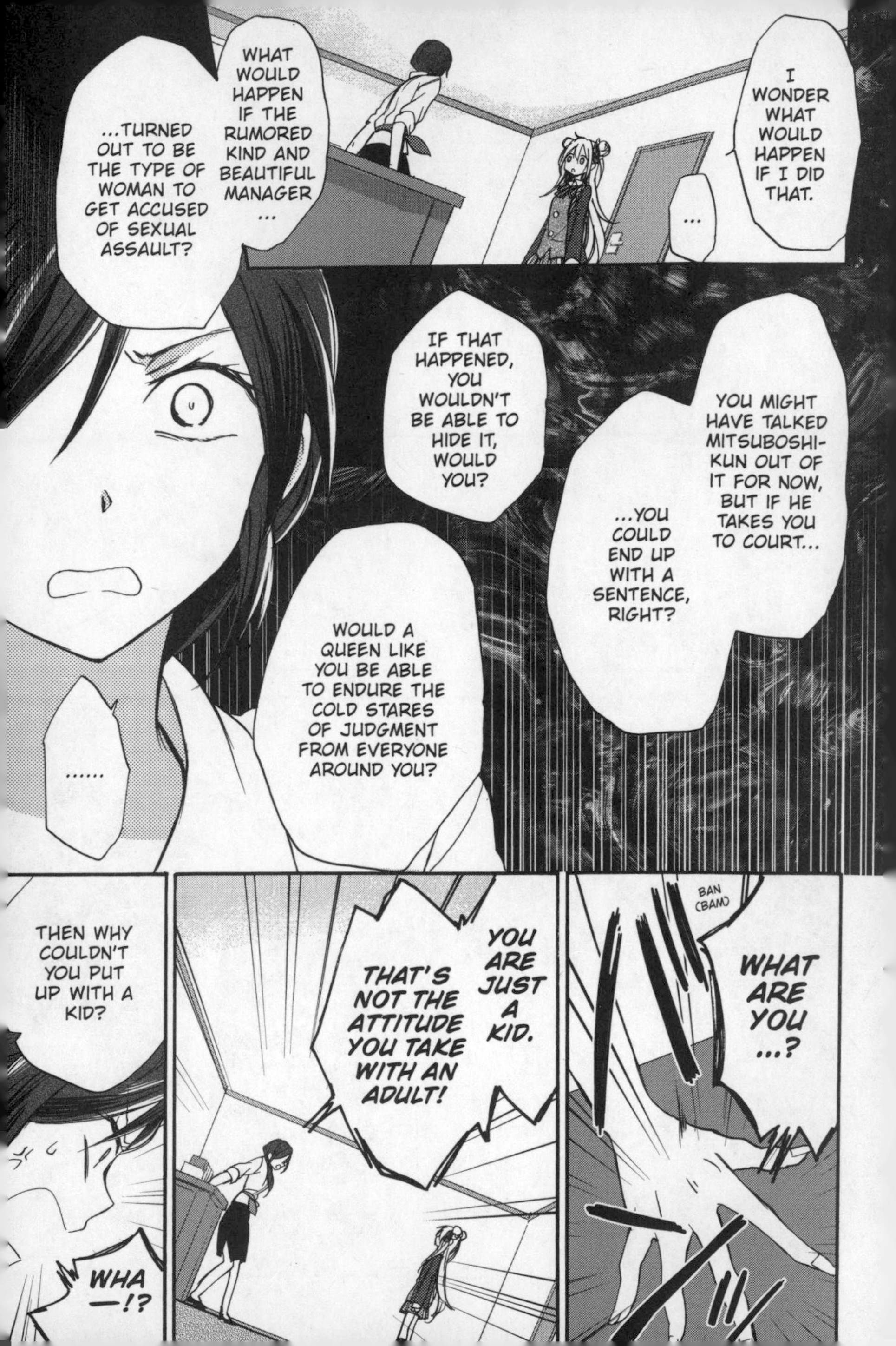
I WONDER WHAT WOULD HAPPEN IF I DID THAT.
...
WHAT WOULD HAPPEN IF THE RUMORED KIND AND BEAUTIFUL MANAGER ...
...TURNED OUT TO BE THE TYPE OF WOMAN TO GET ACCUSED OF SEXUAL ASSAULT?
YOU MIGHT HAVE TALKED MITSUBOSHI-KUN OUT OF IT FOR NOW, BUT IF HE TAKES YOU TO COURT...
...YOU COULD END UP WITH A SENTENCE, RIGHT?
IF THAT HAPPENED, YOU WOULDN'T BE ABLE TO HIDE IT, WOULD YOU?
WOULD A QUEEN LIKE YOU BE ABLE TO ENDURE THE COLD STARES OF JUDGMENT FROM EVERYONE AROUND YOU?
......
BAN (BAM)
WHAT ARE YOU ...?
YOU ARE JUST A KID.
THAT'S NOT THE ATTITUDE YOU TAKE WITH AN ADULT!
THEN WHY COULDN'T YOU PUT UP WITH A KID?
WHA—!?

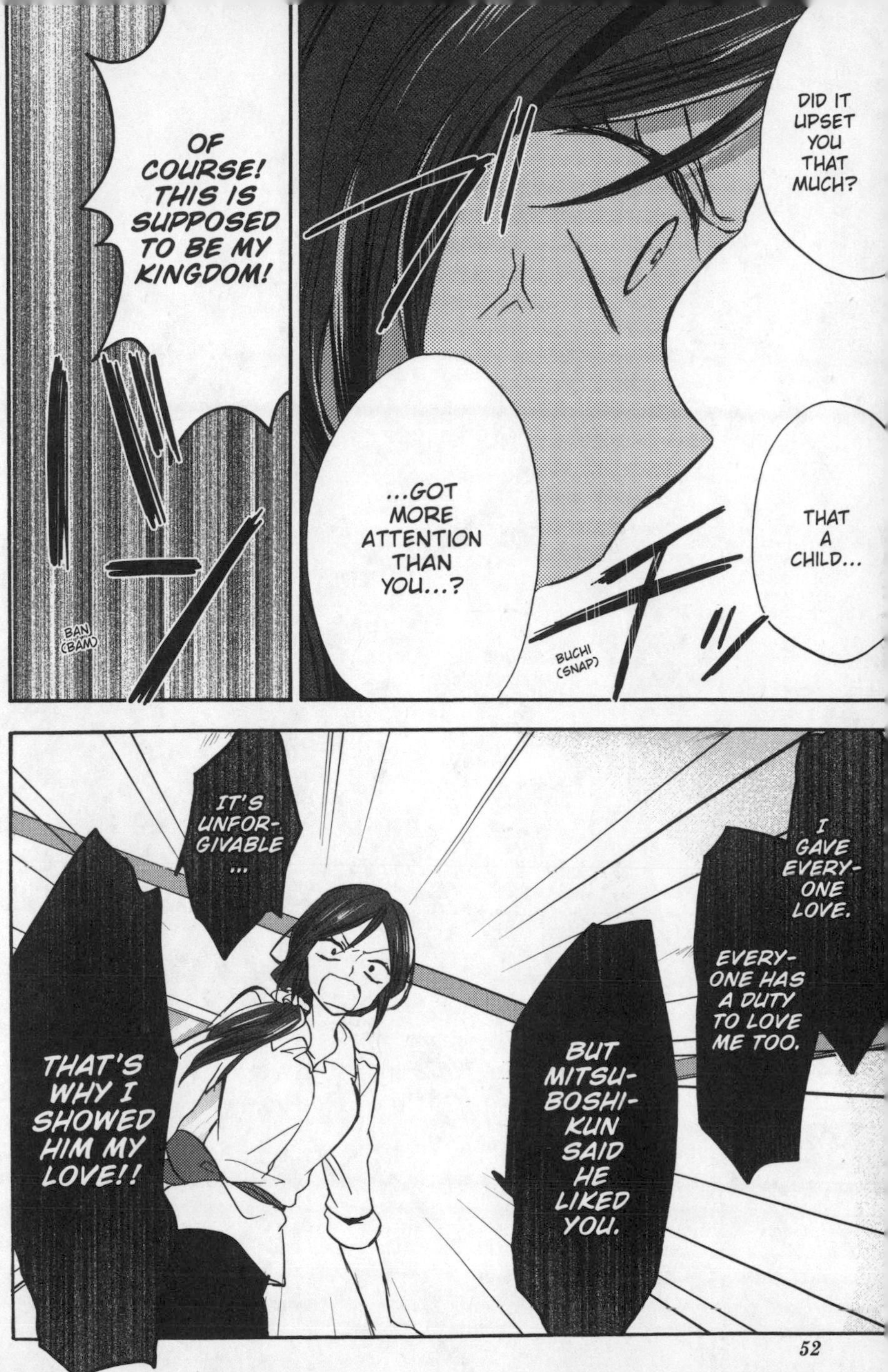
DID IT UPSET YOU THAT MUCH?
THAT A CHILD...
BUCHI (SNAP)
...GOT MORE ATTENTION THAN YOU...?
OF COURSE! THIS IS SUPPOSED TO BE MY KINGDOM!
BAN (BAM)
I GAVE EVERYONE LOVE.
EVERYONE HAS A DUTY TO LOVE ME TOO.
BUT MITSUBOSHI-KUN SAID HE LIKED YOU.
IT'S UNFORGIVABLE...
THAT'S WHY I SHOWED HIM MY LOVE!!

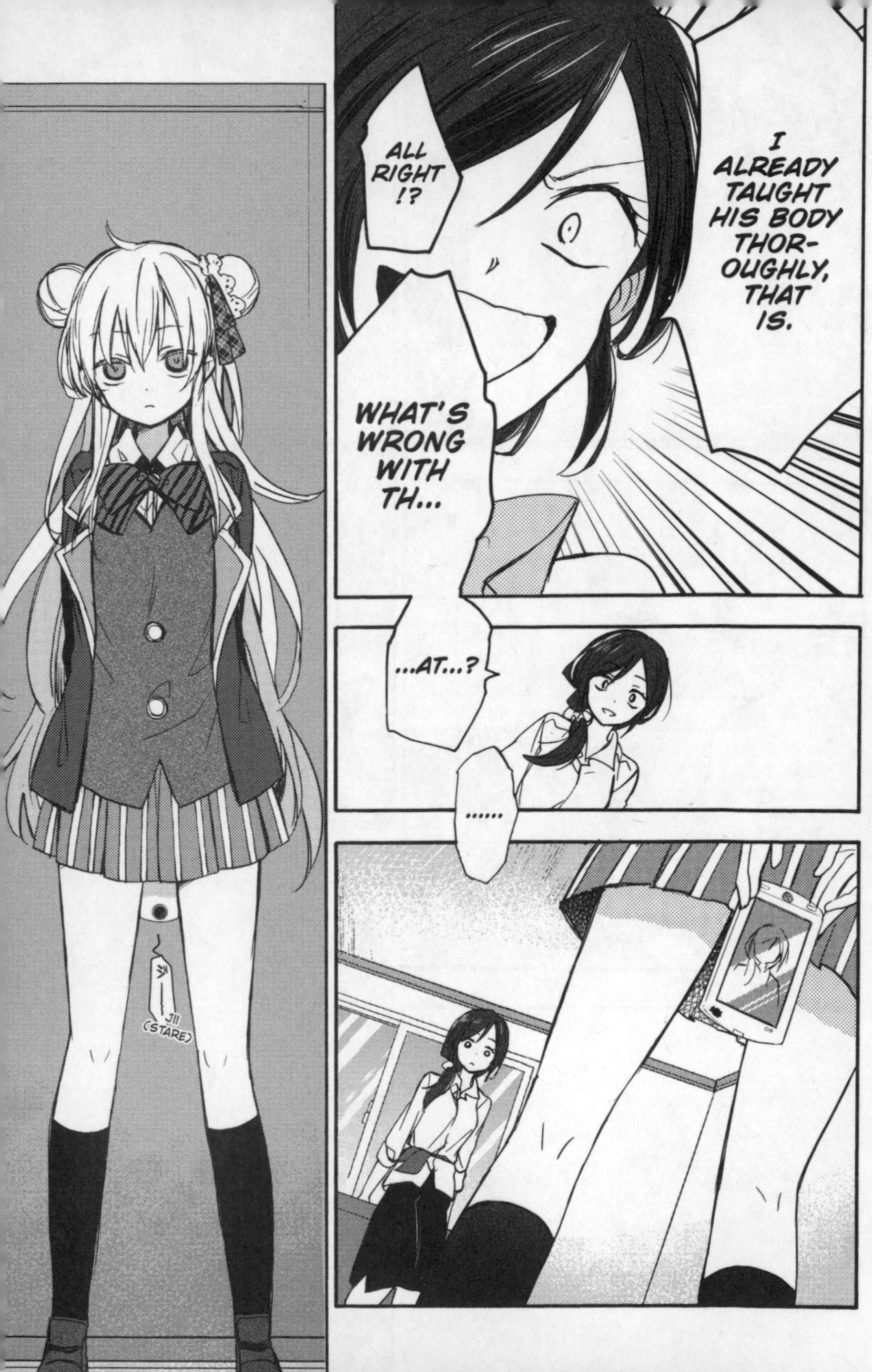
I ALREADY TAUGHT HIS BODY THOR-OUGHLY, THAT IS.
ALL RIGHT!?
WHAT'S WRONG WITH TH...
...AT...?
......
JII (STARE)

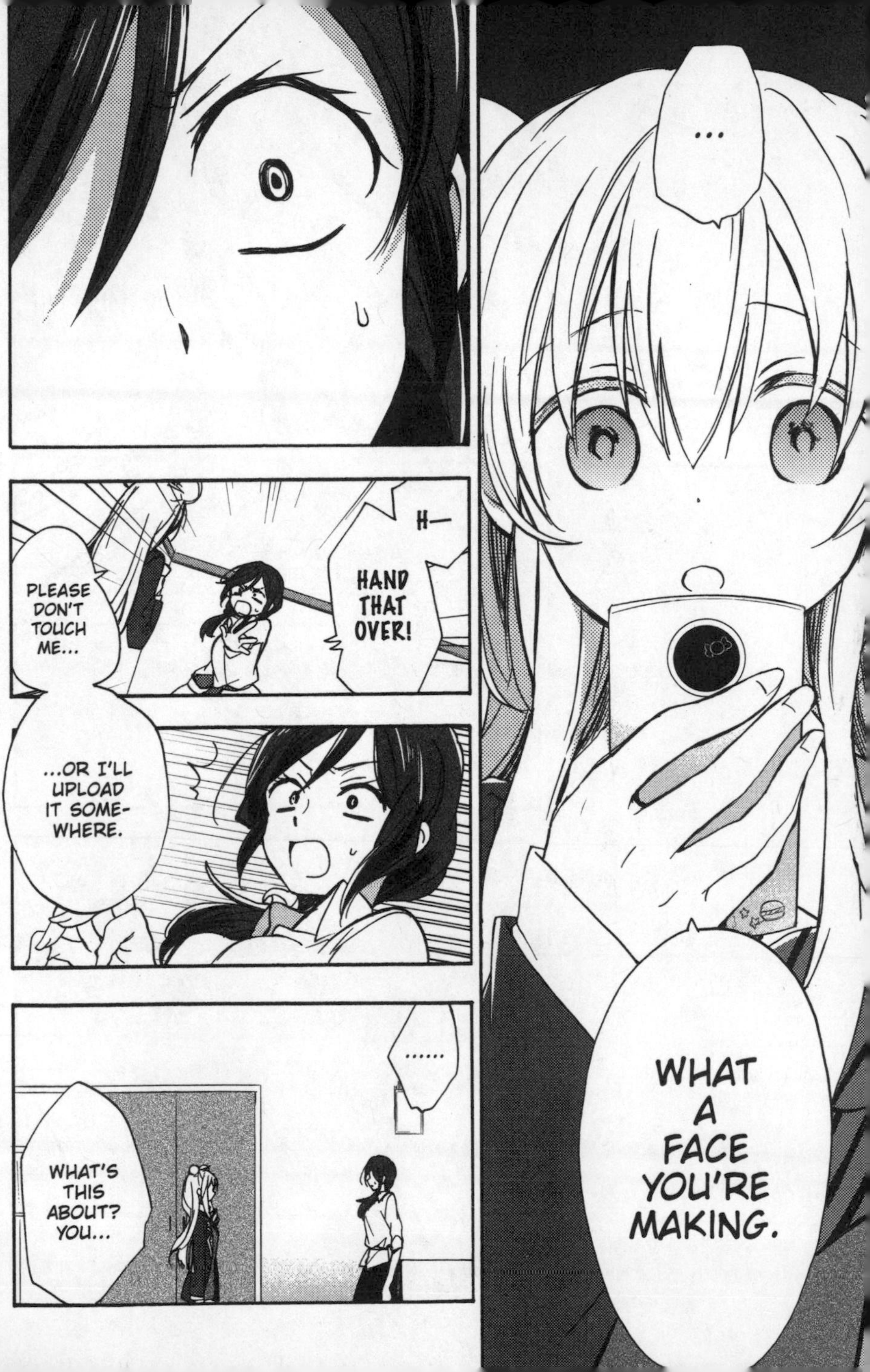
...
WHAT A FACE YOU'RE MAKING.
H—
HAND THAT OVER!
PLEASE DON'T TOUCH ME...
...OR I'LL UPLOAD IT SOME-WHERE.
......
WHAT'S THIS ABOUT? YOU...

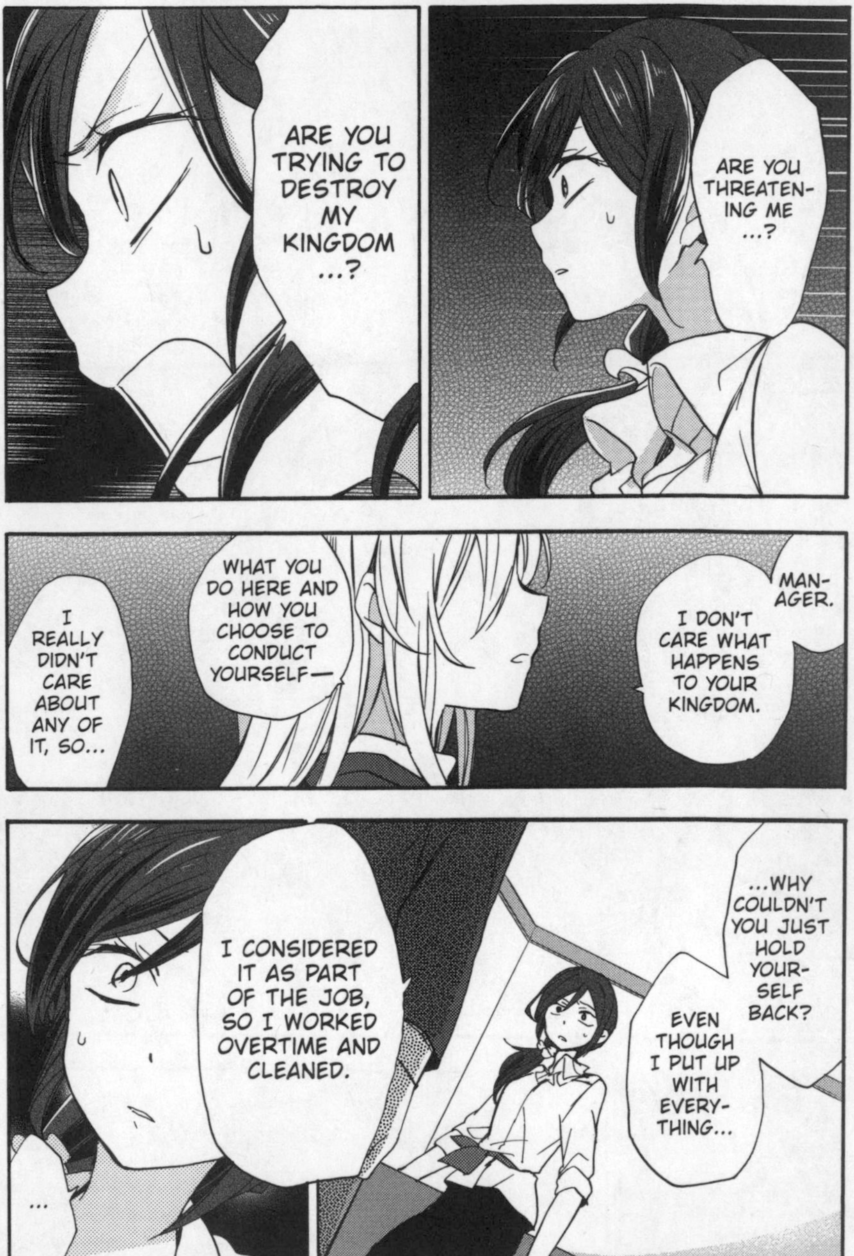
ARE YOU THREATENING ME ...?
ARE YOU TRYING TO DESTROY MY KINGDOM ...?
MANAGER.
I DON'T CARE WHAT HAPPENS TO YOUR KINGDOM.
WHAT YOU DO HERE AND HOW YOU CHOOSE TO CONDUCT YOURSELF—
I REALLY DIDN'T CARE ABOUT ANY OF IT, SO...
...WHY COULDN'T YOU JUST HOLD YOURSELF BACK?
EVEN THOUGH I PUT UP WITH EVERYTHING...
I CONSIDERED IT AS PART OF THE JOB, SO I WORKED OVERTIME AND CLEANED.
...

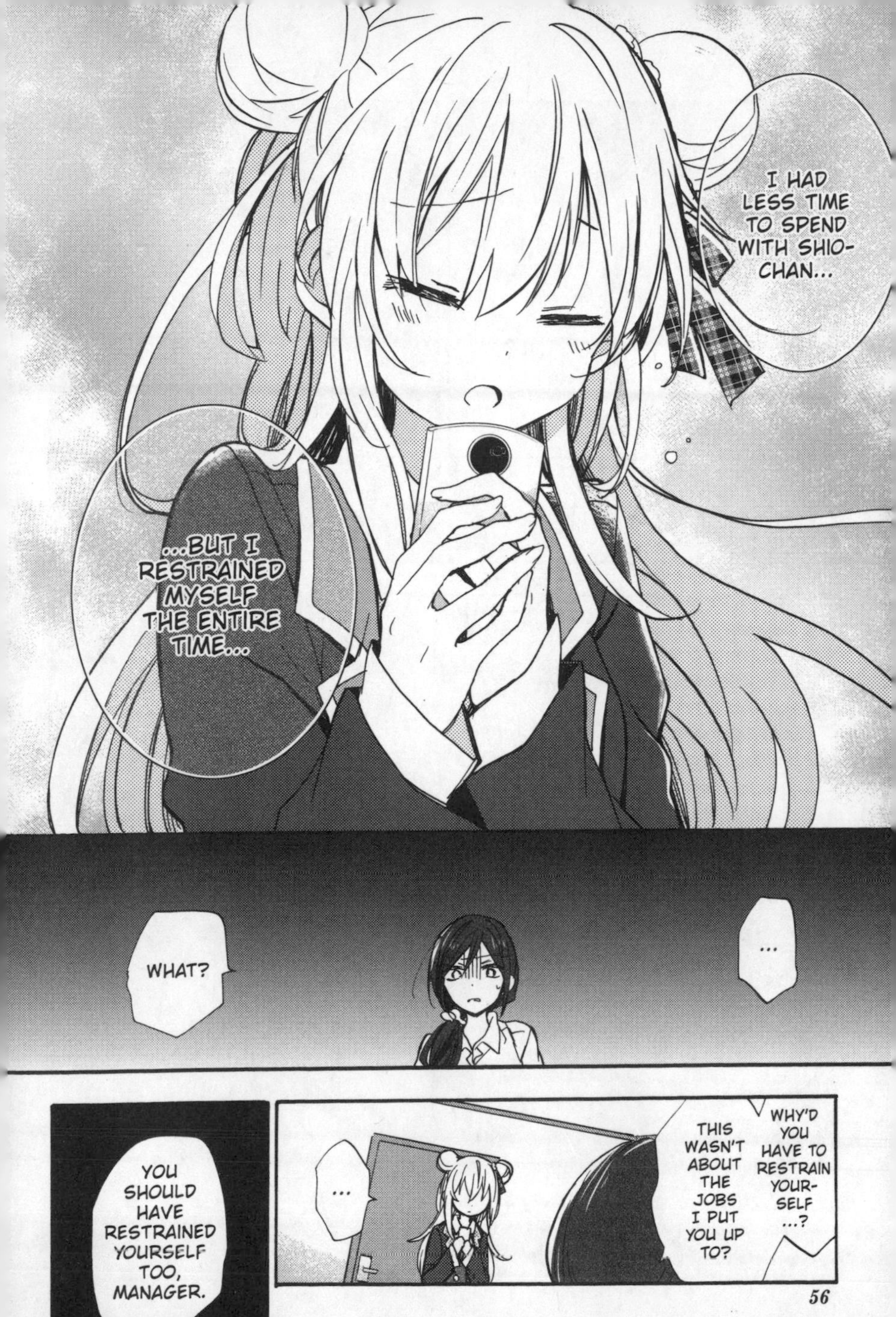
I HAD LESS TIME TO SPEND WITH SHIO-CHAN...
...BUT I RESTRAINED MYSELF THE ENTIRE TIME...
...
WHAT?
WHY'D YOU HAVE TO RESTRAIN YOUR-SELF ...?
THIS WASN'T ABOUT THE JOBS I PUT YOU UP TO?
...
YOU SHOULD HAVE RESTRAINED YOURSELF TOO, MANAGER.

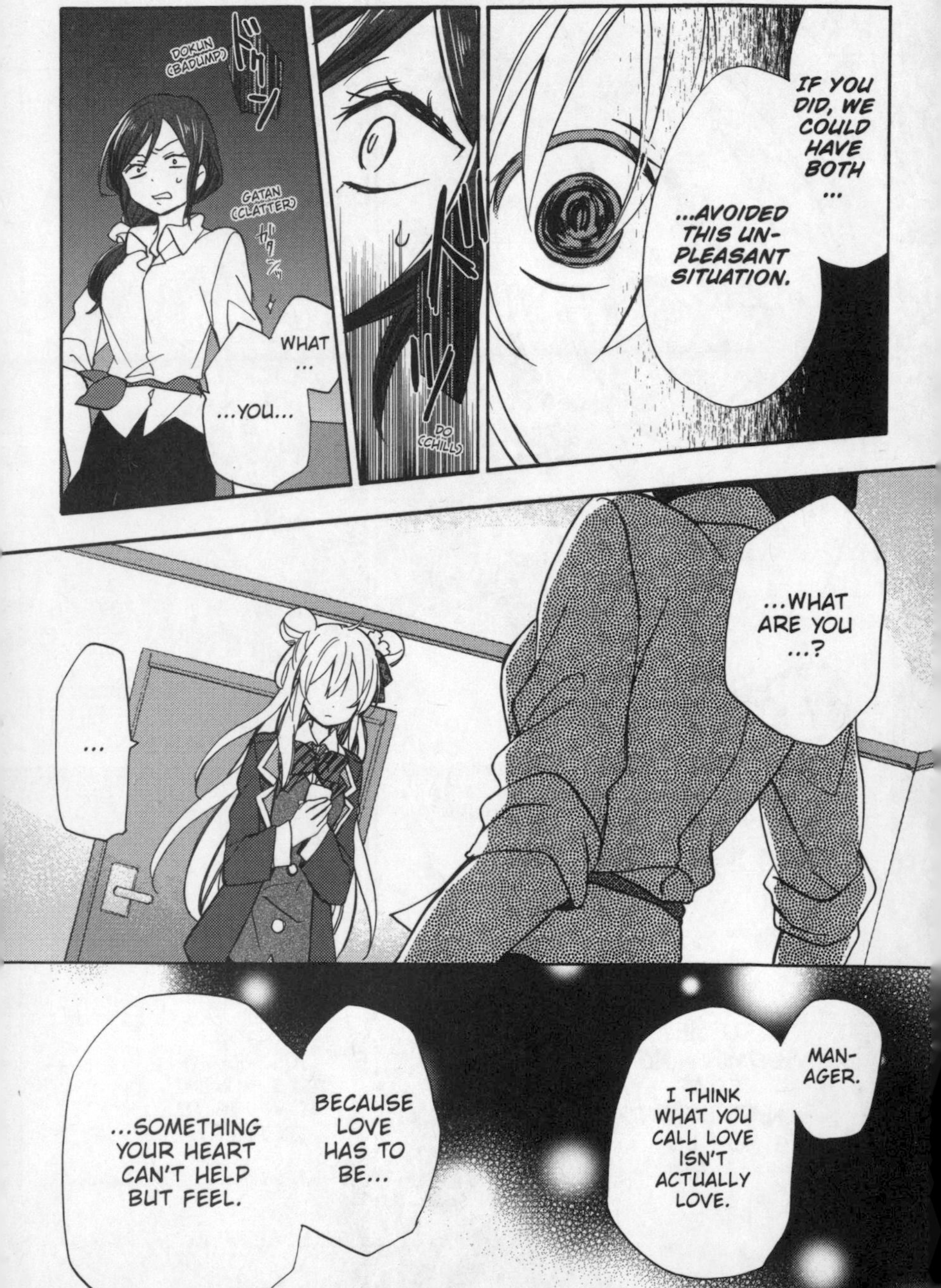
IF YOU DID, WE COULD HAVE BOTH ...
...AVOIDED THIS UN-PLEASANT SITUATION.
DO (CHILL)
DOKUN (BADUMP)
GATAN (CLATTER)
WHAT ...
...YOU...
...WHAT ARE YOU ...?
...
MAN-AGER.
I THINK WHAT YOU CALL LOVE ISN'T ACTUALLY LOVE.
BECAUSE LOVE HAS TO BE...
...SOMETHING YOUR HEART CAN'T HELP BUT FEEL.

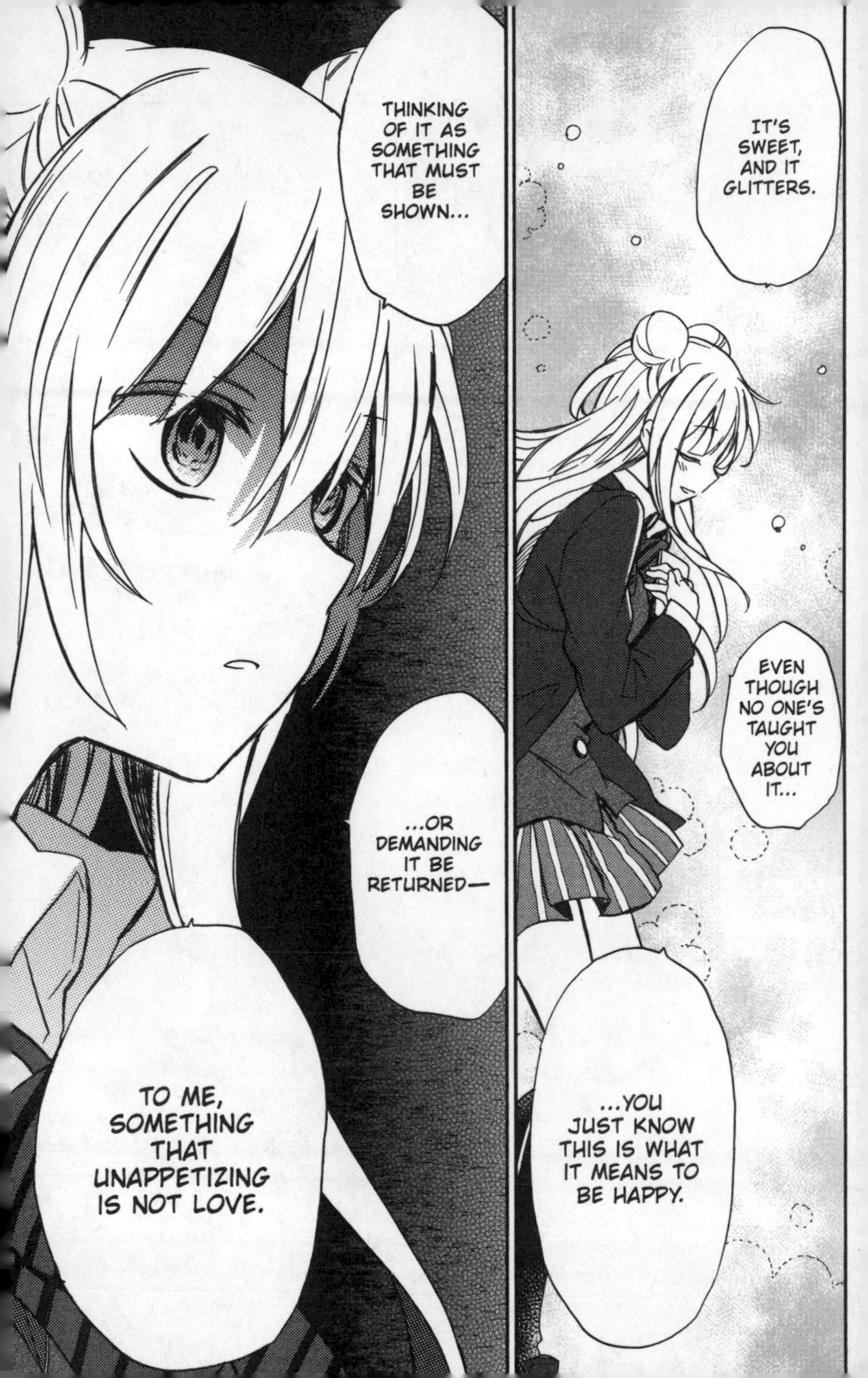
IT'S SWEET, AND IT GLITTERS.
EVEN THOUGH NO ONE'S TAUGHT YOU ABOUT IT...
...YOU JUST KNOW THIS IS WHAT IT MEANS TO BE HAPPY.
THINKING OF IT AS SOMETHING THAT MUST BE SHOWN...
...OR DEMANDING IT BE RETURNED—
TO ME, SOMETHING THAT UNAPPETIZING IS NOT LOVE.

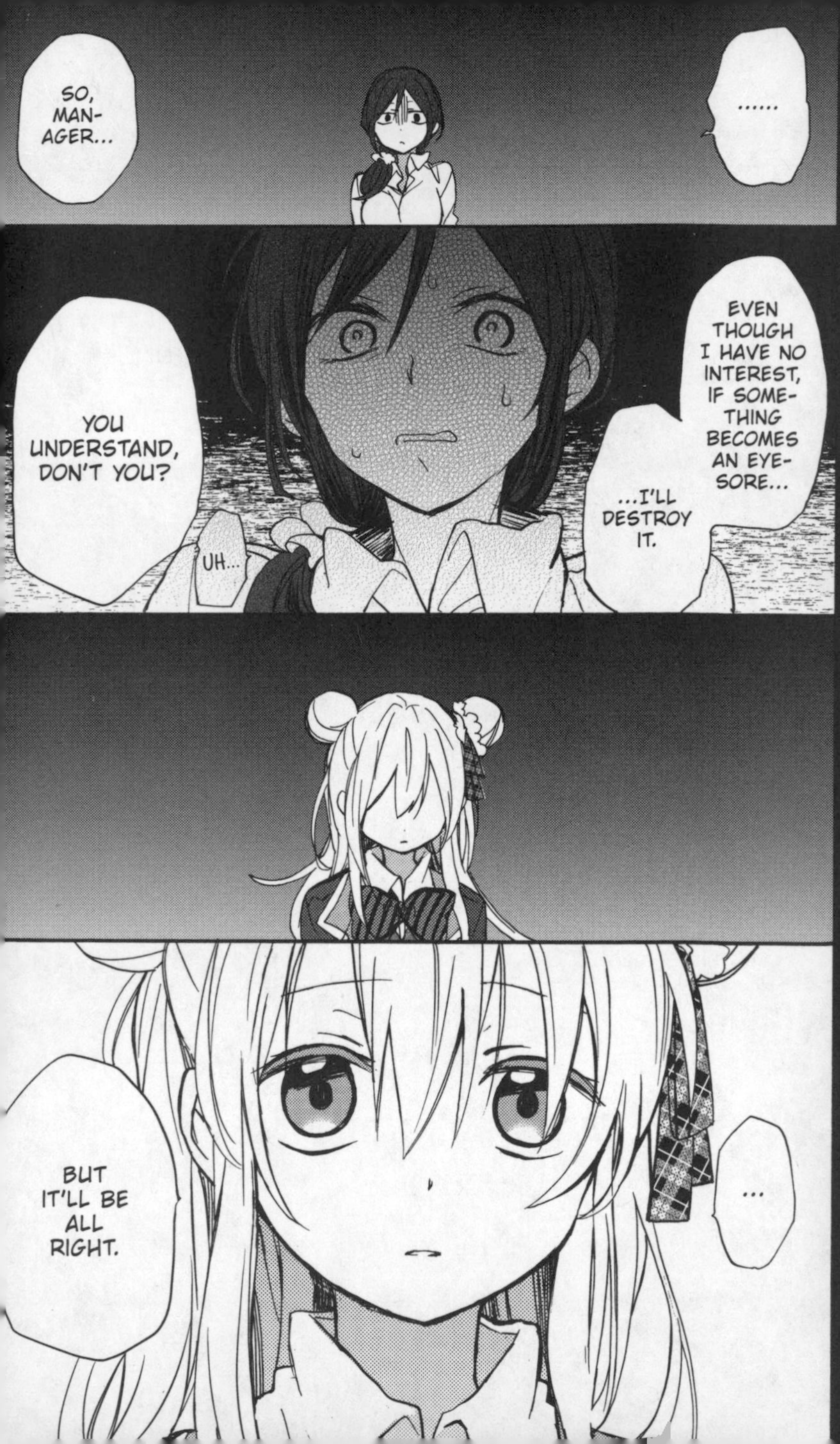
......
SO, MANAGER...
EVEN THOUGH I HAVE NO INTEREST, IF SOMETHING BECOMES AN EYESORE...
...I'LL DESTROY IT.
YOU UNDERSTAND, DON'T YOU?
UH...
...
BUT IT'LL BE ALL RIGHT.

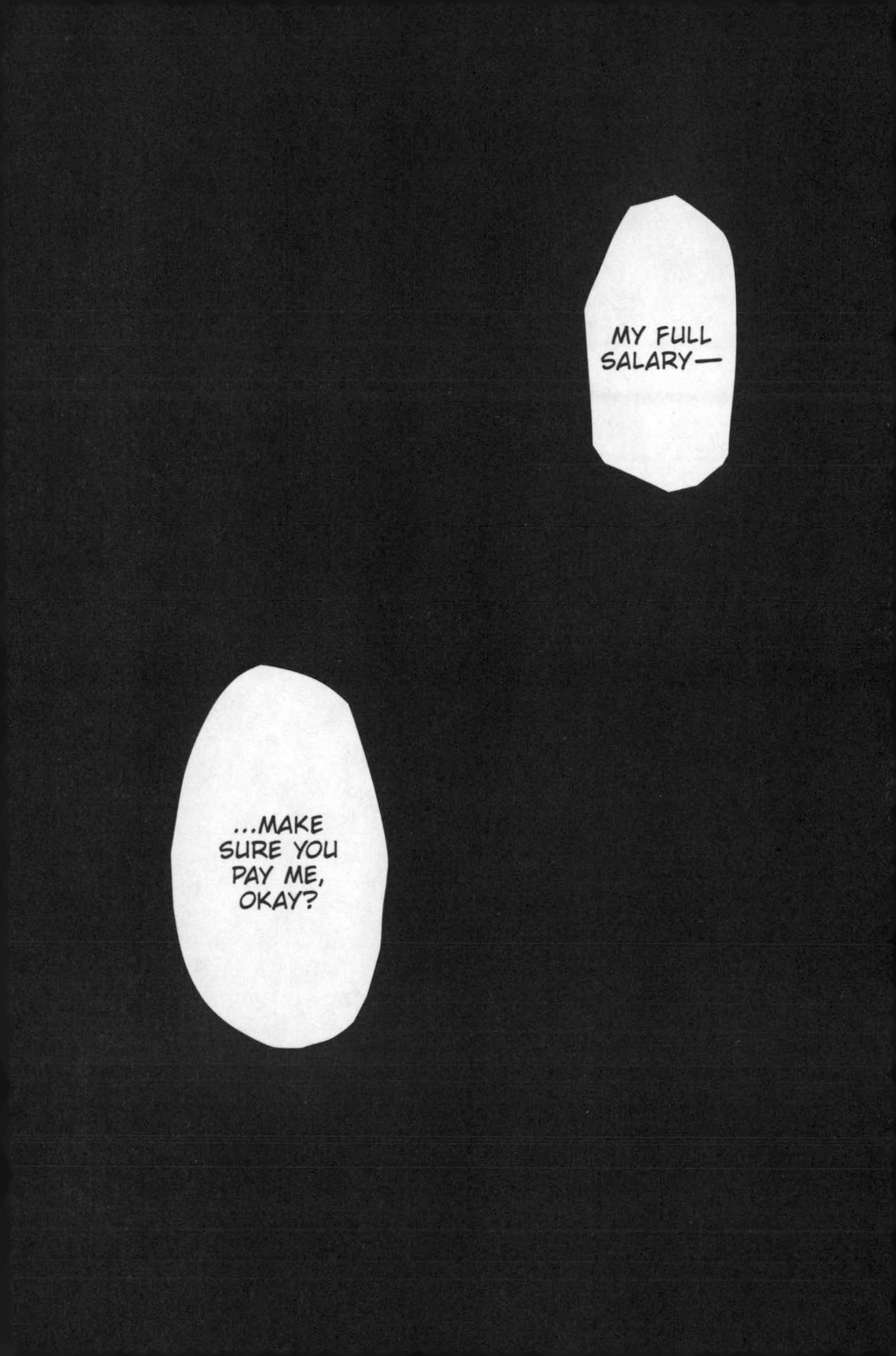
MY FULL SALARY—
...MAKE SURE YOU PAY ME, OKAY?

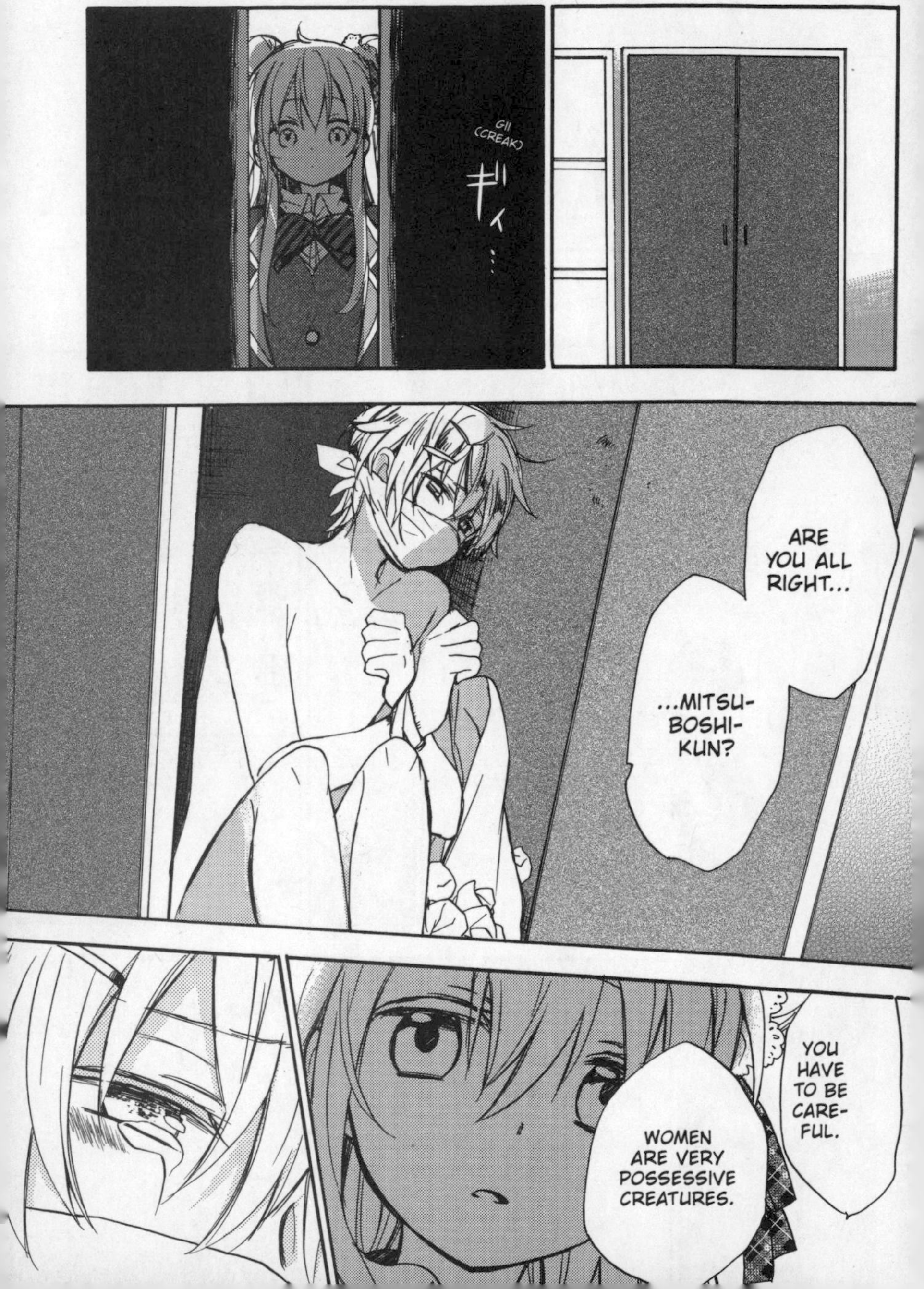
GII (CREAK)
ギィ…
ARE YOU ALL RIGHT...
...MITSU-BOSHI-KUN?
YOU HAVE TO BE CARE-FUL.
WOMEN ARE VERY POSSESSIVE CREATURES.

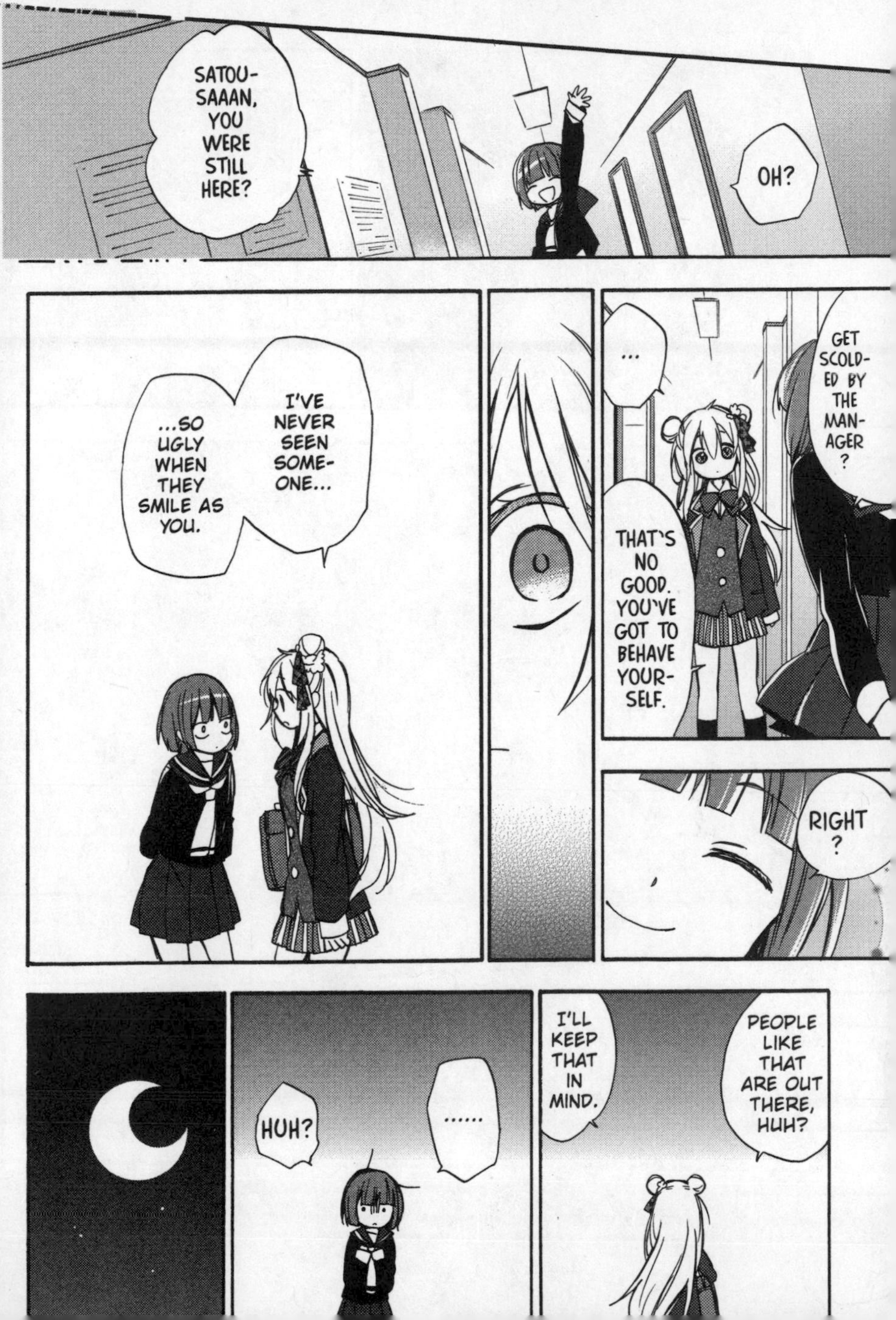
OH?
SATOU-SAAAN, YOU WERE STILL HERE?
GET SCOLDED BY THE MANAGER?
...
THAT'S NO GOOD. YOU'VE GOT TO BEHAVE YOURSELF.
RIGHT?
I'VE NEVER SEEN SOMEONE...
...SO UGLY WHEN THEY SMILE AS YOU.
PEOPLE LIKE THAT ARE OUT THERE, HUH?
I'LL KEEP THAT IN MIND.
......
HUH?

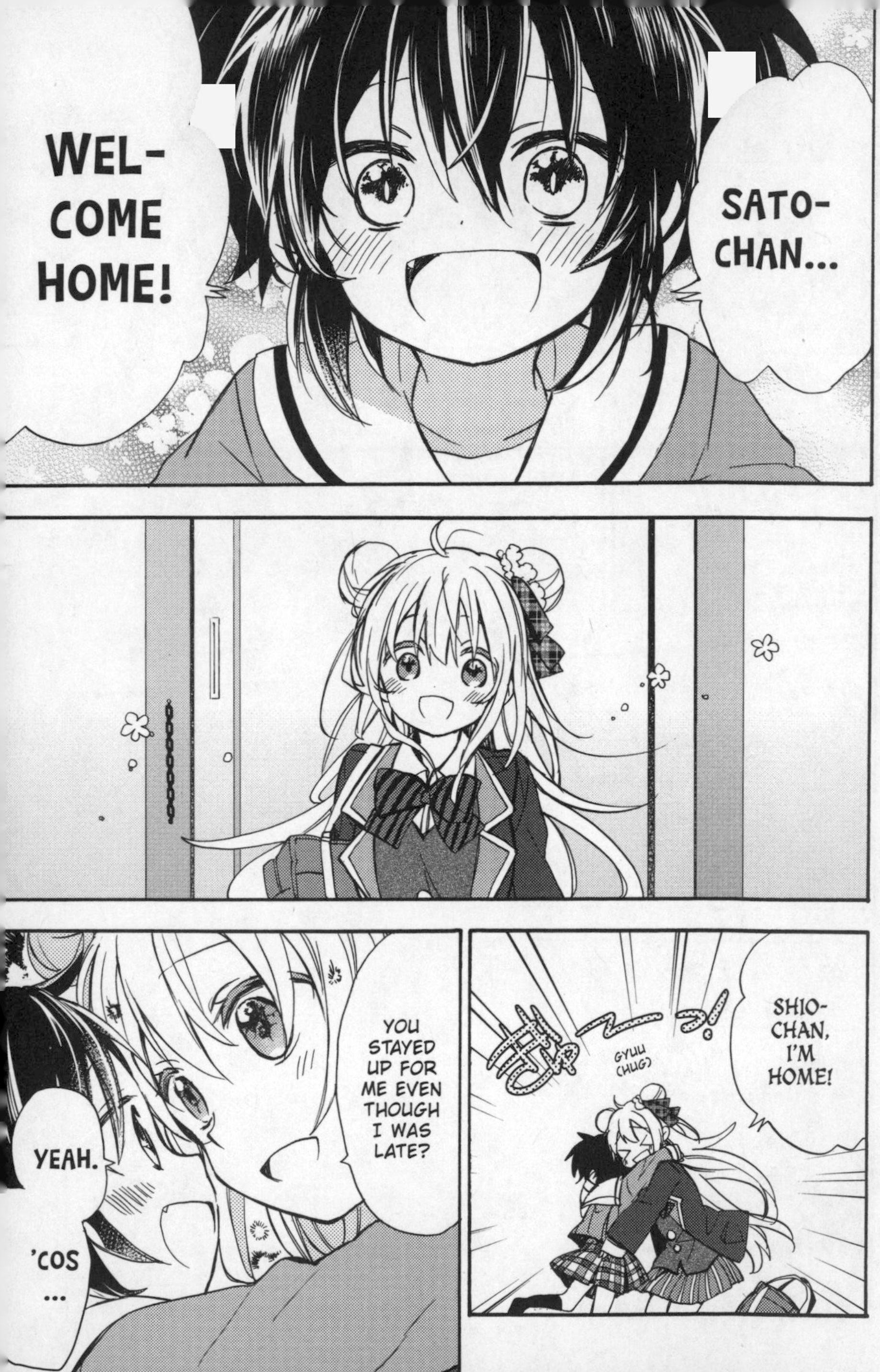
SATO-CHAN...
WEL-COME HOME!
SHIO-CHAN, I'M HOME!
GYUU (HUG)
YOU STAYED UP FOR ME EVEN THOUGH I WAS LATE?
YEAH.
'COS ...

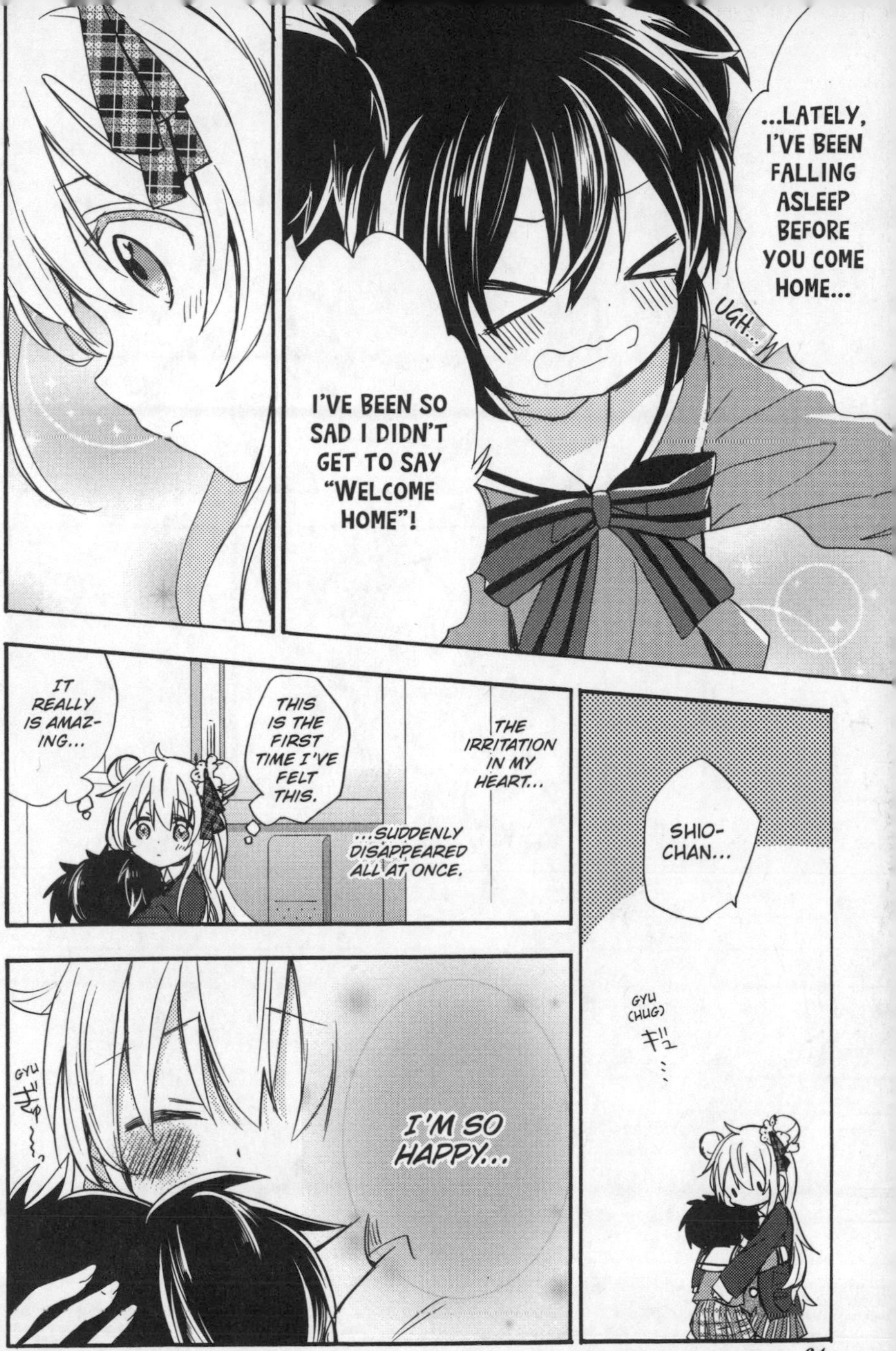
...LATELY, I'VE BEEN FALLING ASLEEP BEFORE YOU COME HOME...
UGH...
I'VE BEEN SO SAD I DIDN'T GET TO SAY "WELCOME HOME"!
SHIO-CHAN...
GYU (HUG)
ギュ
THE IRRITATION IN MY HEART...
THIS IS THE FIRST TIME I'VE FELT THIS.
IT REALLY IS AMAZING...
...SUDDENLY DISAPPEARED ALL AT ONCE.
I'M SO HAPPY...
GYU
ギュ~

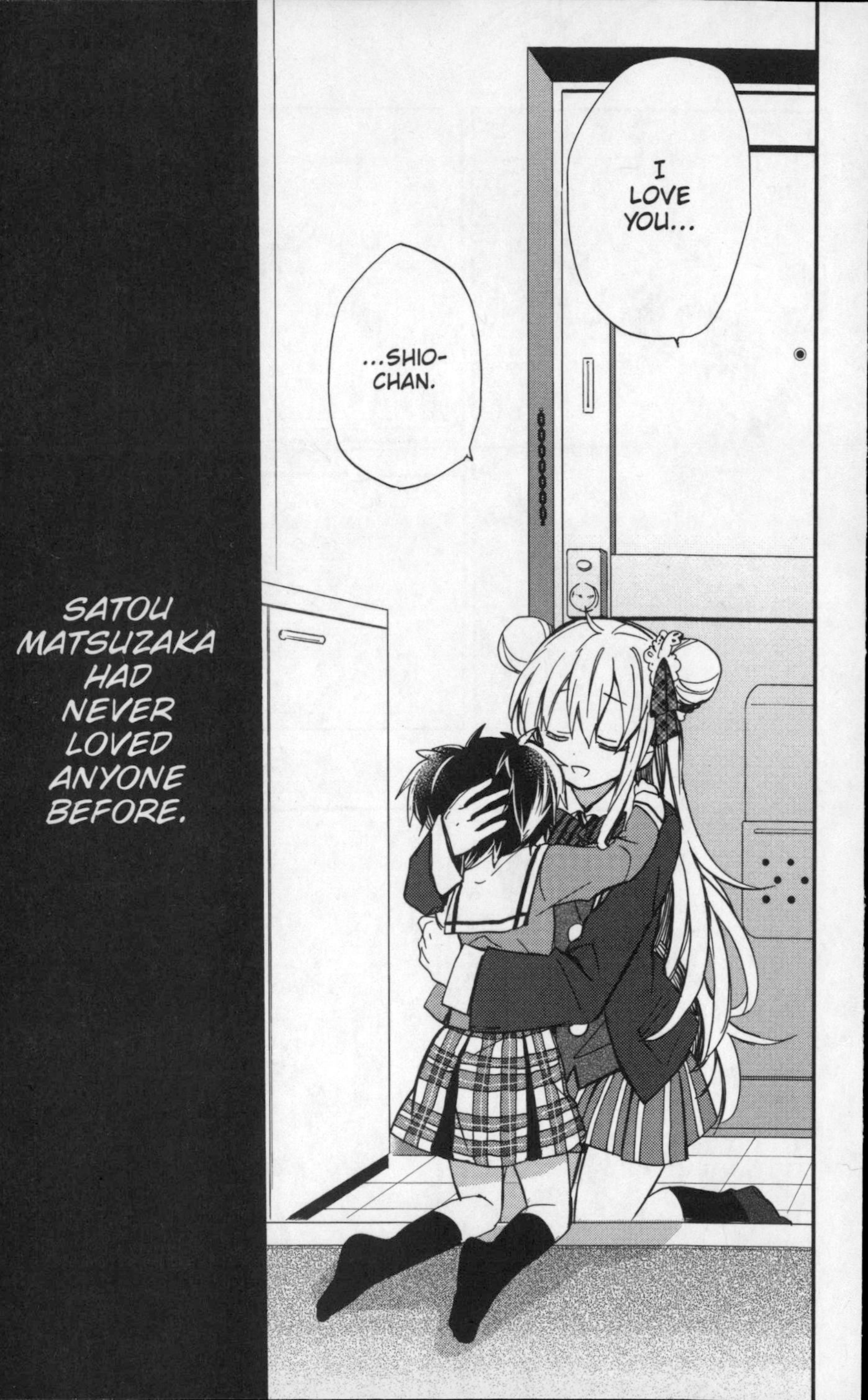
I LOVE YOU...
...SHIO-CHAN.
SATOU MATSUZAKA HAD NEVER LOVED ANYONE BEFORE.

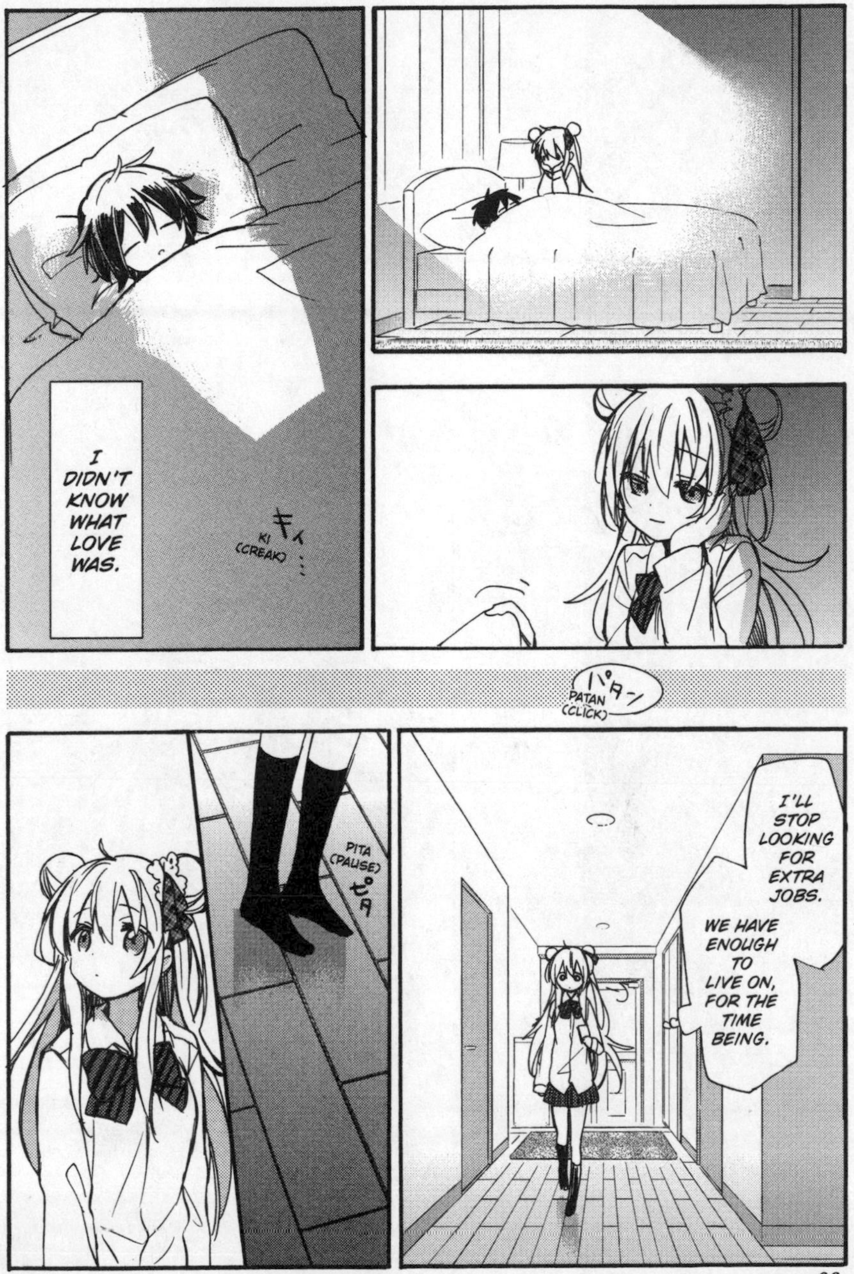
I DIDN'T KNOW WHAT LOVE WAS.
キィ… KI (CREAK)
パタン PATAN (CLICK)
I'LL STOP LOOKING FOR EXTRA JOBS.
WE HAVE ENOUGH TO LIVE ON, FOR THE TIME BEING.
ピタ PITA (PAUSE)

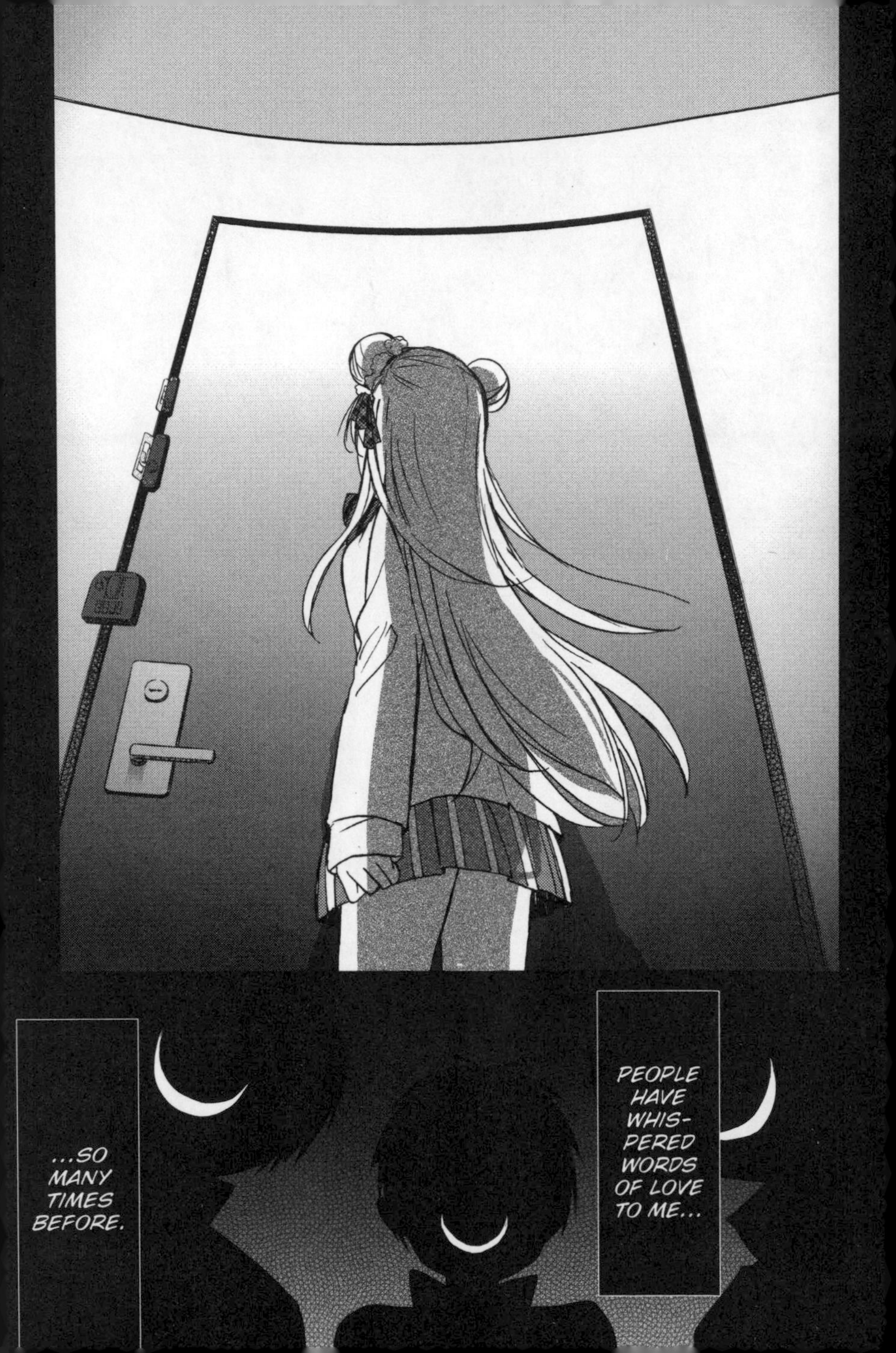
PEOPLE HAVE WHIS-PERED WORDS OF LOVE TO ME...
...SO MANY TIMES BEFORE.

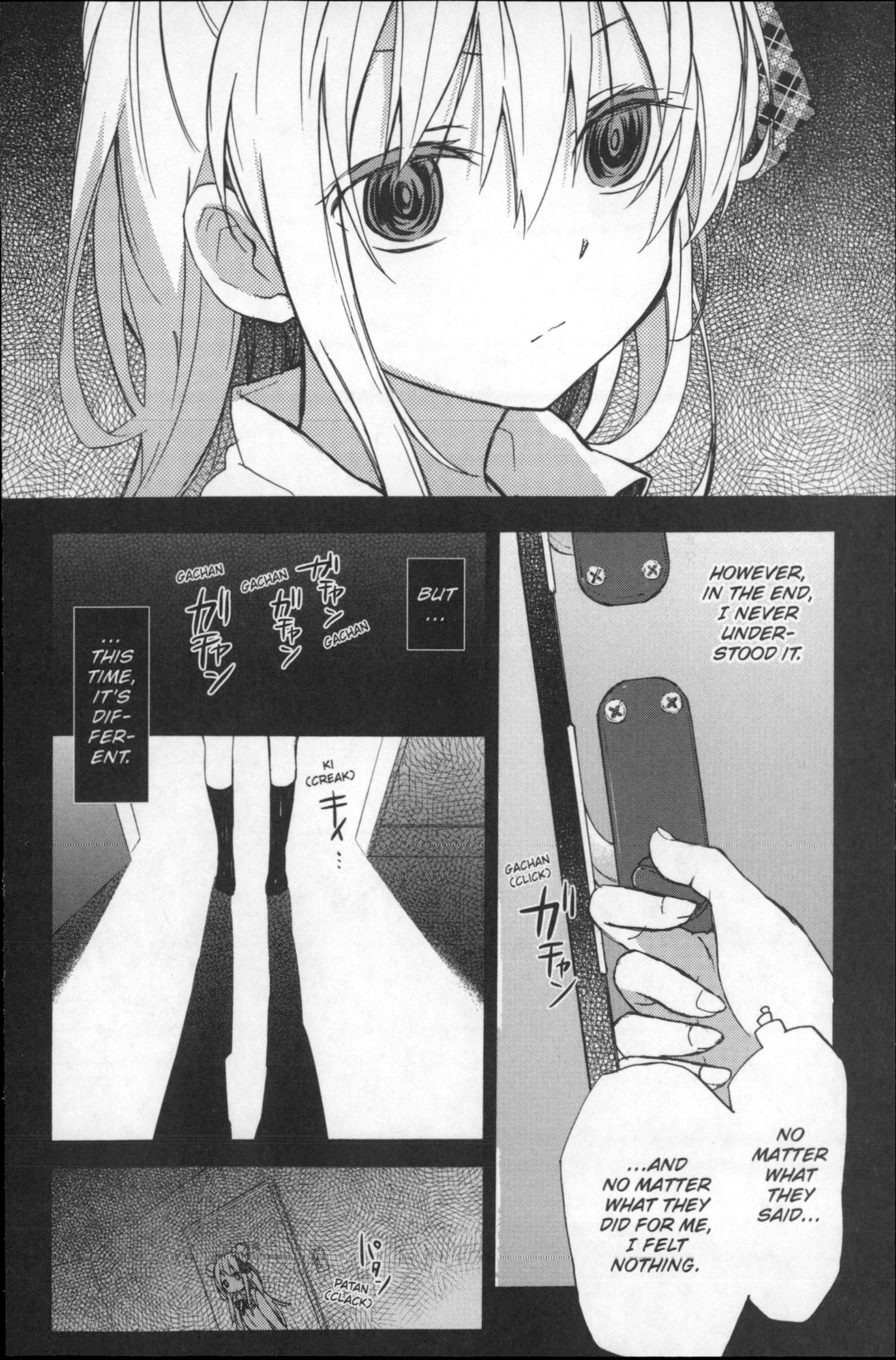
HOWEVER, IN THE END, I NEVER UNDER-STOOD IT.
GACHAN (CLICK)
ガチャン
NO MATTER WHAT THEY SAID...
...AND NO MATTER WHAT THEY DID FOR ME, I FELT NOTHING.
BUT...
ガチャン
GACHAN
GACHAN
ガチャン
GACHAN
ガチャン
...THIS TIME, IT'S DIF-FER-ENT.
KI (CREAK)
キィ…
パタン
PATAN (CLACK)

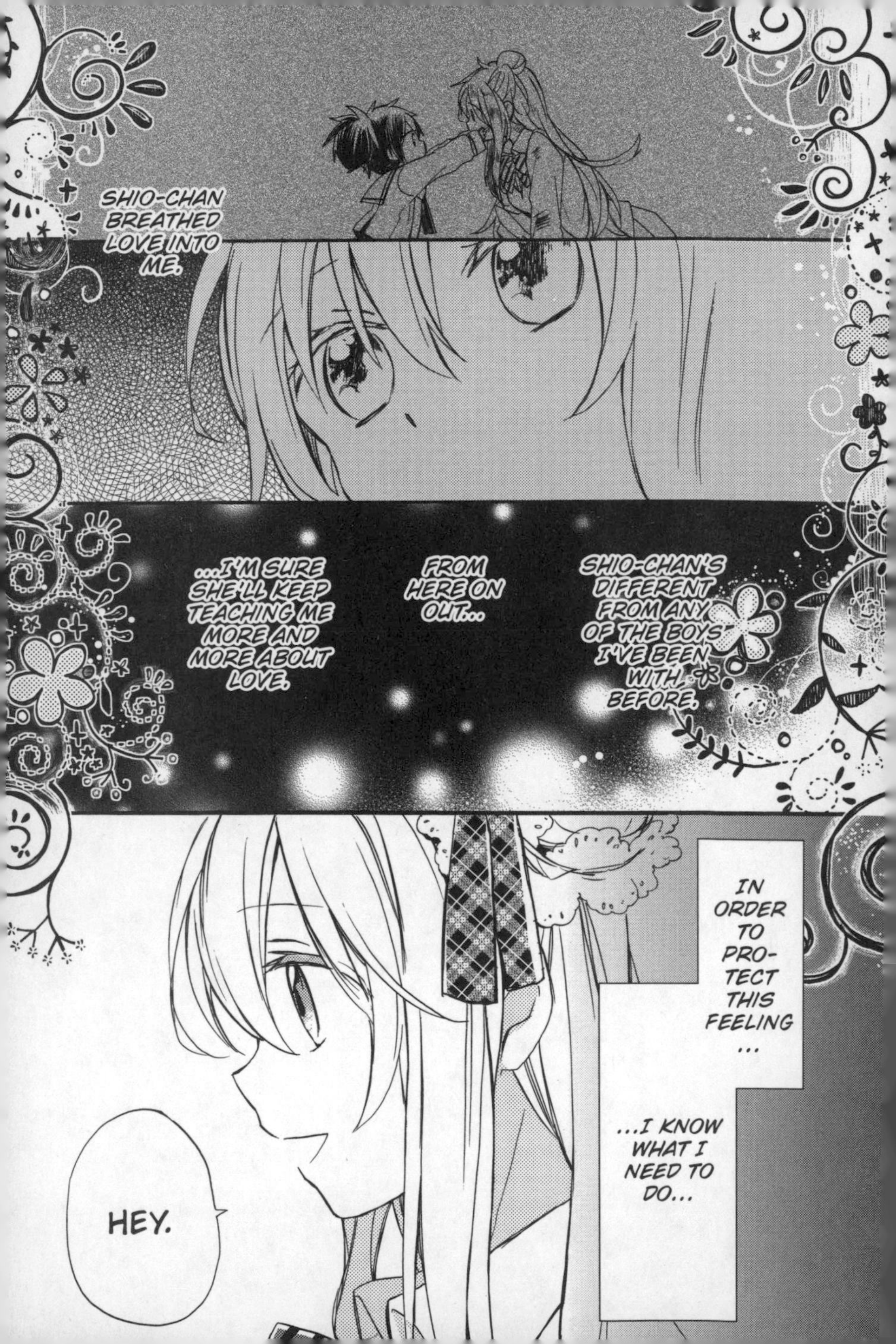
SHIO-CHAN BREATHED LOVE INTO ME.
SHIO-CHAN'S DIFFERENT FROM ANY OF THE BOYS I'VE BEEN WITH BEFORE.
FROM HERE ON OUT...
...I'M SURE SHE'LL KEEP TEACHING ME MORE AND MORE ABOUT LOVE.
IN ORDER TO PRO-TECT THIS FEELING...
...I KNOW WHAT I NEED TO DO...
HEY.

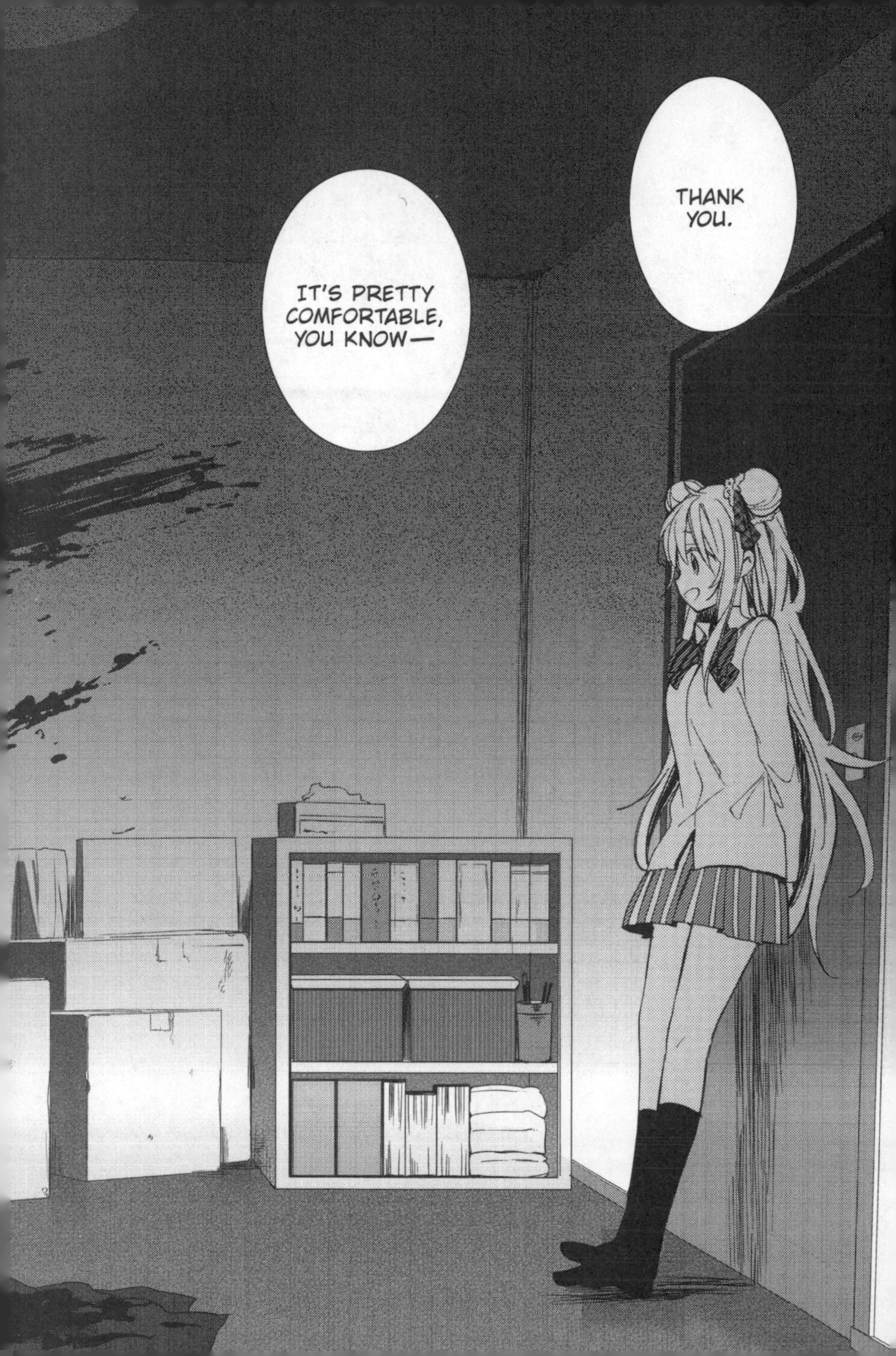
THANK YOU.
IT'S PRETTY COMFORTABLE, YOU KNOW—

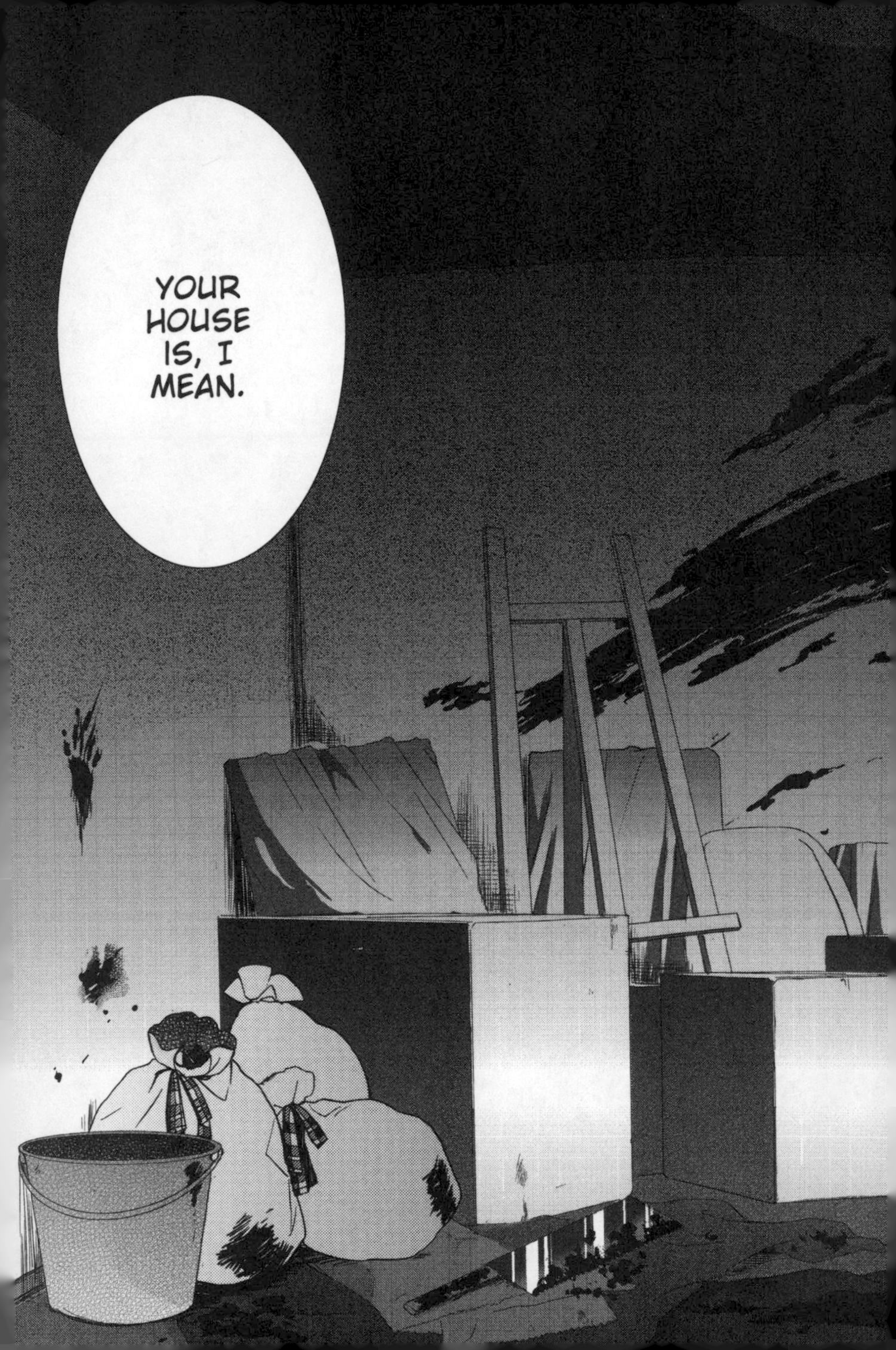
YOUR HOUSE IS, I MEAN.

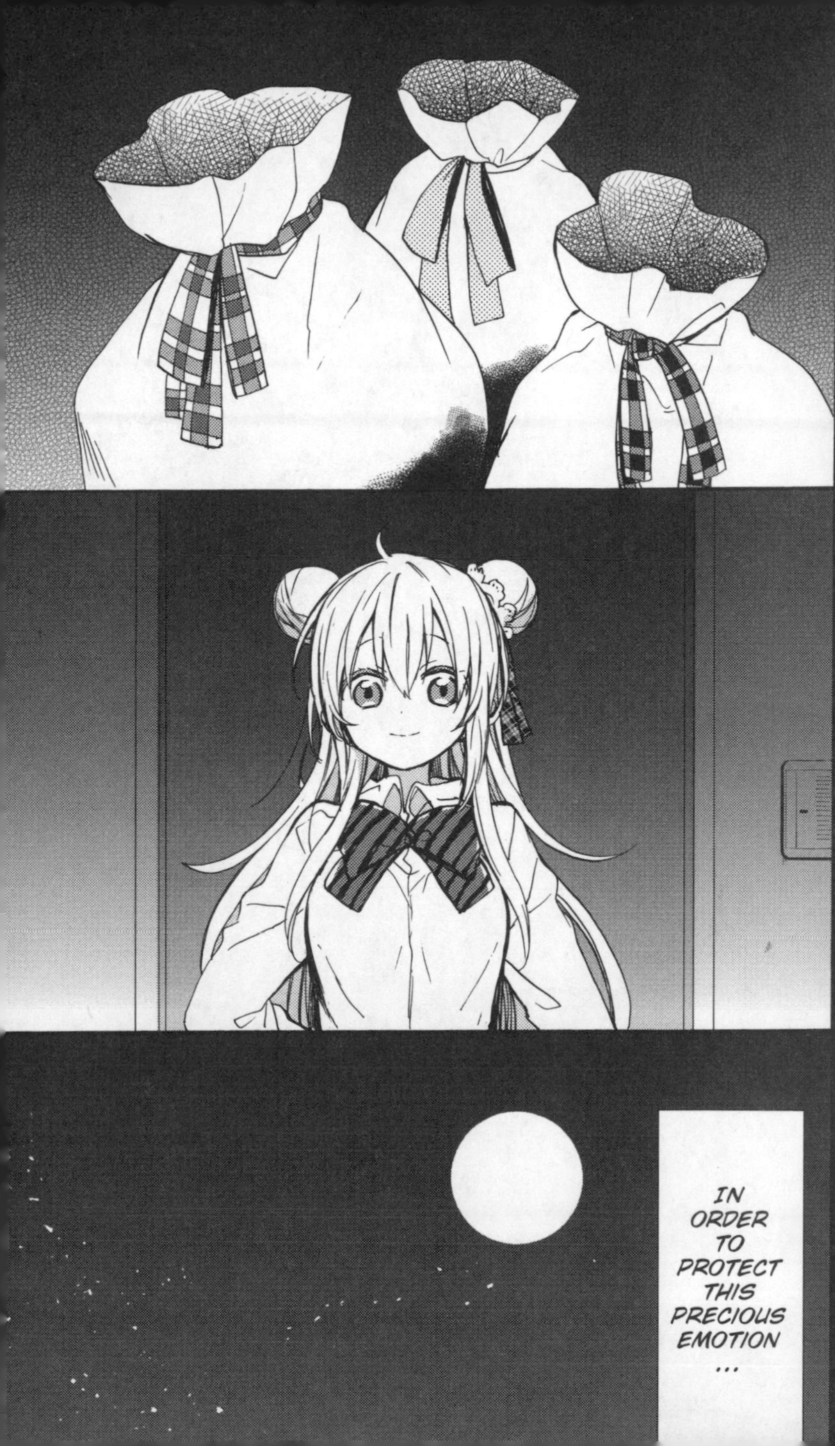
IN ORDER TO PROTECT THIS PRECIOUS EMOTION ...

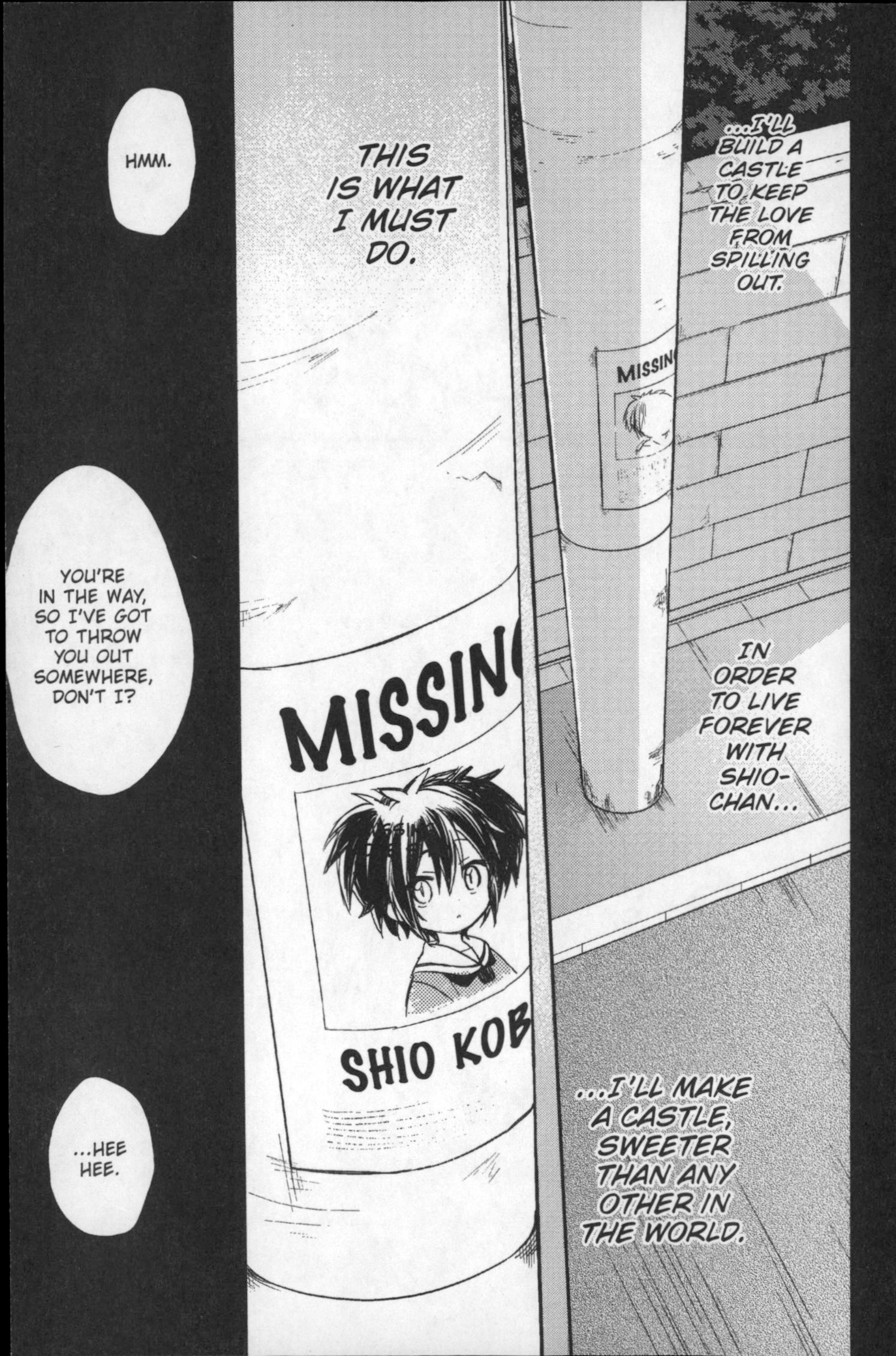
...I'LL BUILD A CASTLE TO KEEP THE LOVE FROM SPILLING OUT.
THIS IS WHAT I MUST DO.
MISSIN
IN ORDER TO LIVE FOREVER WITH SHIO-CHAN...
MISSIN
SHIO KOB
...I'LL MAKE A CASTLE, SWEETER THAN ANY OTHER IN THE WORLD.
HMM.
YOU'RE IN THE WAY, SO I'VE GOT TO THROW YOU OUT SOMEWHERE, DON'T I?
...HEE HEE.

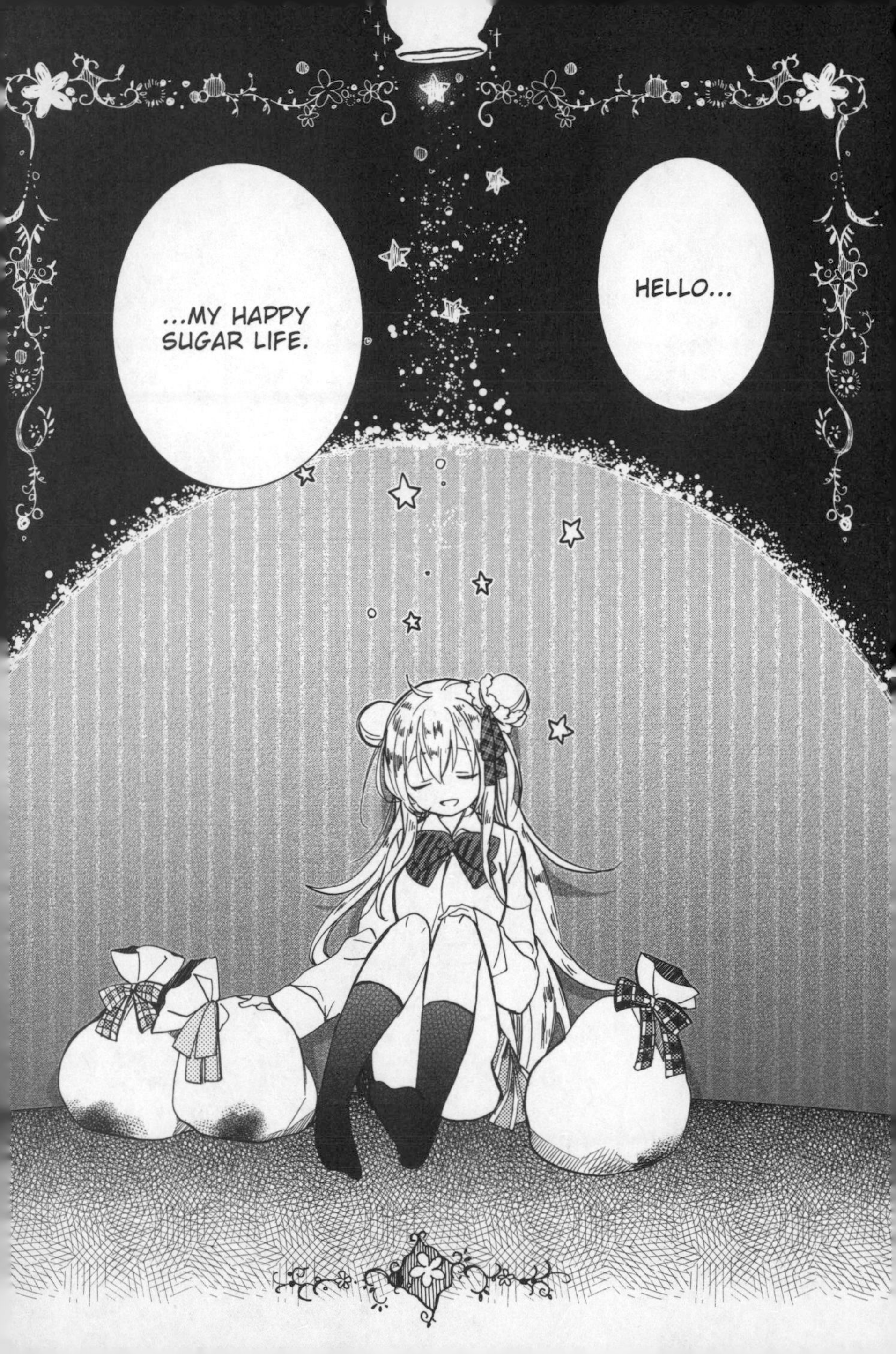
HELLO...
...MY HAPPY SUGAR LIFE.

Happy
Sugar
Life

Happy
Sugar
Life

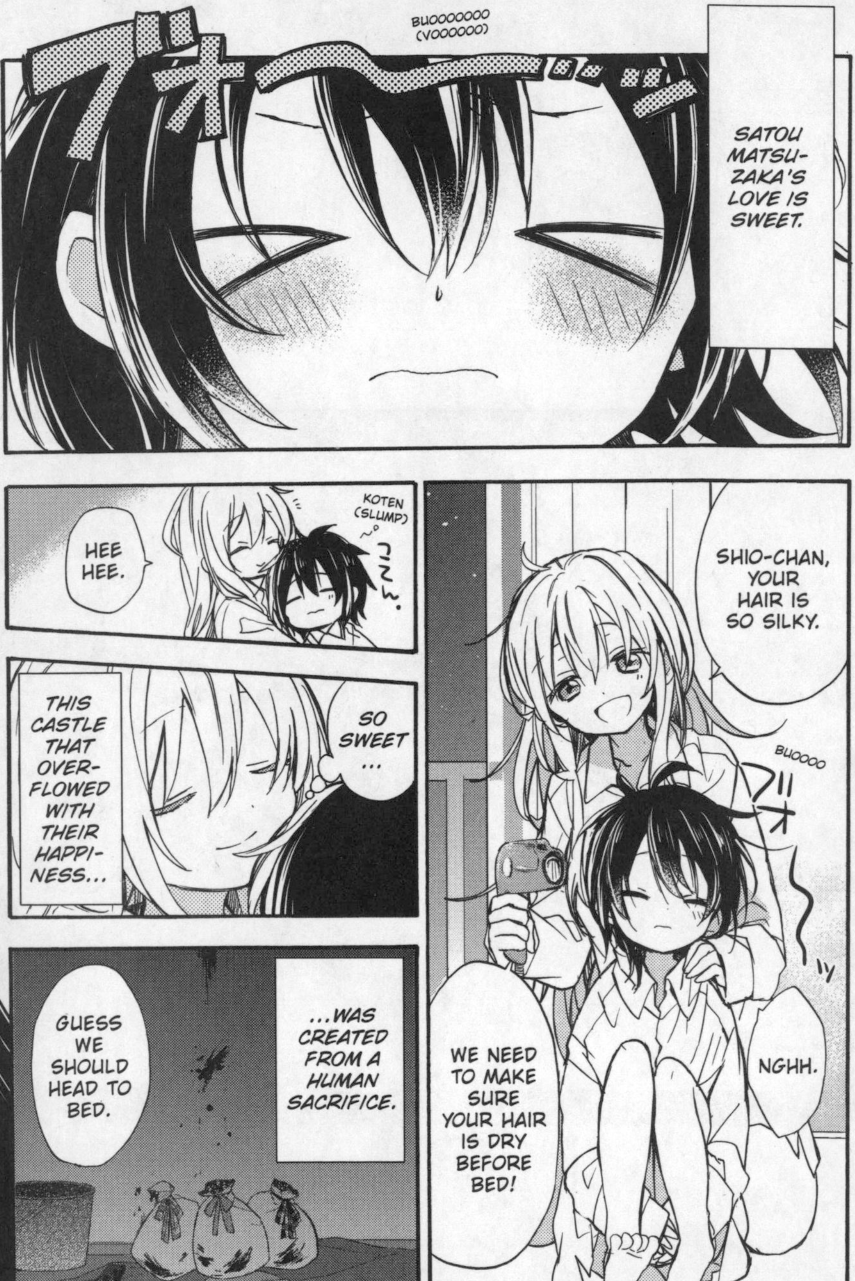
SATOU MATSU-ZAKA'S LOVE IS SWEET.
BUOOOOOOO (VOOOOOOO)
SHIO-CHAN, YOUR HAIR IS SO SILKY.
BUOOOO
NGHH.
WE NEED TO MAKE SURE YOUR HAIR IS DRY BEFORE BED!
KOTEN (SLUMP)
HEE HEE.
SO SWEET...
THIS CASTLE THAT OVER-FLOWED WITH THEIR HAPPI-NESS...
...WAS CREATED FROM A HUMAN SACRIFICE.
GUESS WE SHOULD HEAD TO BED.

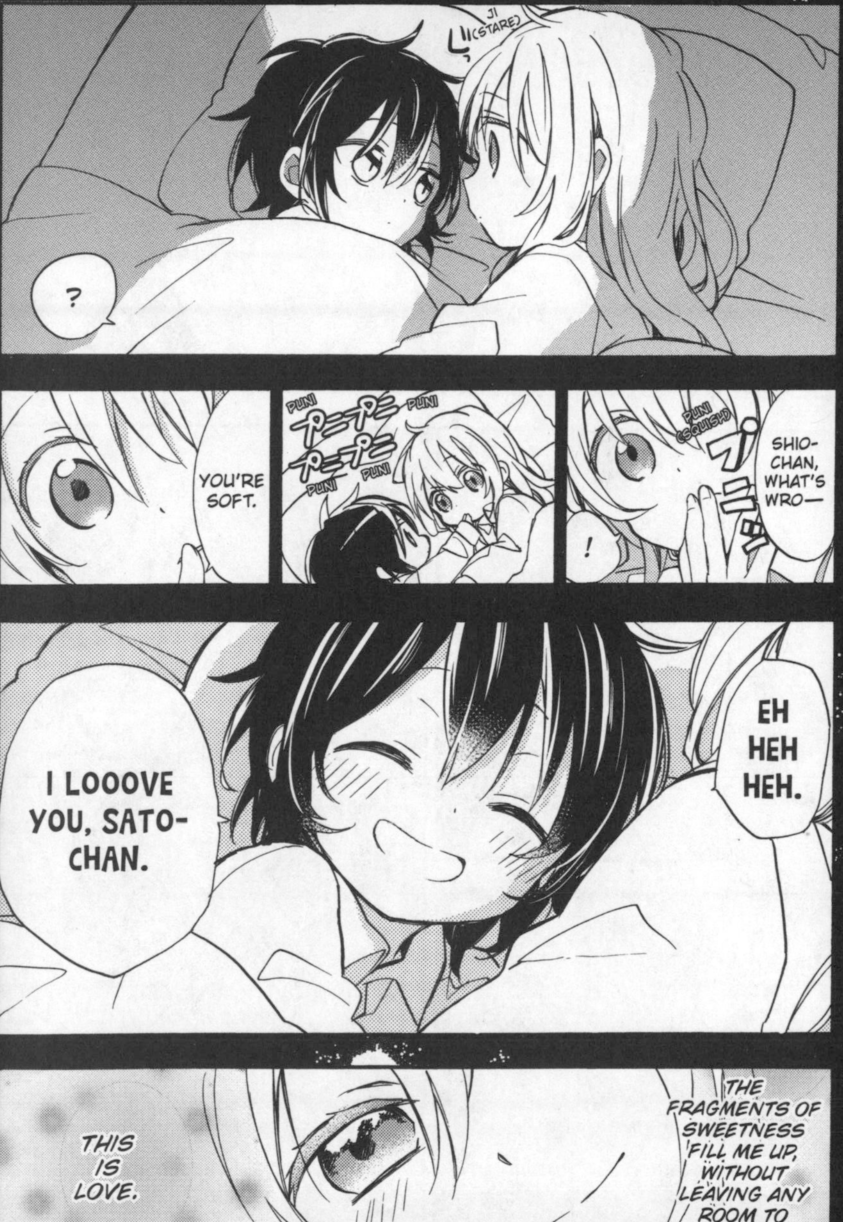
JI (STARE)
?
PUNI (SQUISH)
SHIO-CHAN, WHAT'S WRO—
!
PUNI PUNI
PUNI PUNI
YOU'RE SOFT.
EH HEH HEH.
I LOOOVE YOU, SATO-CHAN.
THE FRAGMENTS OF SWEETNESS FILL ME UP, WITHOUT LEAVING ANY ROOM TO SPARE.
THIS IS LOVE.

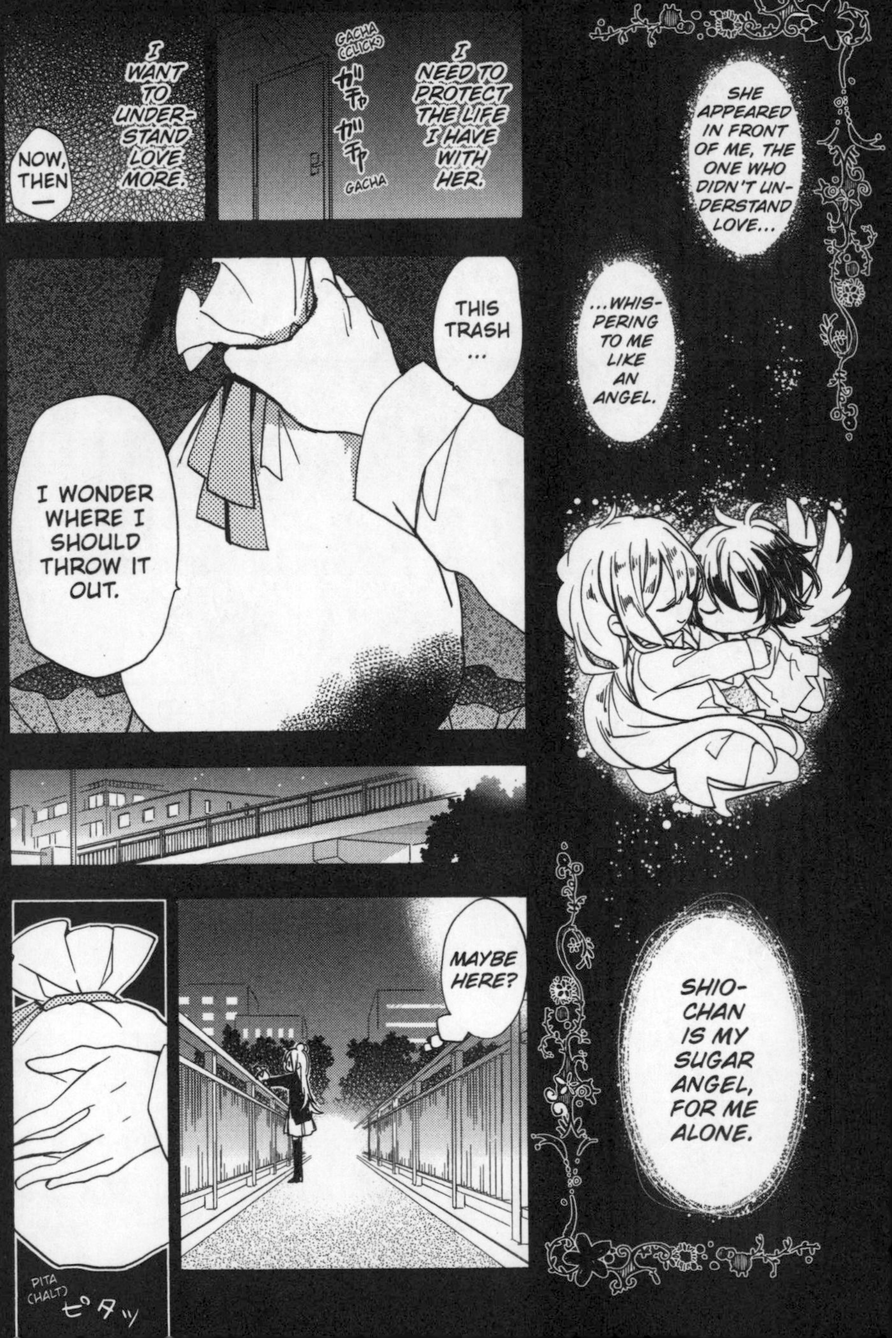
SHE APPEARED IN FRONT OF ME, THE ONE WHO DIDN'T UNDERSTAND LOVE...
...WHISPERING TO ME LIKE AN ANGEL.
SHIO-CHAN IS MY SUGAR ANGEL, FOR ME ALONE.
I NEED TO PROTECT THE LIFE I HAVE WITH HER.
GACHA (CLICK)
ガチャ
ガチャ
GACHA
I WANT TO UNDERSTAND LOVE MORE.
NOW, THEN—
THIS TRASH...
I WONDER WHERE I SHOULD THROW IT OUT.
MAYBE HERE?
PITA (HALT)
ピタッ

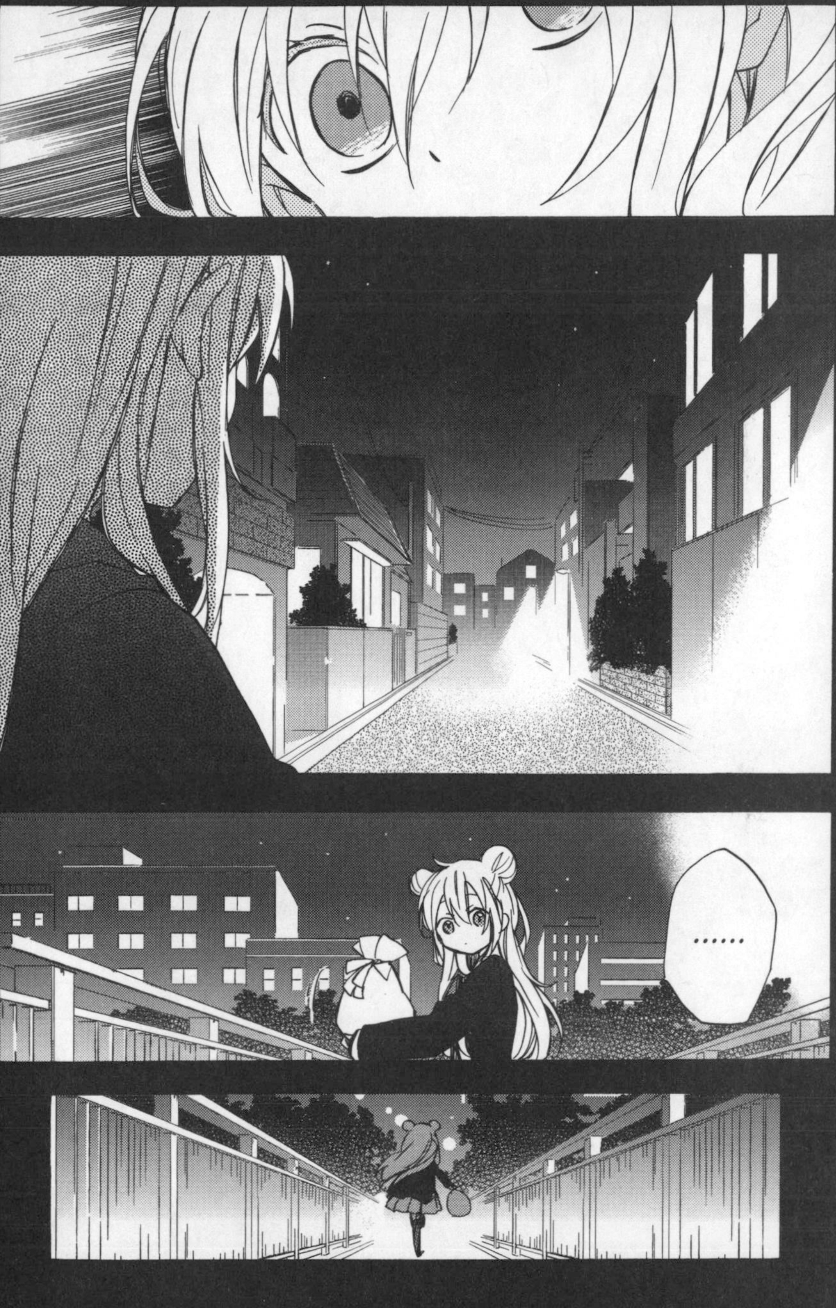
......

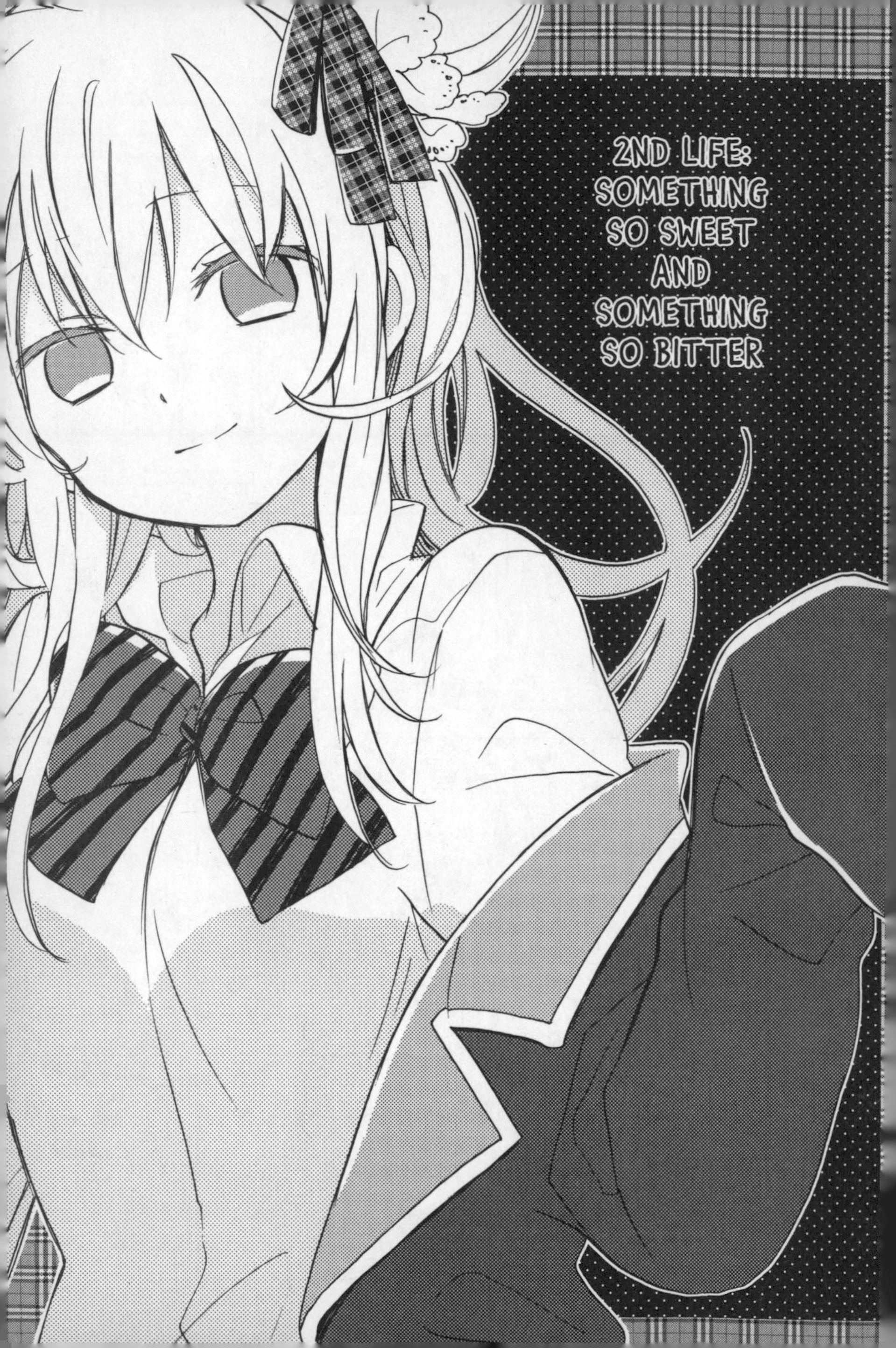
2ND LIFE: SOMETHING SO SWEET AND SOMETHING SO BITTER

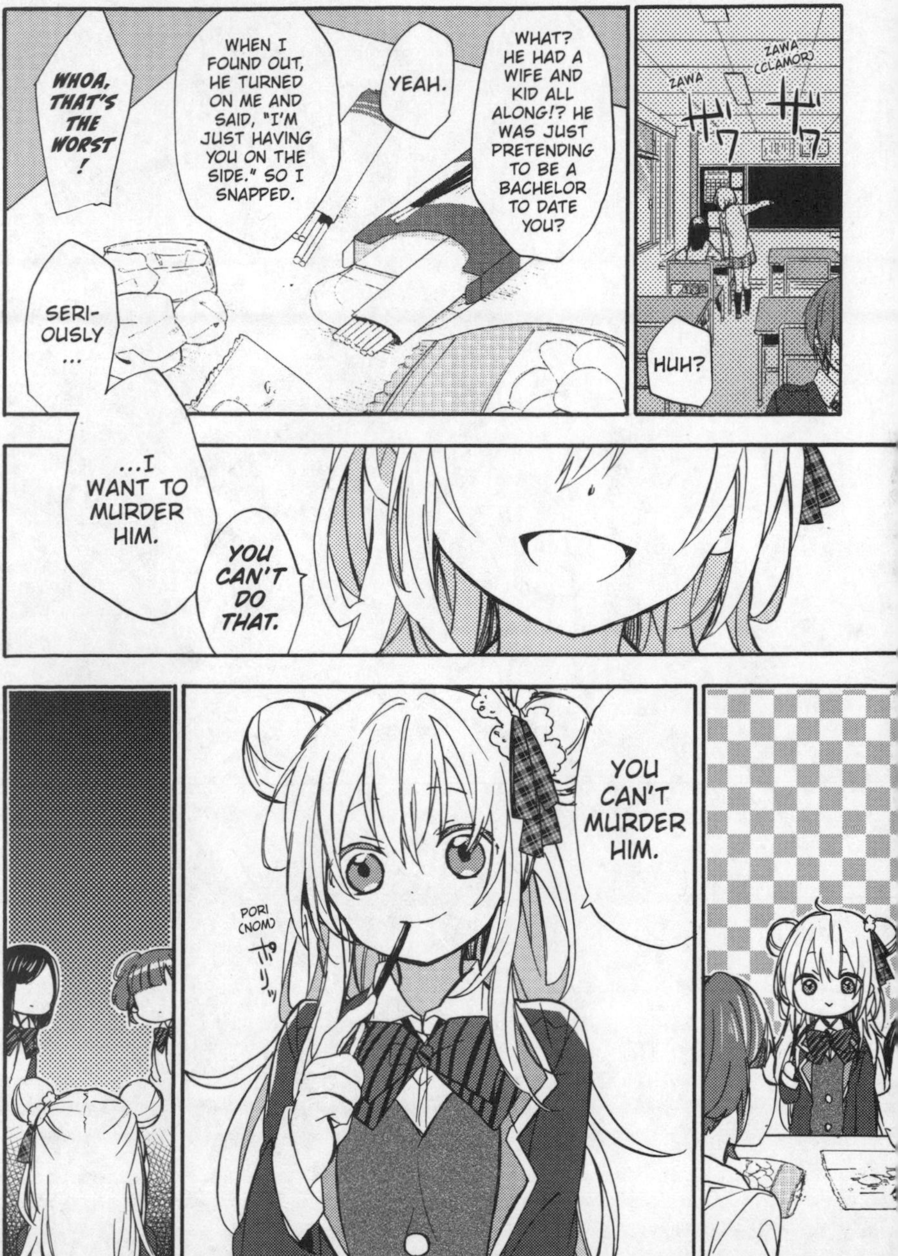
ZAWA (CLAMOR)
ZAWA
ザワ
ザワ
HUH?
WHAT? HE HAD A WIFE AND KID ALL ALONG!? HE WAS JUST PRETENDING TO BE A BACHELOR TO DATE YOU?
YEAH.
WHEN I FOUND OUT, HE TURNED ON ME AND SAID, "I'M JUST HAVING YOU ON THE SIDE." SO I SNAPPED.
WHOA, THAT'S THE WORST!
SERI-OUSLY ...
...I WANT TO MURDER HIM.
YOU CAN'T DO THAT.
YOU CAN'T MURDER HIM.
PORI (NOM)
ポリッ

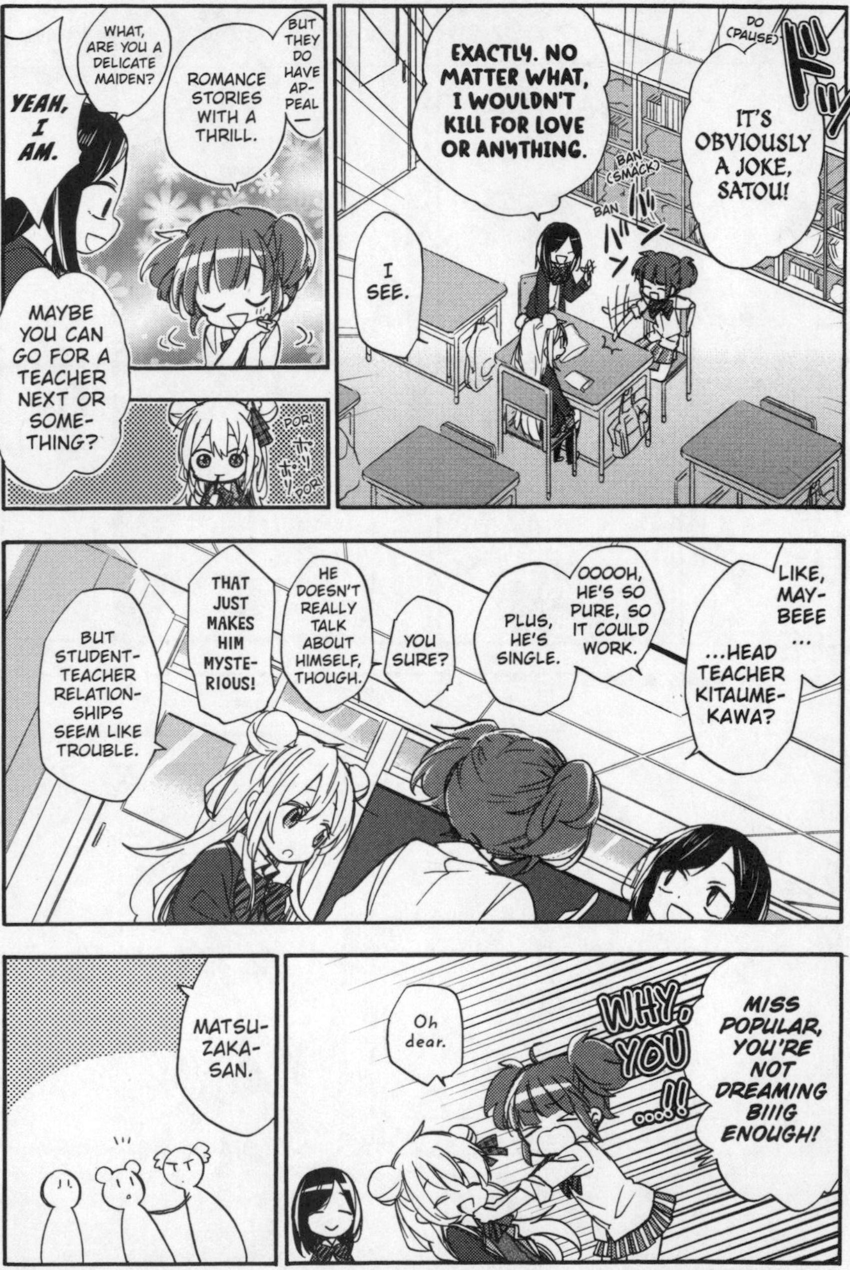
DO (PAUSE)
IT'S OBVIOUSLY A JOKE, SATOU!
BAN (SMACK)
BAN
EXACTLY. NO MATTER WHAT, I WOULDN'T KILL FOR LOVE OR ANYTHING.
I SEE.
BUT THEY DO HAVE AP-PEAL—
ROMANCE STORIES WITH A THRILL.
WHAT, ARE YOU A DELICATE MAIDEN?
YEAH, I AM.
MAYBE YOU CAN GO FOR A TEACHER NEXT OR SOME-THING?
PORI
POR
LIKE, MAY-BEEE...
...HEAD TEACHER KITAUME-KAWA?
OOOOH, HE'S SO PURE, SO IT COULD WORK.
PLUS, HE'S SINGLE.
YOU SURE?
HE DOESN'T REALLY TALK ABOUT HIMSELF, THOUGH.
THAT JUST MAKES HIM MYSTE-RIOUS!
BUT STUDENT-TEACHER RELATION-SHIPS SEEM LIKE TROUBLE.
MISS POPULAR, YOU'RE NOT DREAMING BIIIG ENOUGH!
WHY, YOU ...!!
Oh dear.
MATSU-ZAKA-SAN.

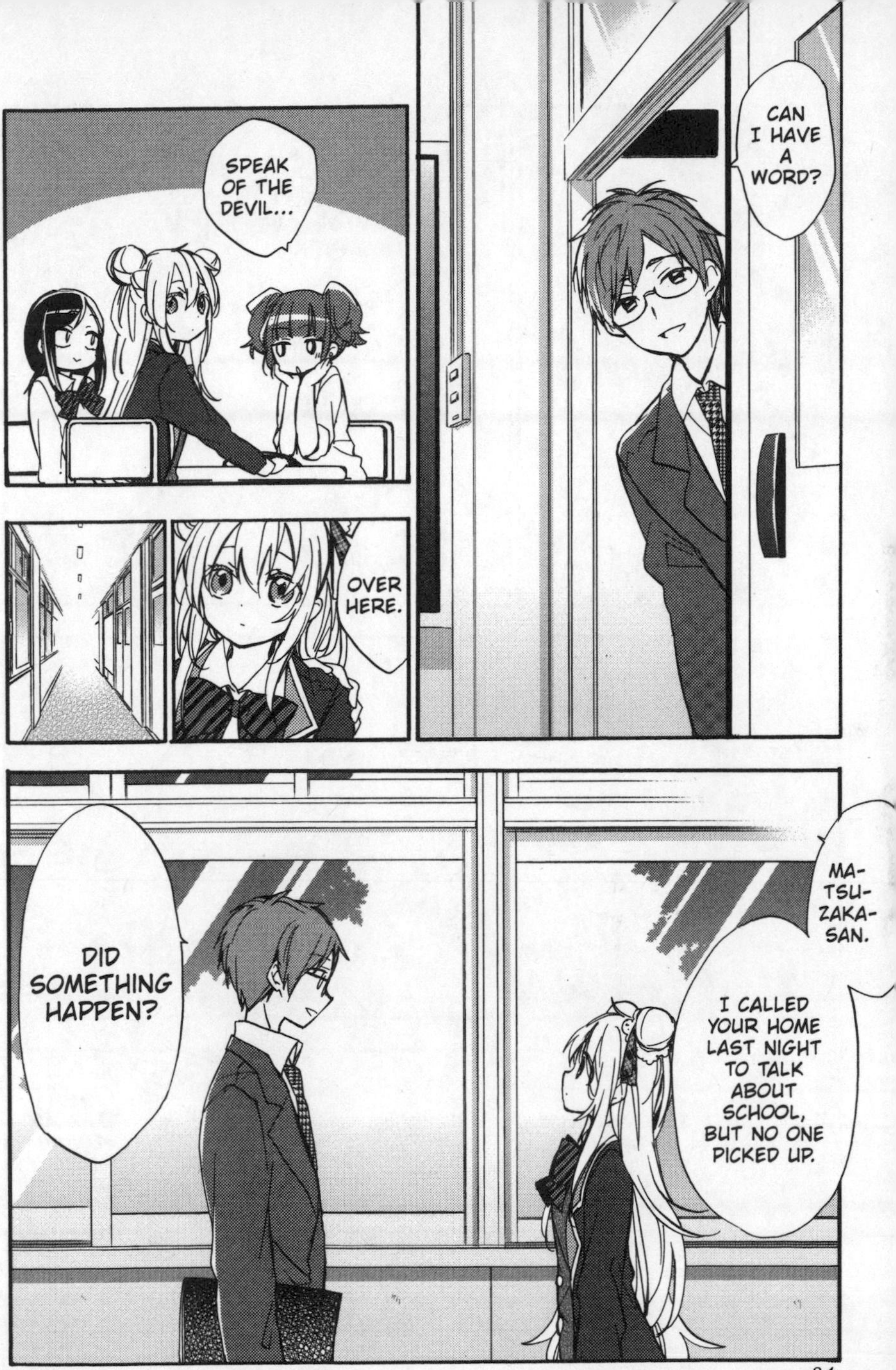
CAN I HAVE A WORD?
SPEAK OF THE DEVIL...
OVER HERE.
MA-TSU-ZAKA-SAN.
I CALLED YOUR HOME LAST NIGHT TO TALK ABOUT SCHOOL, BUT NO ONE PICKED UP.
DID SOMETHING HAPPEN?

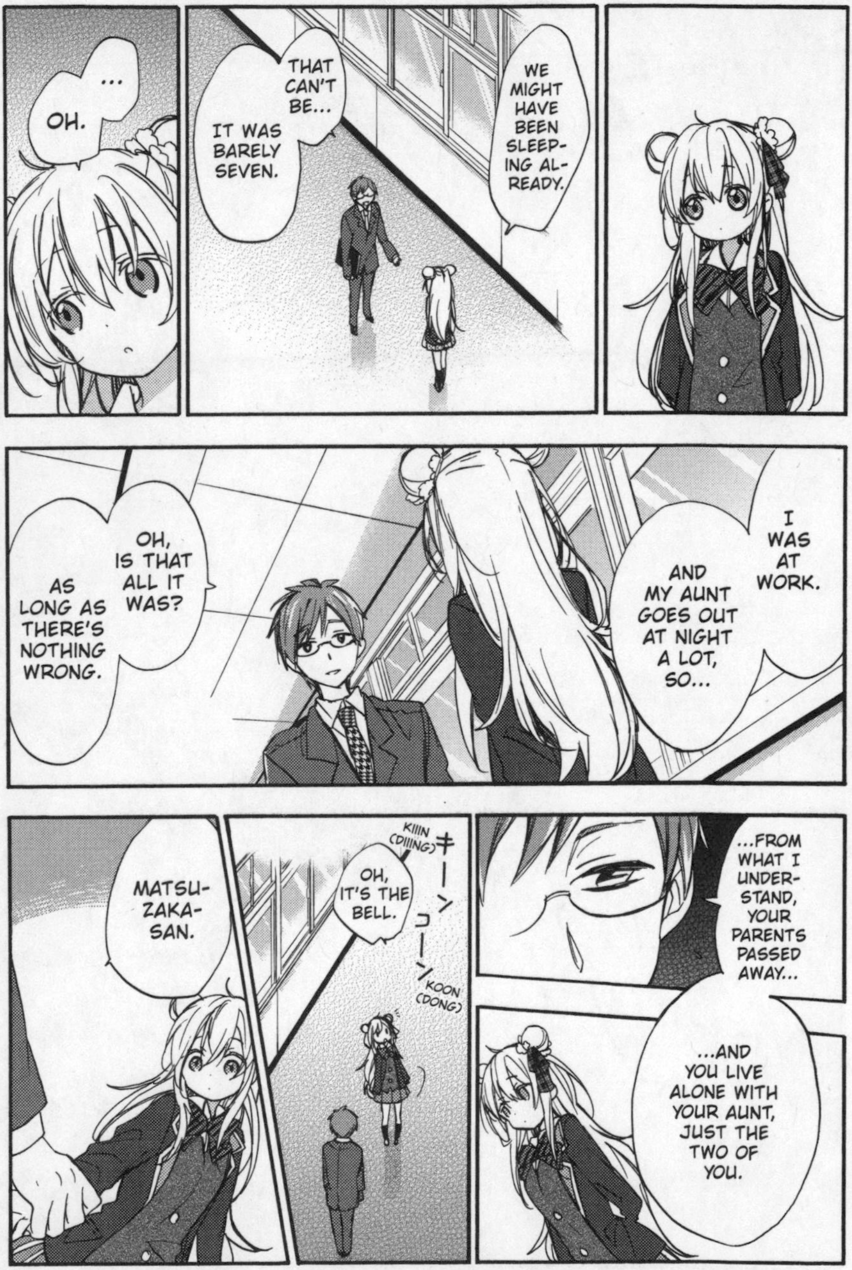
WE MIGHT HAVE BEEN SLEEPING ALREADY.
THAT CAN'T BE... IT WAS BARELY SEVEN.
... OH.
I WAS AT WORK. AND MY AUNT GOES OUT AT NIGHT A LOT, SO...
OH, IS THAT ALL IT WAS? AS LONG AS THERE'S NOTHING WRONG.
...FROM WHAT I UNDERSTAND, YOUR PARENTS PASSED AWAY...
...AND YOU LIVE ALONE WITH YOUR AUNT, JUST THE TWO OF YOU.
キーン KIIIN (DIIING)
コーン KOON (DONG)
OH, IT'S THE BELL.
MATSUZAKA-SAN.

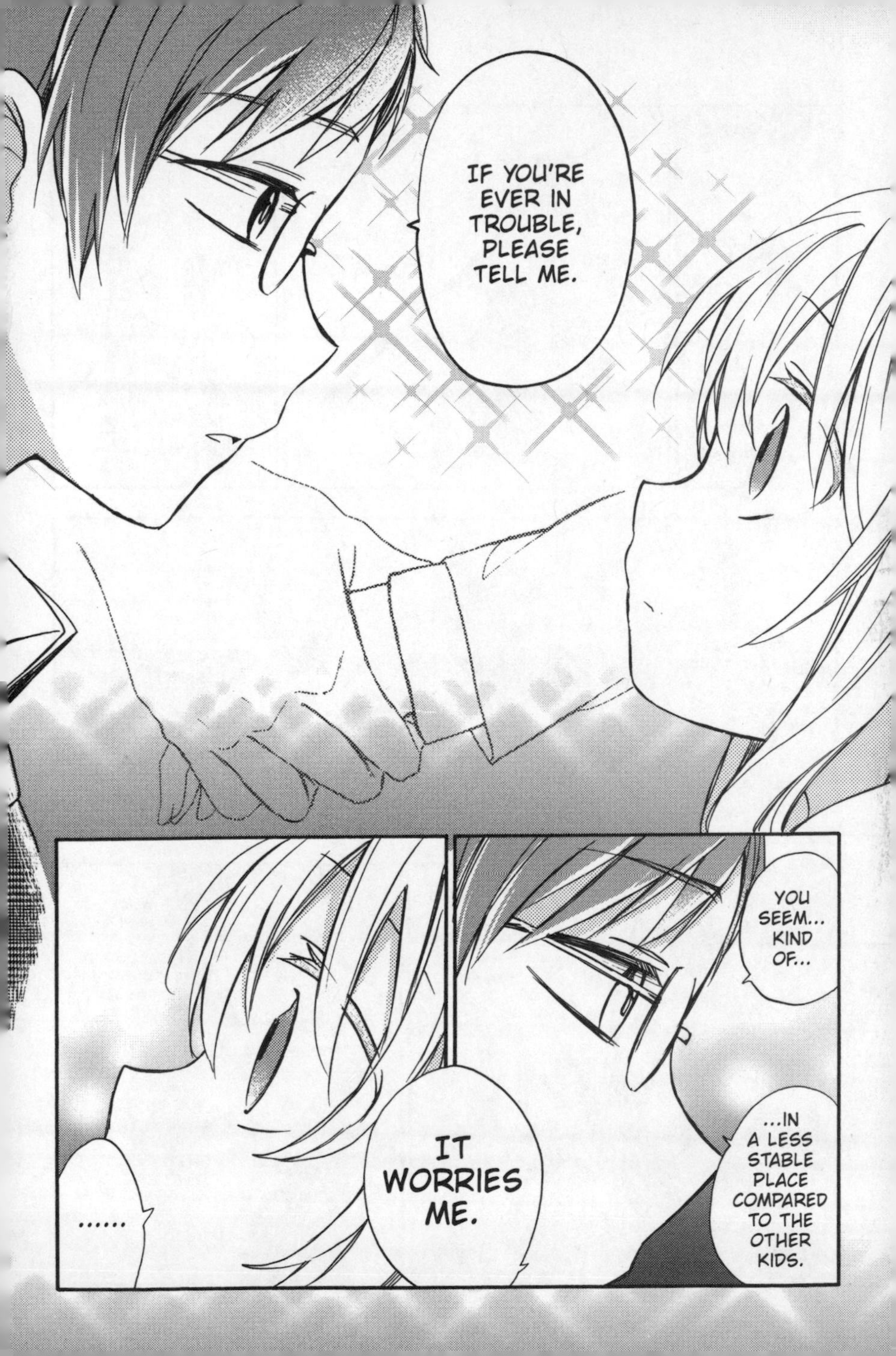
IF YOU'RE EVER IN TROUBLE, PLEASE TELL ME.
YOU SEEM... KIND OF...
...IN A LESS STABLE PLACE COMPARED TO THE OTHER KIDS.
IT WORRIES ME.
......

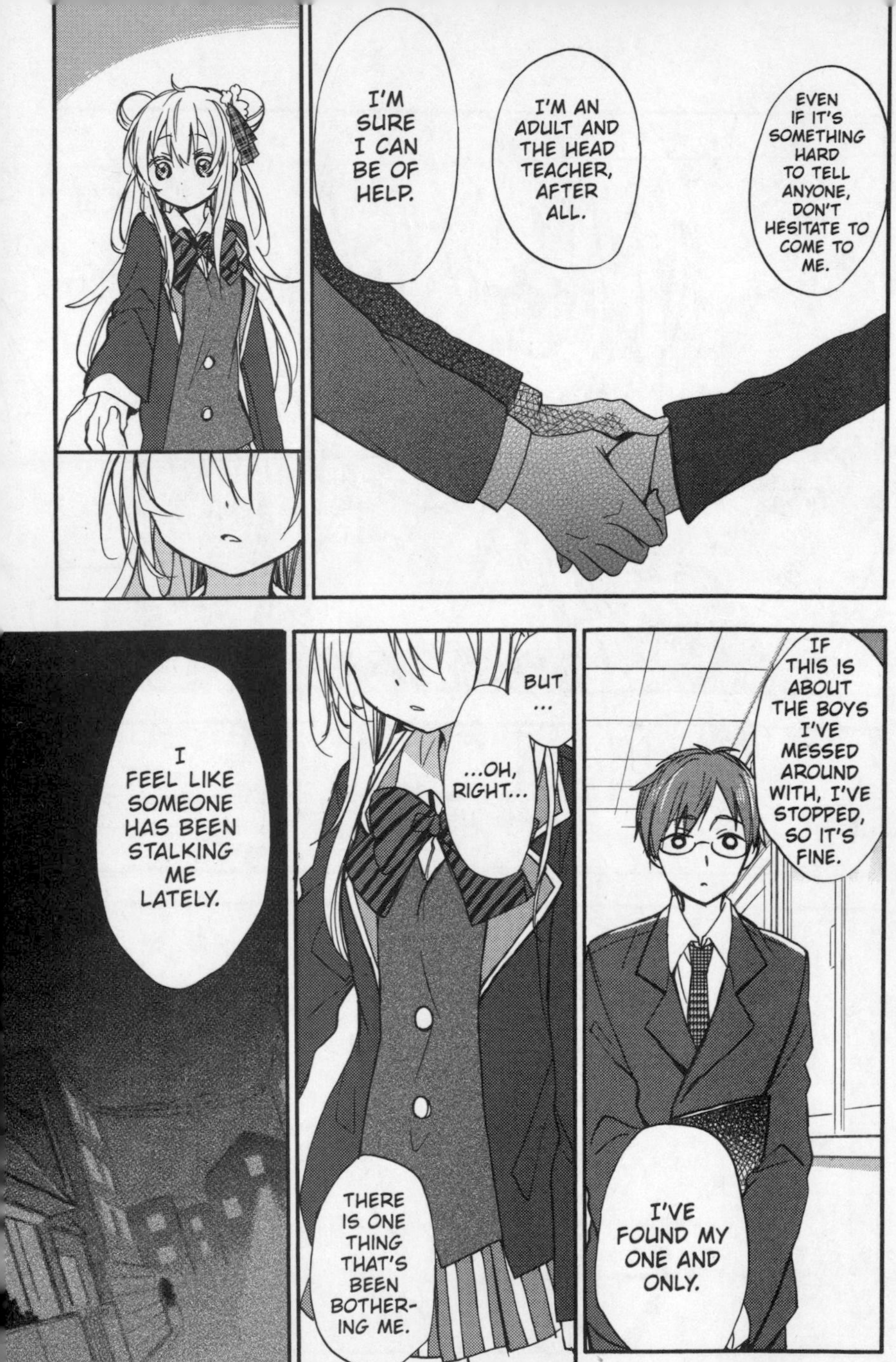
EVEN IF IT'S SOMETHING HARD TO TELL ANYONE, DON'T HESITATE TO COME TO ME.
I'M AN ADULT AND THE HEAD TEACHER, AFTER ALL.
I'M SURE I CAN BE OF HELP.
IF THIS IS ABOUT THE BOYS I'VE MESSED AROUND WITH, I'VE STOPPED, SO IT'S FINE.
I'VE FOUND MY ONE AND ONLY.
BUT ...
...OH, RIGHT...
THERE IS ONE THING THAT'S BEEN BOTHER-ING ME.
I FEEL LIKE SOMEONE HAS BEEN STALKING ME LATELY.

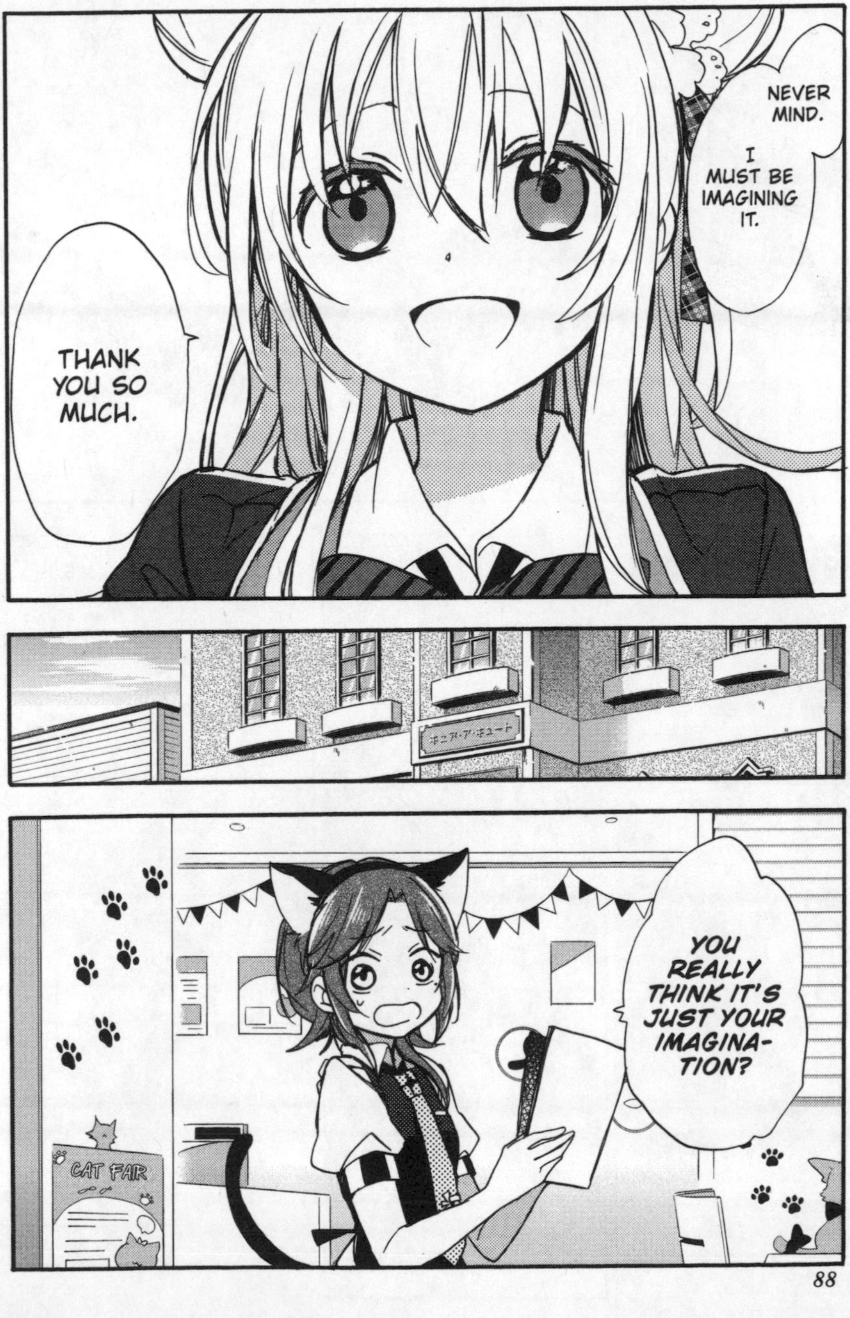
NEVER MIND.
I MUST BE IMAGINING IT.
THANK YOU SO MUCH.
キュア・ア・キュート
YOU REALLY THINK IT'S JUST YOUR IMAGINA-TION?
CAT FAIR

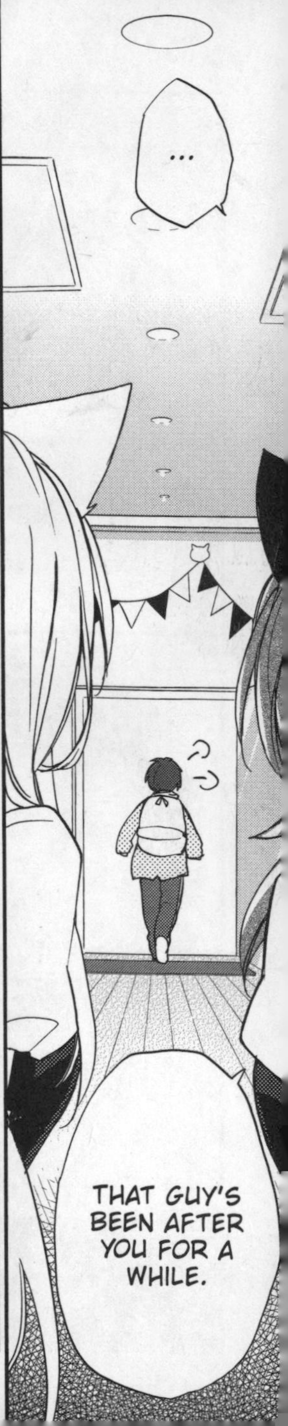
...
THAT GUY'S BEEN AFTER YOU FOR A WHILE.

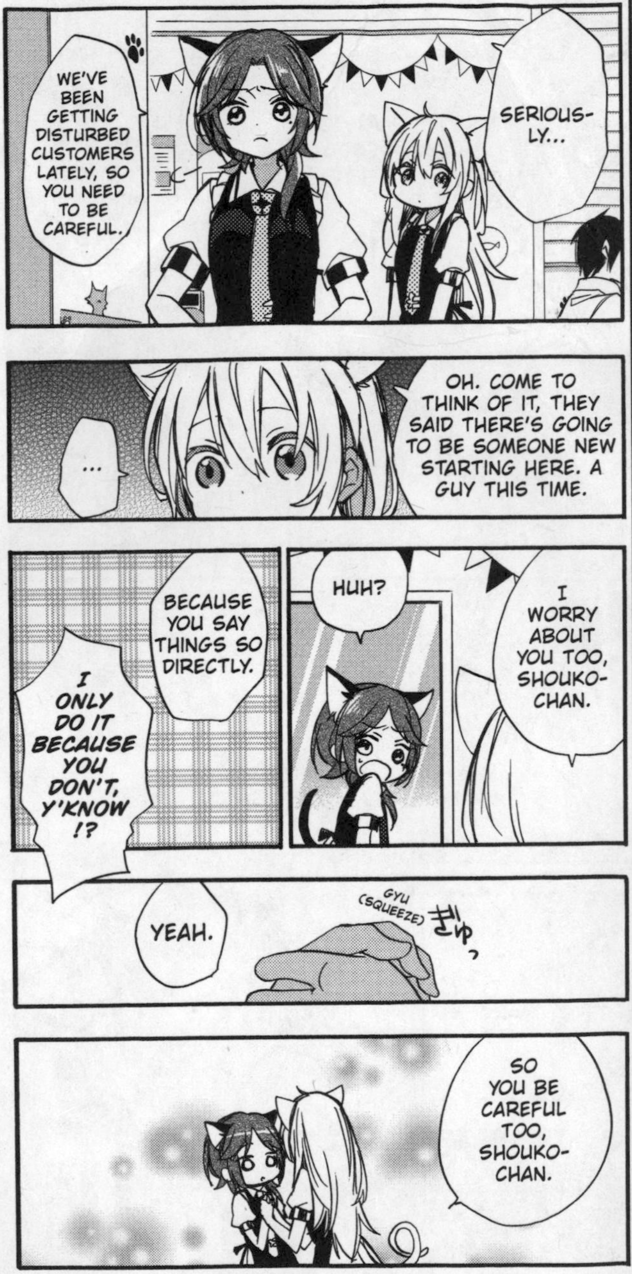
SERIOUSLY...
WE'VE BEEN GETTING DISTURBED CUSTOMERS LATELY, SO YOU NEED TO BE CAREFUL.
OH. COME TO THINK OF IT, THEY SAID THERE'S GOING TO BE SOMEONE NEW STARTING HERE. A GUY THIS TIME.
...
I WORRY ABOUT YOU TOO, SHOUKO-CHAN.
HUH?
BECAUSE YOU SAY THINGS SO DIRECTLY.
I ONLY DO IT BECAUSE YOU DON'T, Y'KNOW!?
GYU (SQUEEZE)
YEAH.
SO YOU BE CAREFUL TOO, SHOUKO-CHAN.

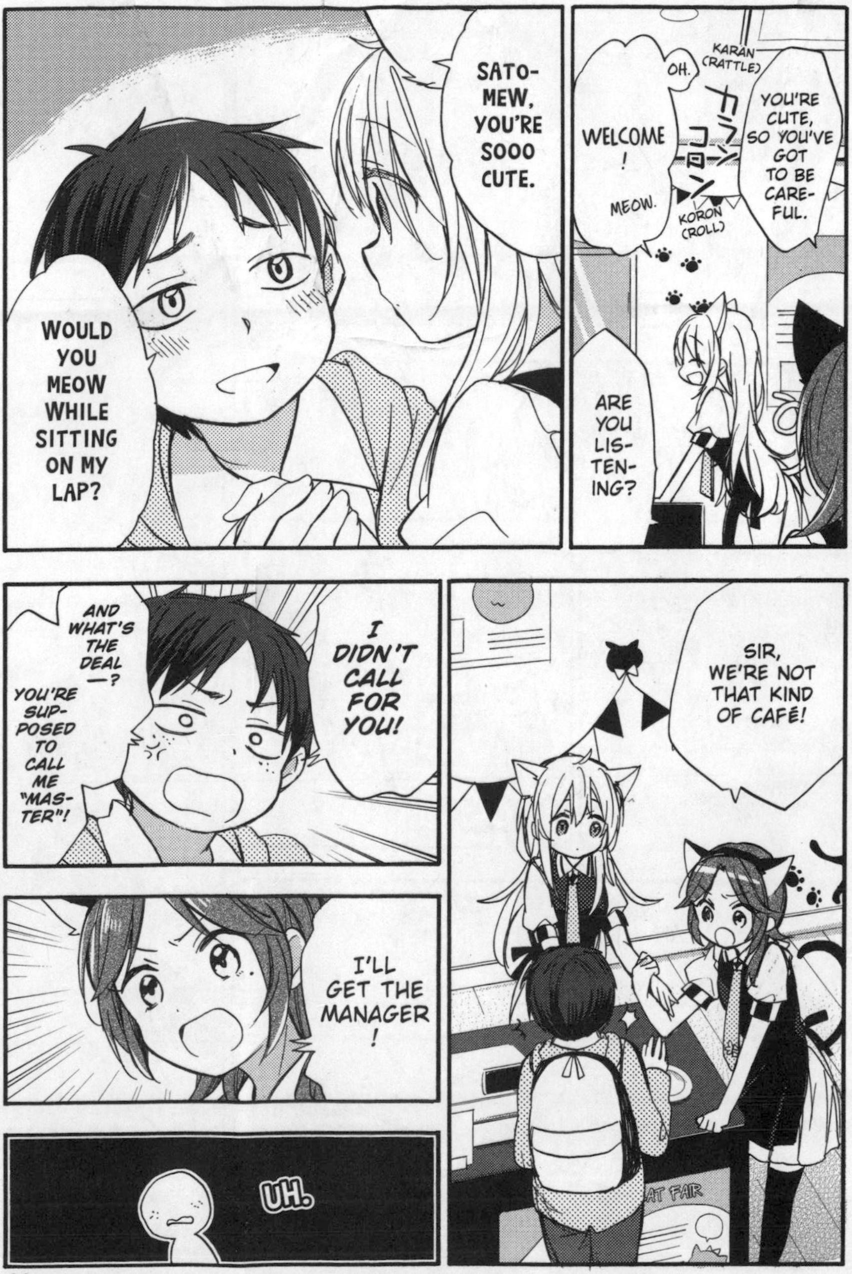
YOU'RE CUTE, SO YOU'VE GOT TO BE CAREFUL.
KARAN (RATTLE)
カラン
OH.
WELCOME! MEOW.
コロン
KORON (ROLL)
ARE YOU LISTENING?
SATO-MEW, YOU'RE SOOO CUTE.
WOULD YOU MEOW WHILE SITTING ON MY LAP?
SIR, WE'RE NOT THAT KIND OF CAFÉ!
I DIDN'T CALL FOR YOU!
AND WHAT'S THE DEAL—? YOU'RE SUPPOSED TO CALL ME "MASTER"!
I'LL GET THE MANAGER!
UH.

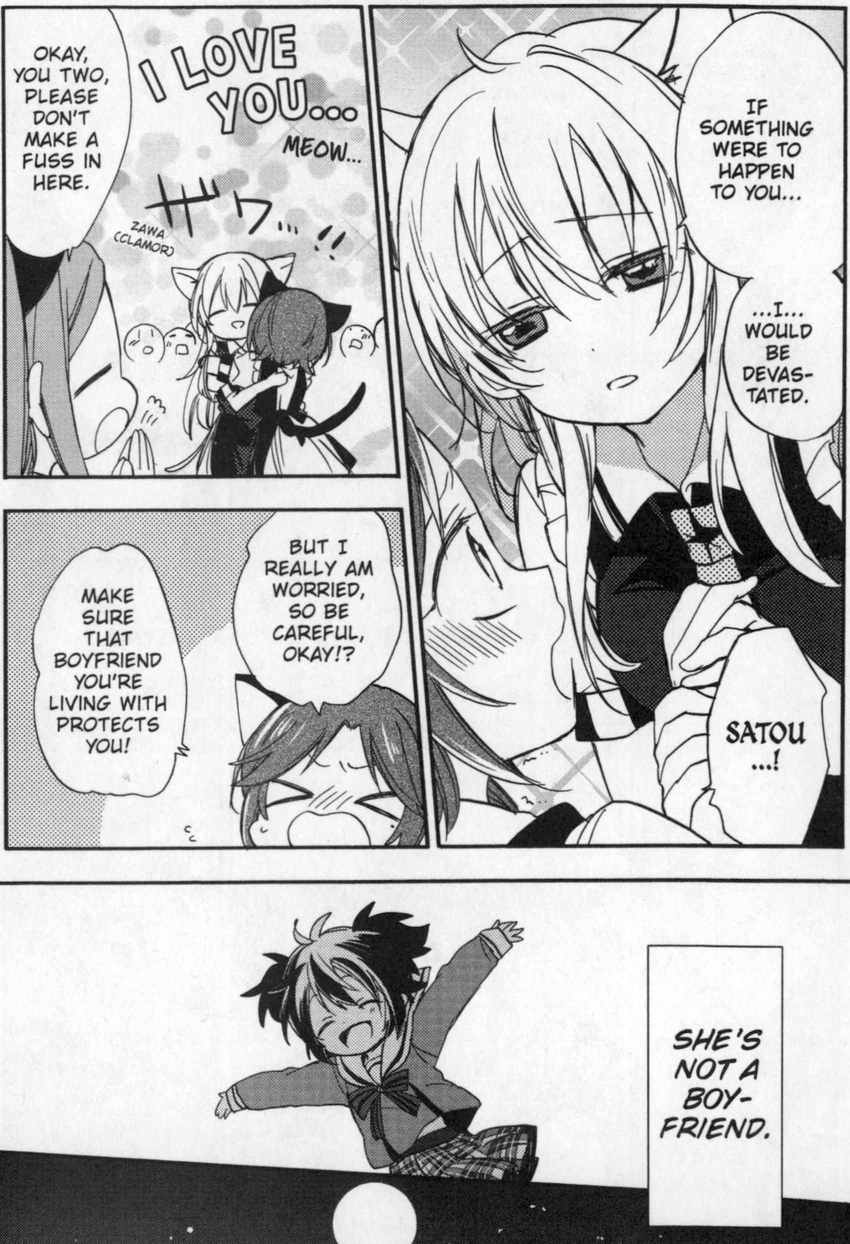
IF SOMETHING WERE TO HAPPEN TO YOU...
...I... WOULD BE DEVAS-TATED.
SATOU ...!
I LOVE YOU...
MEOW...
OKAY, YOU TWO, PLEASE DON'T MAKE A FUSS IN HERE.
ZAWA (CLAMOR)
BUT I REALLY AM WORRIED, SO BE CAREFUL, OKAY!?
MAKE SURE THAT BOYFRIEND YOU'RE LIVING WITH PROTECTS YOU!
SHE'S NOT A BOY-FRIEND.

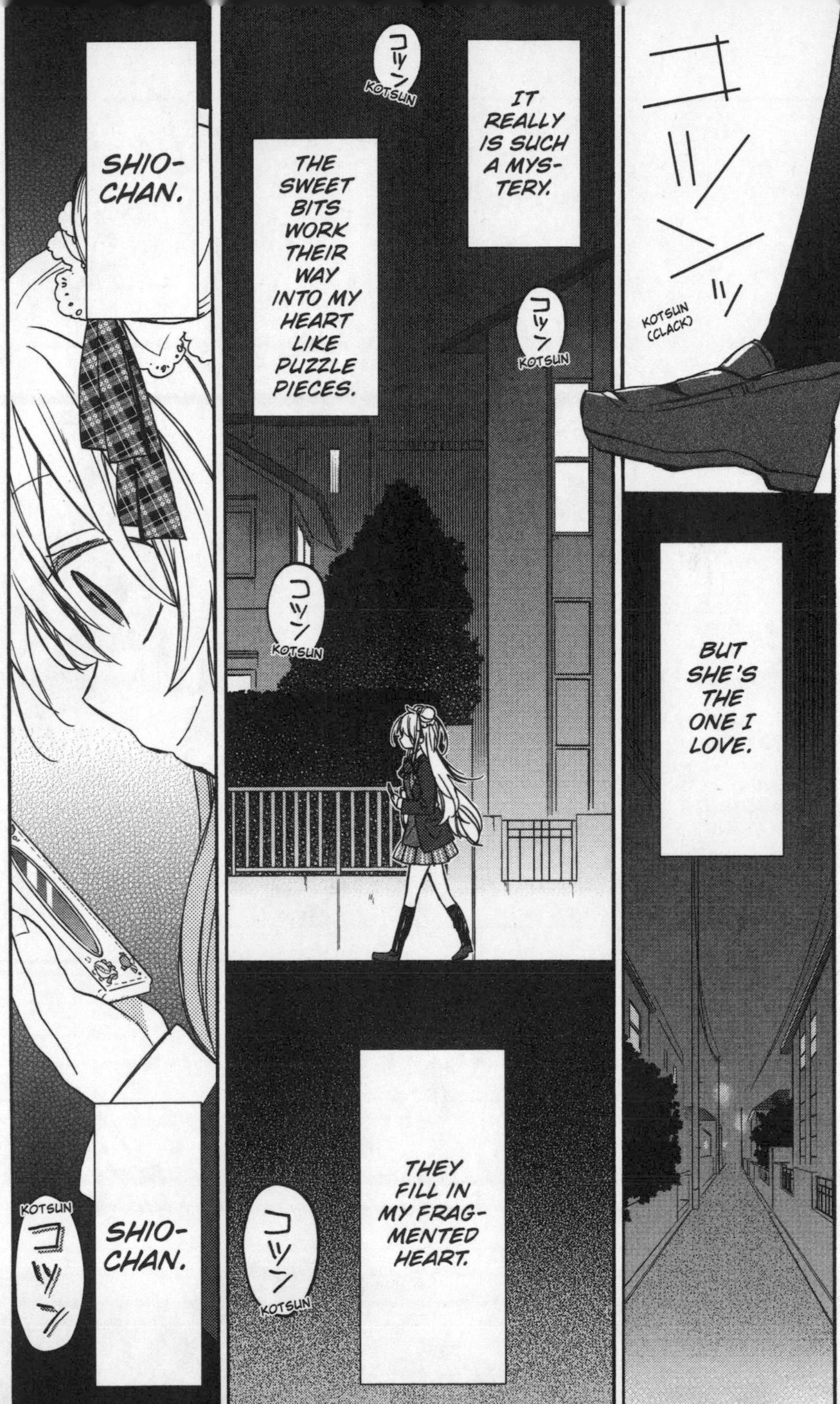
KOTSUN (CLACK)
BUT SHE'S THE ONE I LOVE.
IT REALLY IS SUCH A MYSTERY.
コツン KOTSUN
THE SWEET BITS WORK THEIR WAY INTO MY HEART LIKE PUZZLE PIECES.
コツン KOTSUN
コツン KOTSUN
THEY FILL IN MY FRAGMENTED HEART.
コツン KOTSUN
SHIO-CHAN.
SHIO-CHAN.
KOTSUN コツン

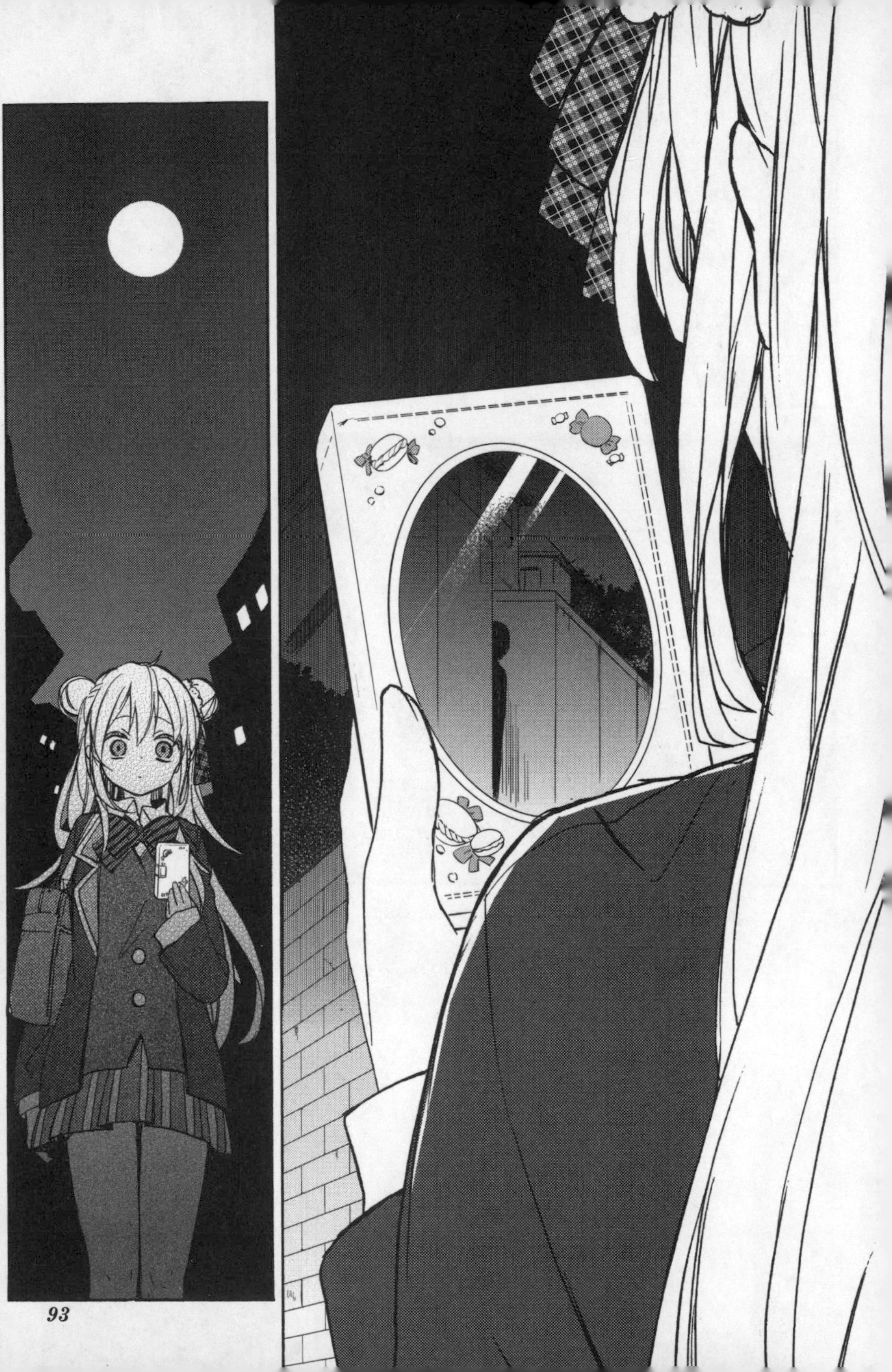

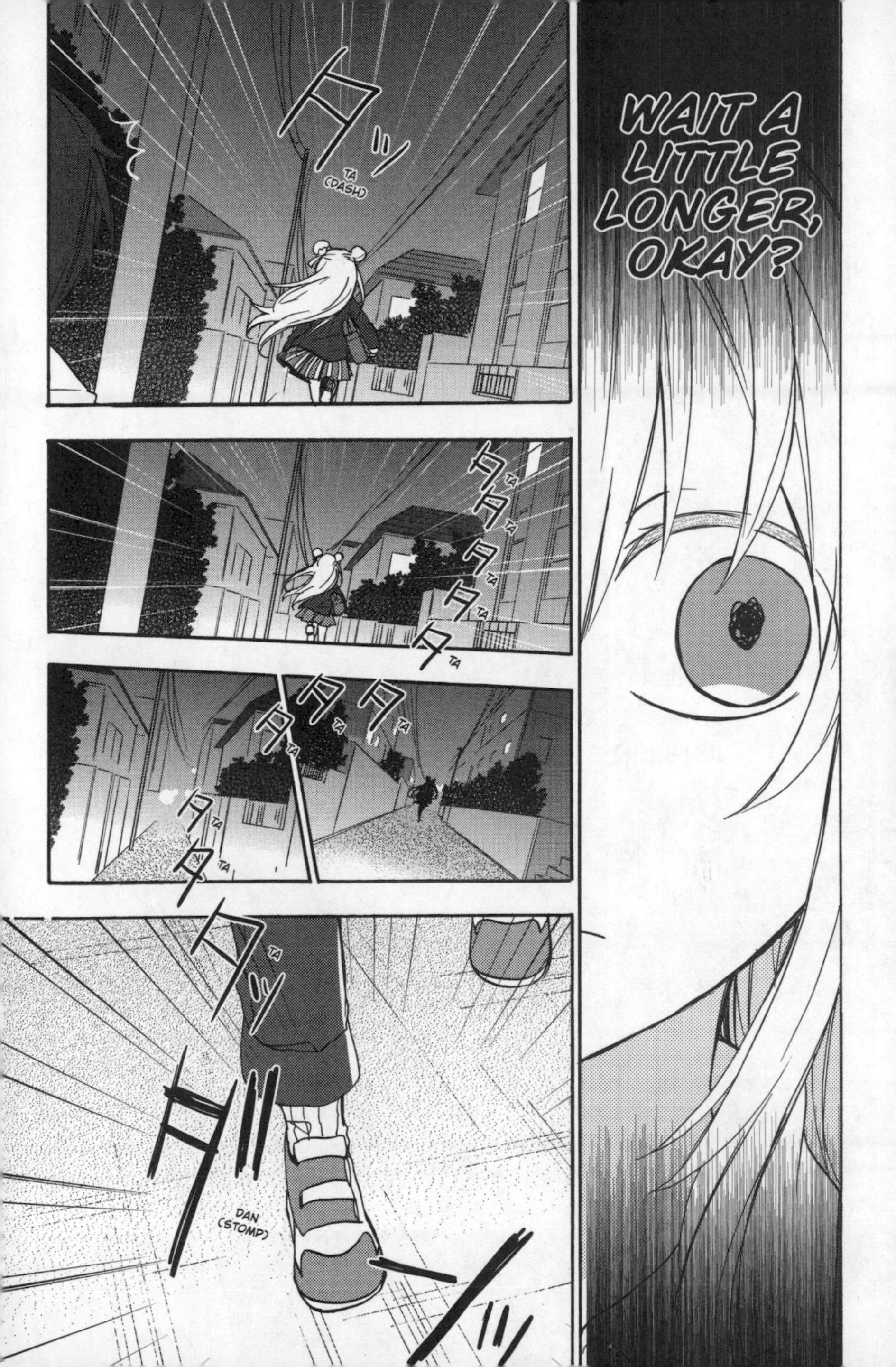

WAIT A LITTLE LONGER, OKAY?
TA (DASH)
TA
TA
TA
TA
TA
TA
TA
TA
TA
TA
TA
DAN (STOMP)

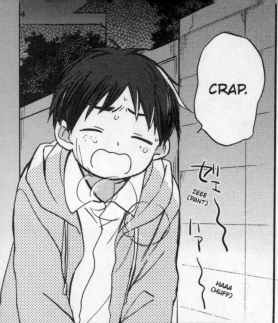

CRAP.

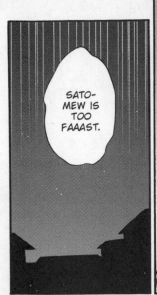

SATO-MEW IS TOO FAAAST.

ZEEE (PANT)

HAAA (CHUFF)

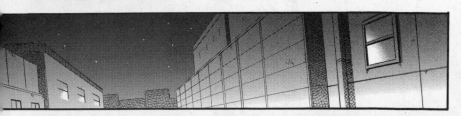

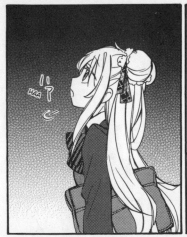

HAA

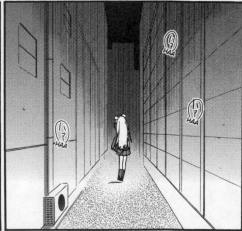

HAA

HAA

HAA

HAA

95

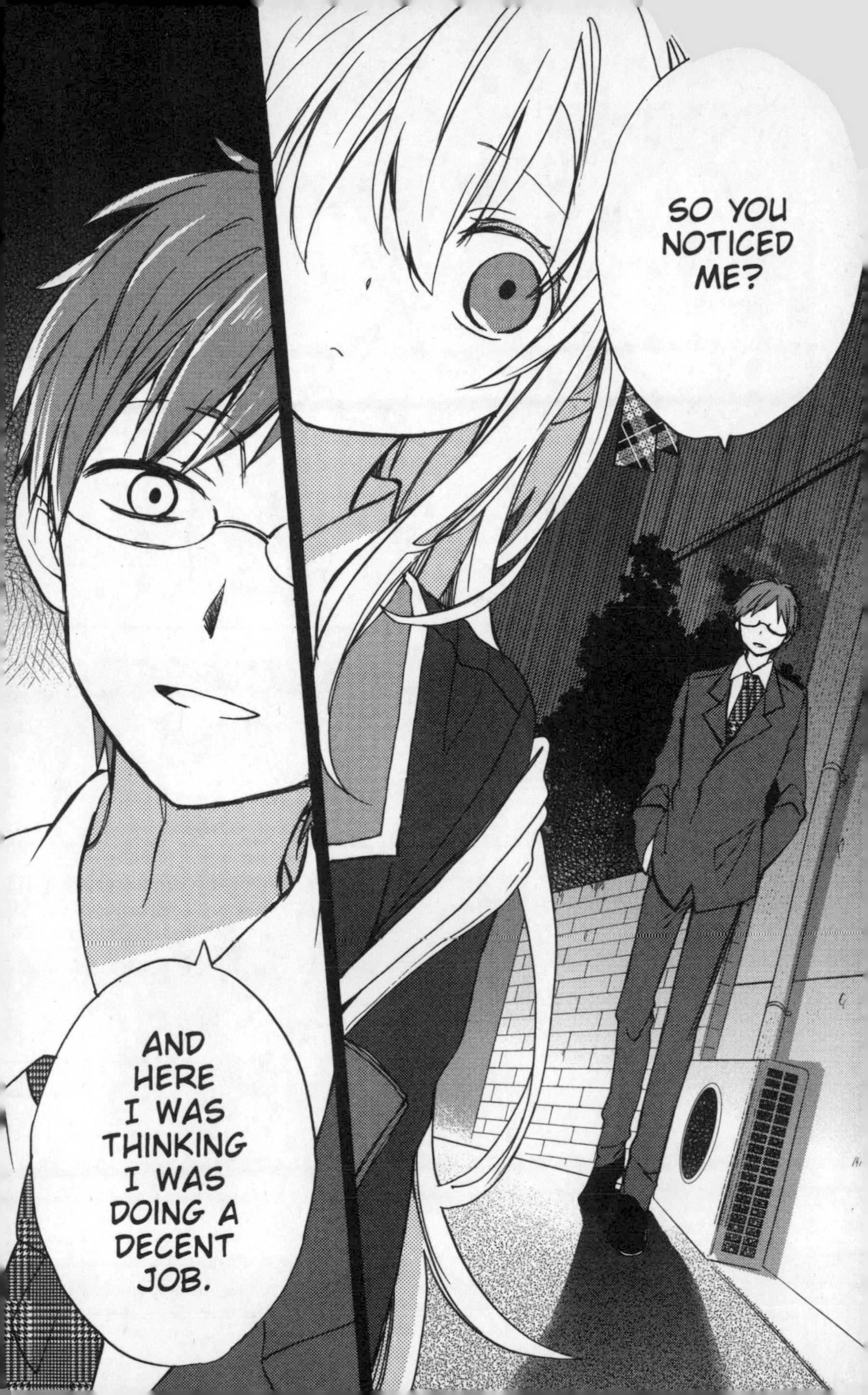
SO YOU NOTICED ME?
AND HERE I WAS THINKING I WAS DOING A DECENT JOB.

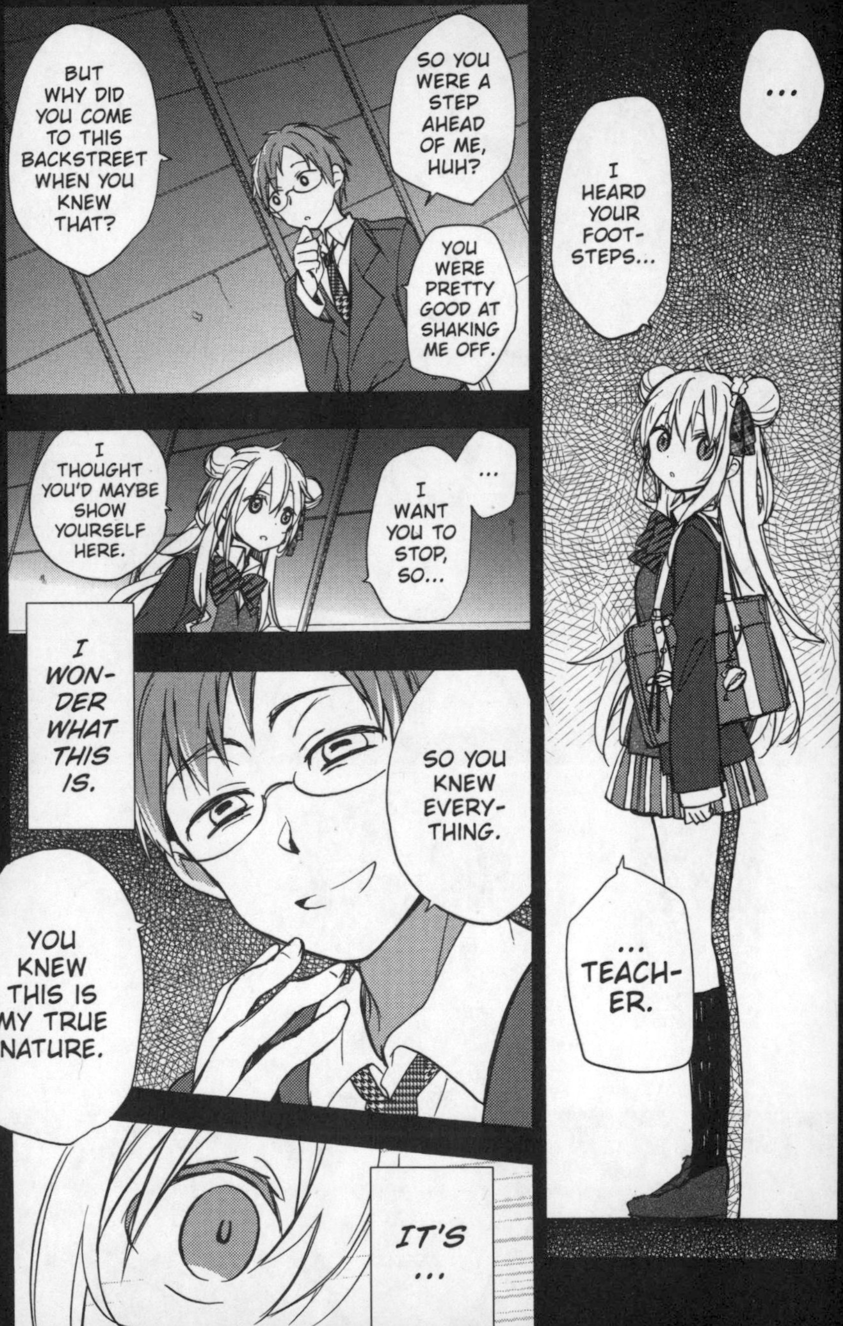
...
I HEARD YOUR FOOT-STEPS...
... TEACH-ER.
SO YOU WERE A STEP AHEAD OF ME, HUH?
YOU WERE PRETTY GOOD AT SHAKING ME OFF.
BUT WHY DID YOU COME TO THIS BACKSTREET WHEN YOU KNEW THAT?
... I WANT YOU TO STOP, SO...
I THOUGHT YOU'D MAYBE SHOW YOURSELF HERE.
SO YOU KNEW EVERY-THING.
YOU KNEW THIS IS MY TRUE NATURE.
I WON-DER WHAT THIS IS.
IT'S ...

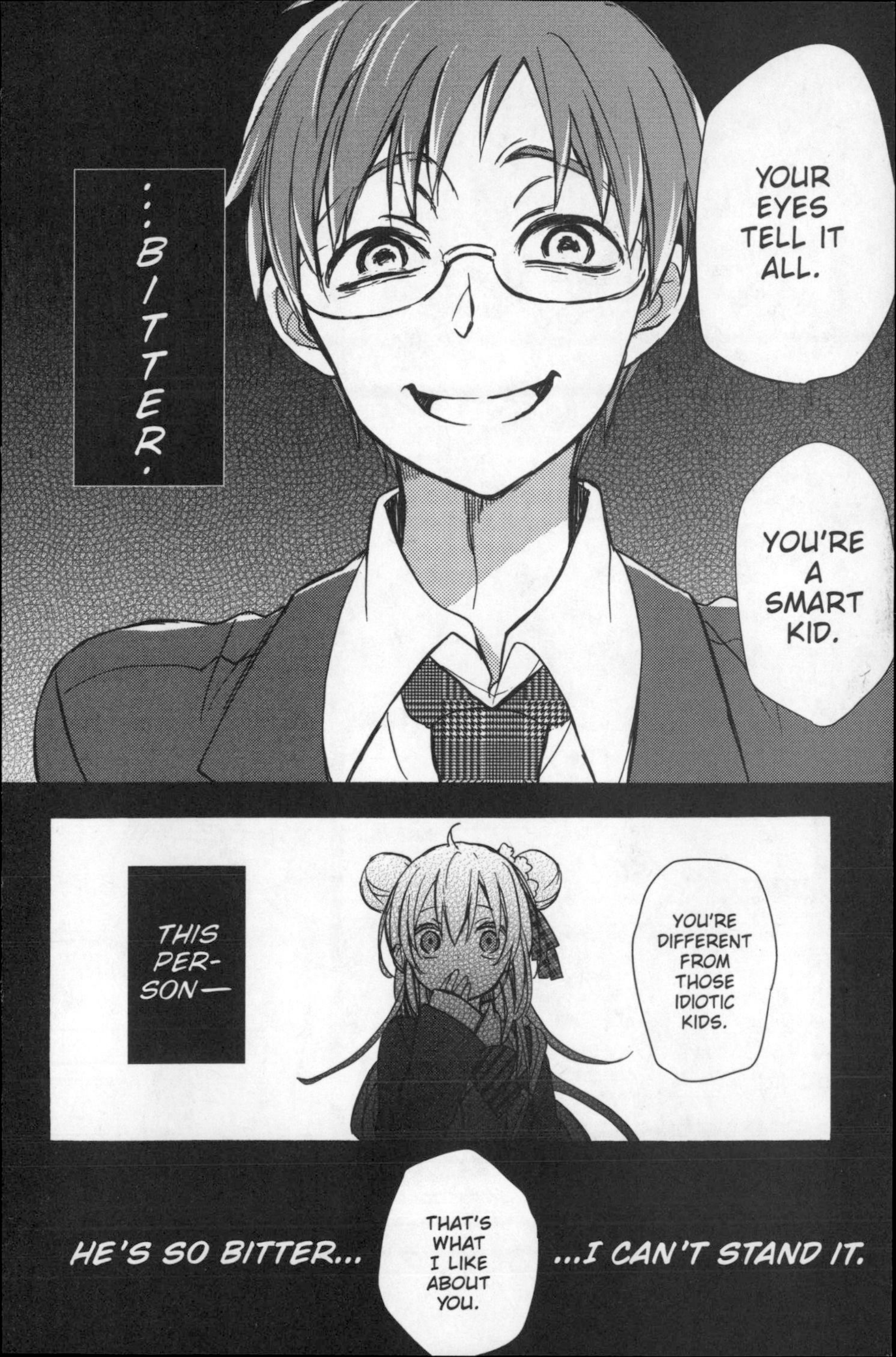
YOUR EYES TELL IT ALL.
YOU'RE A SMART KID.
...BITTER.
YOU'RE DIFFERENT FROM THOSE IDIOTIC KIDS.
THIS PER-SON—
THAT'S WHAT I LIKE ABOUT YOU.
HE'S SO BITTER...
...I CAN'T STAND IT.

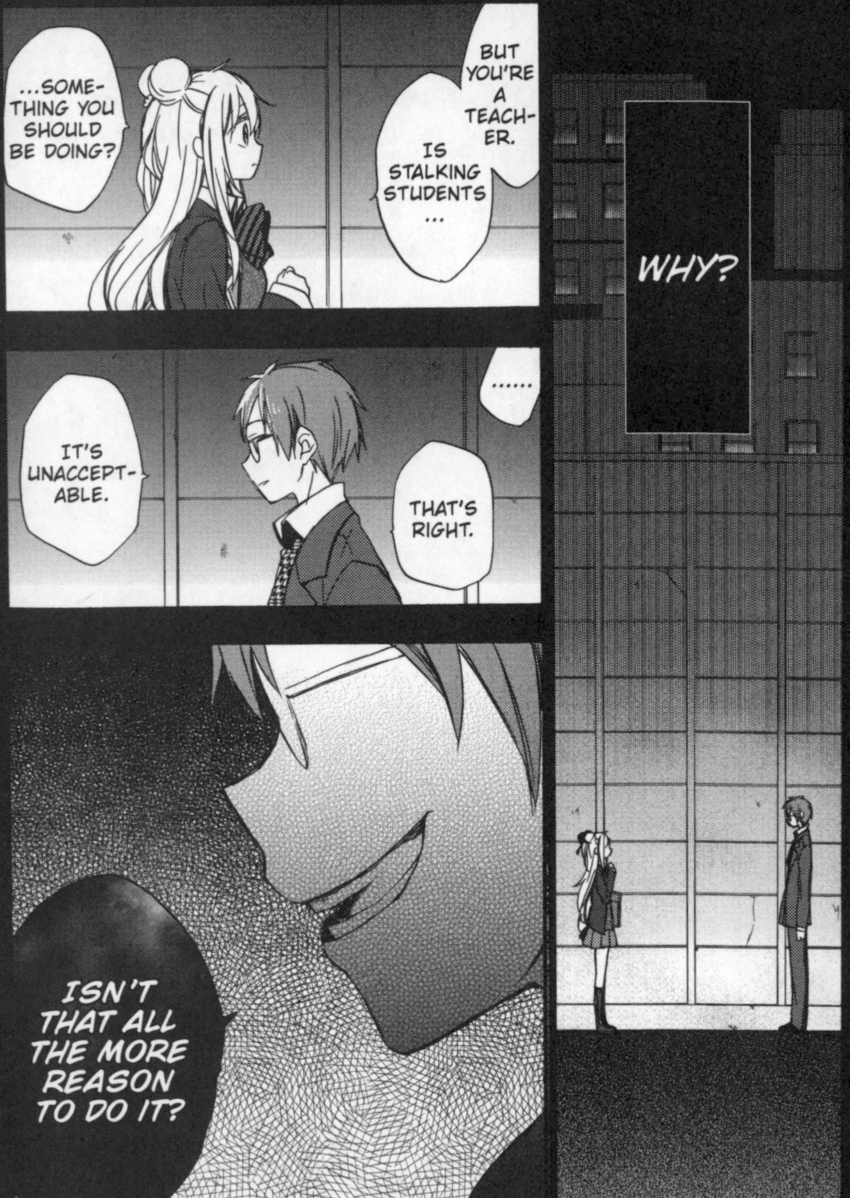
WHY?
BUT YOU'RE A TEACHER.
IS STALKING STUDENTS...
...SOMETHING YOU SHOULD BE DOING?
......
THAT'S RIGHT.
IT'S UNACCEPTABLE.
ISN'T THAT ALL THE MORE REASON TO DO IT?

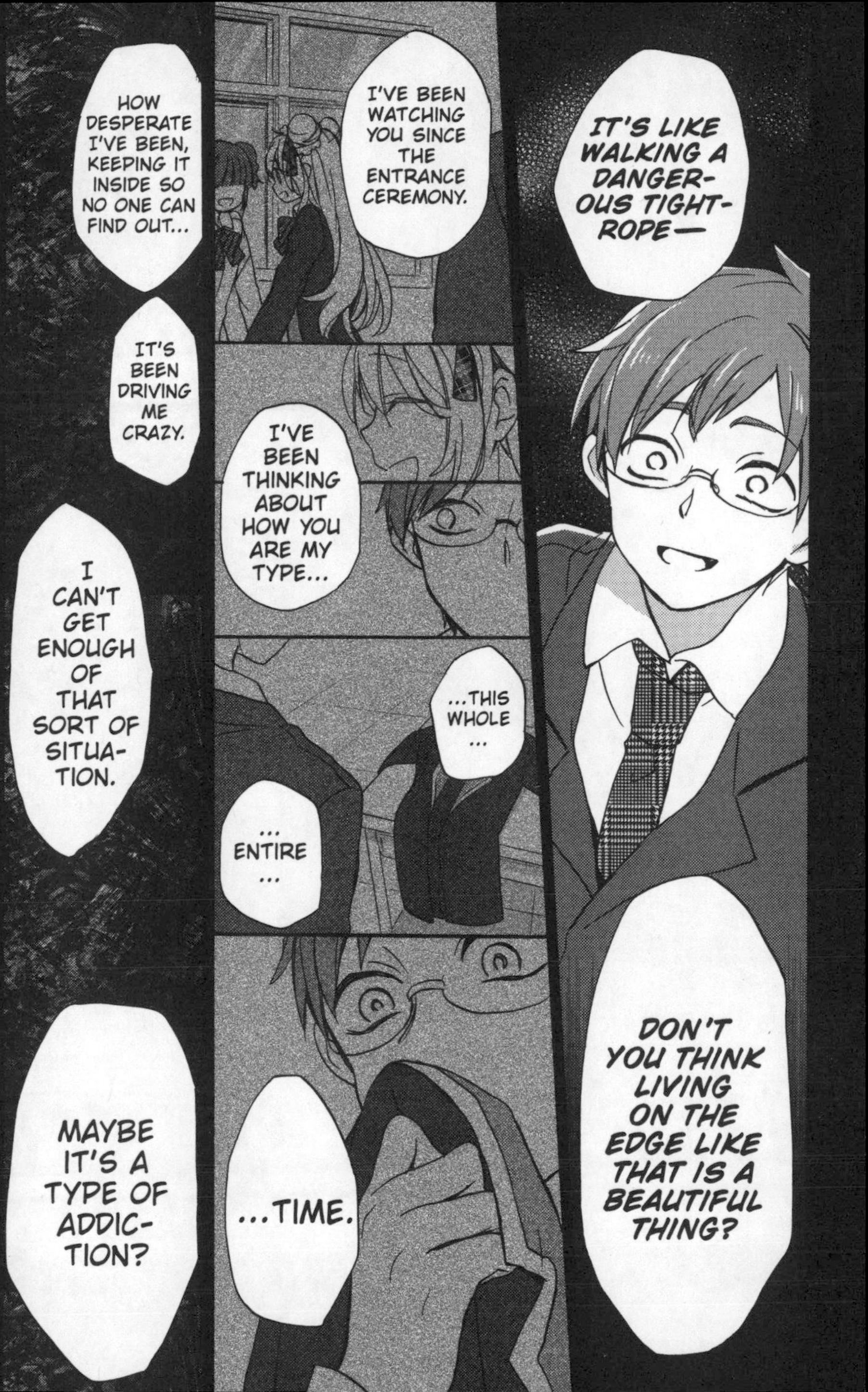
IT'S LIKE WALKING A DANGER-OUS TIGHT-ROPE—
I'VE BEEN WATCHING YOU SINCE THE ENTRANCE CEREMONY.
HOW DESPERATE I'VE BEEN, KEEPING IT INSIDE SO NO ONE CAN FIND OUT...
IT'S BEEN DRIVING ME CRAZY.
I'VE BEEN THINKING ABOUT HOW YOU ARE MY TYPE...
I CAN'T GET ENOUGH OF THAT SORT OF SITUA-TION.
...THIS WHOLE ...
... ENTIRE ...
DON'T YOU THINK LIVING ON THE EDGE LIKE THAT IS A BEAUTIFUL THING?
...TIME.
MAYBE IT'S A TYPE OF ADDIC-TION?

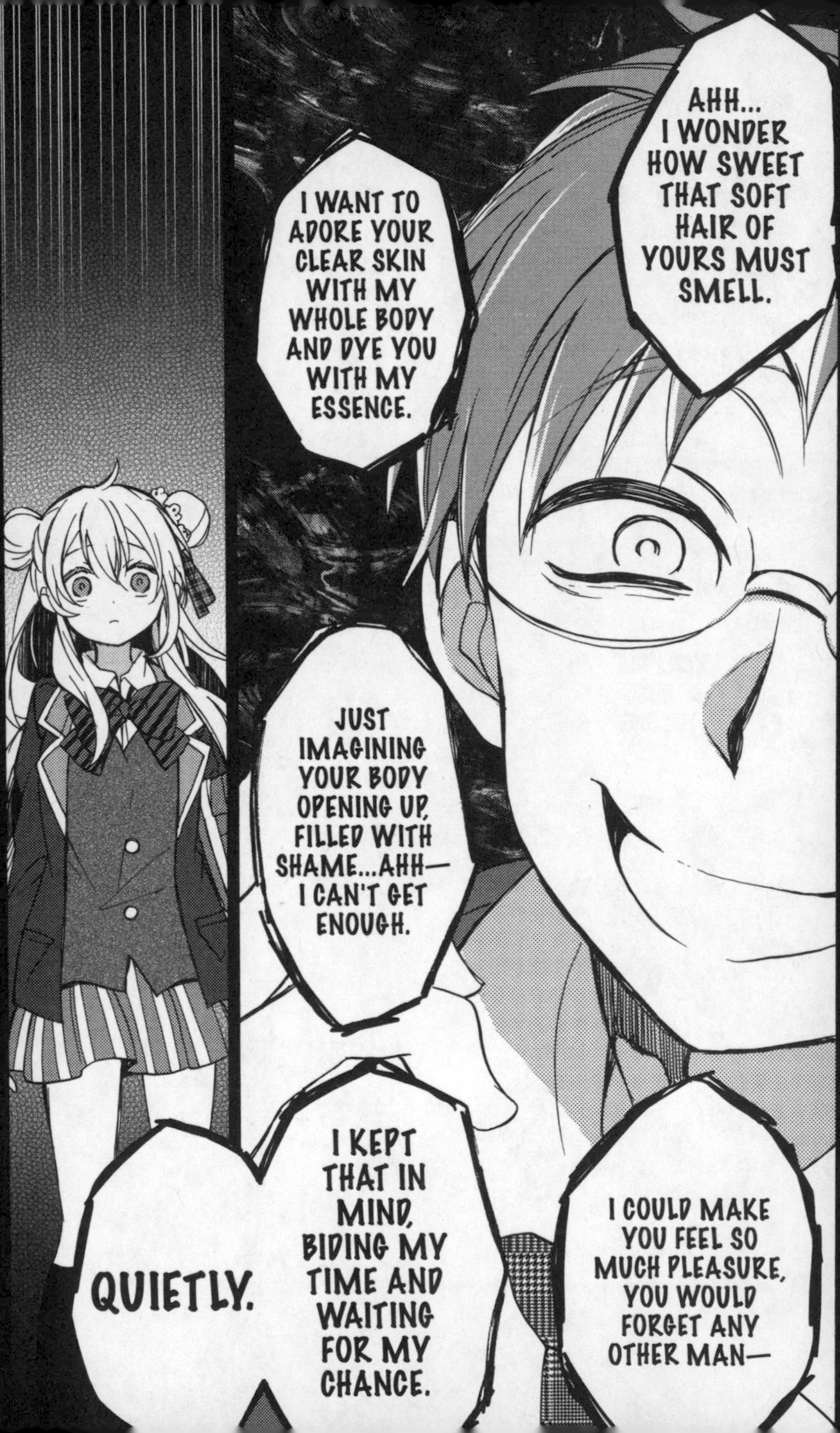
AHH... I WONDER HOW SWEET THAT SOFT HAIR OF YOURS MUST SMELL.
I WANT TO ADORE YOUR CLEAR SKIN WITH MY WHOLE BODY AND DYE YOU WITH MY ESSENCE.
JUST IMAGINING YOUR BODY OPENING UP, FILLED WITH SHAME...AHH— I CAN'T GET ENOUGH.
I COULD MAKE YOU FEEL SO MUCH PLEASURE, YOU WOULD FORGET ANY OTHER MAN—
I KEPT THAT IN MIND, BIDING MY TIME AND WAITING FOR MY CHANCE.
QUIETLY.

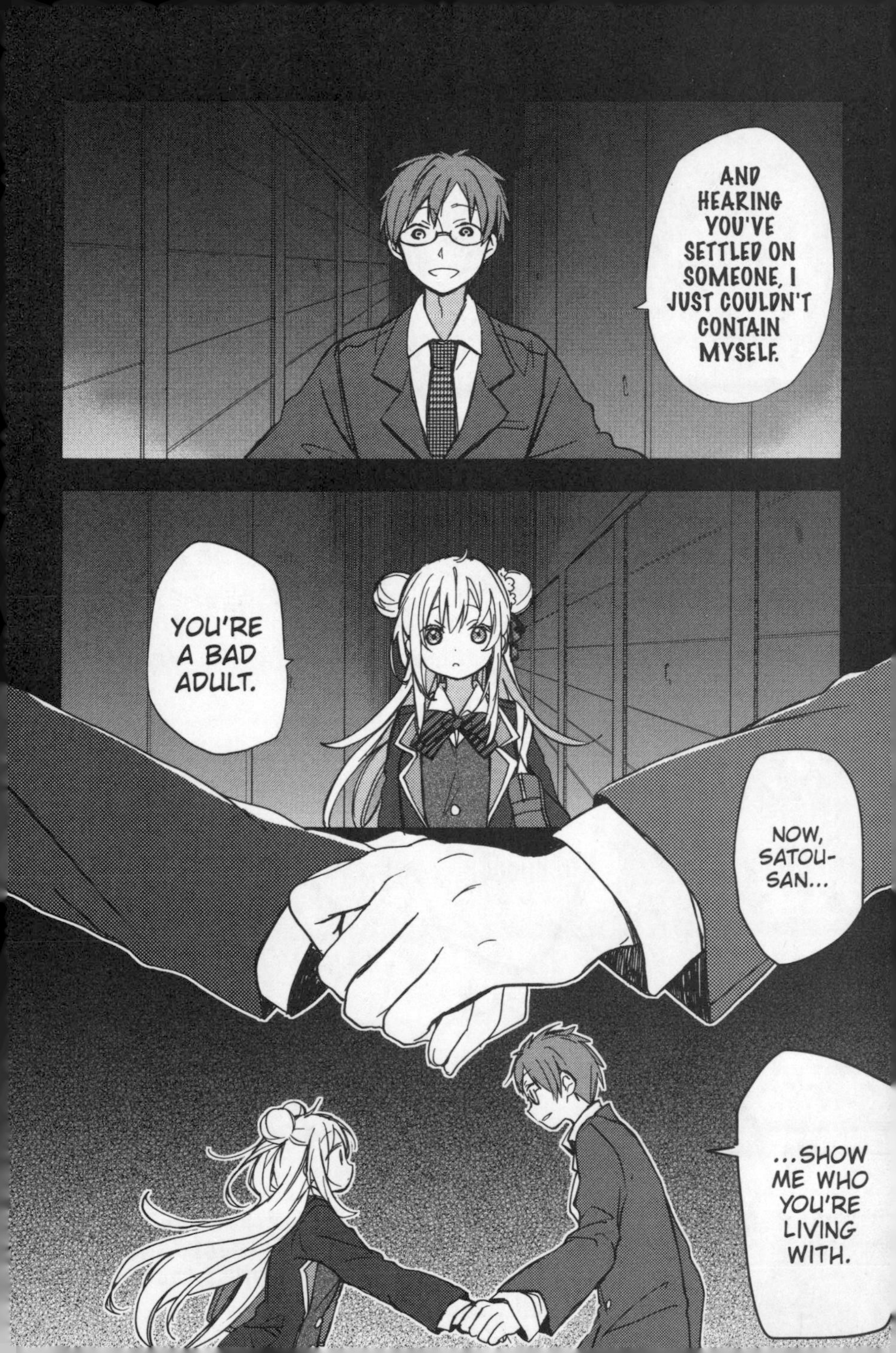
AND HEARING YOU'VE SETTLED ON SOMEONE, I JUST COULDN'T CONTAIN MYSELF.
YOU'RE A BAD ADULT.
NOW, SATOU-SAN...
...SHOW ME WHO YOU'RE LIVING WITH.

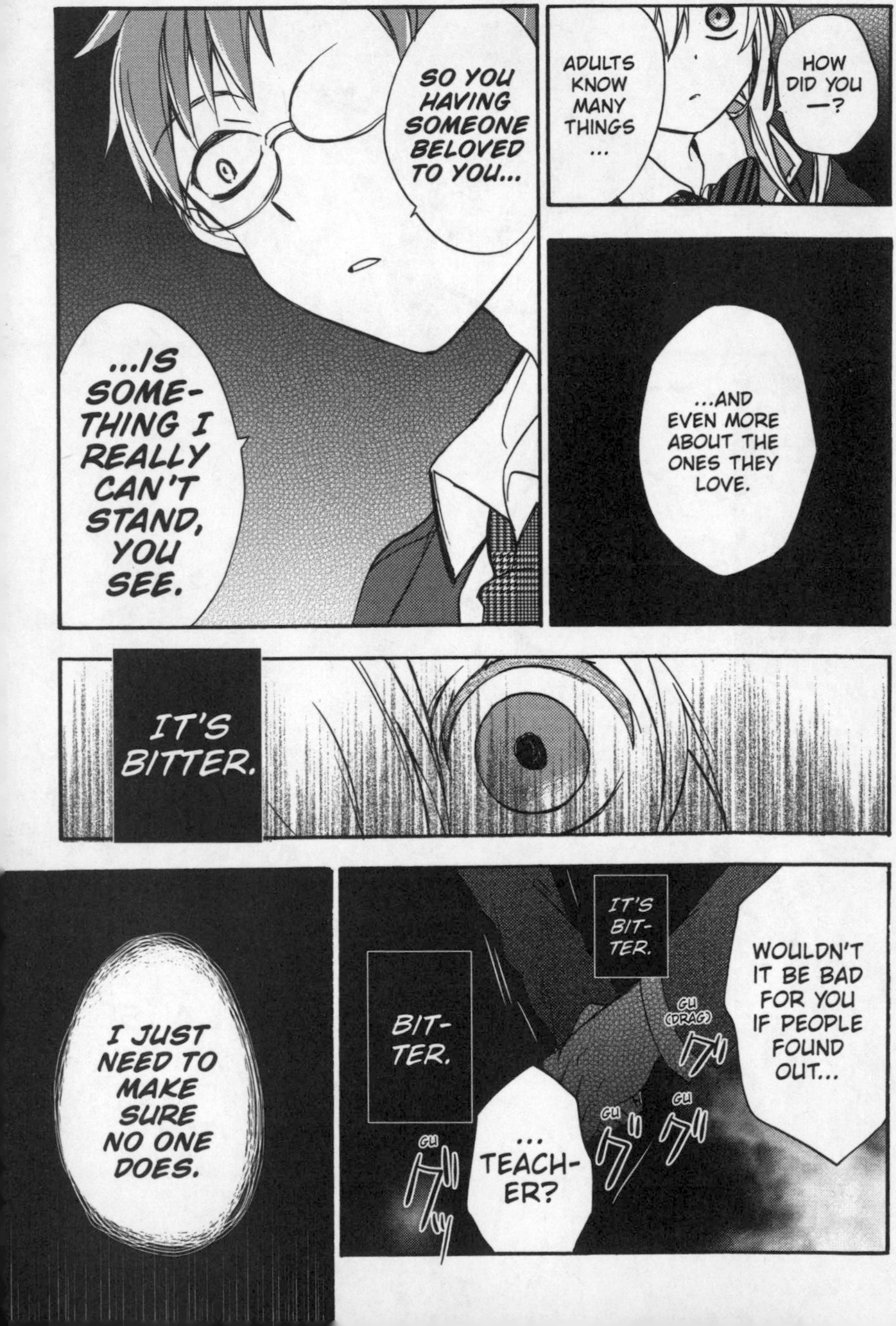
HOW DID YOU —?
ADULTS KNOW MANY THINGS ...
...AND EVEN MORE ABOUT THE ONES THEY LOVE.
SO YOU HAVING SOMEONE BELOVED TO YOU...
...IS SOMETHING I REALLY CAN'T STAND, YOU SEE.
IT'S BITTER.
WOULDN'T IT BE BAD FOR YOU IF PEOPLE FOUND OUT...
IT'S BITTER.
GU (DRAG)
GU
GU
BITTER.
...TEACHER?
GU
I JUST NEED TO MAKE SURE NO ONE DOES.

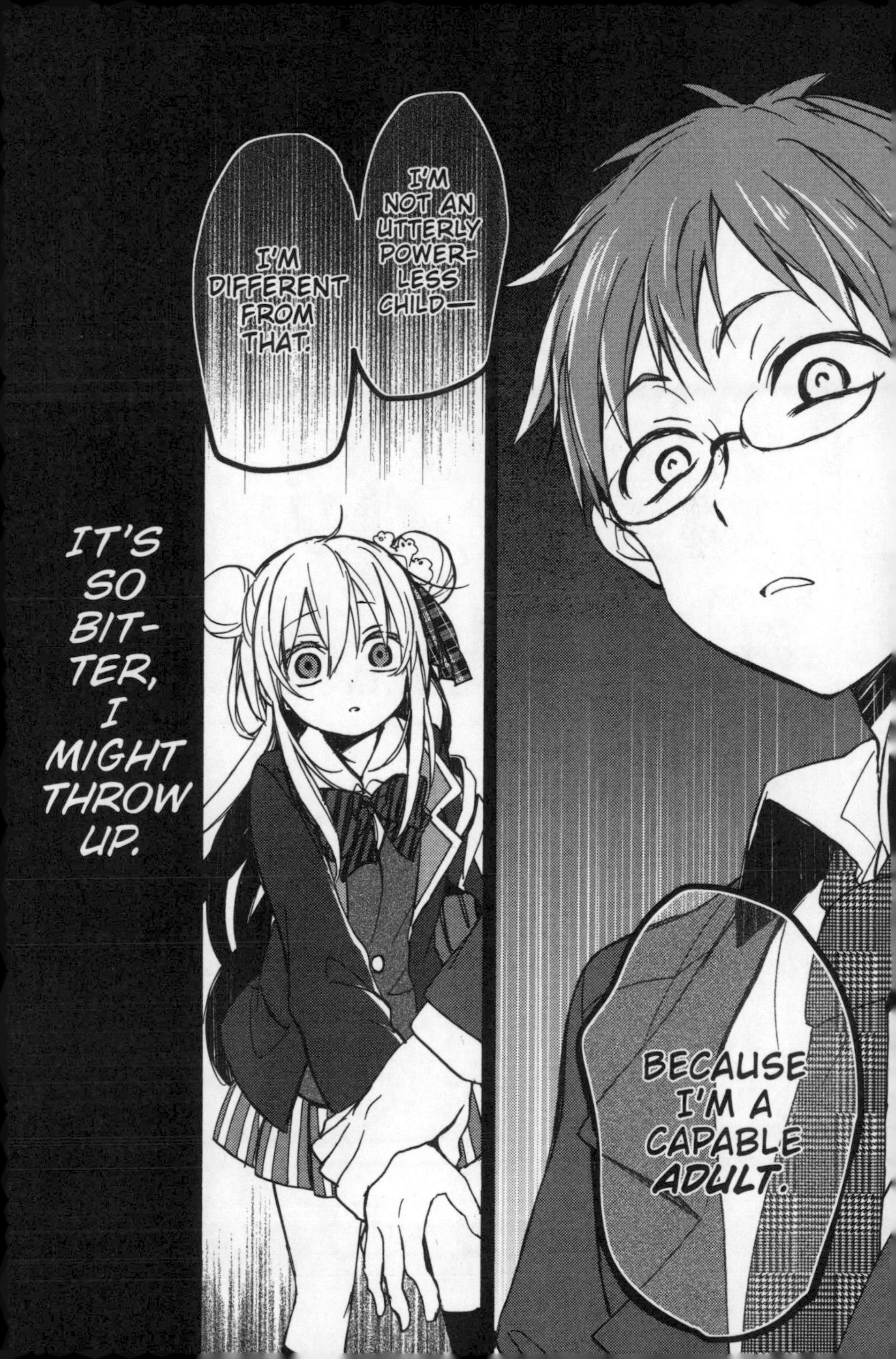
BECAUSE I'M A CAPABLE ADULT.
I'M NOT AN UTTERLY POWER-LESS CHILD—
I'M DIFFERENT FROM THAT.
IT'S SO BIT-TER, I MIGHT THROW UP.

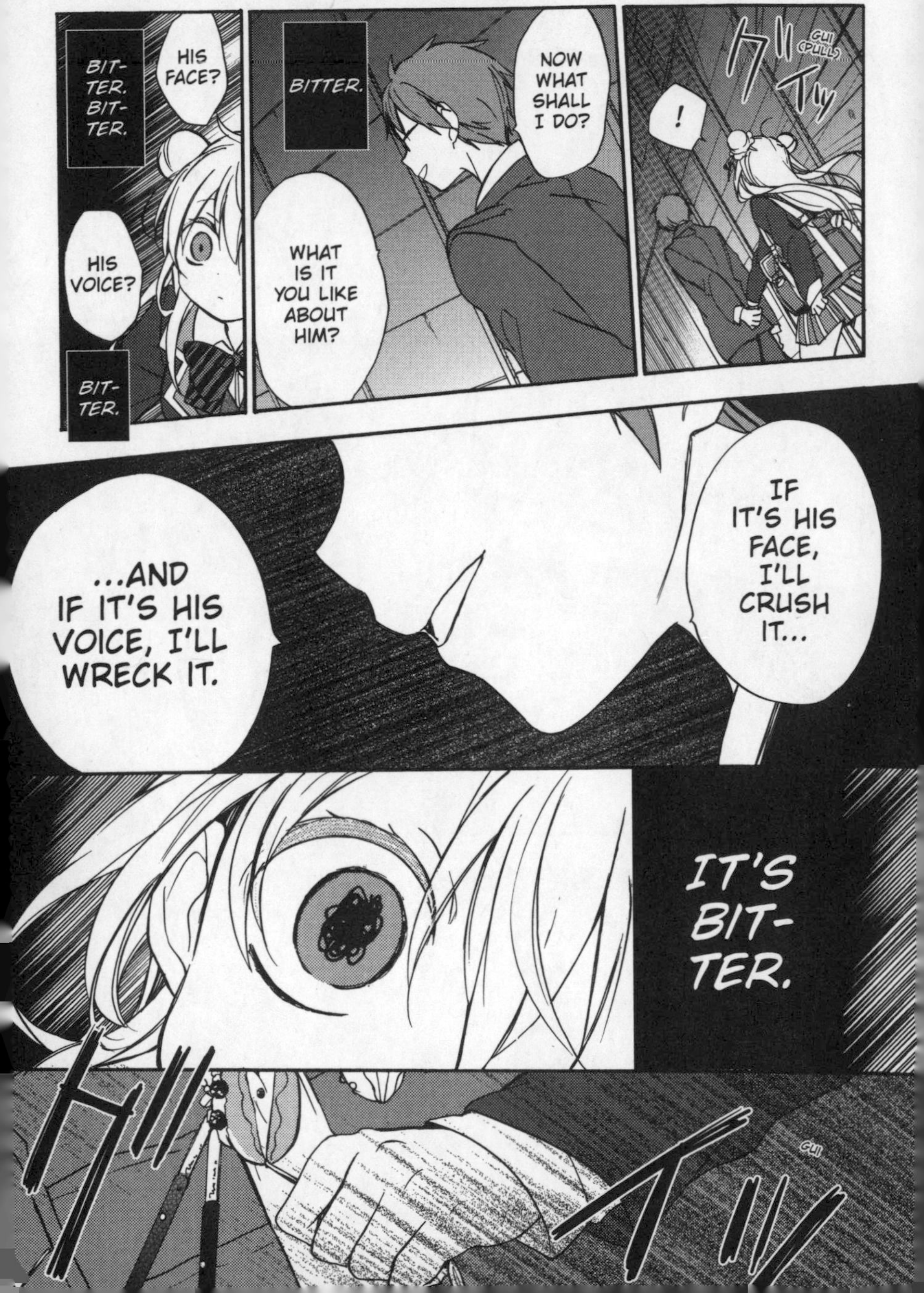GUI (PULL)
!
NOW WHAT SHALL I DO?
BITTER.
WHAT IS IT YOU LIKE ABOUT HIM?
HIS FACE?
BIT-TER. BIT-TER.
HIS VOICE?
BIT-TER.
IF IT'S HIS FACE, I'LL CRUSH IT...
...AND IF IT'S HIS VOICE, I'LL WRECK IT.
IT'S BIT-TER.
GUI

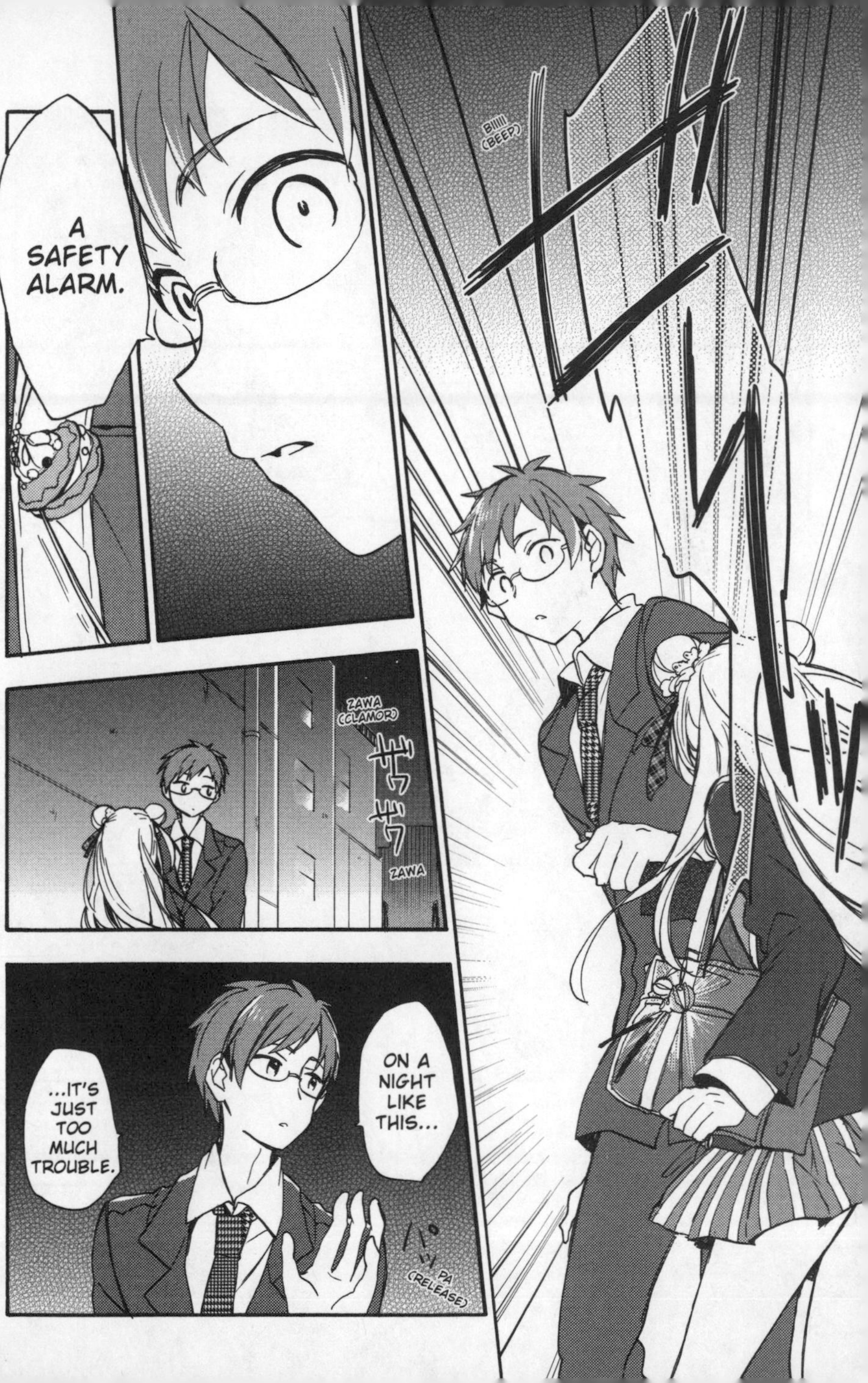
BIIIII (BEEP)
A SAFETY ALARM.
ZAWA (CLAMOR)
ザワ
ザワ
ZAWA
ON A NIGHT LIKE THIS...
...IT'S JUST TOO MUCH TROUBLE.
パッ
PA (RELEASE)

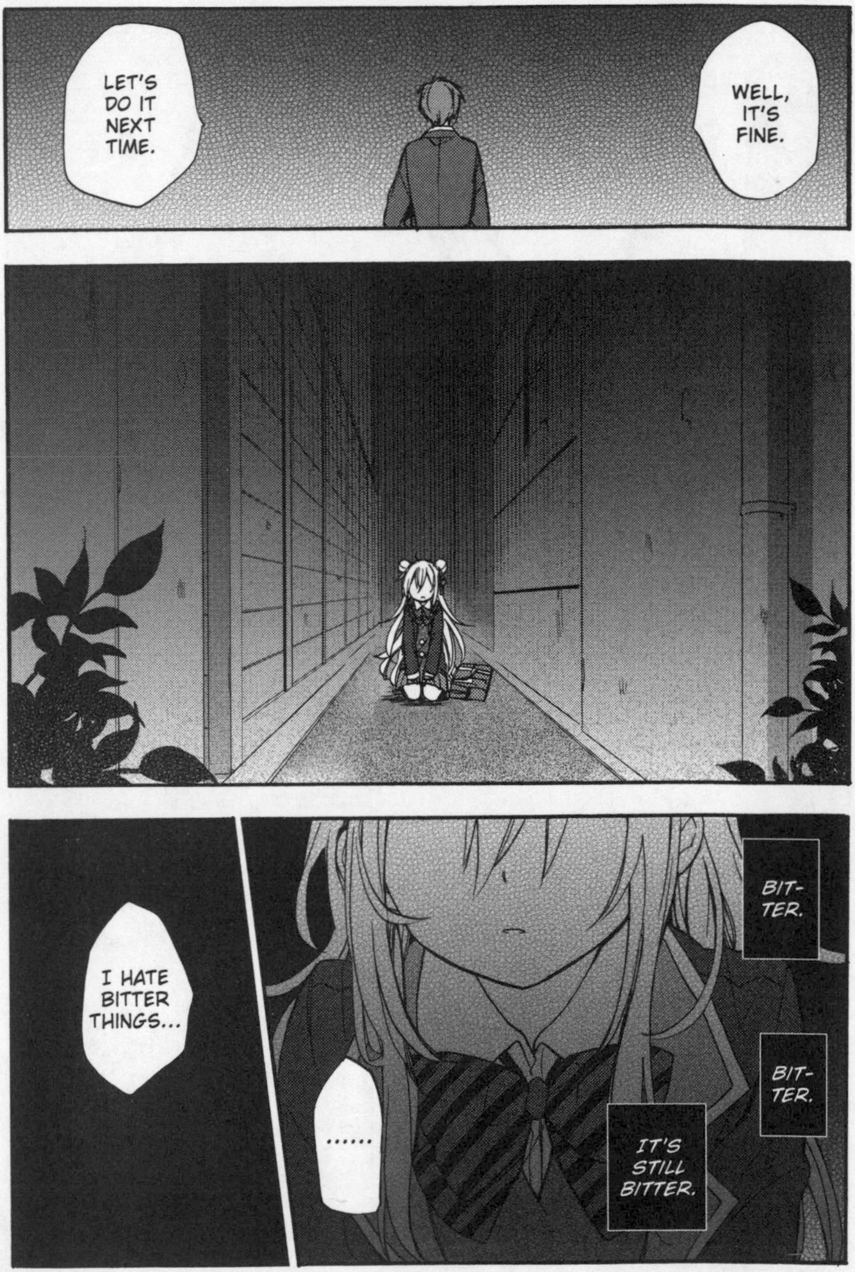
WELL, IT'S FINE.
LET'S DO IT NEXT TIME.
BIT-TER.
BIT-TER.
IT'S STILL BITTER.
......
I HATE BITTER THINGS...

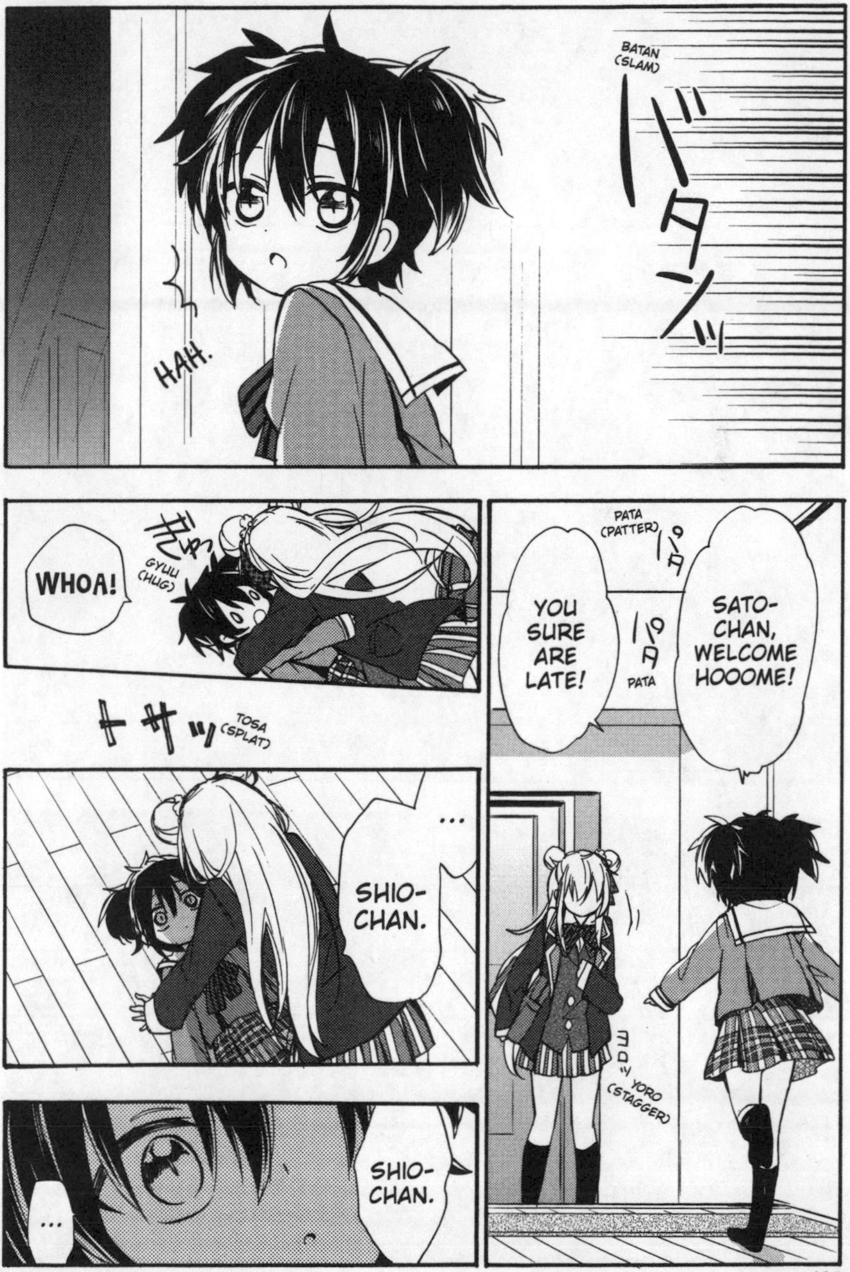

BATAN (SLAM)
バタンッ
HAH.
SATO-CHAN, WELCOME HOOOME!
パタ
PATA (PATTER)
YOU SURE ARE LATE!
パタ
PATA
ヨロッ
YORO (STAGGER)
ぎゅっ
GYUU (HUG)
WHOA!
トサッ
TOSA (SPLAT)
...
SHIO-CHAN.
SHIO-CHAN.
...

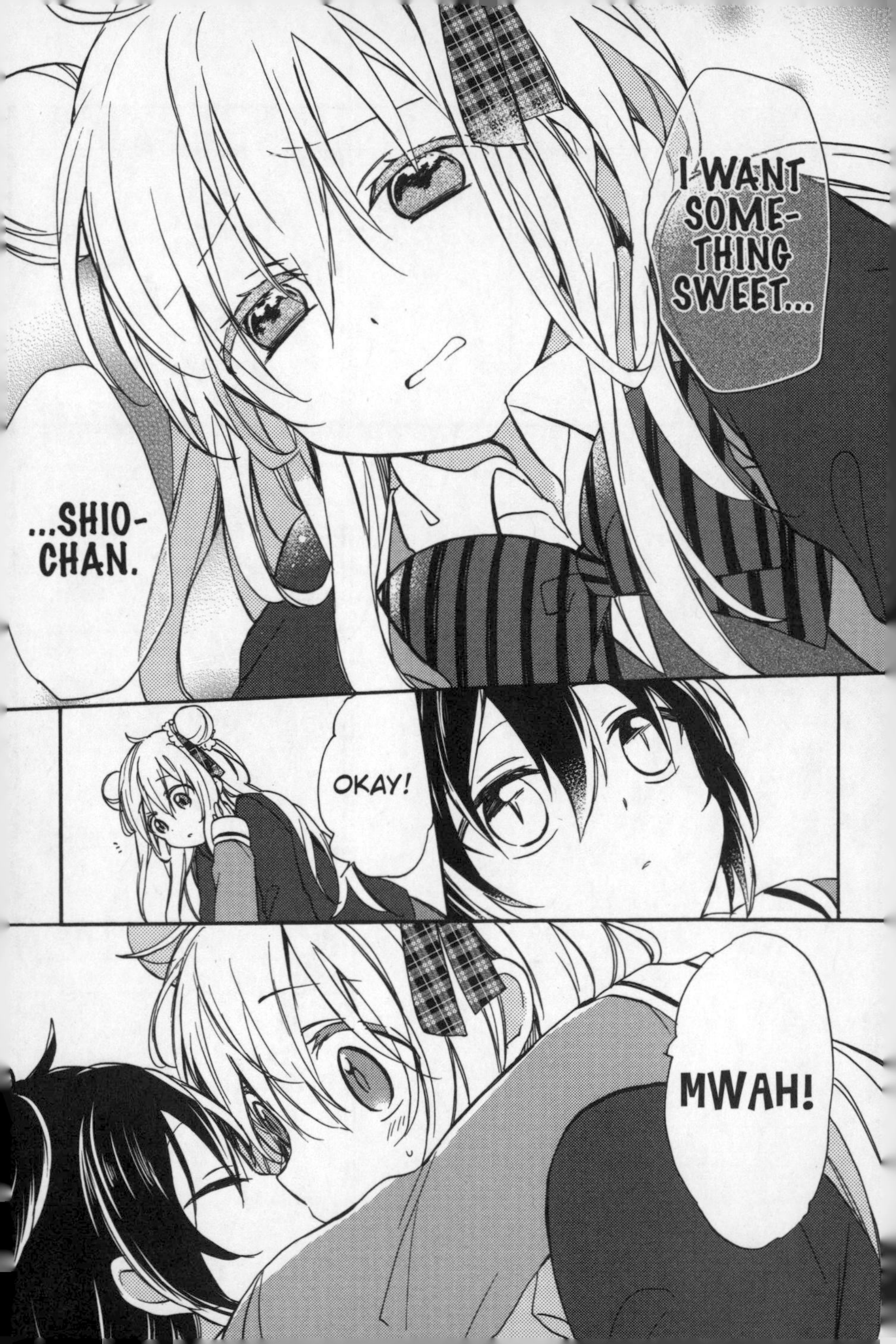
I WANT SOME-THING SWEET...
...SHIO-CHAN.
OKAY!
MWAH!

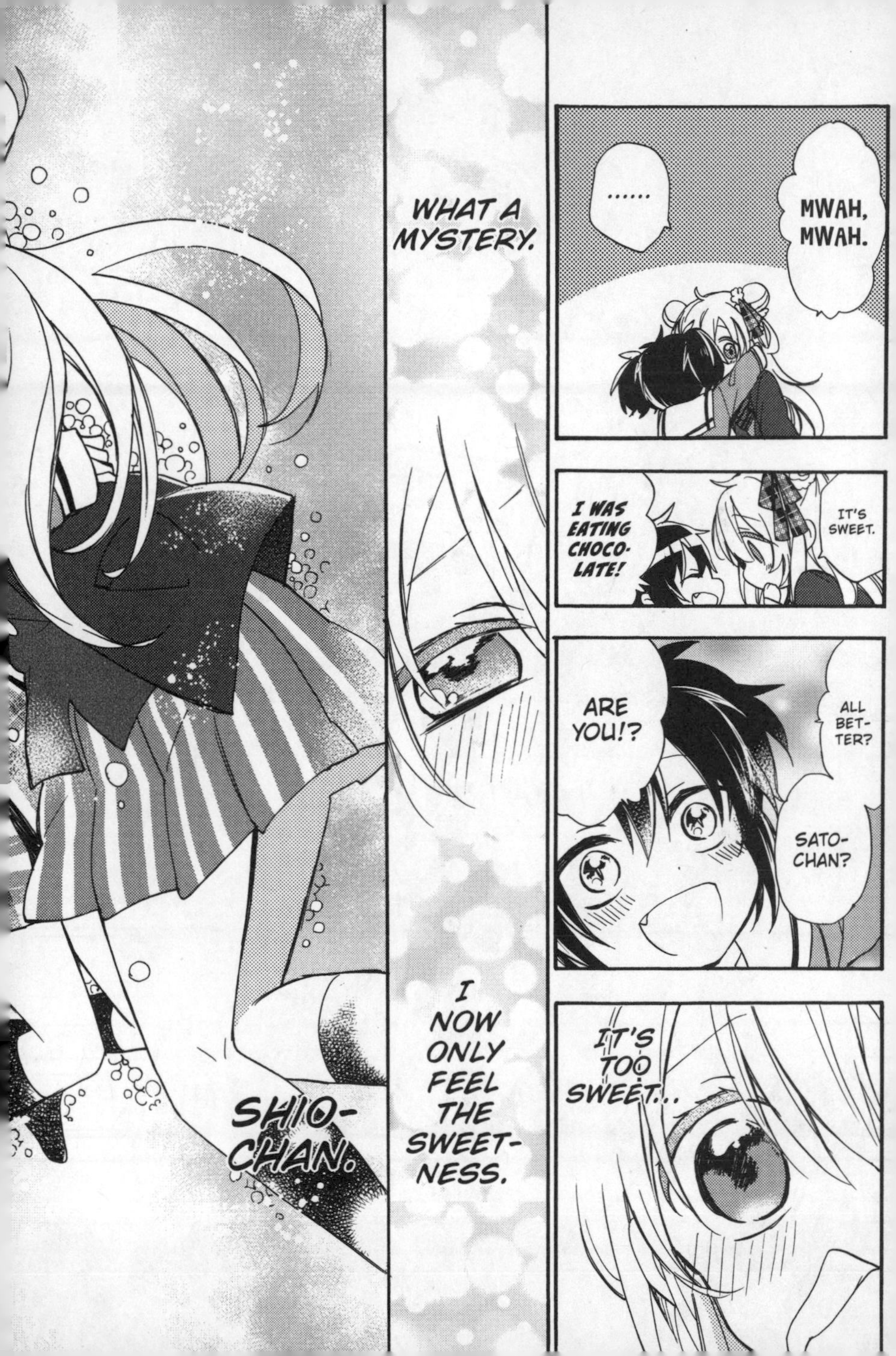

MWAH, MWAH.
......
IT'S SWEET.
I WAS EATING CHOCO-LATE!
ALL BET-TER?
SATO-CHAN?
ARE YOU!?
IT'S TOO SWEET...
WHAT A MYSTERY.
I NOW ONLY FEEL THE SWEET-NESS.
SHIO-CHAN.

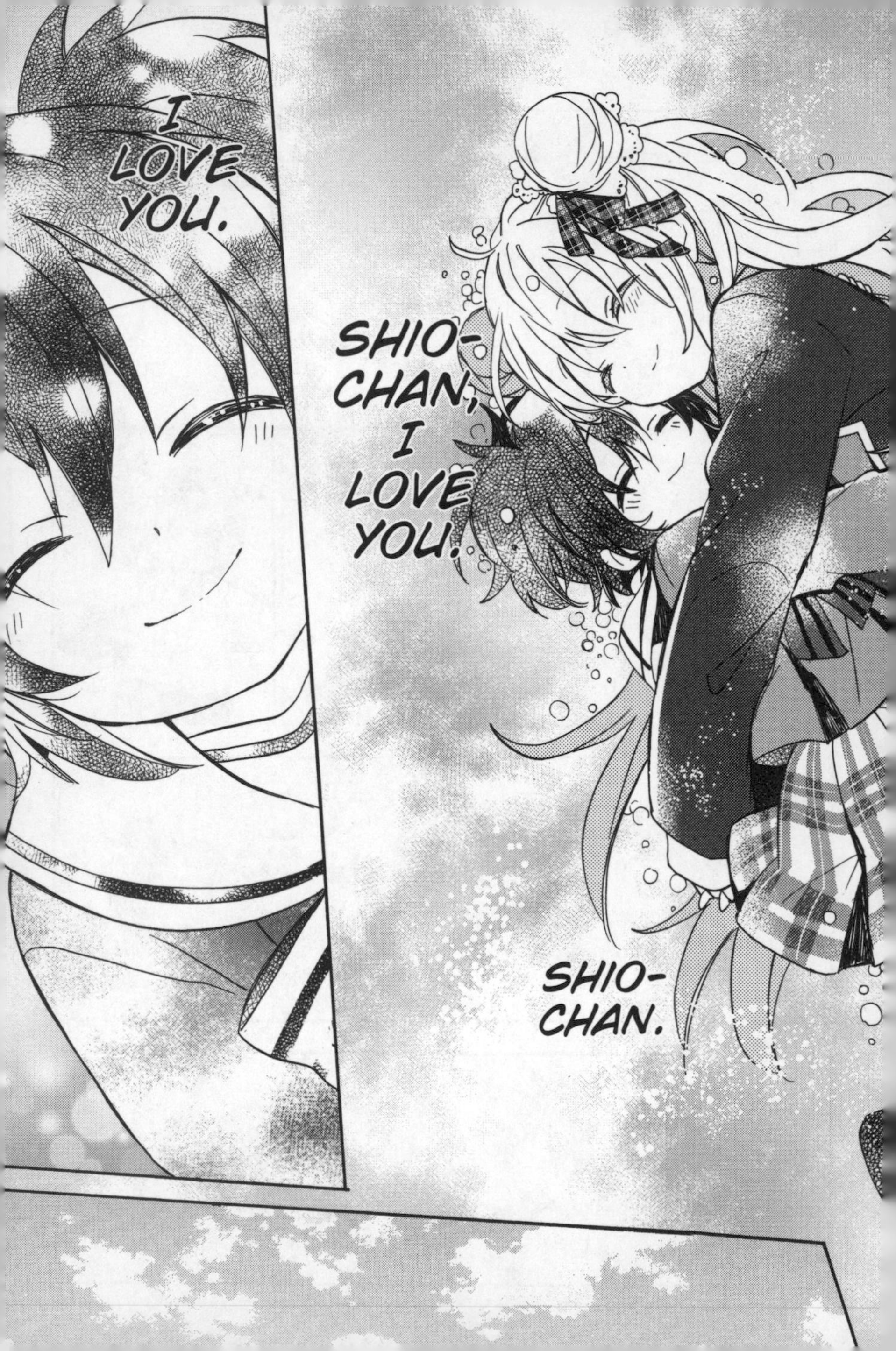
SHIO-CHAN, I LOVE YOU.
SHIO-CHAN.
I LOVE YOU.

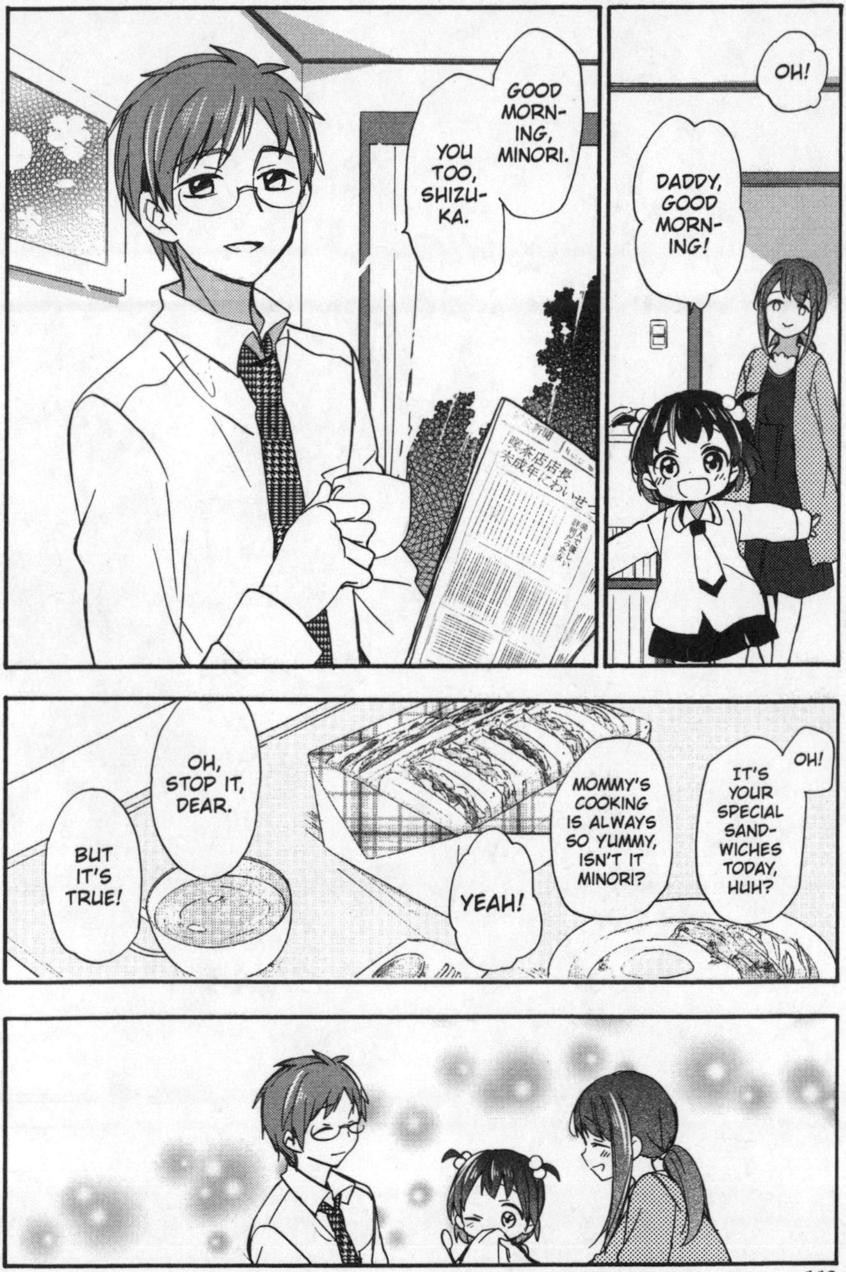
OH!
DADDY, GOOD MORNING!
GOOD MORNING, MINORI.
YOU TOO, SHIZUKA.
OH!
IT'S YOUR SPECIAL SANDWICHES TODAY, HUH?
MOMMY'S COOKING IS ALWAYS SO YUMMY, ISN'T IT MINORI?
YEAH!
OH, STOP IT, DEAR.
BUT IT'S TRUE!

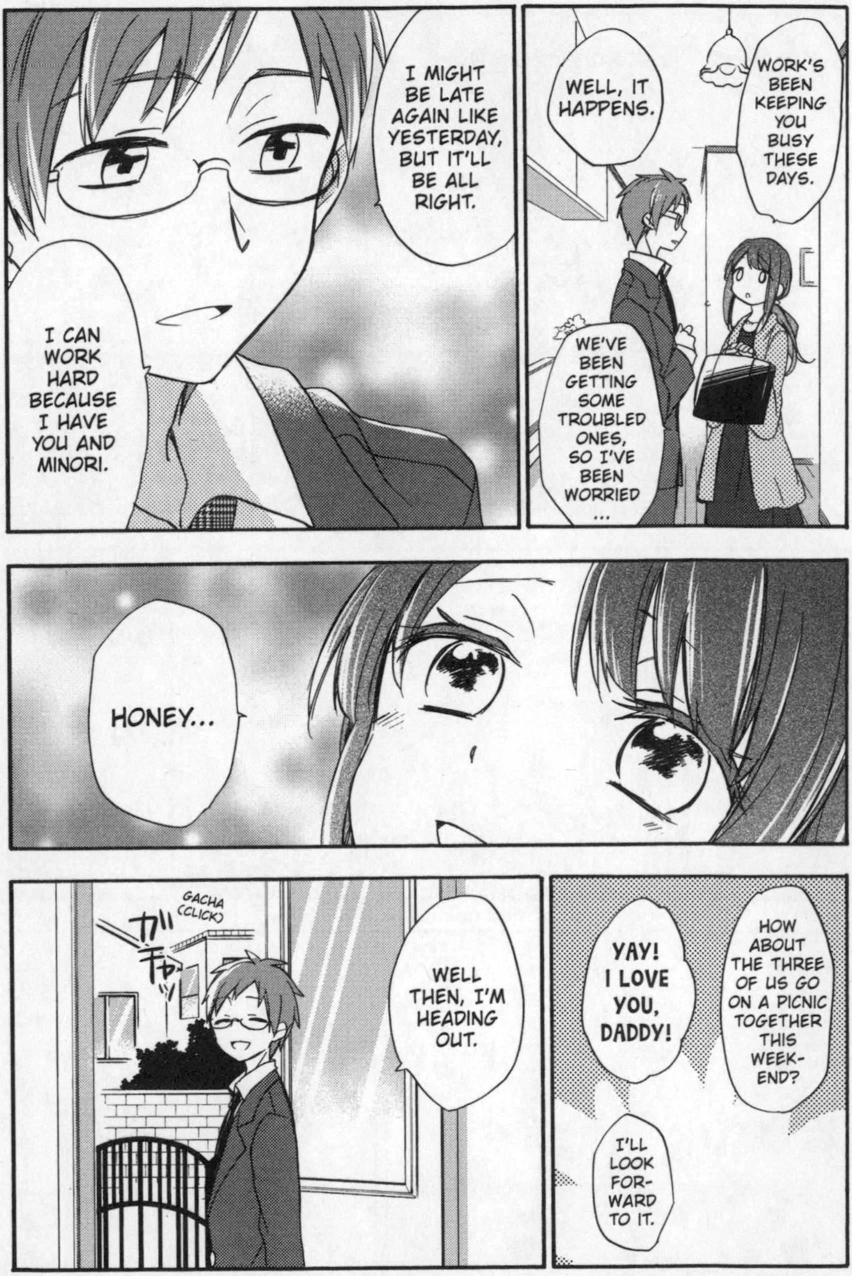
WORK'S BEEN KEEPING YOU BUSY THESE DAYS.
WELL, IT HAPPENS.
WE'VE BEEN GETTING SOME TROUBLED ONES, SO I'VE BEEN WORRIED...
I MIGHT BE LATE AGAIN LIKE YESTERDAY, BUT IT'LL BE ALL RIGHT.
I CAN WORK HARD BECAUSE I HAVE YOU AND MINORI.
HONEY...
HOW ABOUT THE THREE OF US GO ON A PICNIC TOGETHER THIS WEEK-END?
YAY! I LOVE YOU, DADDY!
I'LL LOOK FOR-WARD TO IT.
WELL THEN, I'M HEADING OUT.
GACHA (CLICK)

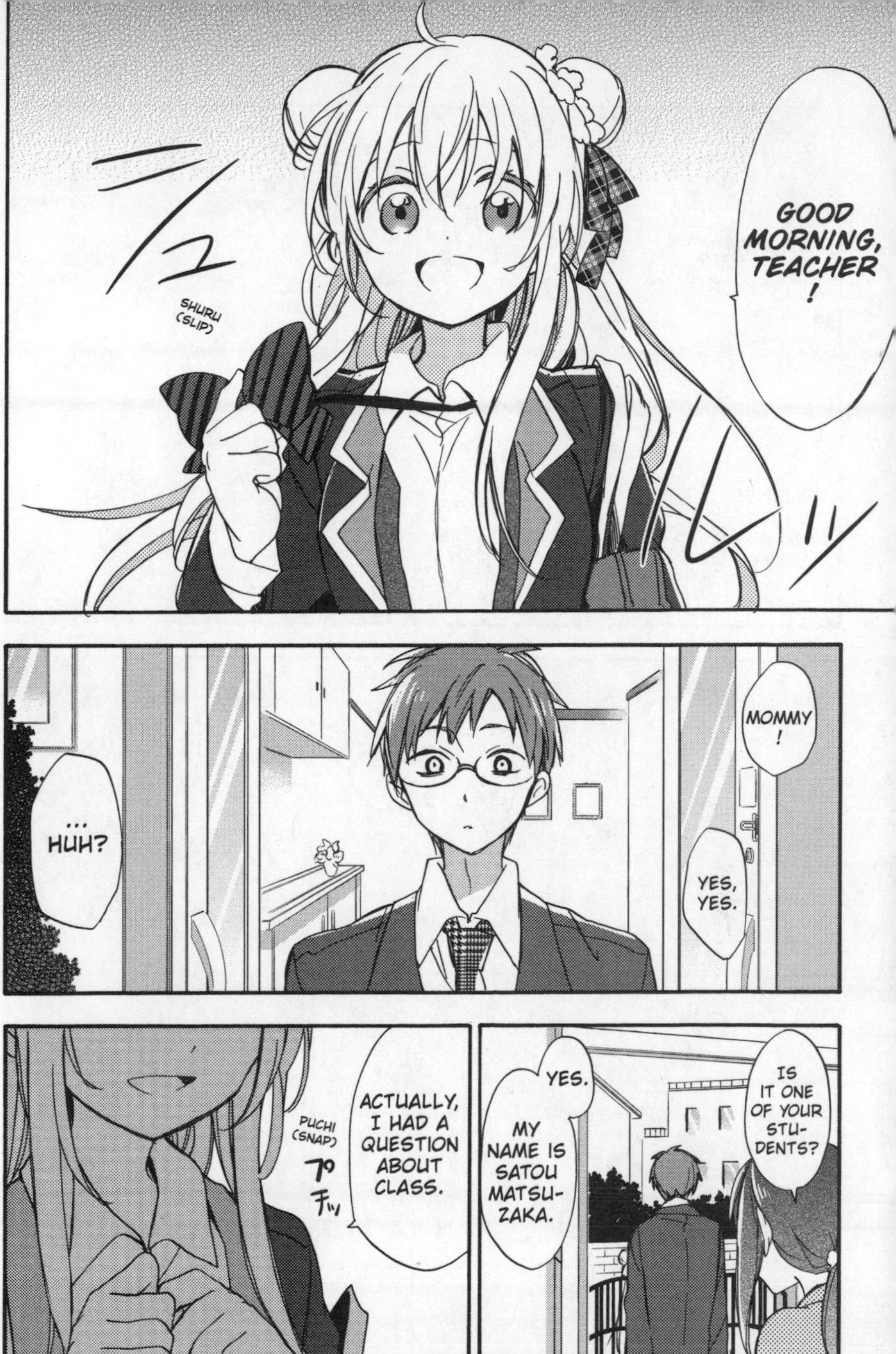
GOOD MORNING, TEACHER!
SHURU (SLIP)
MOMMY!
YES, YES.
... HUH?
IS IT ONE OF YOUR STUDENTS?
YES.
MY NAME IS SATOU MATSUZAKA.
ACTUALLY, I HAD A QUESTION ABOUT CLASS.
PUCHI (SNAP)
プチッ

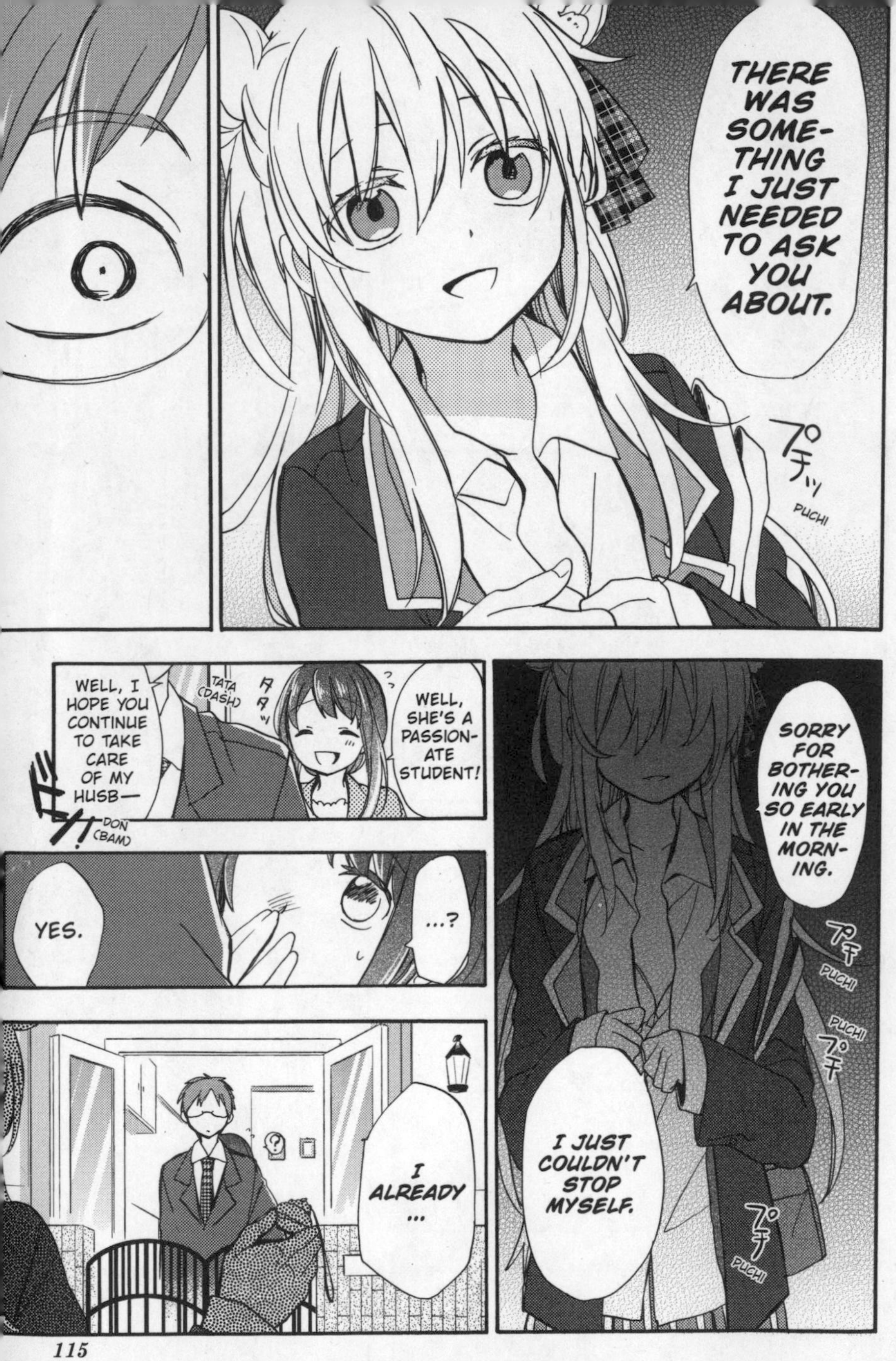
THERE WAS SOMETHING I JUST NEEDED TO ASK YOU ABOUT.
プチッ
PUCHI
SORRY FOR BOTHERING YOU SO EARLY IN THE MORNING.
プチ
PUCHI
PUCHI
プチ
I JUST COULDN'T STOP MYSELF.
プチ
PUCHI
WELL, SHE'S A PASSIONATE STUDENT!
タタッ
TATA (DASH)
WELL, I HOPE YOU CONTINUE TO TAKE CARE OF MY HUSB—
DON (BAM)
...?
YES.
I ALREADY ...

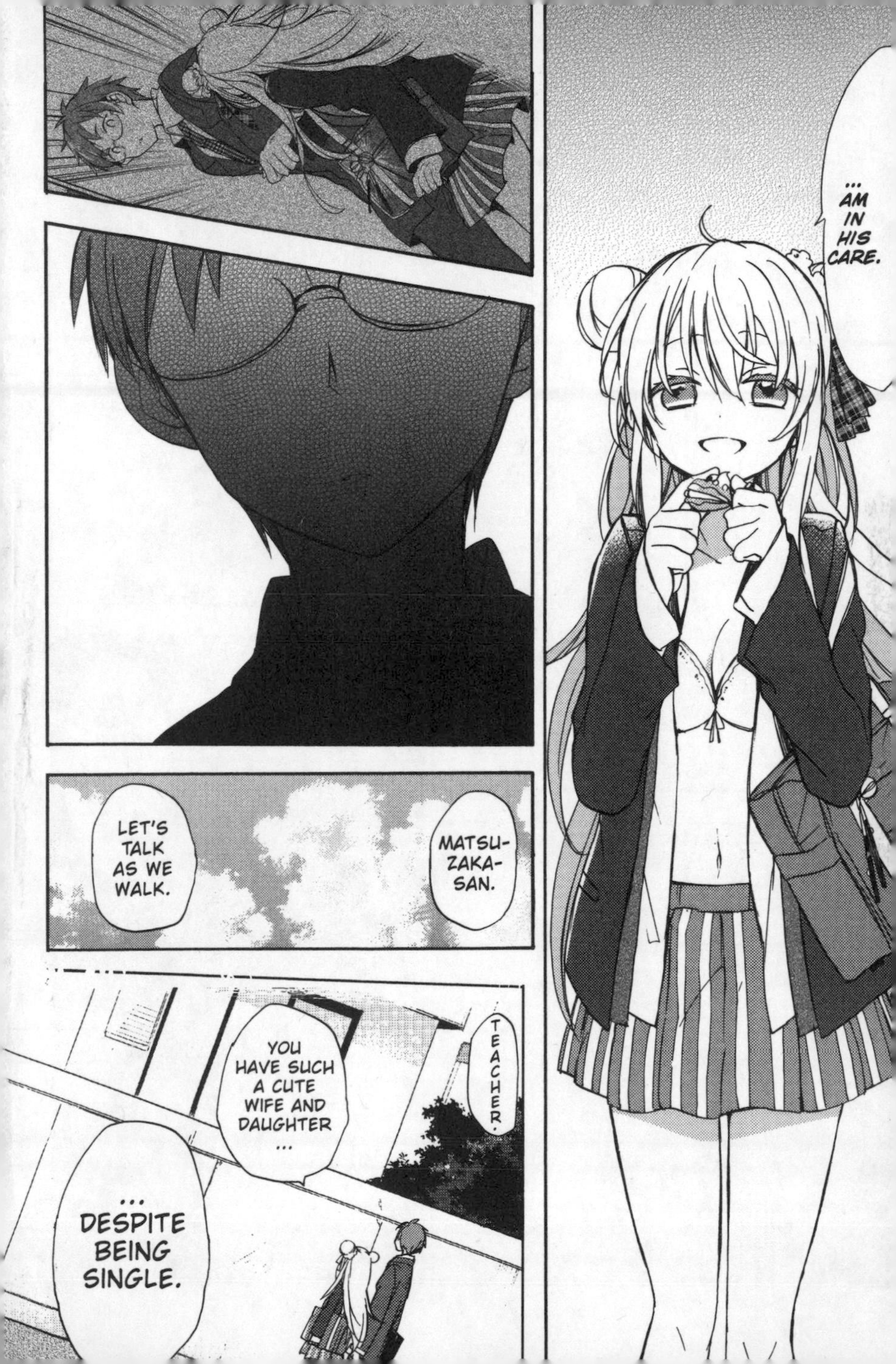
...AM IN HIS CARE.
MATSU-ZAKA-SAN.
LET'S TALK AS WE WALK.
TEACHER.
YOU HAVE SUCH A CUTE WIFE AND DAUGHTER...
...DESPITE BEING SINGLE.

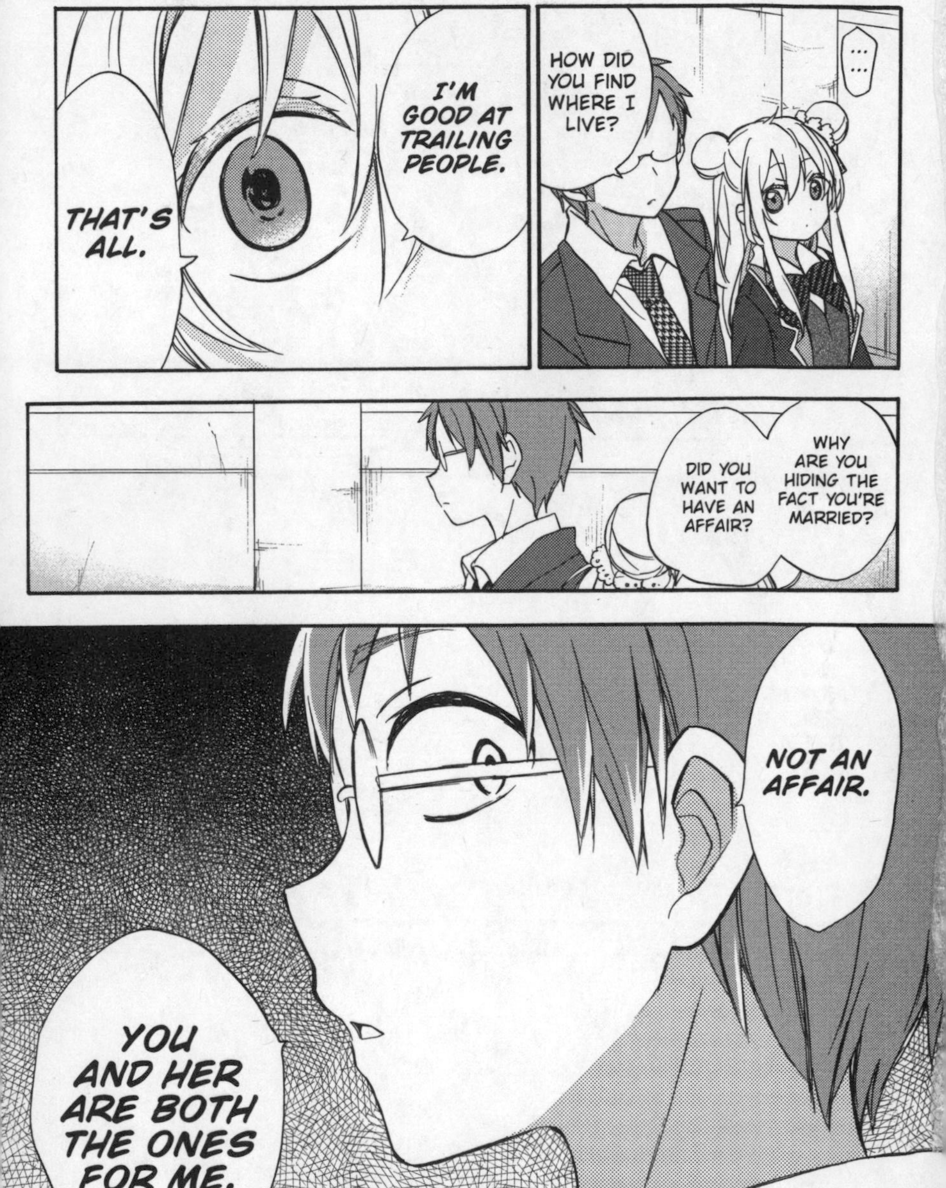
HOW DID YOU FIND WHERE I LIVE?
... ...
I'M GOOD AT TRAILING PEOPLE.
THAT'S ALL.
WHY ARE YOU HIDING THE FACT YOU'RE MARRIED?
DID YOU WANT TO HAVE AN AFFAIR?
NOT AN AFFAIR.
YOU AND HER ARE BOTH THE ONES FOR ME.

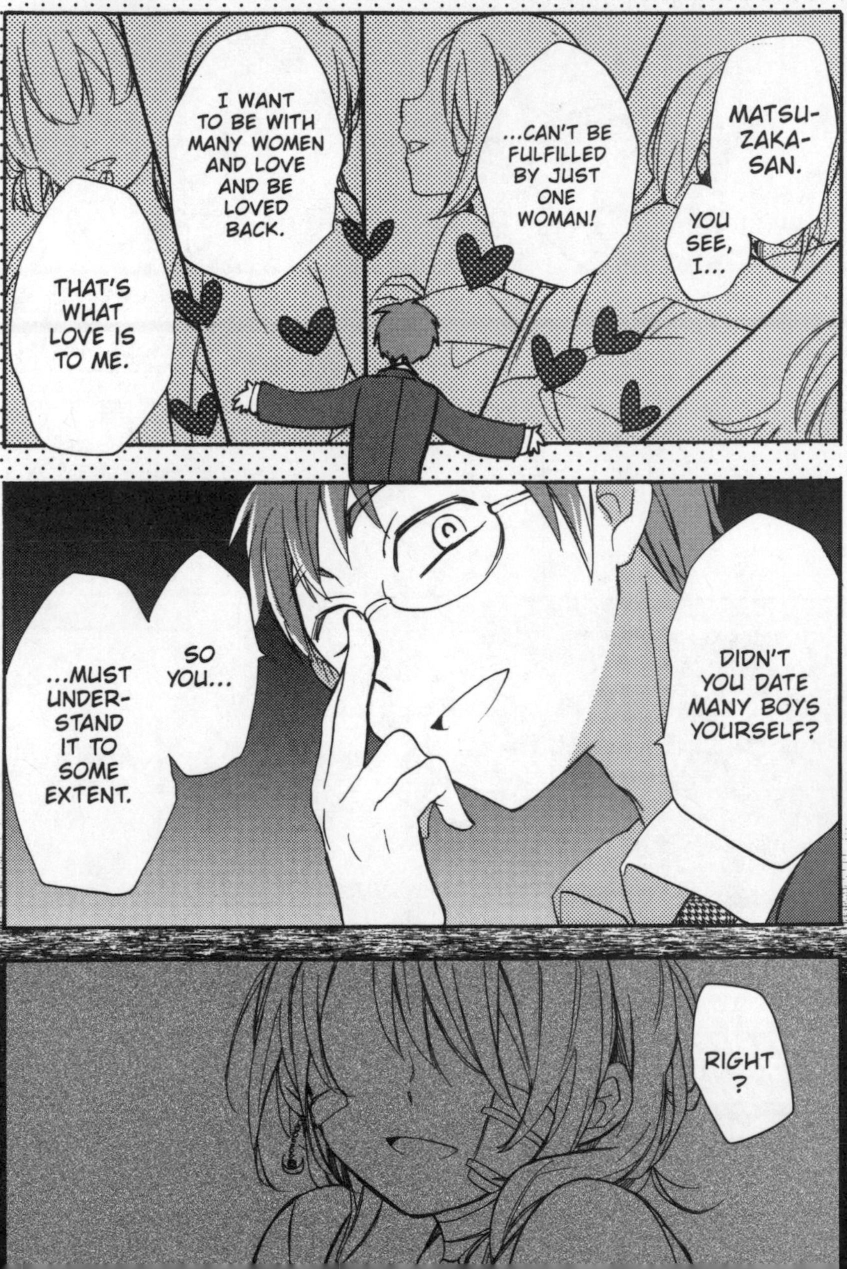
MATSU-ZAKA-SAN.
YOU SEE, I...
...CAN'T BE FULFILLED BY JUST ONE WOMAN!
I WANT TO BE WITH MANY WOMEN AND LOVE AND BE LOVED BACK.
THAT'S WHAT LOVE IS TO ME.
DIDN'T YOU DATE MANY BOYS YOURSELF?
SO YOU...
...MUST UNDER-STAND IT TO SOME EXTENT.
RIGHT?

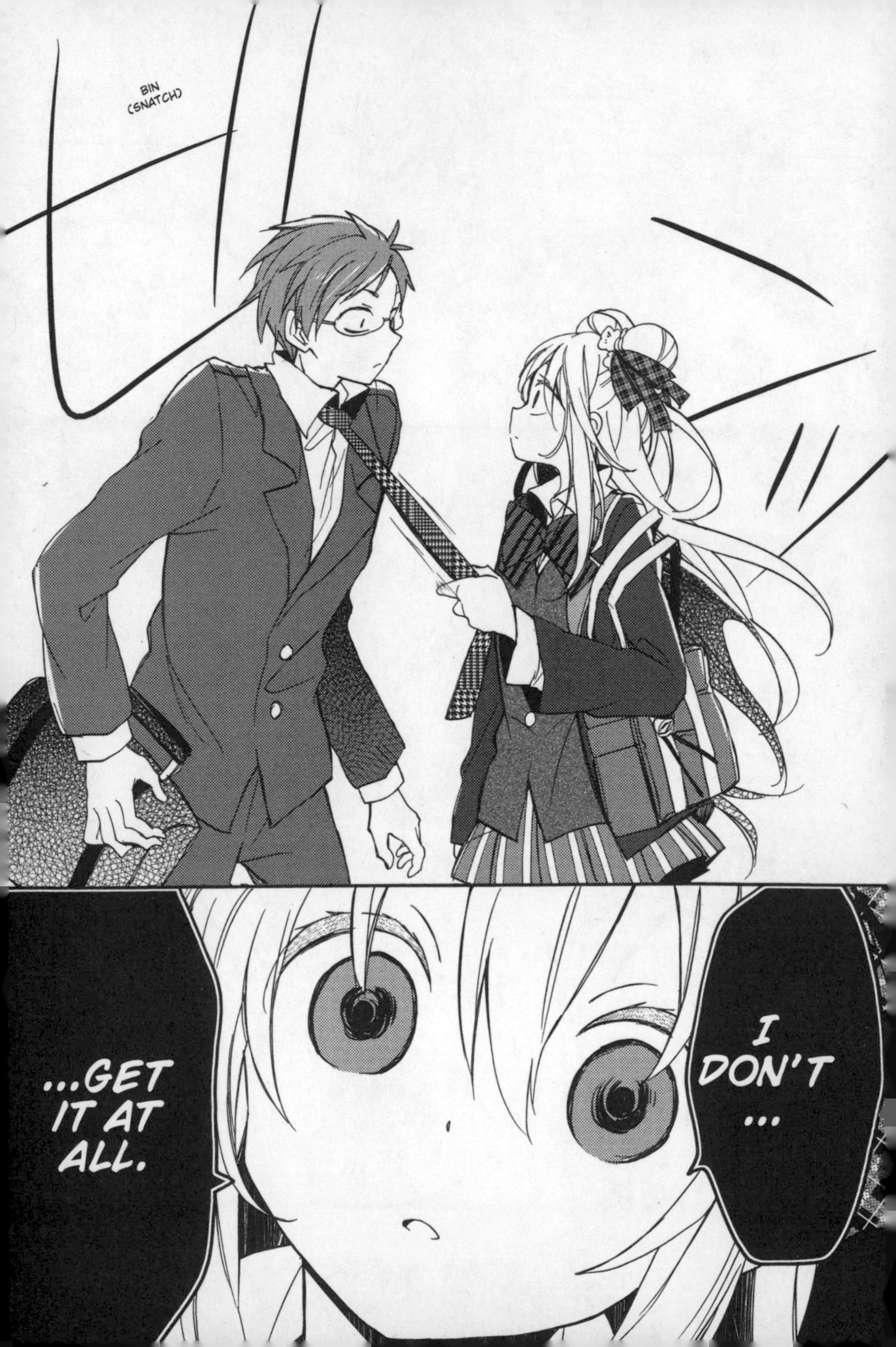
BIN (SNATCH)
I DON'T ...
...GET IT AT ALL.

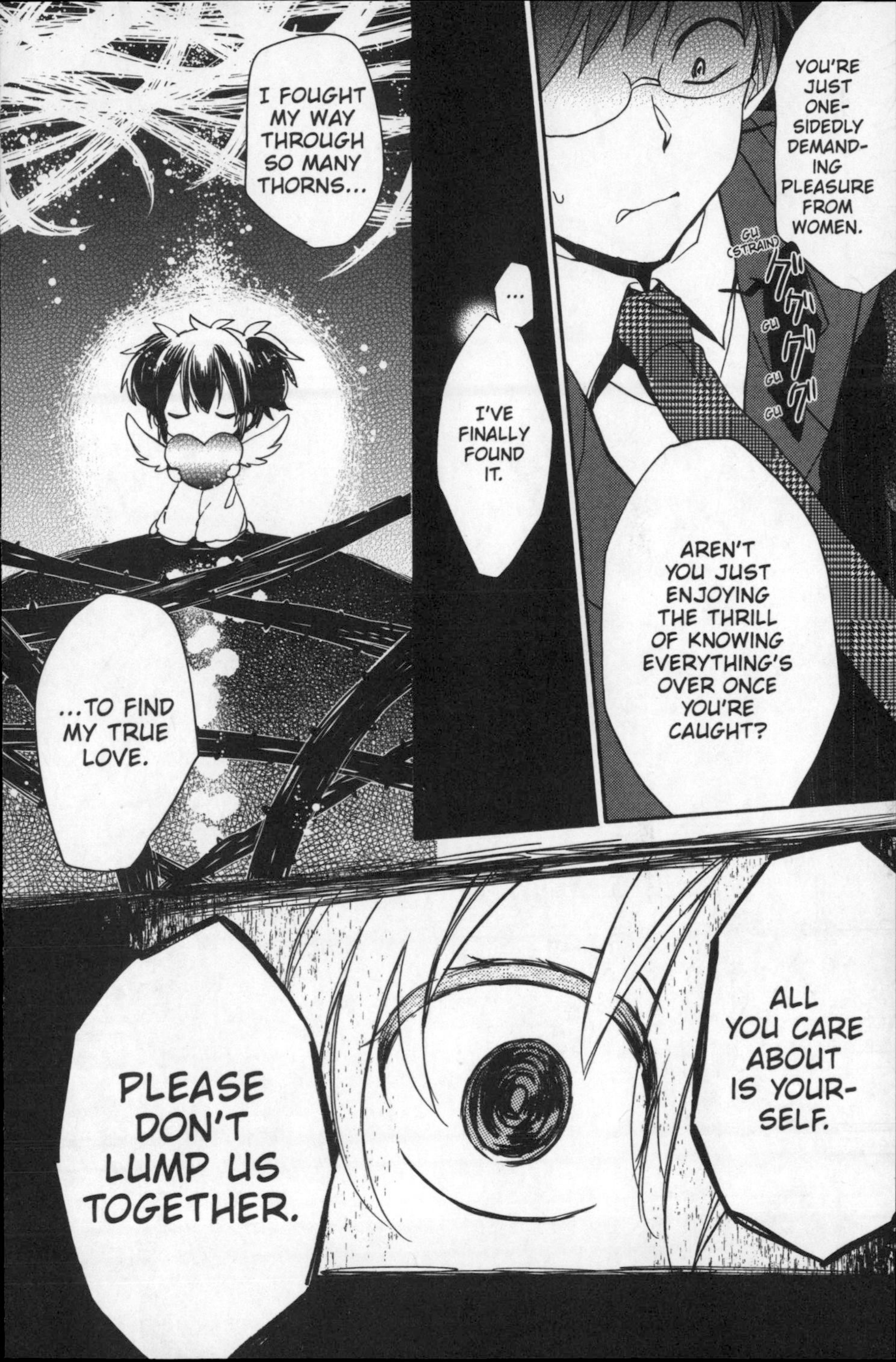

YOU'RE JUST ONE-SIDEDLY DEMANDING PLEASURE FROM WOMEN.
GU (STRAIN)
GU
GU
GU
...
AREN'T YOU JUST ENJOYING THE THRILL OF KNOWING EVERYTHING'S OVER ONCE YOU'RE CAUGHT?
I'VE FINALLY FOUND IT.
I FOUGHT MY WAY THROUGH SO MANY THORNS...
...TO FIND MY TRUE LOVE.
ALL YOU CARE ABOUT IS YOURSELF.
PLEASE DON'T LUMP US TOGETHER.

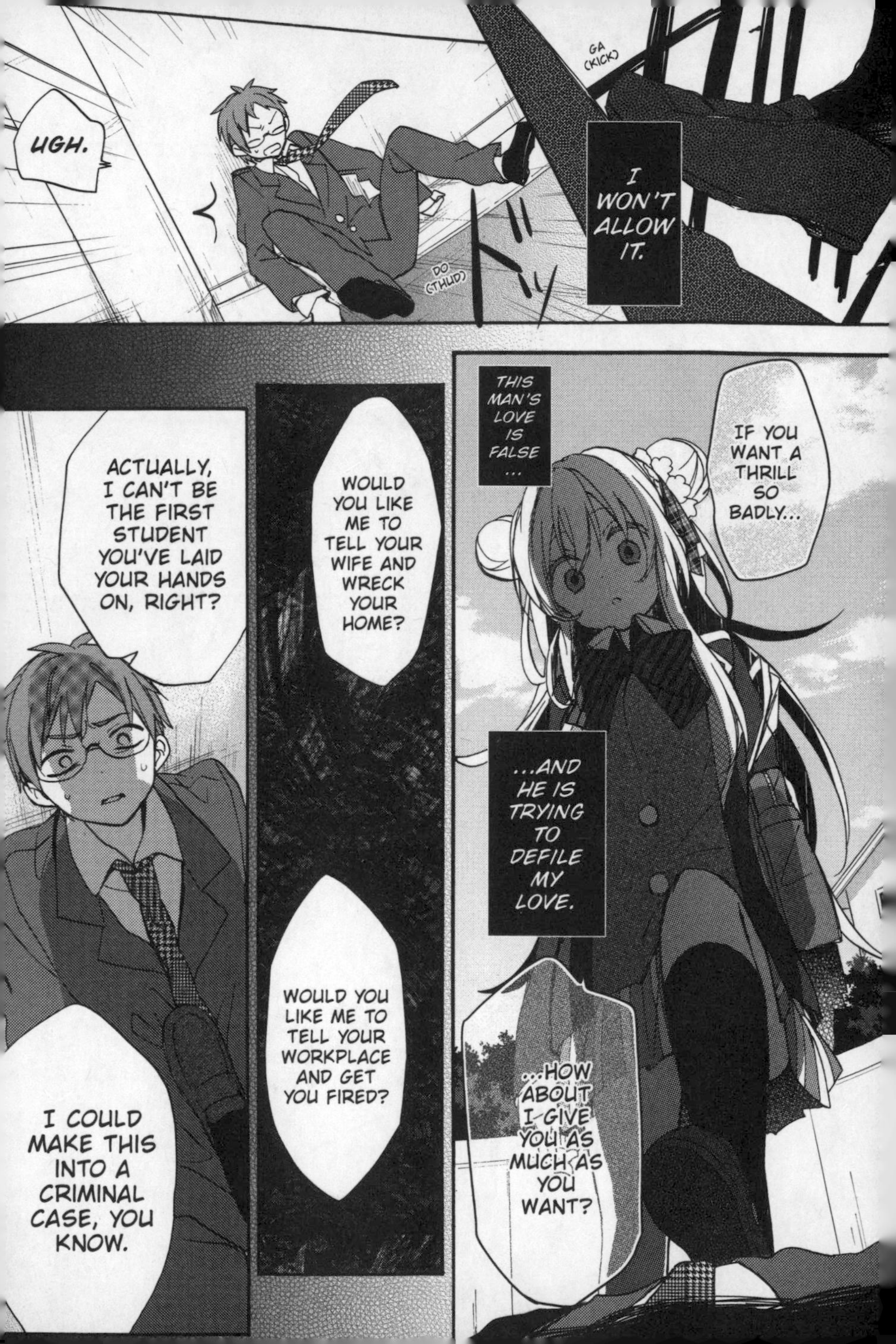
GA (KICK)
I WON'T ALLOW IT.
DO (THUD)
UGH.
IF YOU WANT A THRILL SO BADLY...
THIS MAN'S LOVE IS FALSE...
...AND HE IS TRYING TO DEFILE MY LOVE.
...HOW ABOUT I GIVE YOU AS MUCH AS YOU WANT?
WOULD YOU LIKE ME TO TELL YOUR WIFE AND WRECK YOUR HOME?
WOULD YOU LIKE ME TO TELL YOUR WORKPLACE AND GET YOU FIRED?
ACTUALLY, I CAN'T BE THE FIRST STUDENT YOU'VE LAID YOUR HANDS ON, RIGHT?
I COULD MAKE THIS INTO A CRIMINAL CASE, YOU KNOW.

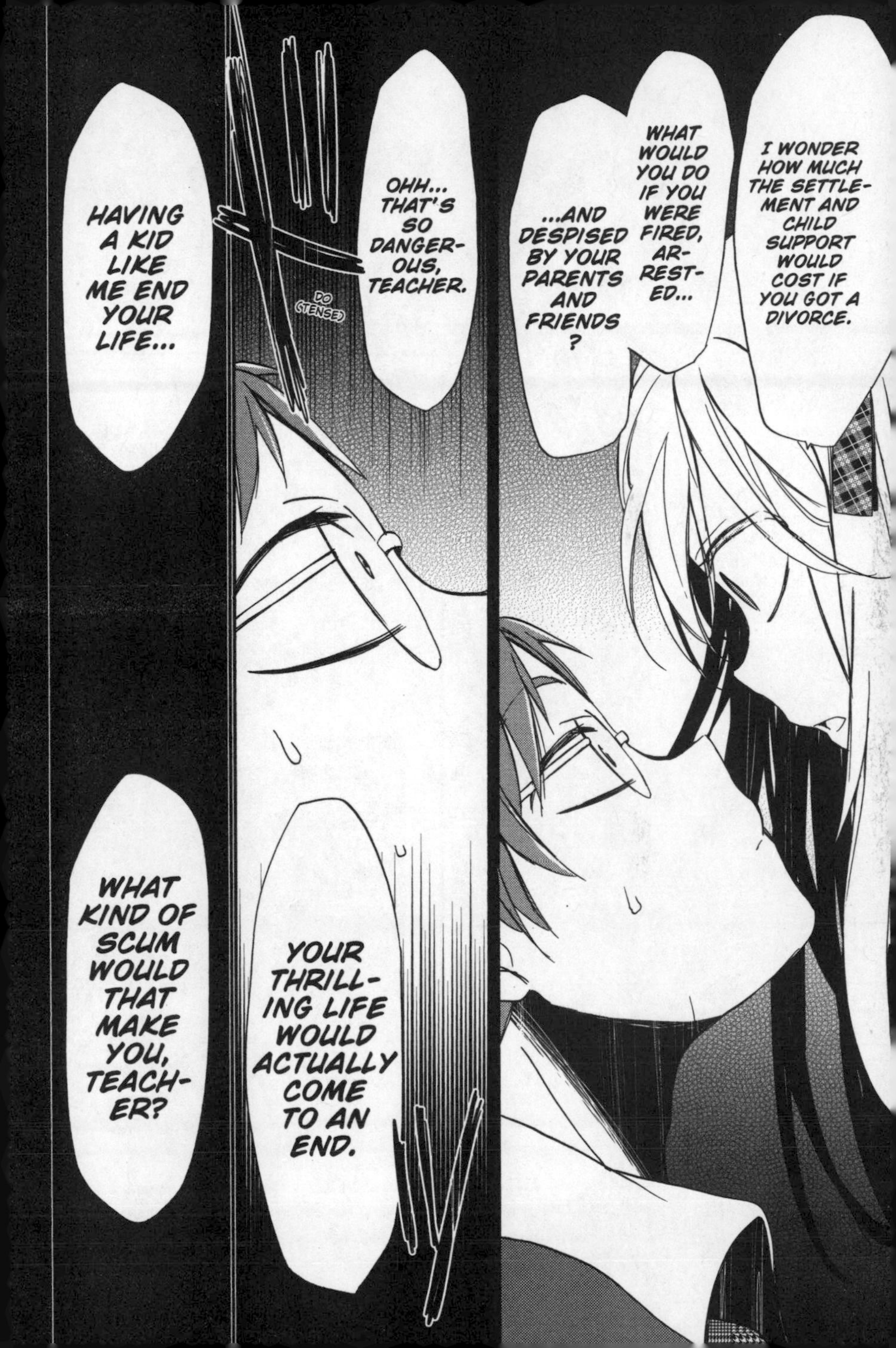
I WONDER HOW MUCH THE SETTLEMENT AND CHILD SUPPORT WOULD COST IF YOU GOT A DIVORCE.
WHAT WOULD YOU DO IF YOU WERE FIRED, ARRESTED...
...AND DESPISED BY YOUR PARENTS AND FRIENDS?
OHH... THAT'S SO DANGEROUS, TEACHER.
DO (TENSE)
YOUR THRILLING LIFE WOULD ACTUALLY COME TO AN END.
HAVING A KID LIKE ME END YOUR LIFE...
WHAT KIND OF SCUM WOULD THAT MAKE YOU, TEACHER?

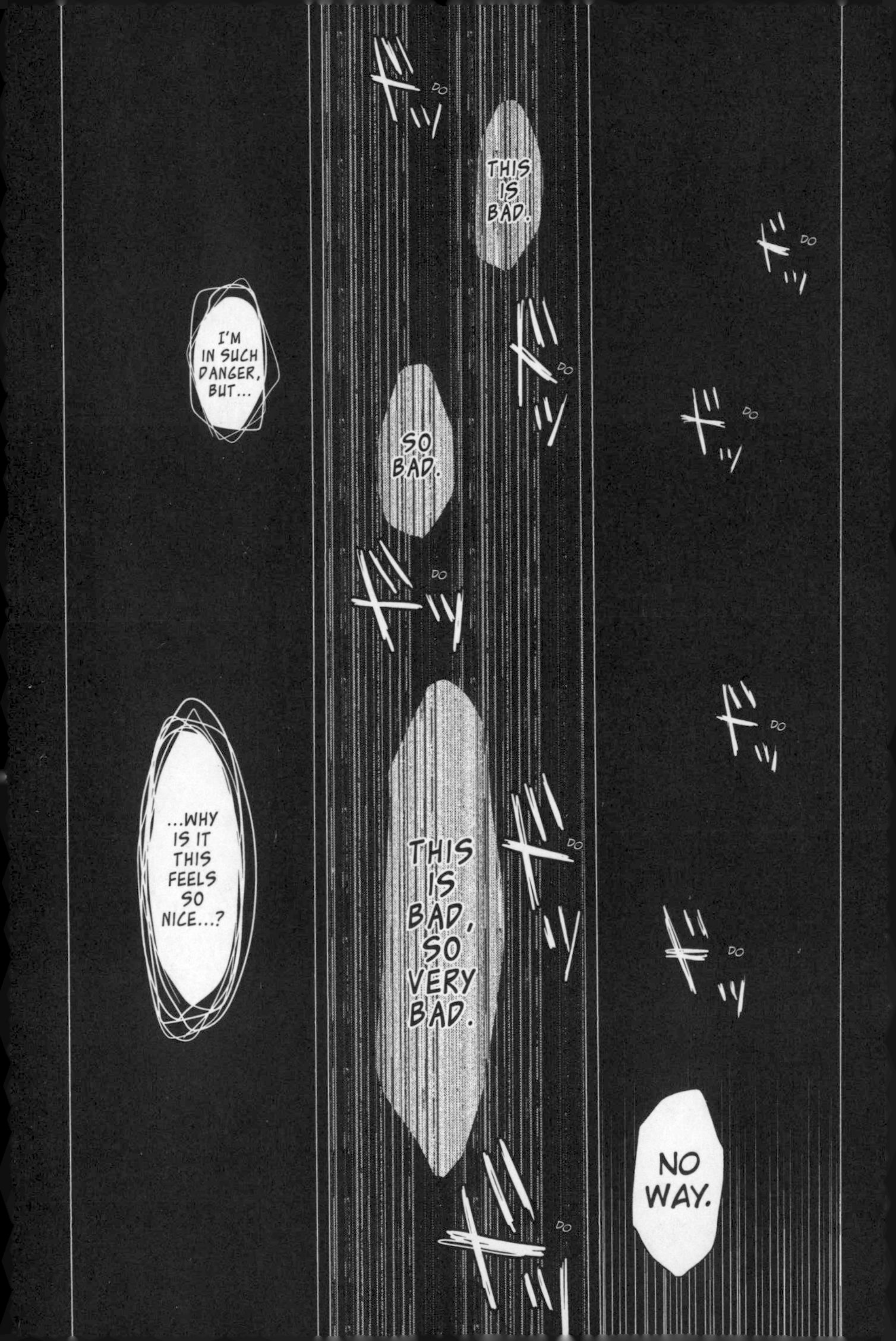
DO
DO
DO
DO
NO WAY.
DO
THIS IS BAD.
DO
SO BAD.
DO
THIS IS BAD, SO VERY BAD.
DO
DO
I'M IN SUCH DANGER, BUT...
...WHY IS IT THIS FEELS SO NICE...?

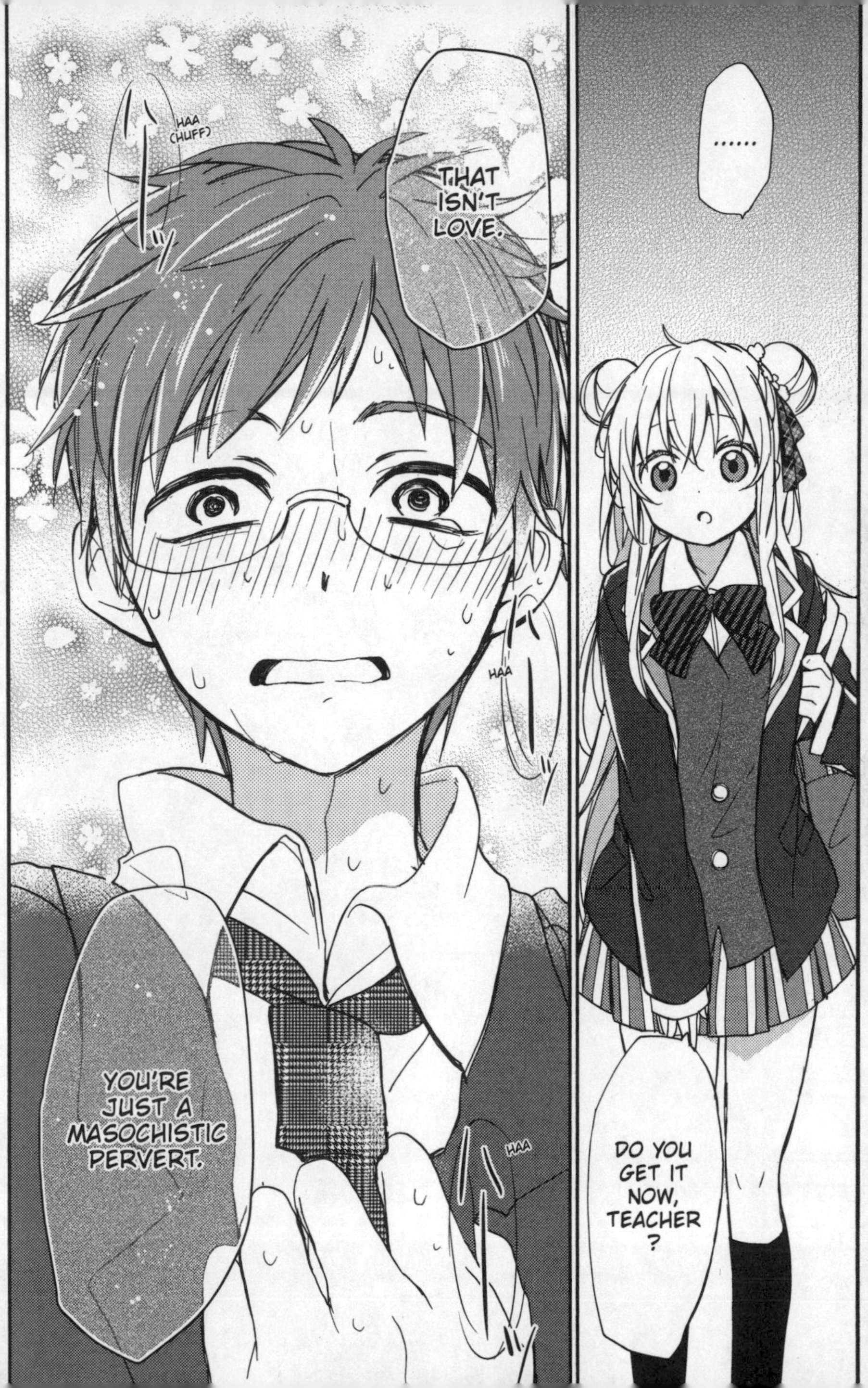
......
DO YOU GET IT NOW, TEACHER?
THAT ISN'T LOVE.
HAA (HUFF)
HAA
HAA
YOU'RE JUST A MASOCHISTIC PERVERT.

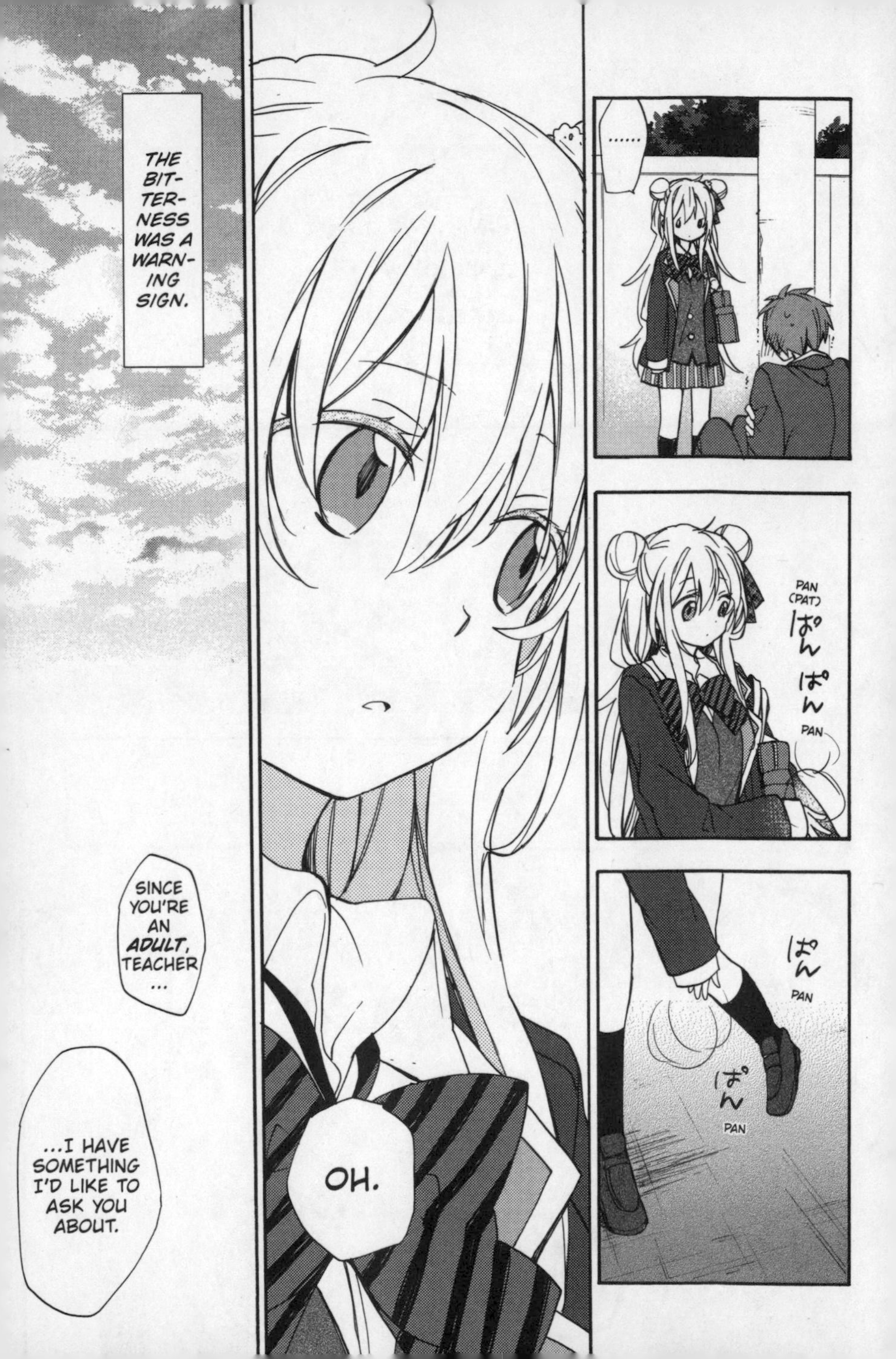
......
PAN (PAT)
ぱん
ぱん
PAN
ぱん
PAN
ぱん
PAN
OH.
THE BIT-TER-NESS WAS A WARN-ING SIGN.
SINCE YOU'RE AN ADULT, TEACHER...
...I HAVE SOMETHING I'D LIKE TO ASK YOU ABOUT.

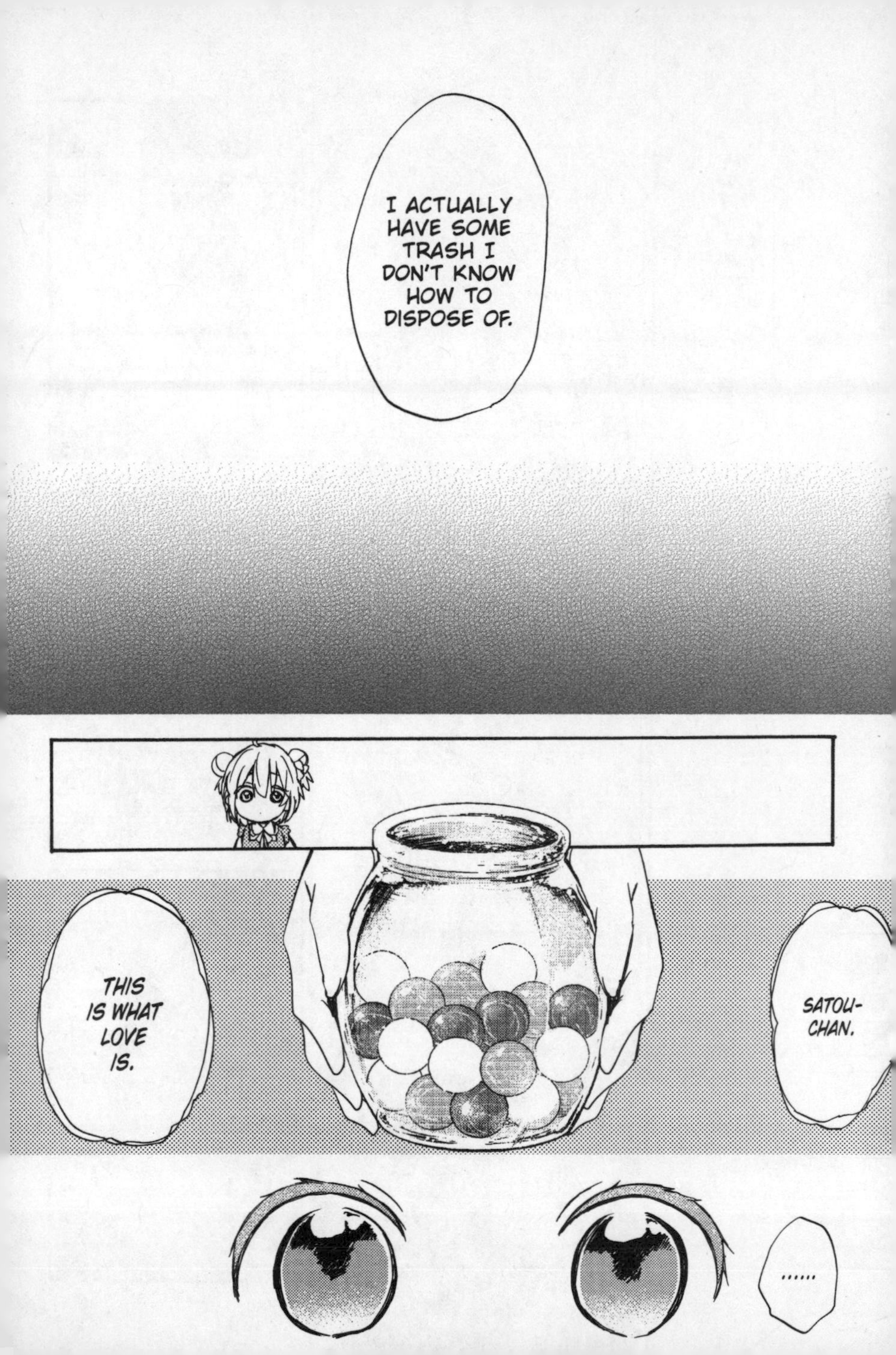
I ACTUALLY HAVE SOME TRASH I DON'T KNOW HOW TO DISPOSE OF.
SATOU-CHAN.
THIS IS WHAT LOVE IS.
......

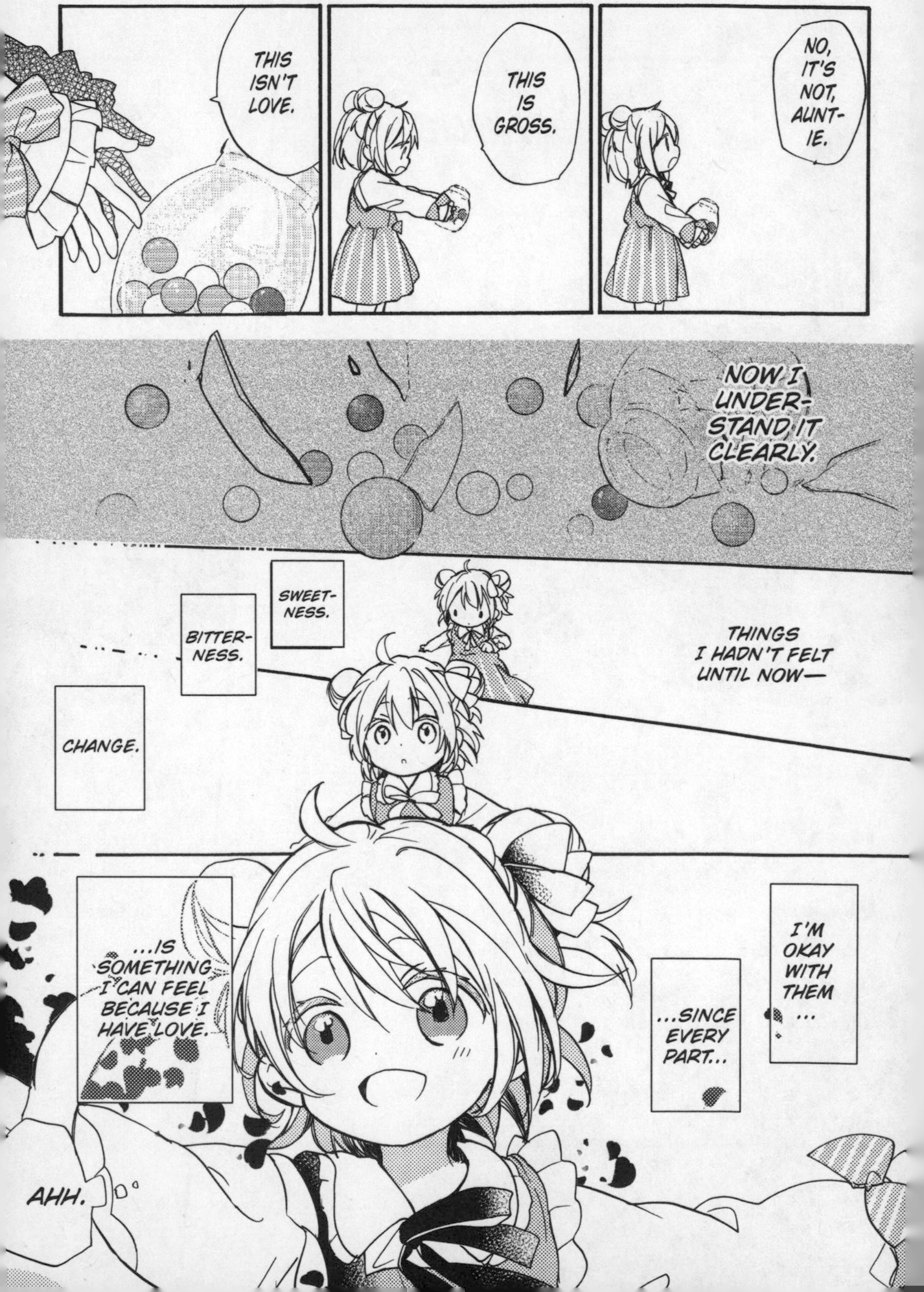
NO, IT'S NOT, AUNT-IE.
THIS IS GROSS.
THIS ISN'T LOVE.
NOW I UNDER-STAND IT CLEARLY.
THINGS I HADN'T FELT UNTIL NOW—
SWEET-NESS.
BITTER-NESS.
CHANGE.
I'M OKAY WITH THEM ...
...SINCE EVERY PART...
...IS SOMETHING I CAN FEEL BECAUSE I HAVE LOVE.
AHH.

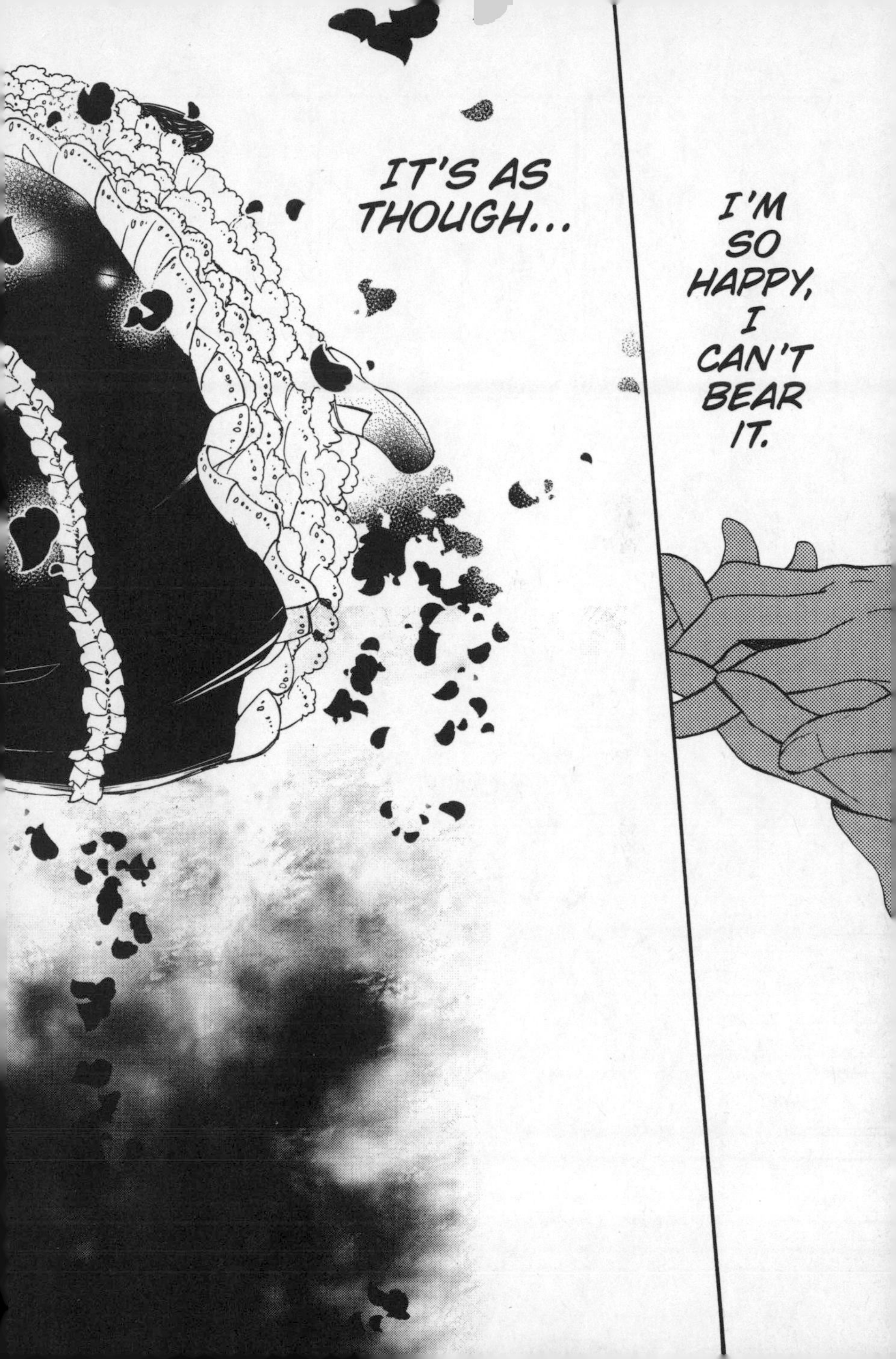
I'M SO HAPPY, I CAN'T BEAR IT.
IT'S AS THOUGH...

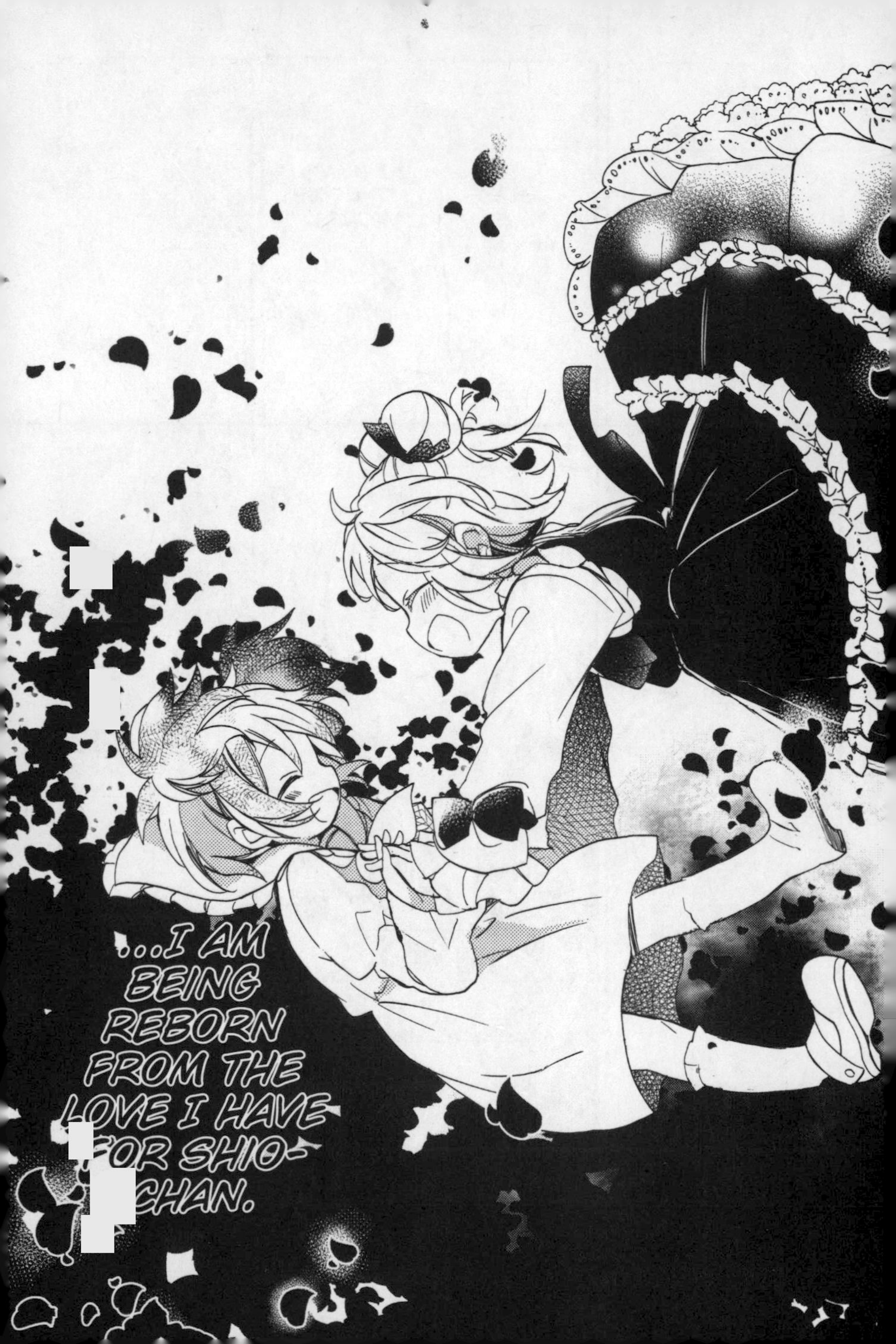
...I AM BEING REBORN FROM THE LOVE I HAVE FOR SHIO-CHAN.

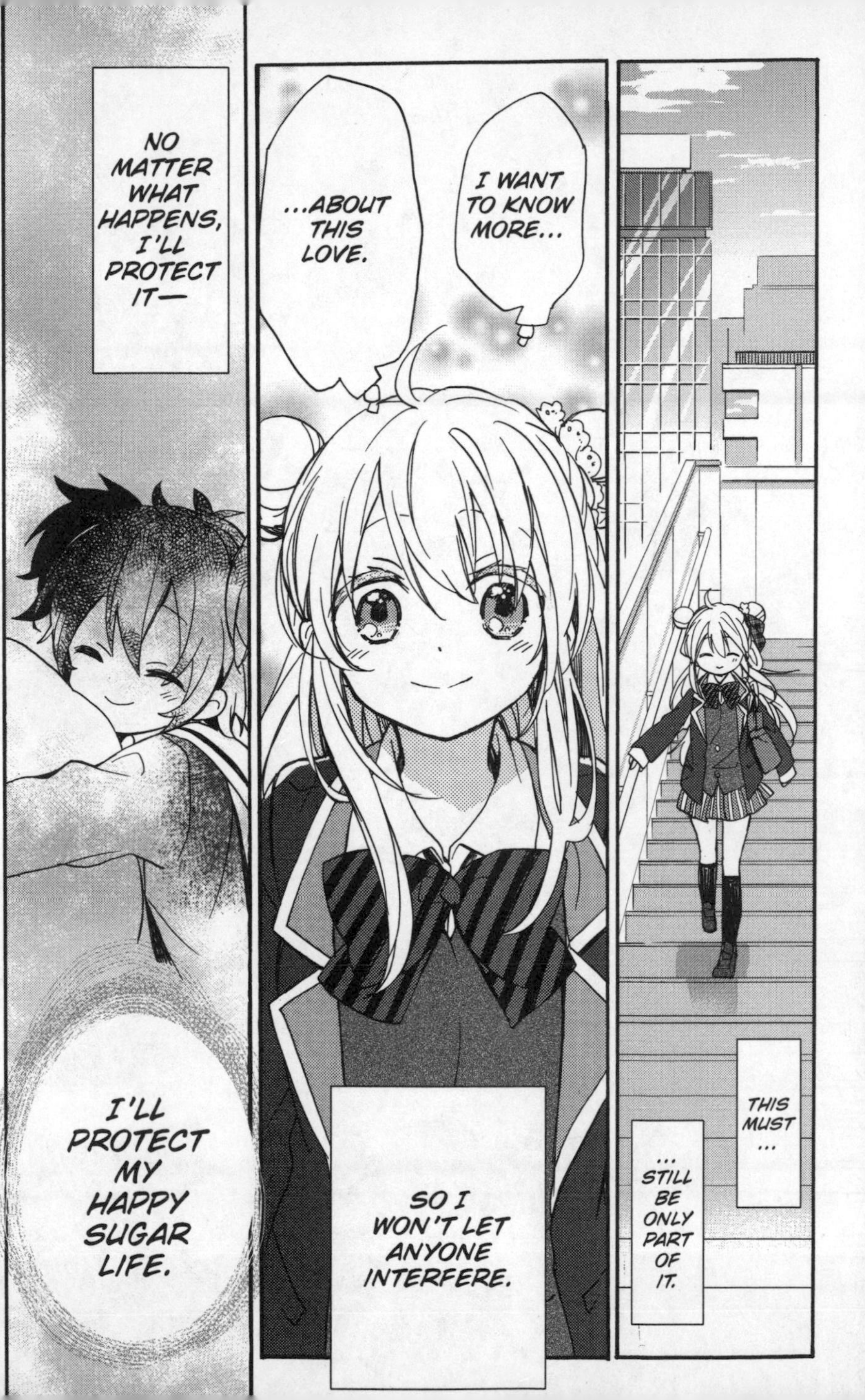
THIS MUST...
...STILL BE ONLY PART OF IT.
I WANT TO KNOW MORE...
...ABOUT THIS LOVE.
SO I WON'T LET ANYONE INTERFERE.
NO MATTER WHAT HAPPENS, I'LL PROTECT IT—
I'LL PROTECT MY HAPPY SUGAR LIFE.

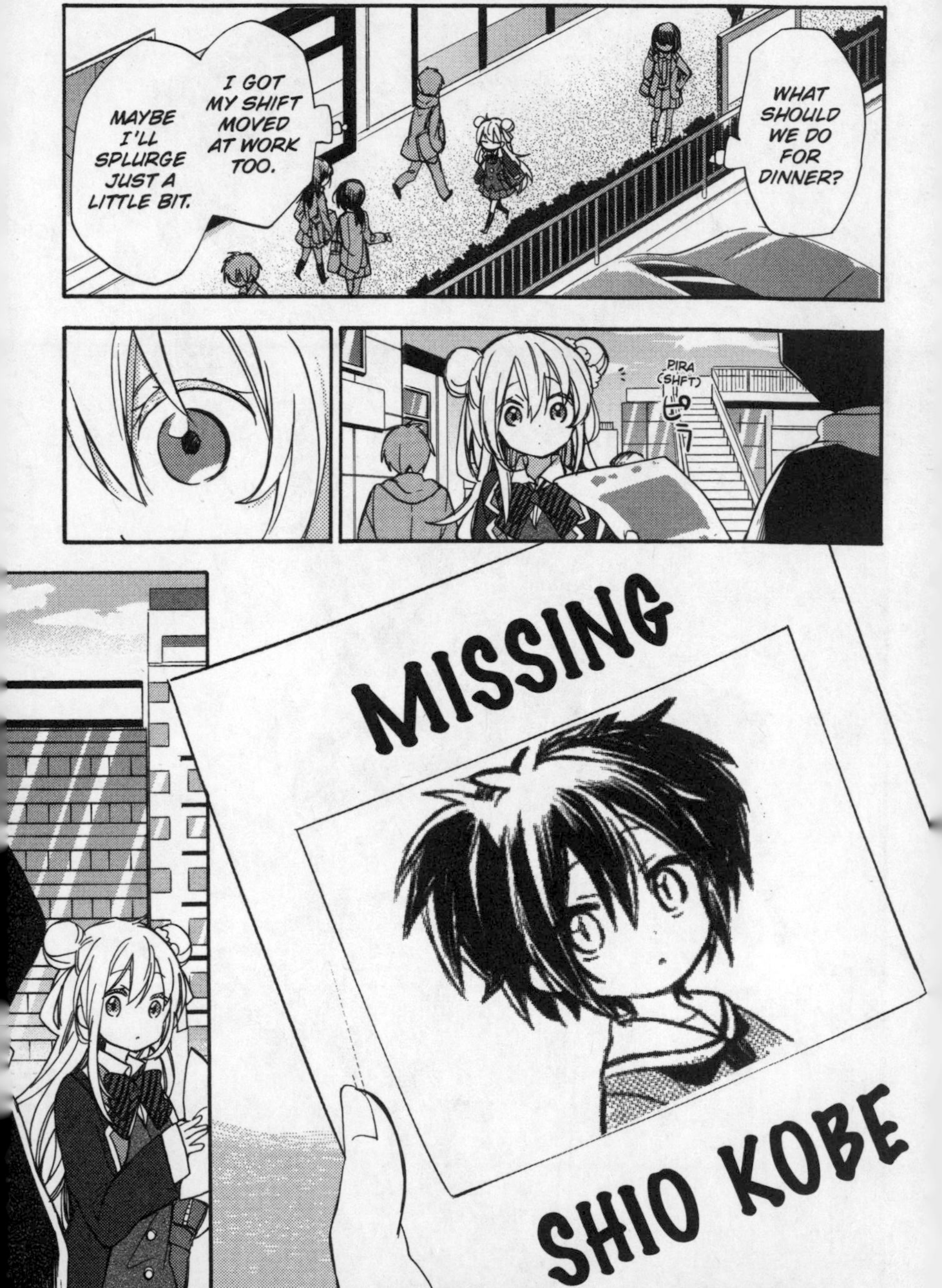
WHAT SHOULD WE DO FOR DINNER?
I GOT MY SHIFT MOVED AT WORK TOO.
MAYBE I'LL SPLURGE JUST A LITTLE BIT.
PIRA (SHFT)
MISSING
SHIO KOBE

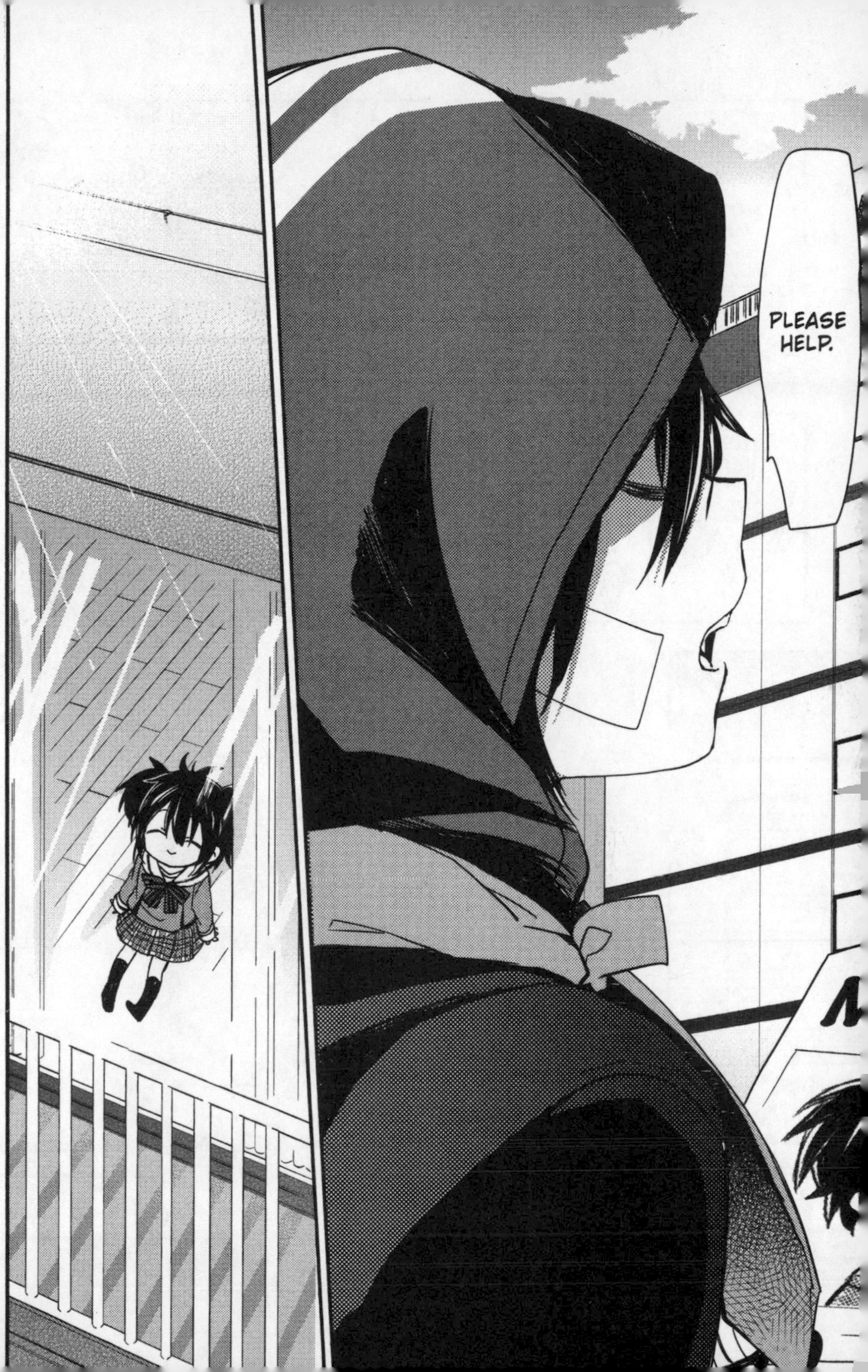
PLEASE HELP.

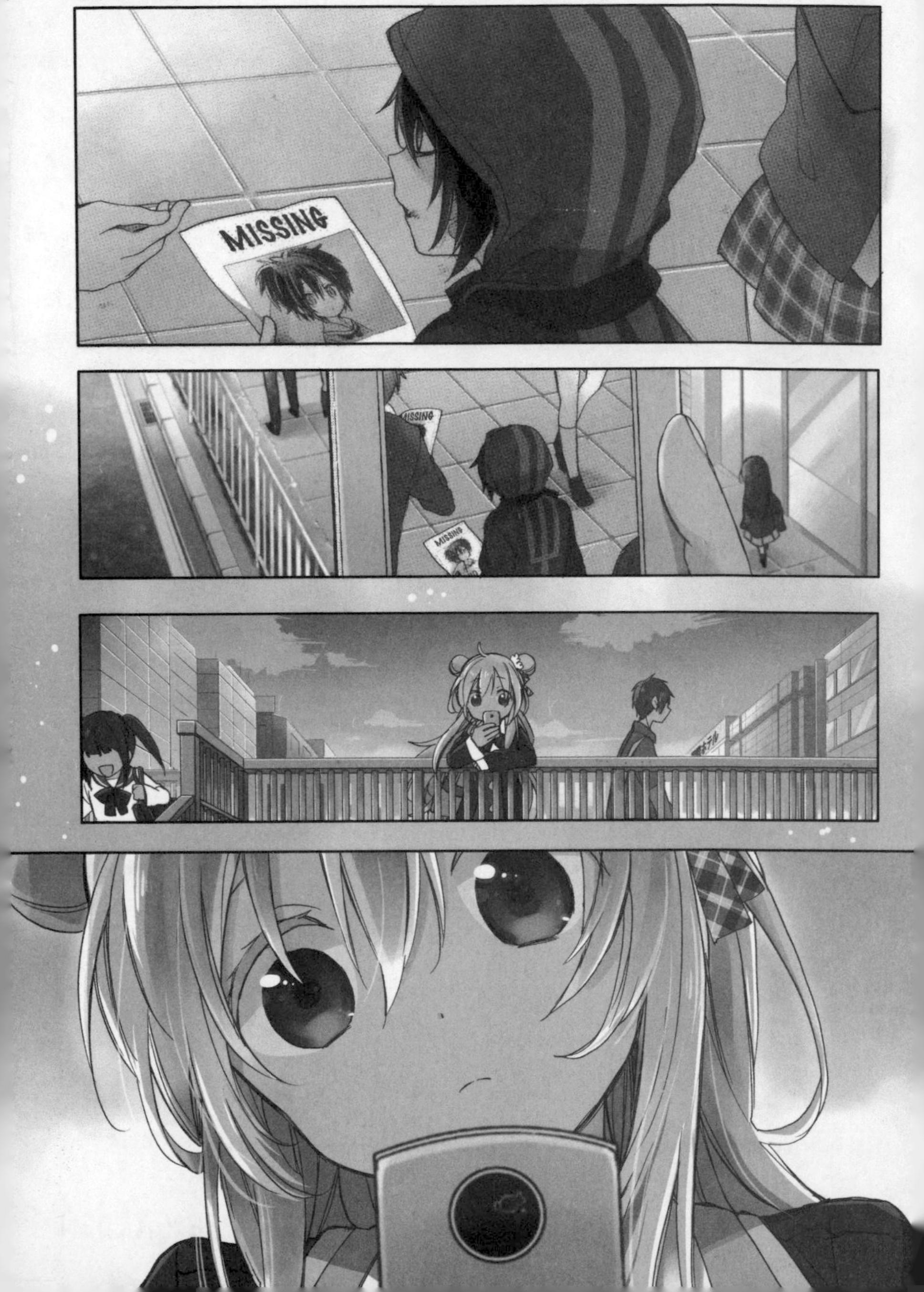
MISSING
MISSING
MISSING

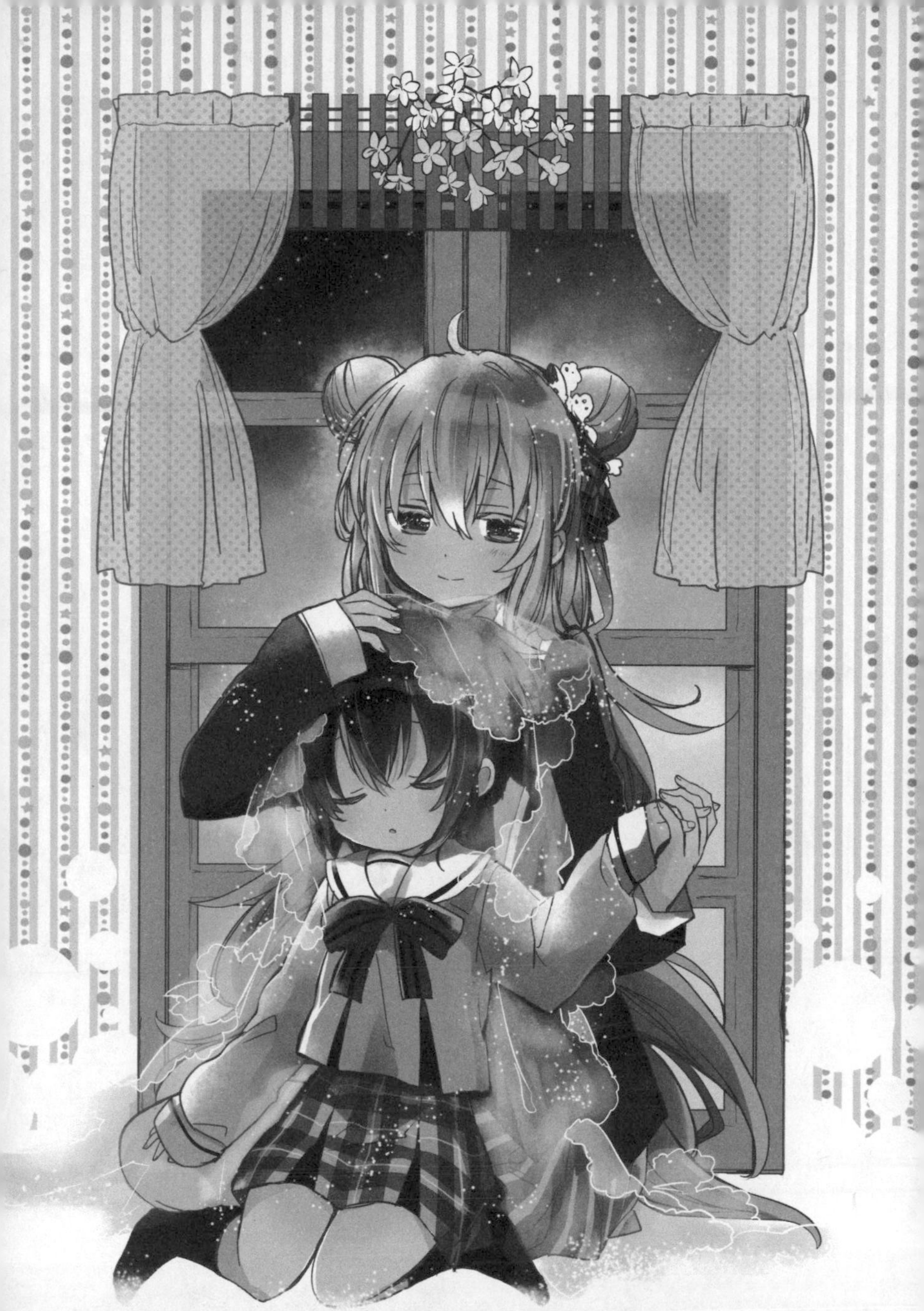

3RD LIFE: SHIO'S MINIATURE GARDEN

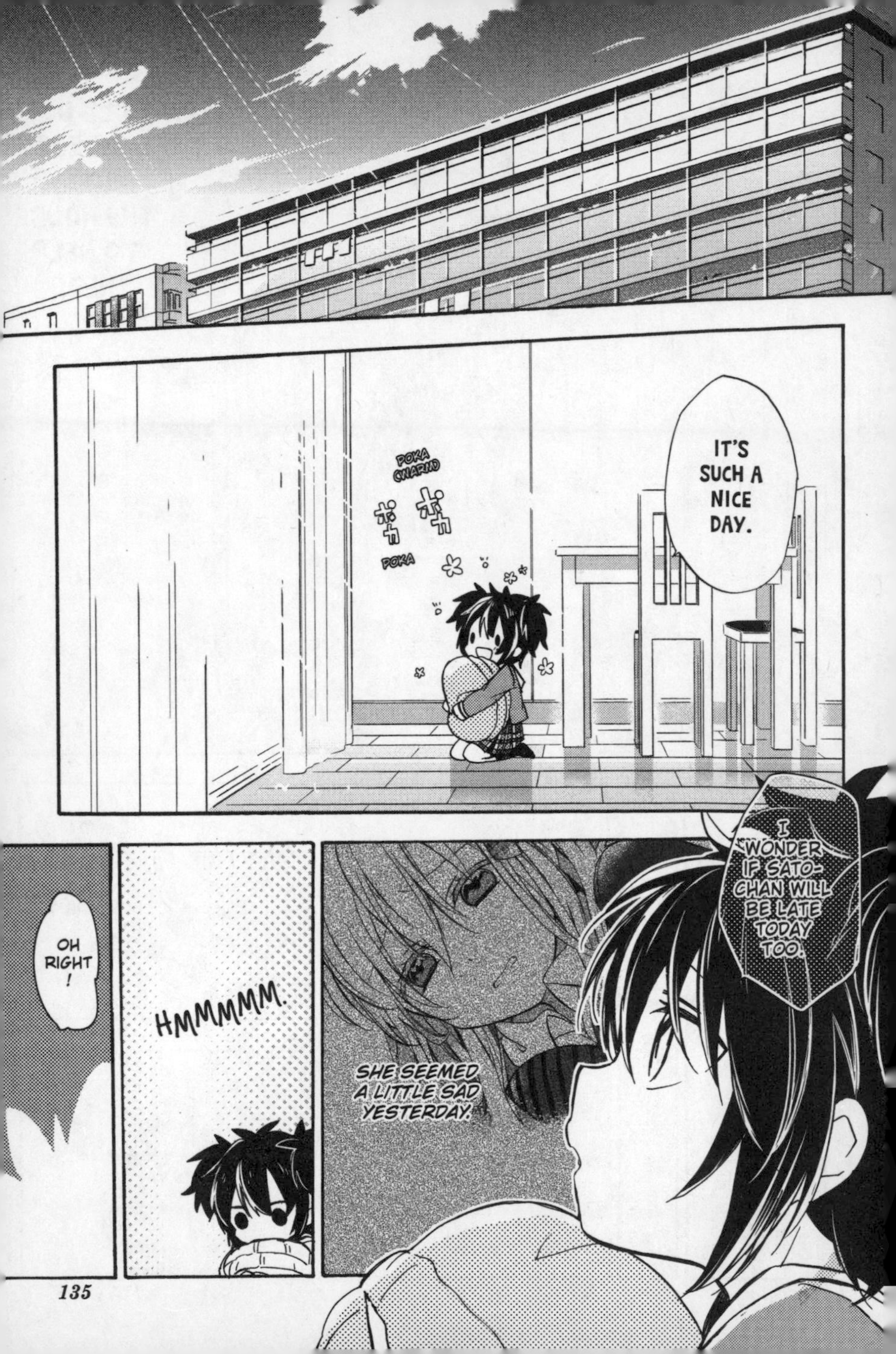
IT'S SUCH A NICE DAY.
POKA (WARM)
ポカ
ポカ
POKA
I WONDER IF SATO-CHAN WILL BE LATE TODAY TOO.
SHE SEEMED A LITTLE SAD YESTERDAY.
HMMMMM.
OH RIGHT!

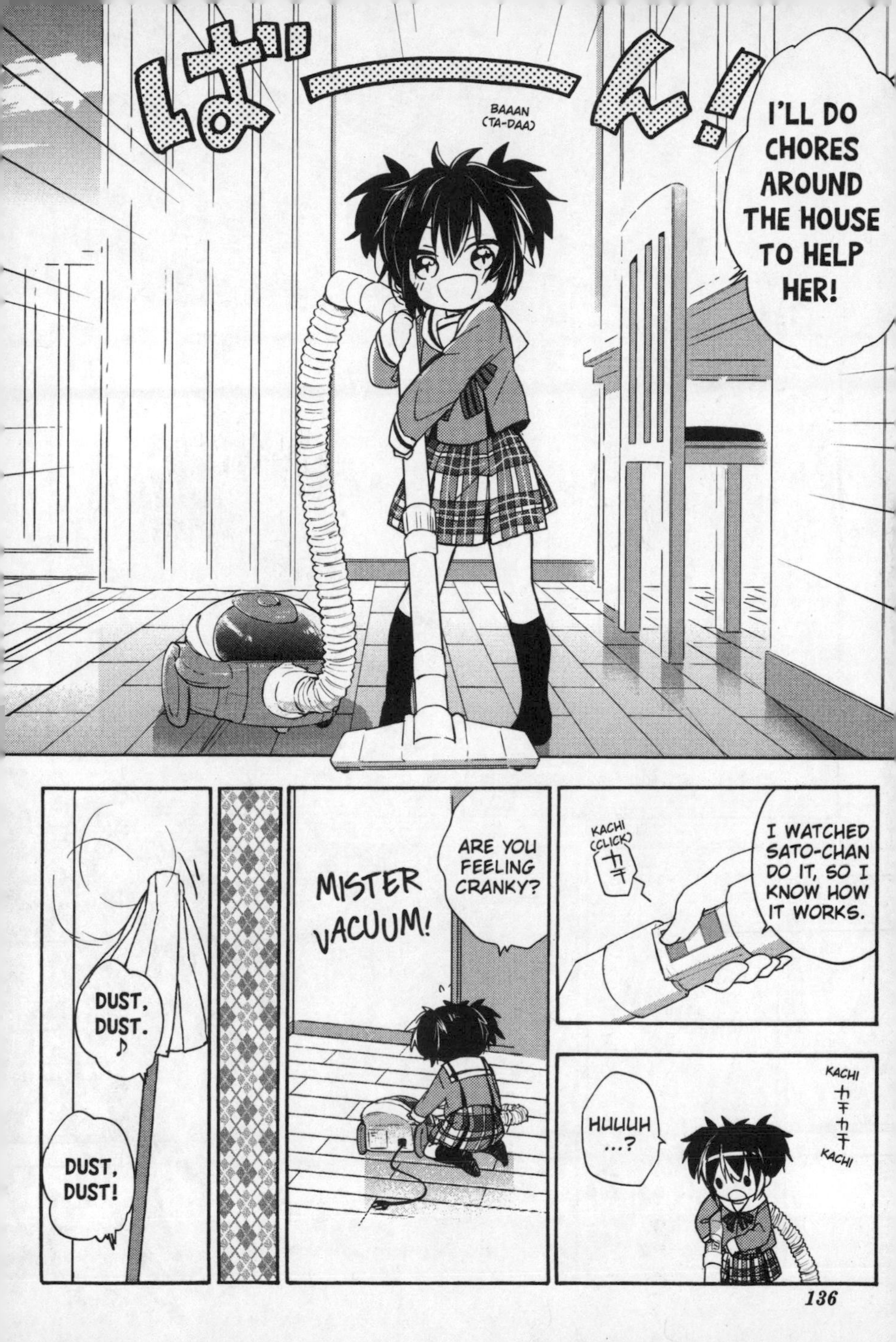
I'LL DO CHORES AROUND THE HOUSE TO HELP HER!
ばーーん!
BAAAN (TA-DAA)
I WATCHED SATO-CHAN DO IT, SO I KNOW HOW IT WORKS.
KACHI (CLICK)
カチ
KACHI
カチカチ
KACHI
HUUUH ...?
ARE YOU FEELING CRANKY?
MISTER VACUUM!
DUST, DUST. ♪
DUST, DUST!

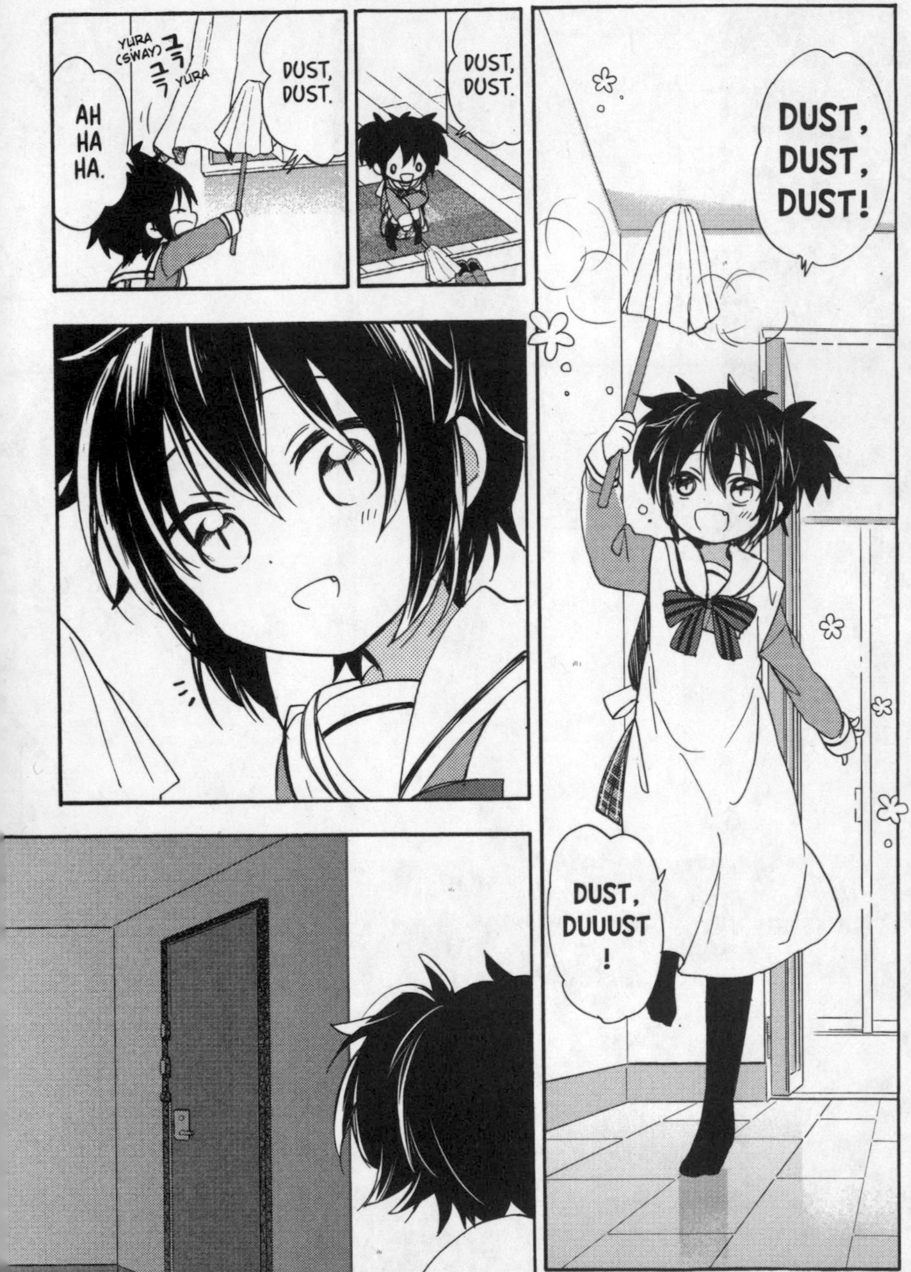
DUST, DUST, DUST!
DUST, DUUUST!
DUST, DUST.
DUST, DUST.
YURA (SWAY) ユラ
ユラ YURA
AH HA HA.

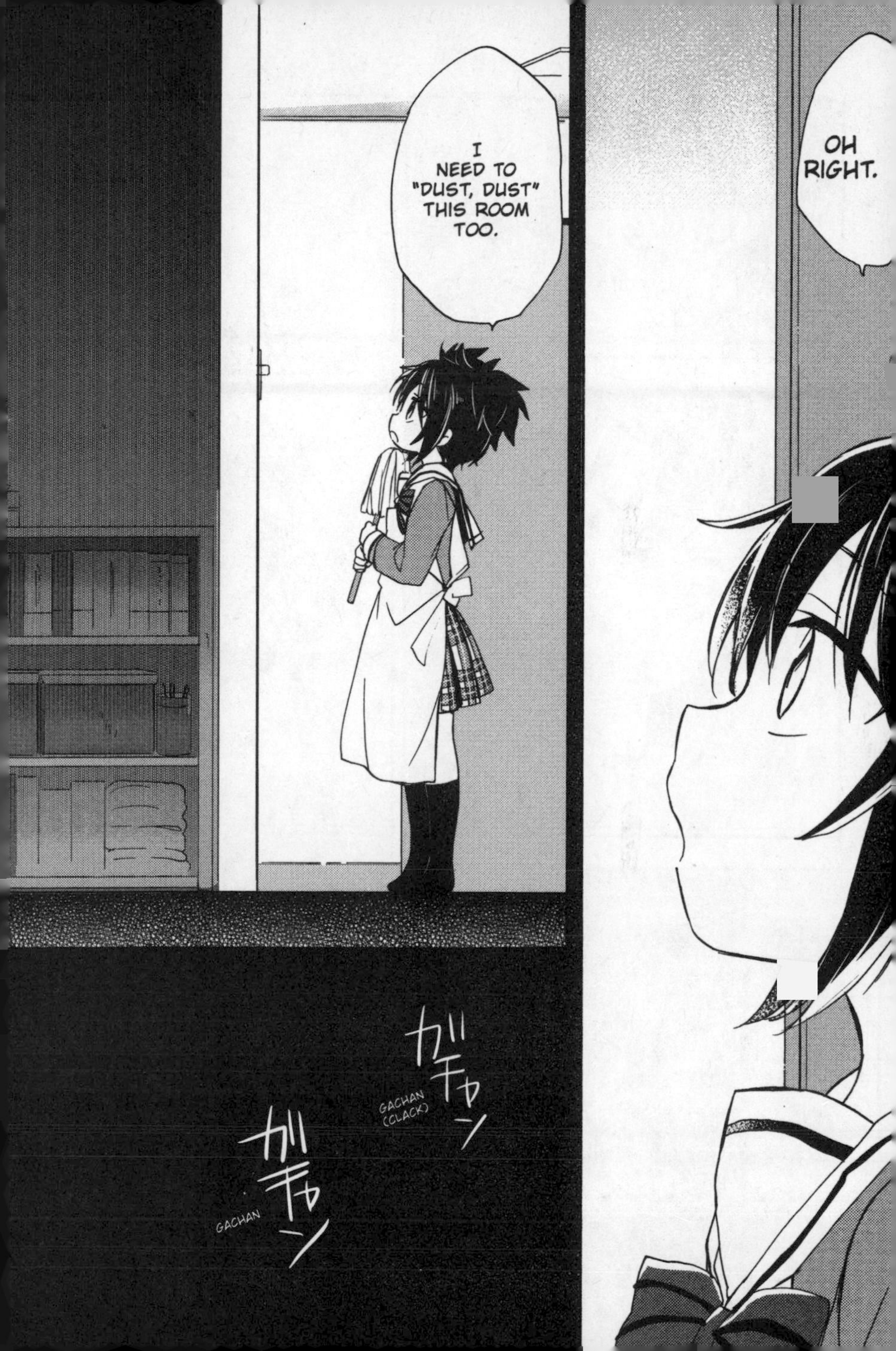
OH RIGHT.
I NEED TO "DUST, DUST" THIS ROOM TOO.
ガチャン
GACHAN (CLACK)
ガチャン
GACHAN

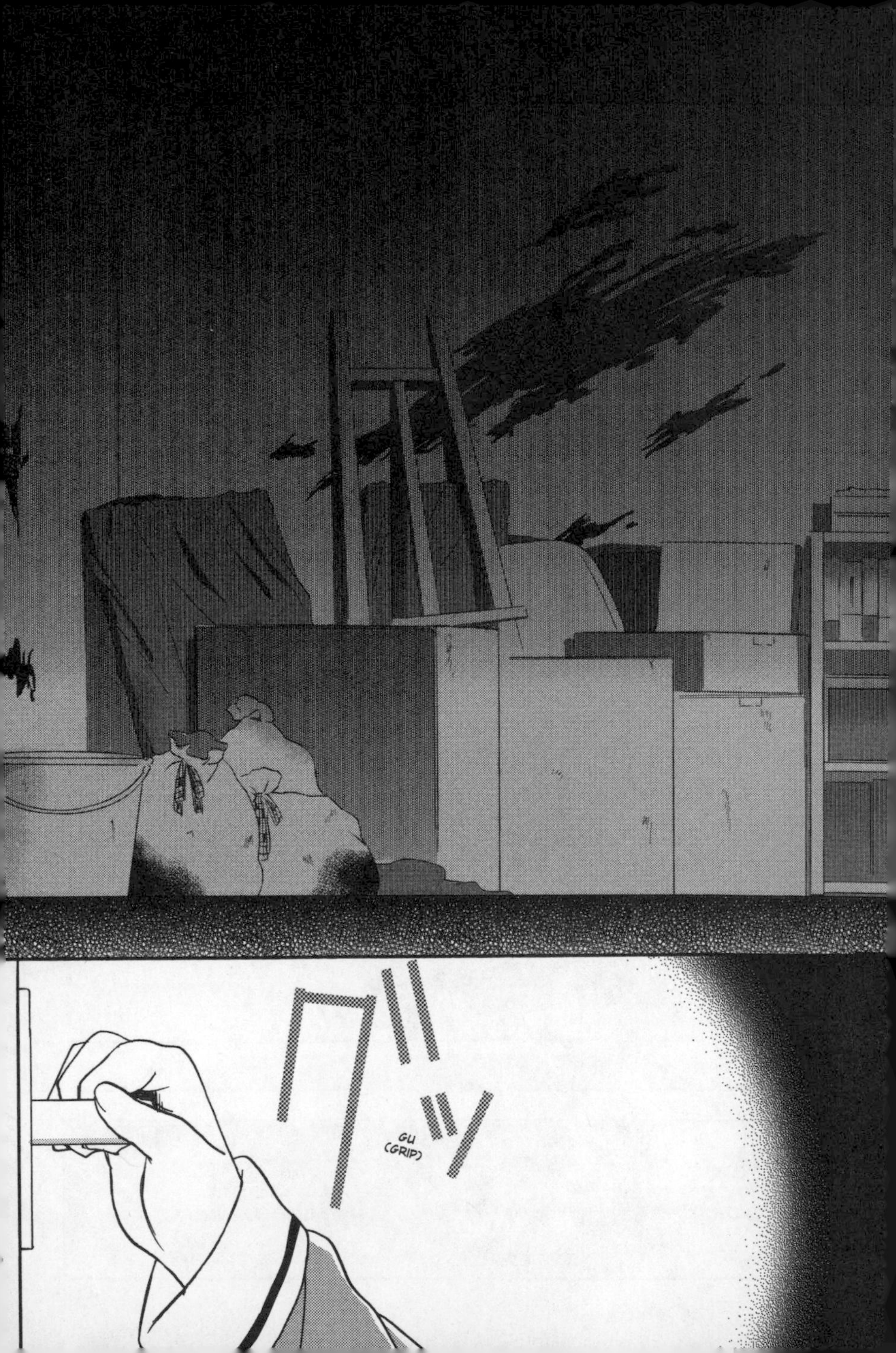
グッ
GU
(GRIP)

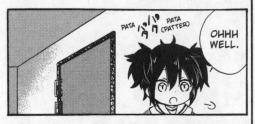

PATA PATA (PATTER)

OHHH WELL.

IT WON'T OPEN.

...

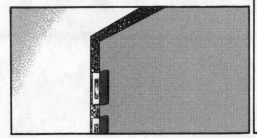

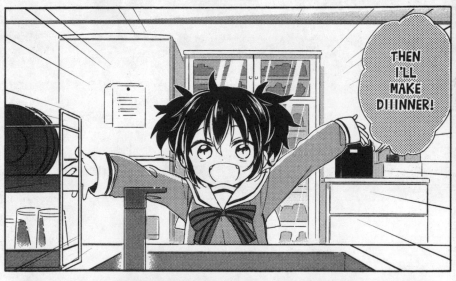

THEN I'LL MAKE DIIINNER!

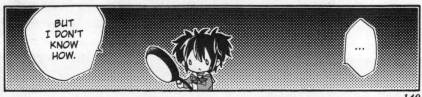

BUT I DON'T KNOW HOW.

...

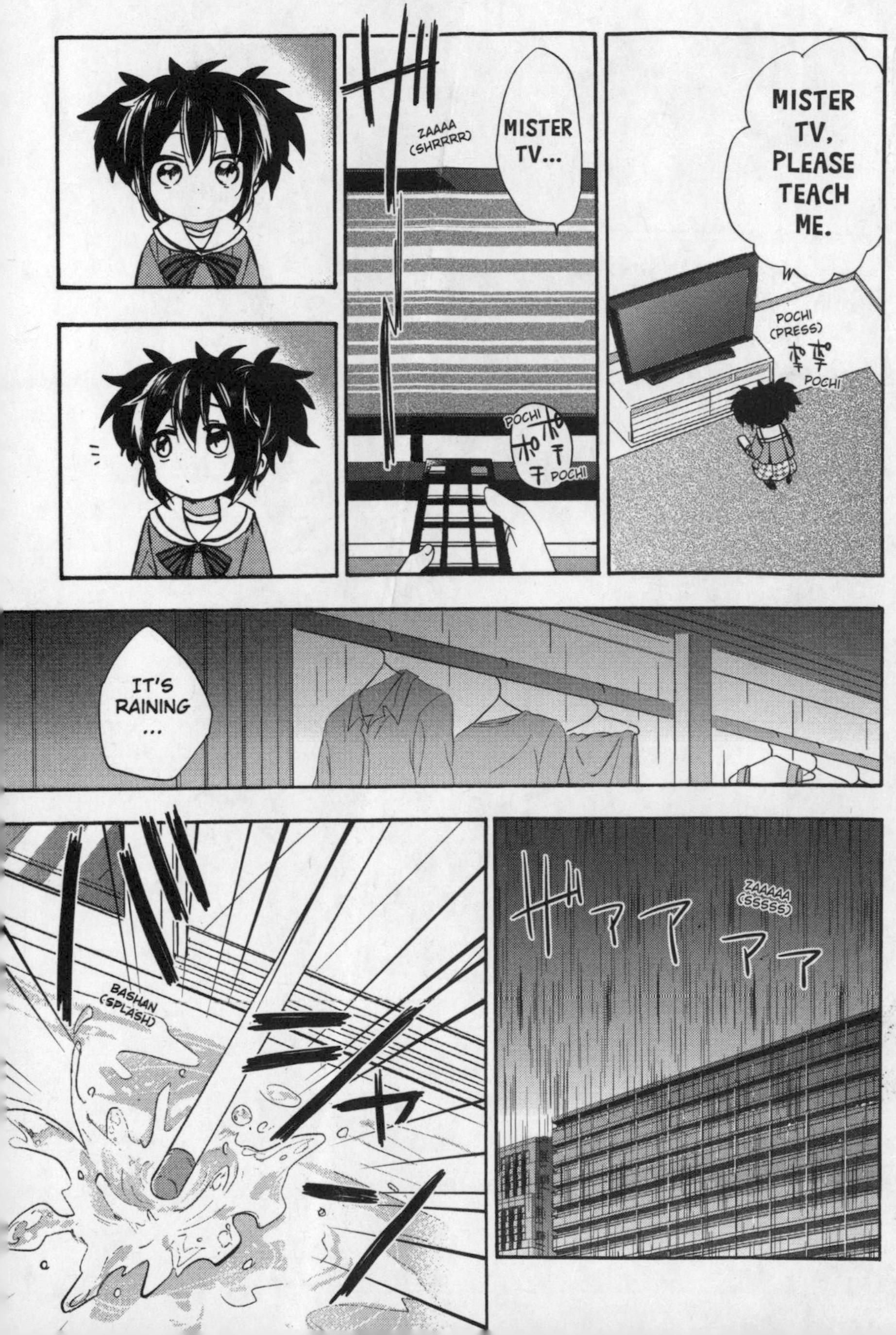
MISTER TV, PLEASE TEACH ME.
POCHI (PRESS)
POCHI
MISTER TV...
ZAAAA (SHRRRR)
POCHI
POCHI
IT'S RAINING ...
ZAAAAA (SSSSS)
BASHAN (SPLASH)

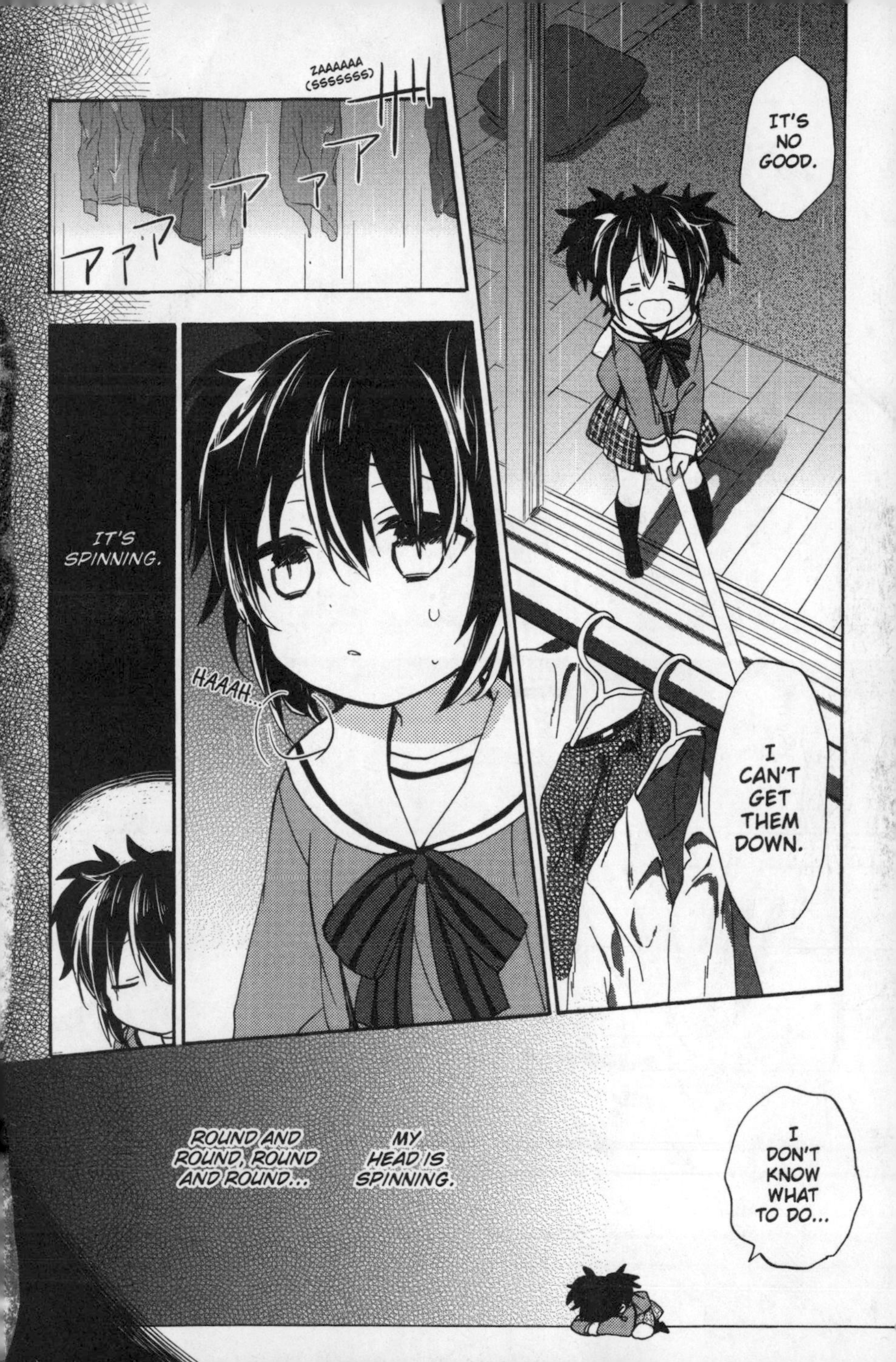
IT'S NO GOOD.
I CAN'T GET THEM DOWN.
ZAAAAAA (SSSSSSS)
HAAAH...
IT'S SPINNING.
I DON'T KNOW WHAT TO DO...
MY HEAD IS SPINNING.
ROUND AND ROUND, ROUND AND ROUND...

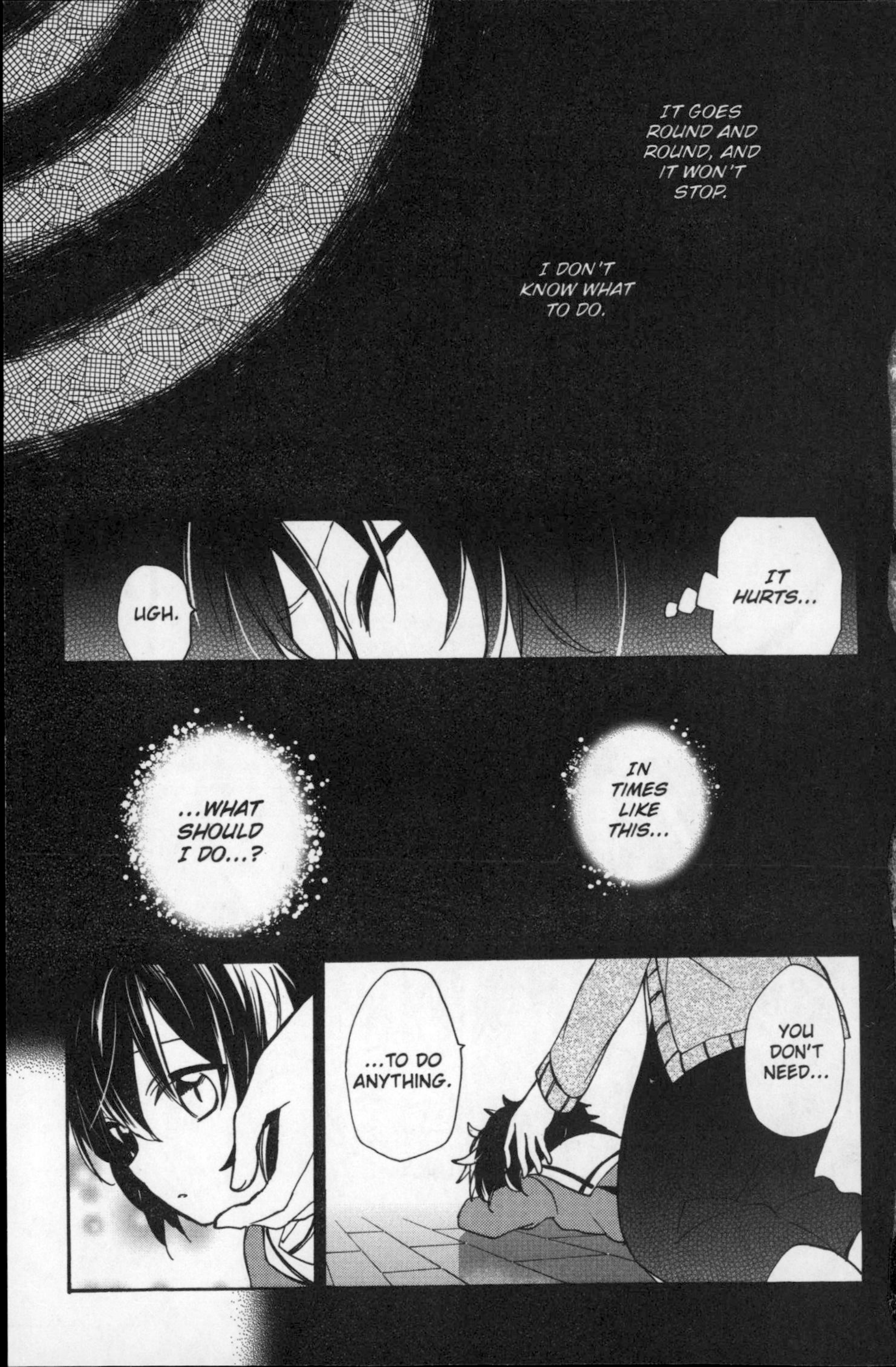
IT GOES ROUND AND ROUND, AND IT WON'T STOP.
I DON'T KNOW WHAT TO DO.
IT HURTS...
UGH.
IN TIMES LIKE THIS...
...WHAT SHOULD I DO...?
YOU DON'T NEED...
...TO DO ANYTHING.

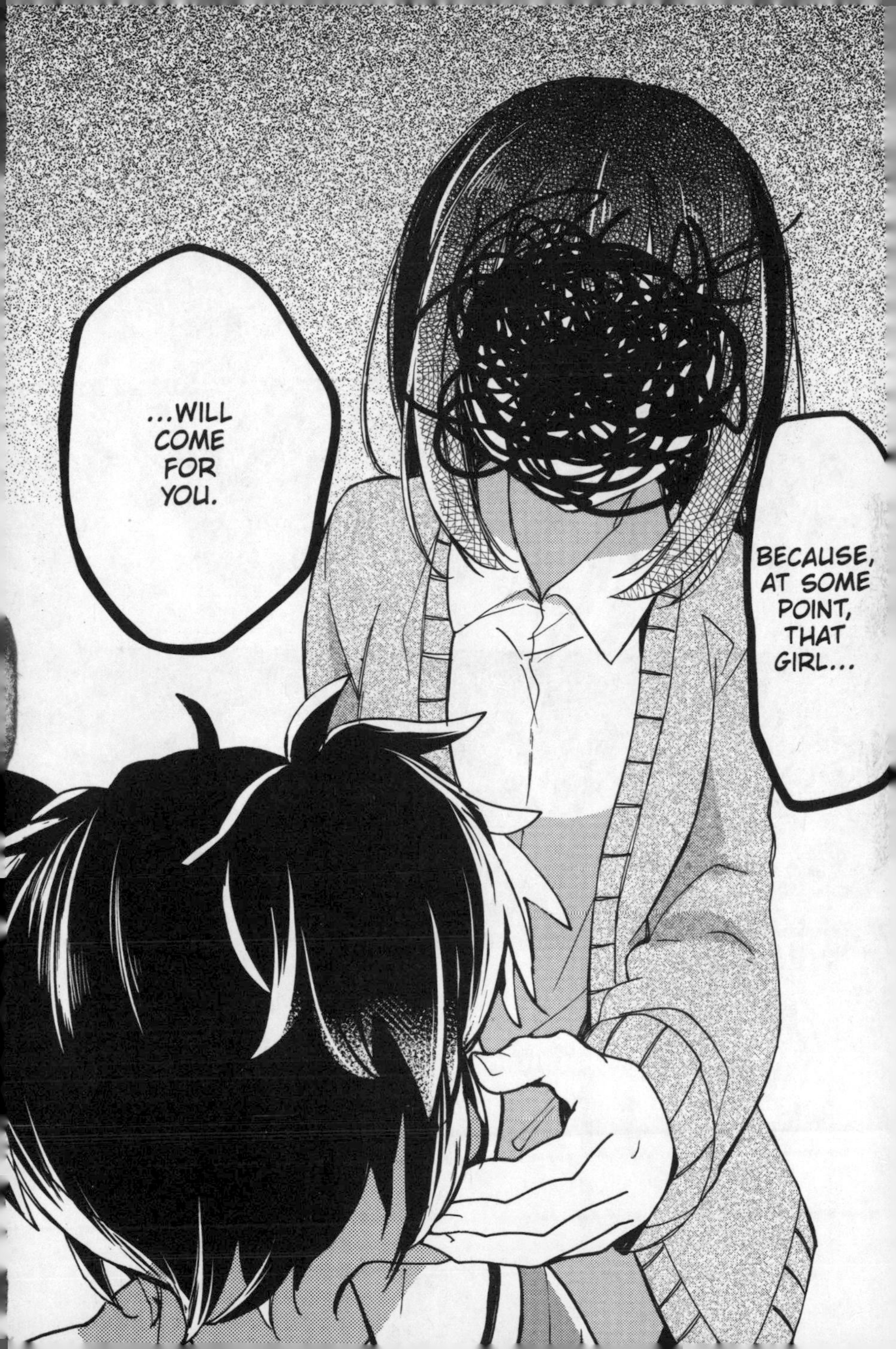
BECAUSE, AT SOME POINT, THAT GIRL...
...WILL COME FOR YOU.

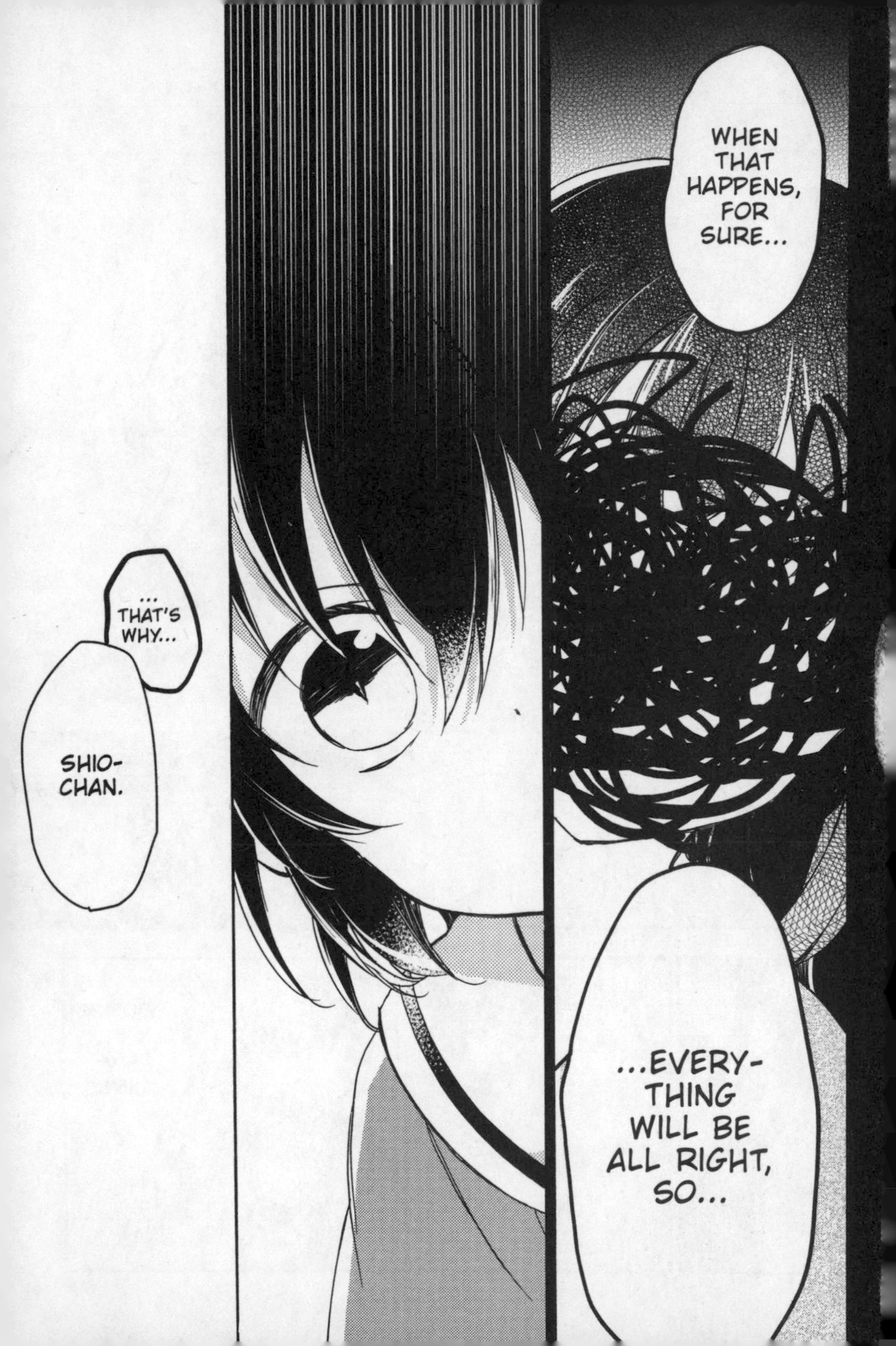
WHEN THAT HAPPENS, FOR SURE...
...EVERY-THING WILL BE ALL RIGHT, SO...
...THAT'S WHY...
SHIO-CHAN.

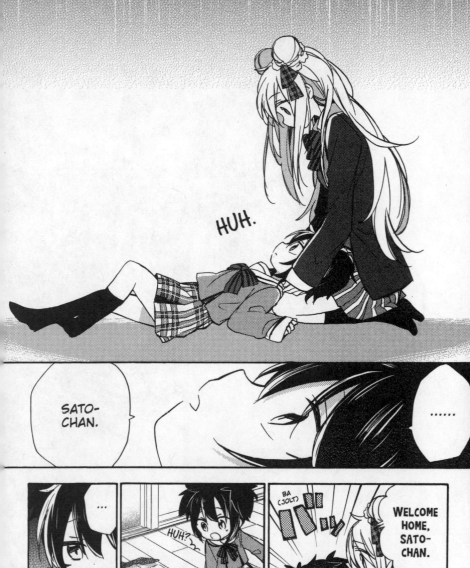

HUH.

SATO-CHAN.

......

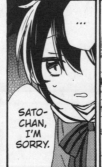

...

SATO-CHAN, I'M SORRY.

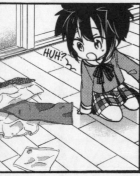

HUH?

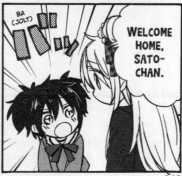

BA (JOLT)

WELCOME HOME, SATO-CHAN.

146

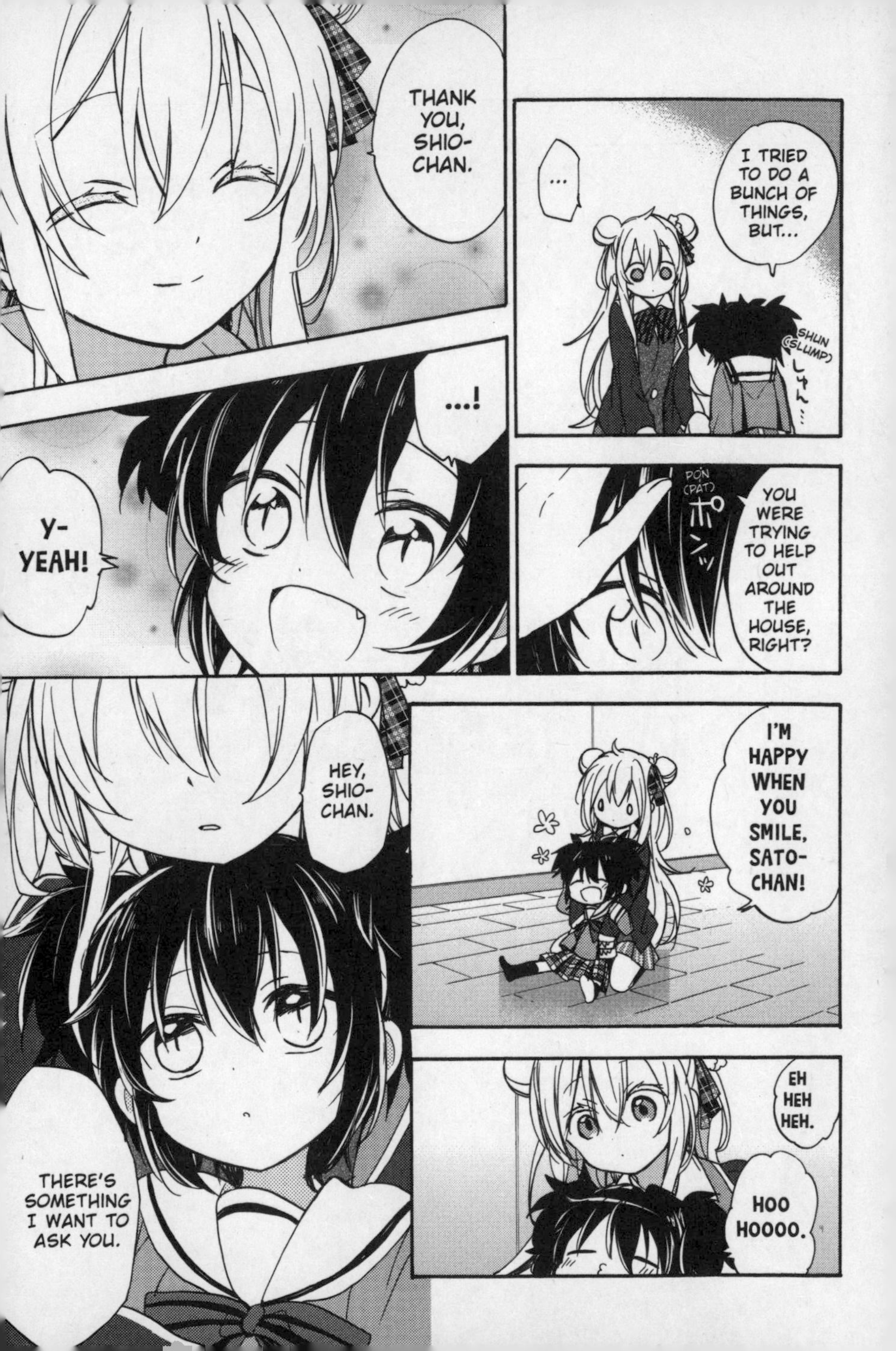
I TRIED TO DO A BUNCH OF THINGS, BUT...
...
SHUN (SLUMP)
しゅん…
THANK YOU, SHIO-CHAN.
PON (PAT)
ポンッ
YOU WERE TRYING TO HELP OUT AROUND THE HOUSE, RIGHT?
...!
Y-YEAH!
I'M HAPPY WHEN YOU SMILE, SATO-CHAN!
EH HEH HEH.
HOO HOOOO.
HEY, SHIO-CHAN.
THERE'S SOMETHING I WANT TO ASK YOU.

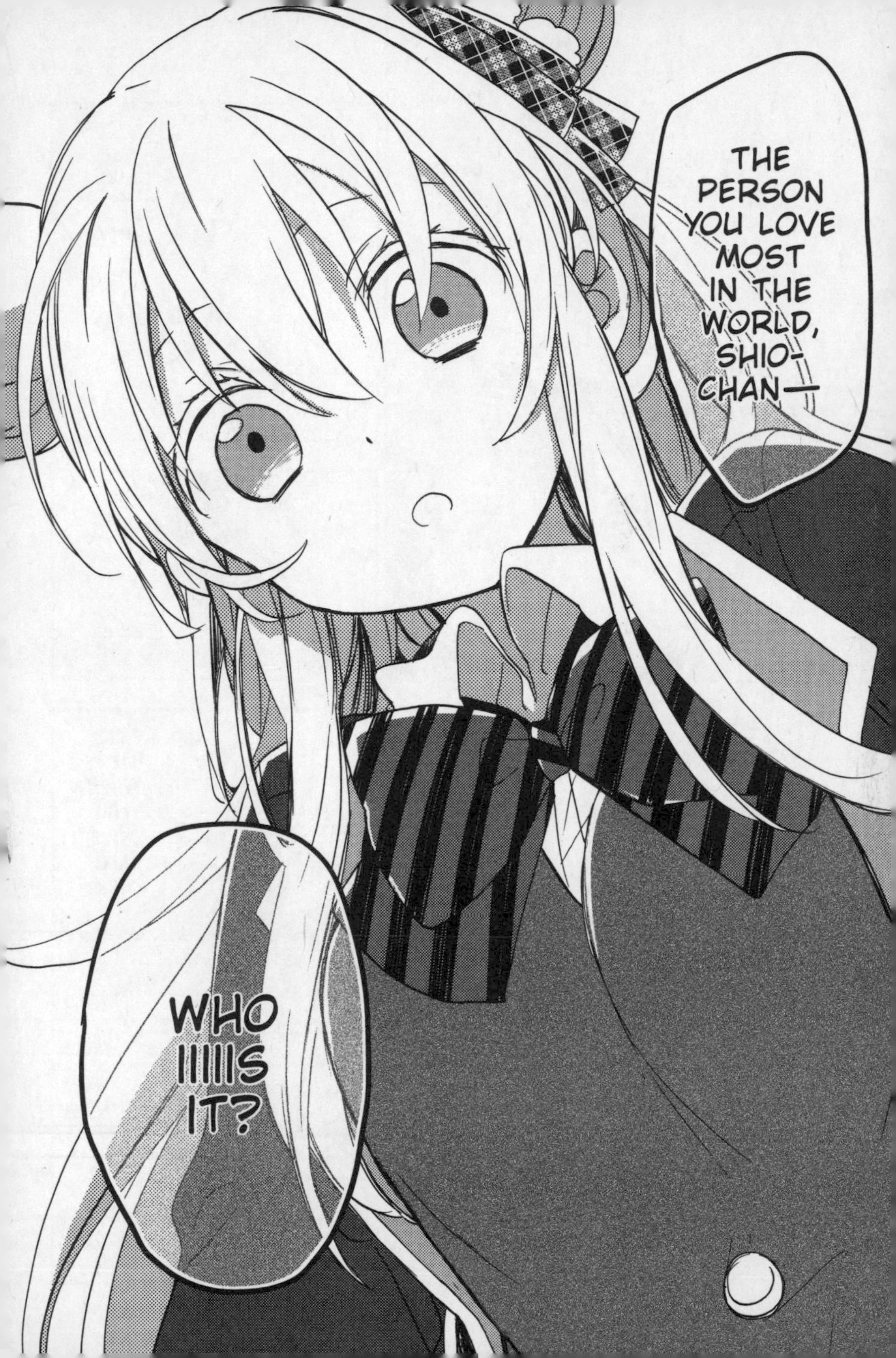
THE PERSON YOU LOVE MOST IN THE WORLD, SHIO-CHAN—
WHO IIIIS IT?

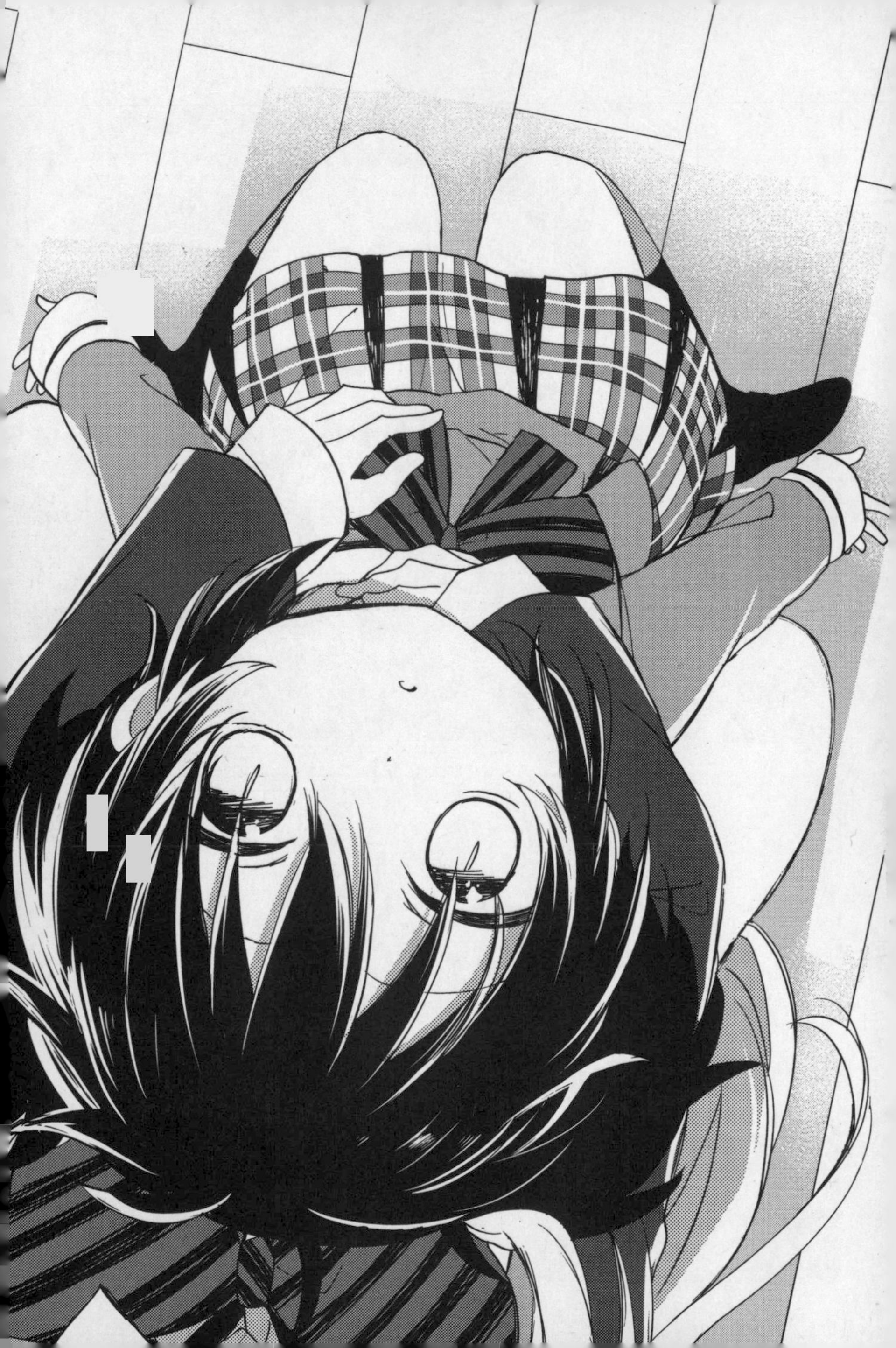

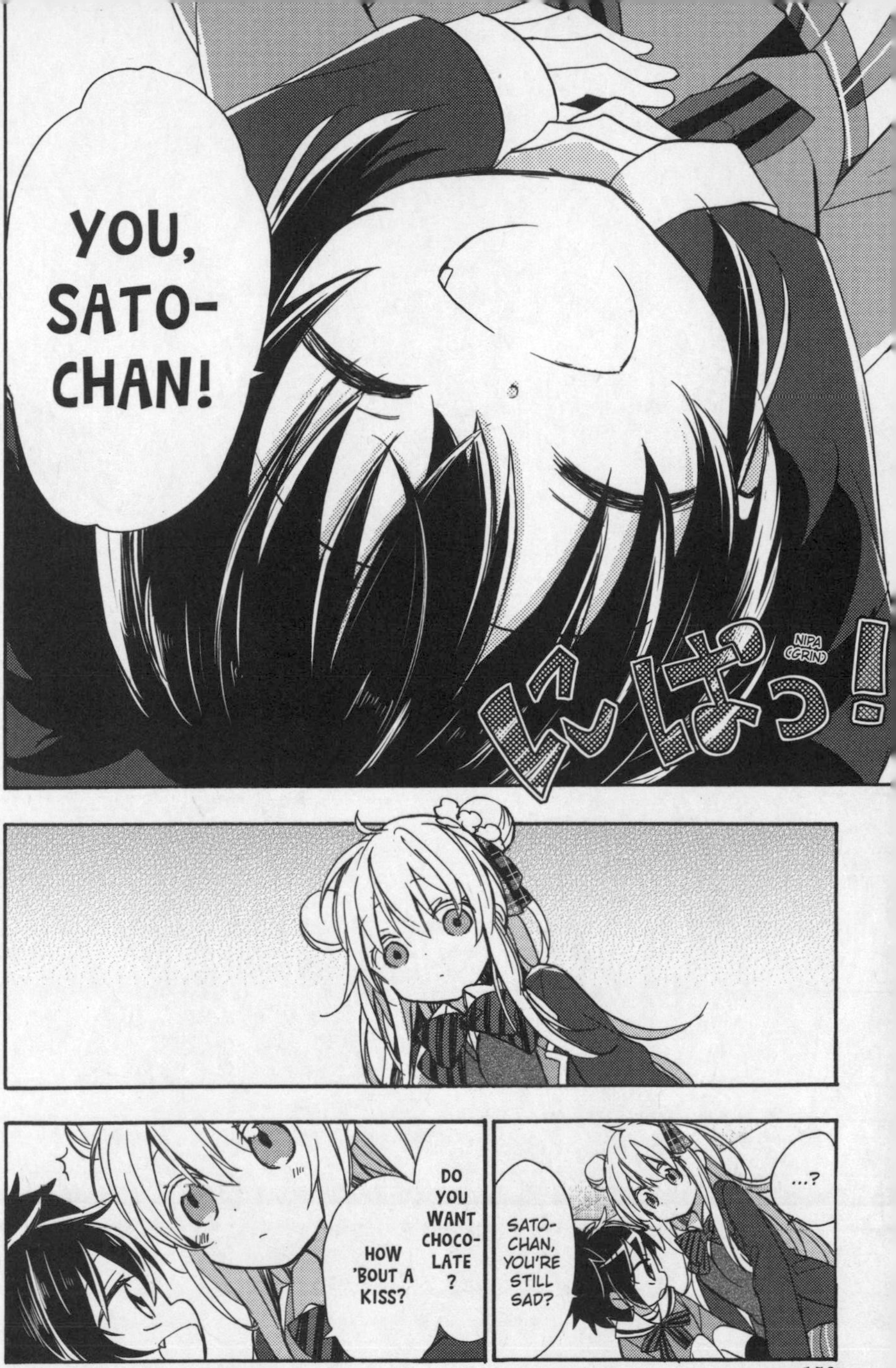
YOU, SATO-CHAN!
NIPA (GRIN)
にぱっ!
...?
SATO-CHAN, YOU'RE STILL SAD?
DO YOU WANT CHOCOLATE?
HOW 'BOUT A KISS?

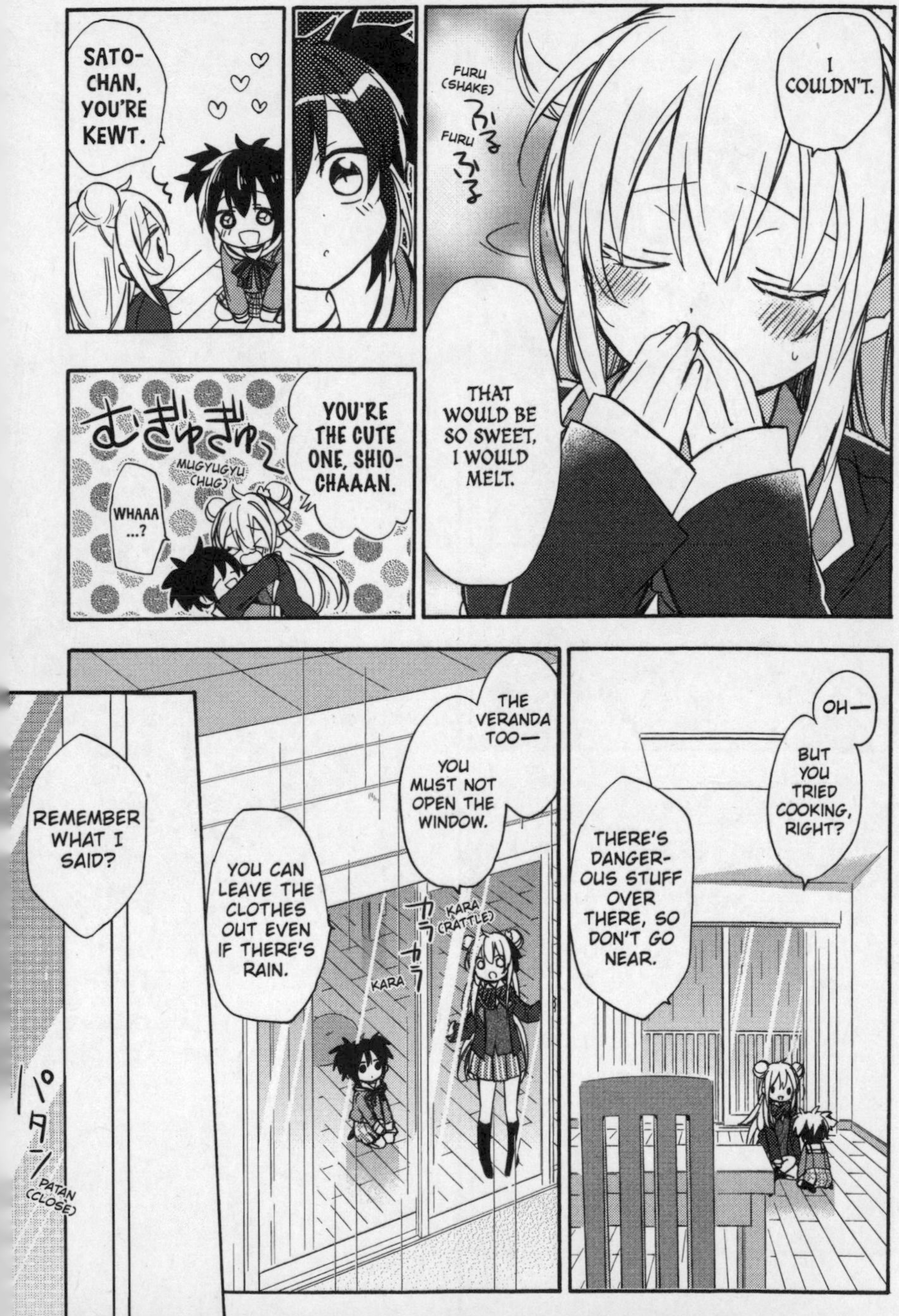
FURU (SHAKE) ふる
FURU ふる
I COULDN'T.
THAT WOULD BE SO SWEET, I WOULD MELT.
SATO-CHAN, YOU'RE KEWT.
YOU'RE THE CUTE ONE, SHIO-CHAAAN.
むぎゅぎゅ MUGYUGYU (HUG)
WHAAA ...?
OH—
BUT YOU TRIED COOKING, RIGHT?
THERE'S DANGER-OUS STUFF OVER THERE, SO DON'T GO NEAR.
THE VERANDA TOO—
YOU MUST NOT OPEN THE WINDOW.
YOU CAN LEAVE THE CLOTHES OUT EVEN IF THERE'S RAIN.
カラ KARA (RATTLE)
カラ KARA
REMEMBER WHAT I SAID?
パタン PATAN (CLOSE)

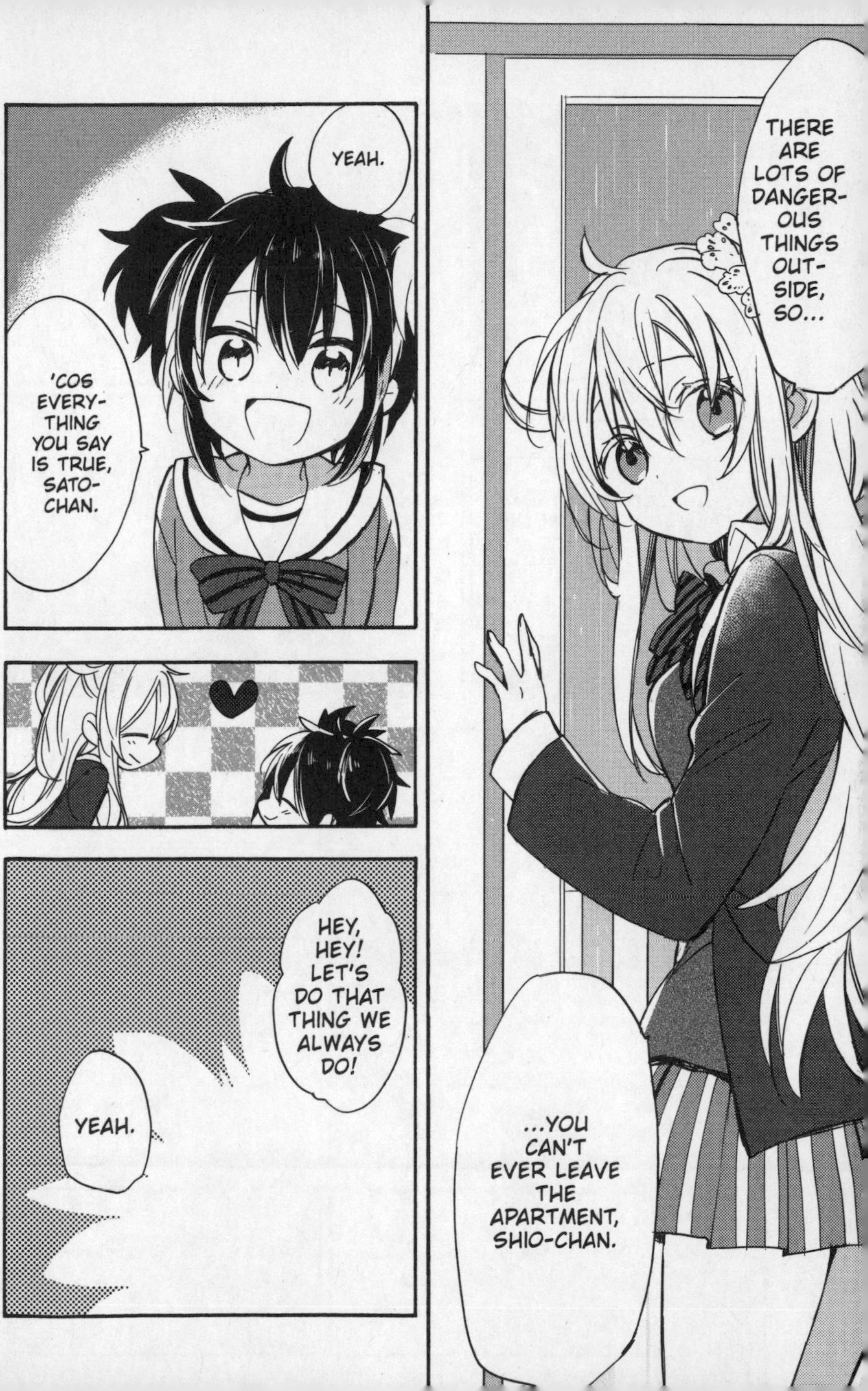
THERE ARE LOTS OF DANGER-OUS THINGS OUT-SIDE, SO...
...YOU CAN'T EVER LEAVE THE APARTMENT, SHIO-CHAN.
YEAH.
'COS EVERY-THING YOU SAY IS TRUE, SATO-CHAN.
HEY, HEY! LET'S DO THAT THING WE ALWAYS DO!
YEAH.

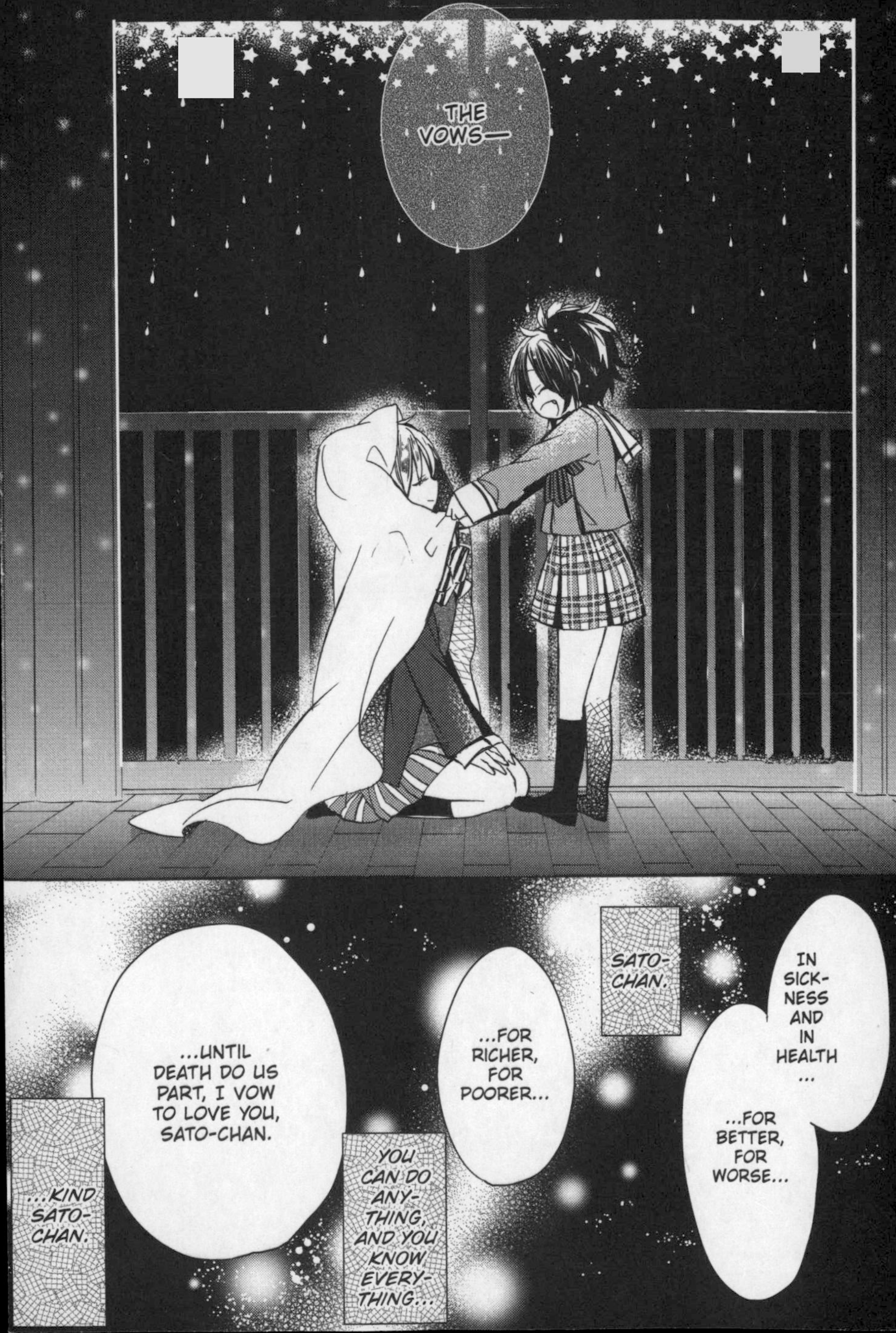
THE VOWS—
IN SICKNESS AND IN HEALTH...
...FOR BETTER, FOR WORSE...
SATO-CHAN.
...FOR RICHER, FOR POORER...
YOU CAN DO ANYTHING, AND YOU KNOW EVERYTHING...
...UNTIL DEATH DO US PART, I VOW TO LOVE YOU, SATO-CHAN.
...KIND SATO-CHAN.

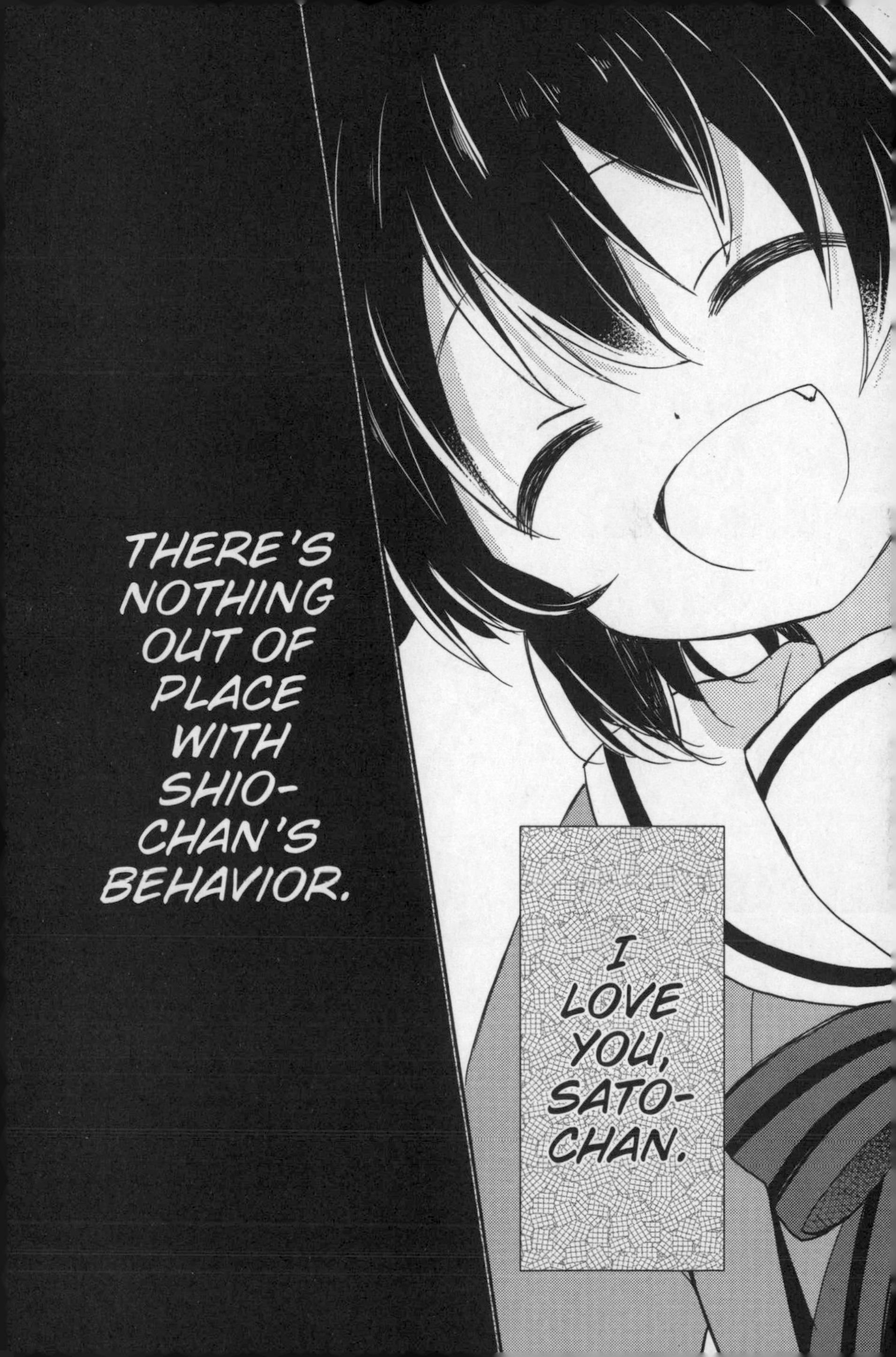
THERE'S NOTHING OUT OF PLACE WITH SHIO-CHAN'S BEHAVIOR.
I LOVE YOU, SATO-CHAN.

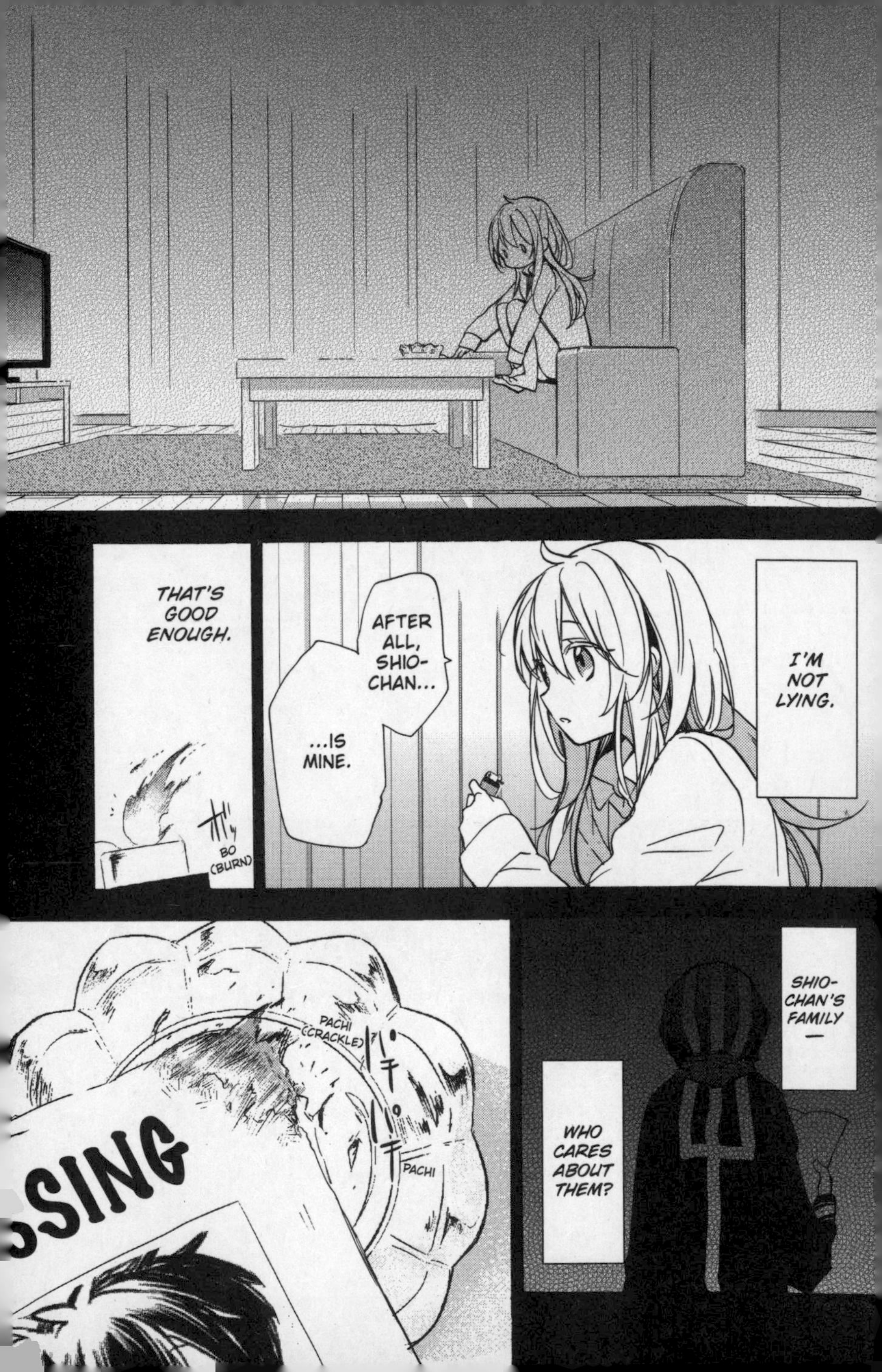
I'M NOT LYING.
AFTER ALL, SHIO-CHAN...
...IS MINE.
THAT'S GOOD ENOUGH.
BO (BURN)
SHIO-CHAN'S FAMILY —
WHO CARES ABOUT THEM?
PACHI (CRACKLE)
PACHI
SSING

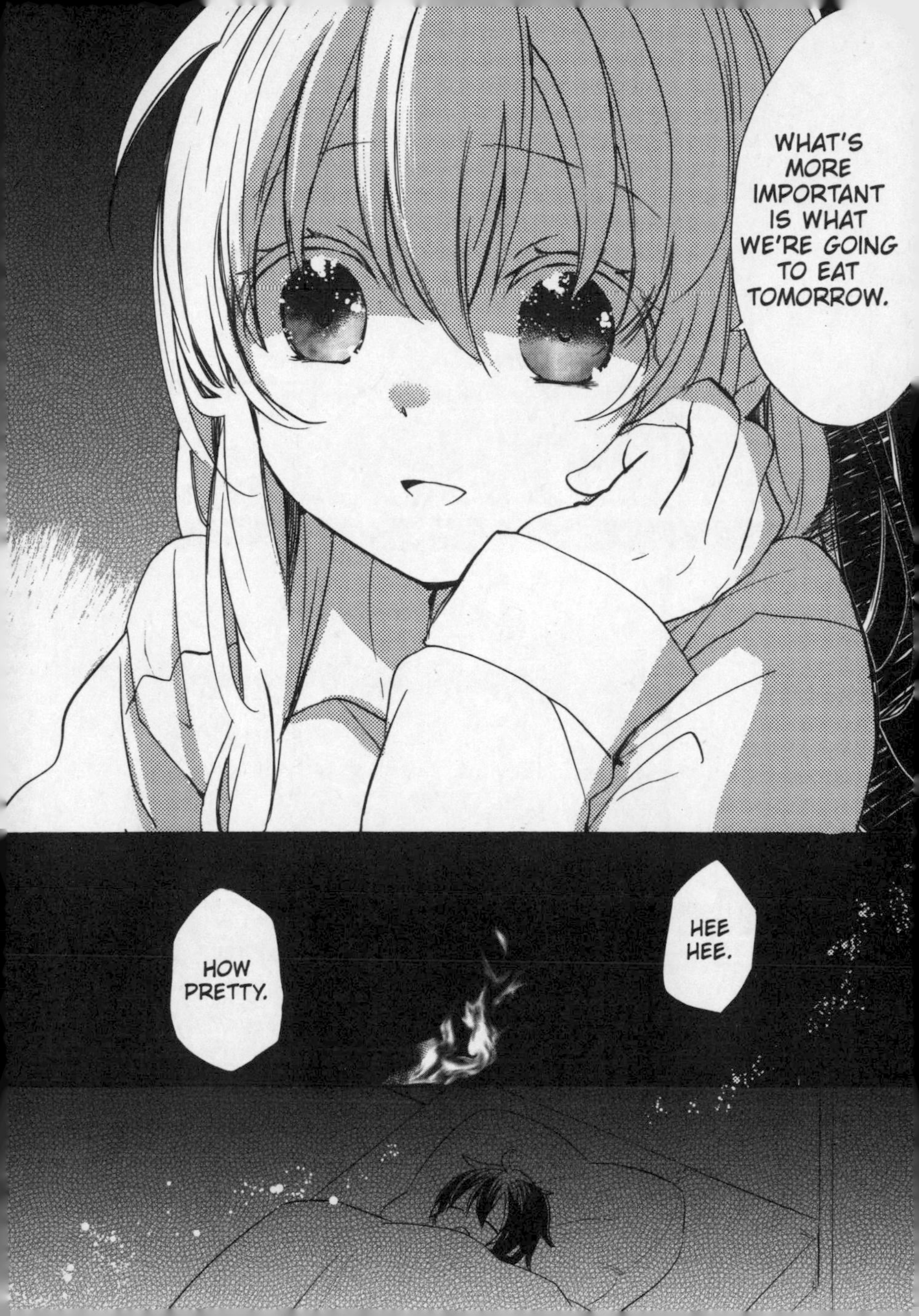
WHAT'S MORE IMPORTANT IS WHAT WE'RE GOING TO EAT TOMORROW.
HEE HEE.
HOW PRETTY.

Happy
Sugar
Life

Happy
Sugar
Life

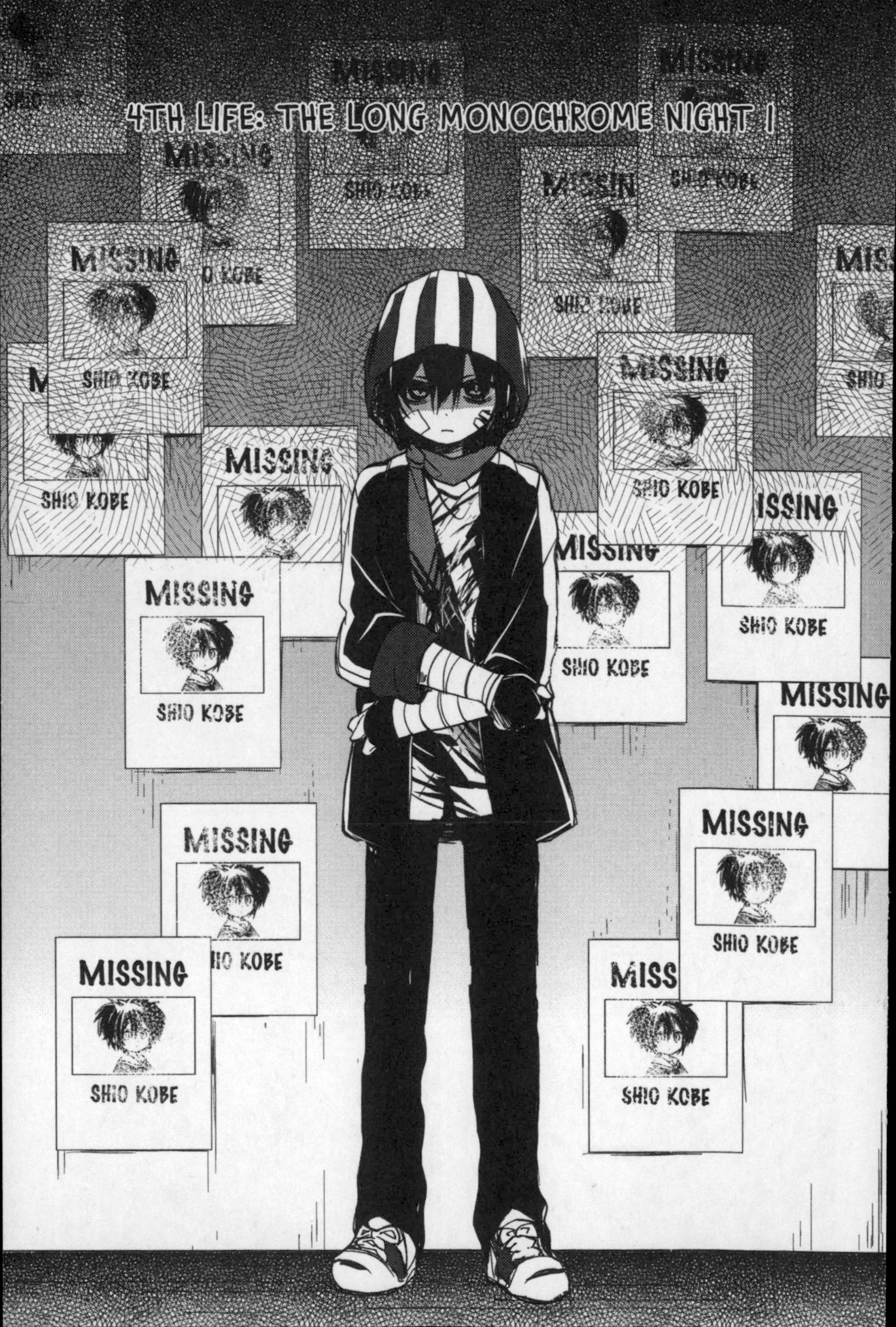
4TH LIFE: THE LONG MONOCHROME NIGHT I
MISSING
SHIO KOBE

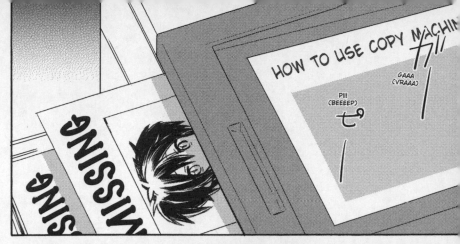

HOW TO USE COPY MACHINE

GAAA (VRAAA)

PIII (BEEEEP)

MISSING

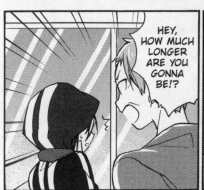

HEY, HOW MUCH LONGER ARE YOU GONNA BE!?

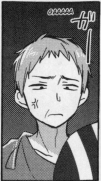

GAAAAA

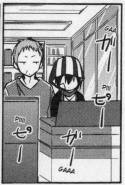

GAA

PIII

PIIII

GAAA

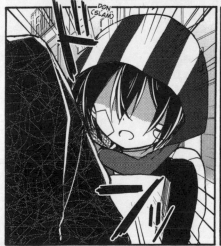

DON (SLAM)

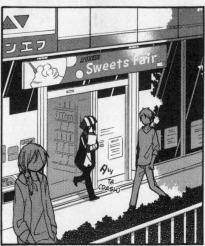

Sweets Fair

TA (DASH)

160

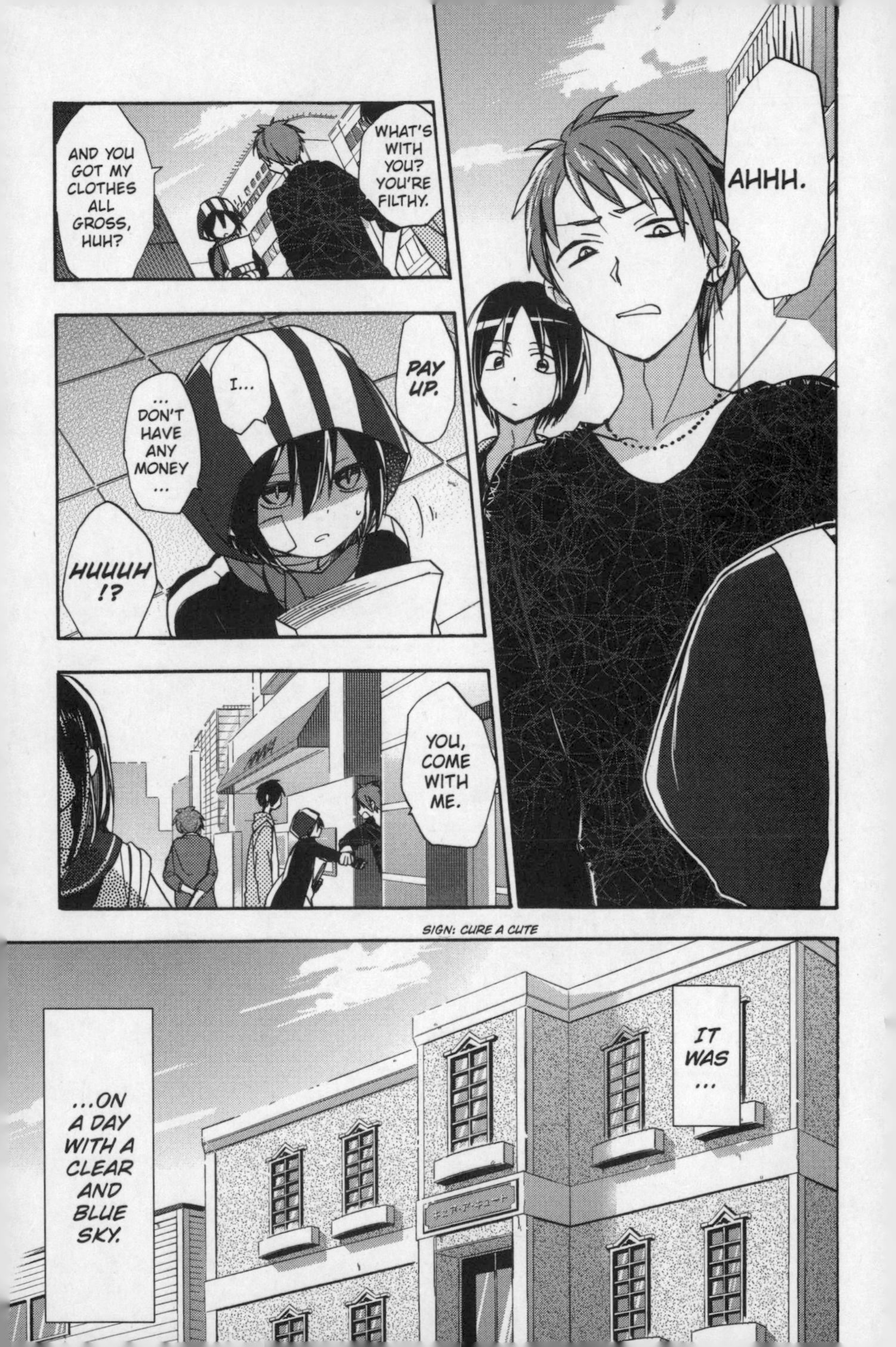
AHHH.
WHAT'S WITH YOU? YOU'RE FILTHY.
AND YOU GOT MY CLOTHES ALL GROSS, HUH?
PAY UP.
I...
...DON'T HAVE ANY MONEY...
HUUUH!?
YOU, COME WITH ME.
SIGN: CURE A CUTE
IT WAS...
...ON A DAY WITH A CLEAR AND BLUE SKY.

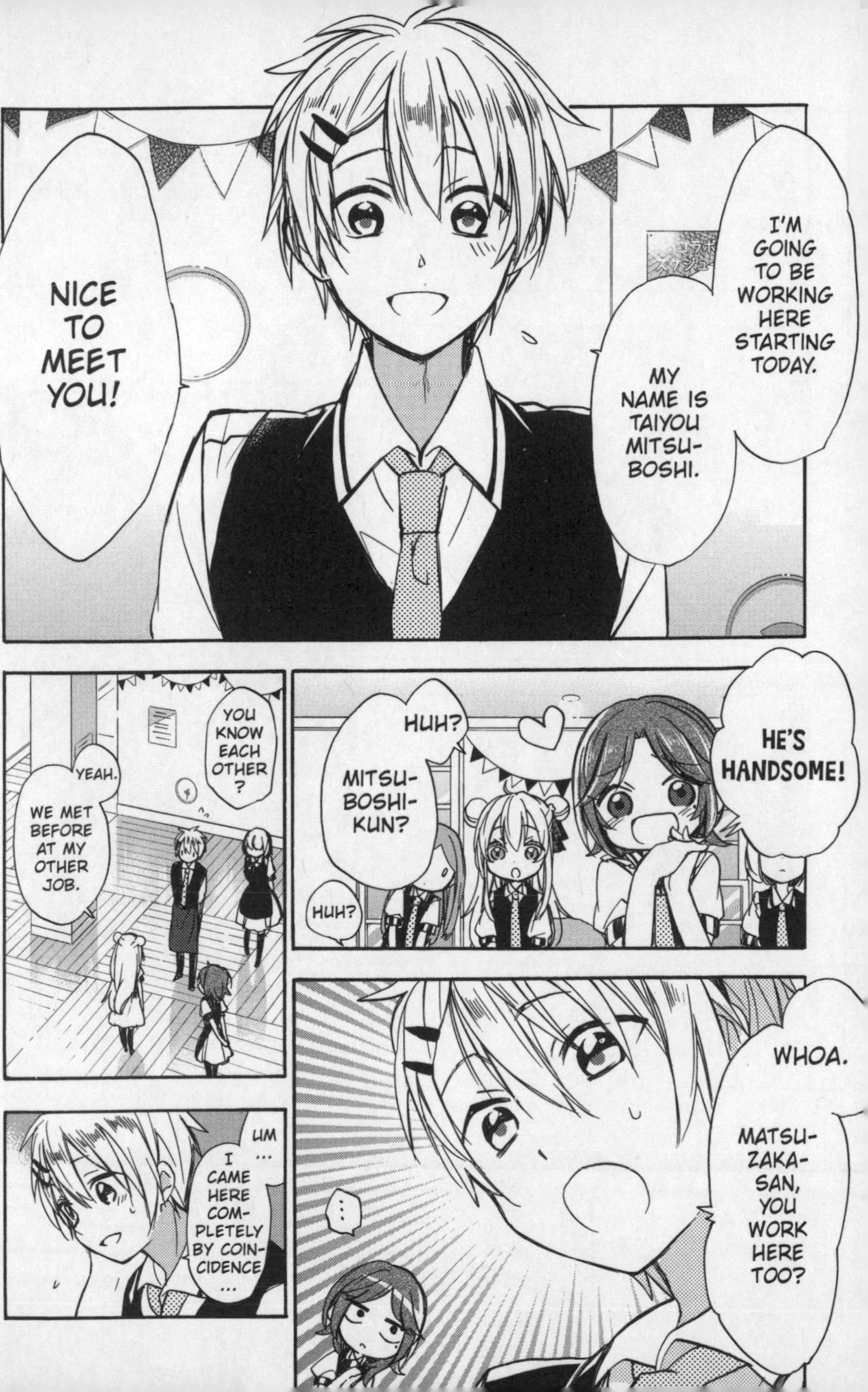
I'M GOING TO BE WORKING HERE STARTING TODAY.
MY NAME IS TAIYOU MITSU-BOSHI.
NICE TO MEET YOU!
HE'S HANDSOME!
HUH?
MITSU-BOSHI-KUN?
HUH?
YOU KNOW EACH OTHER?
YEAH.
WE MET BEFORE AT MY OTHER JOB.
WHOA.
MATSU-ZAKA-SAN, YOU WORK HERE TOO?
...
UM ... I CAME HERE COM-PLETELY BY COIN-CIDENCE ...

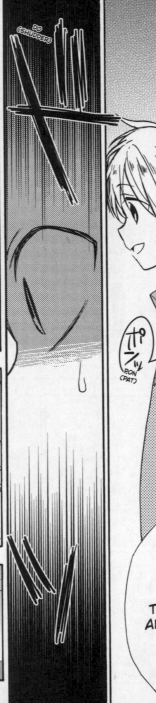

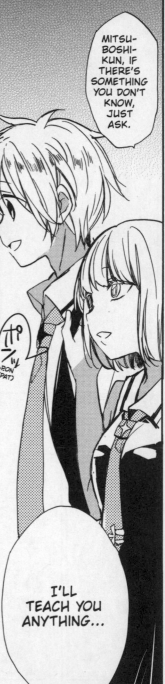

MITSU-BOSHI-KUN, IF THERE'S SOMETHING YOU DON'T KNOW, JUST ASK.

DO (SHUDDER)

PON (PAT)

I'LL TEACH YOU ANYTHING...

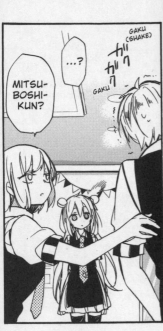

GAKU (SHAKE)

GAKU

...?

MITSU-BOSHI-KUN?

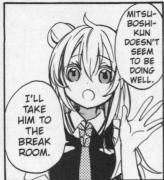

MITSU-BOSHI-KUN DOESN'T SEEM TO BE DOING WELL.

I'LL TAKE HIM TO THE BREAK ROOM.

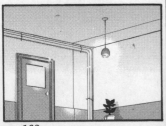

163

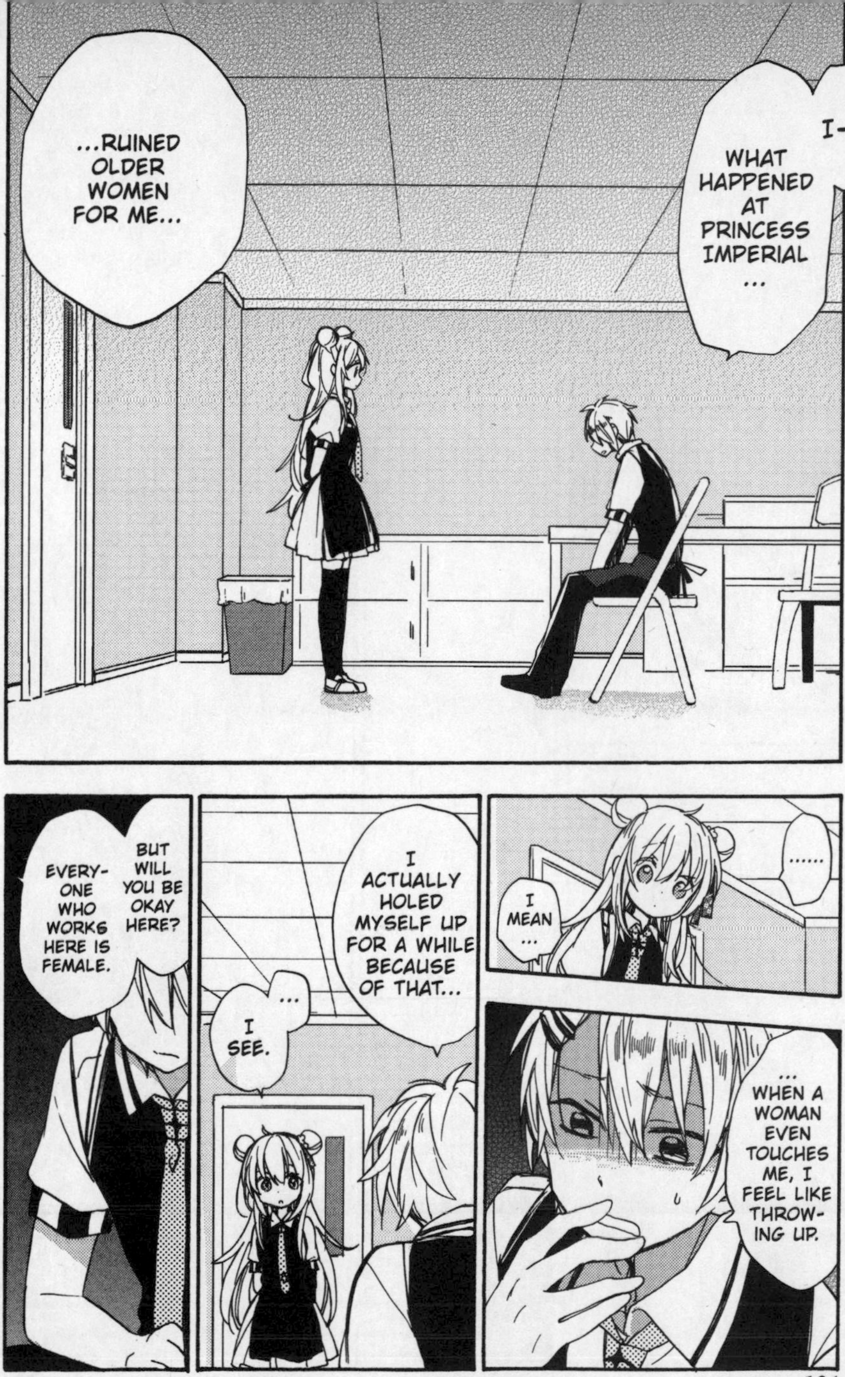
I—
WHAT HAPPENED AT PRINCESS IMPERIAL ...
...RUINED OLDER WOMEN FOR ME...
......
I MEAN ...
... WHEN A WOMAN EVEN TOUCHES ME, I FEEL LIKE THROWING UP.
I ACTUALLY HOLED MYSELF UP FOR A WHILE BECAUSE OF THAT...
... I SEE.
BUT WILL YOU BE OKAY HERE?
EVERYONE WHO WORKS HERE IS FEMALE.

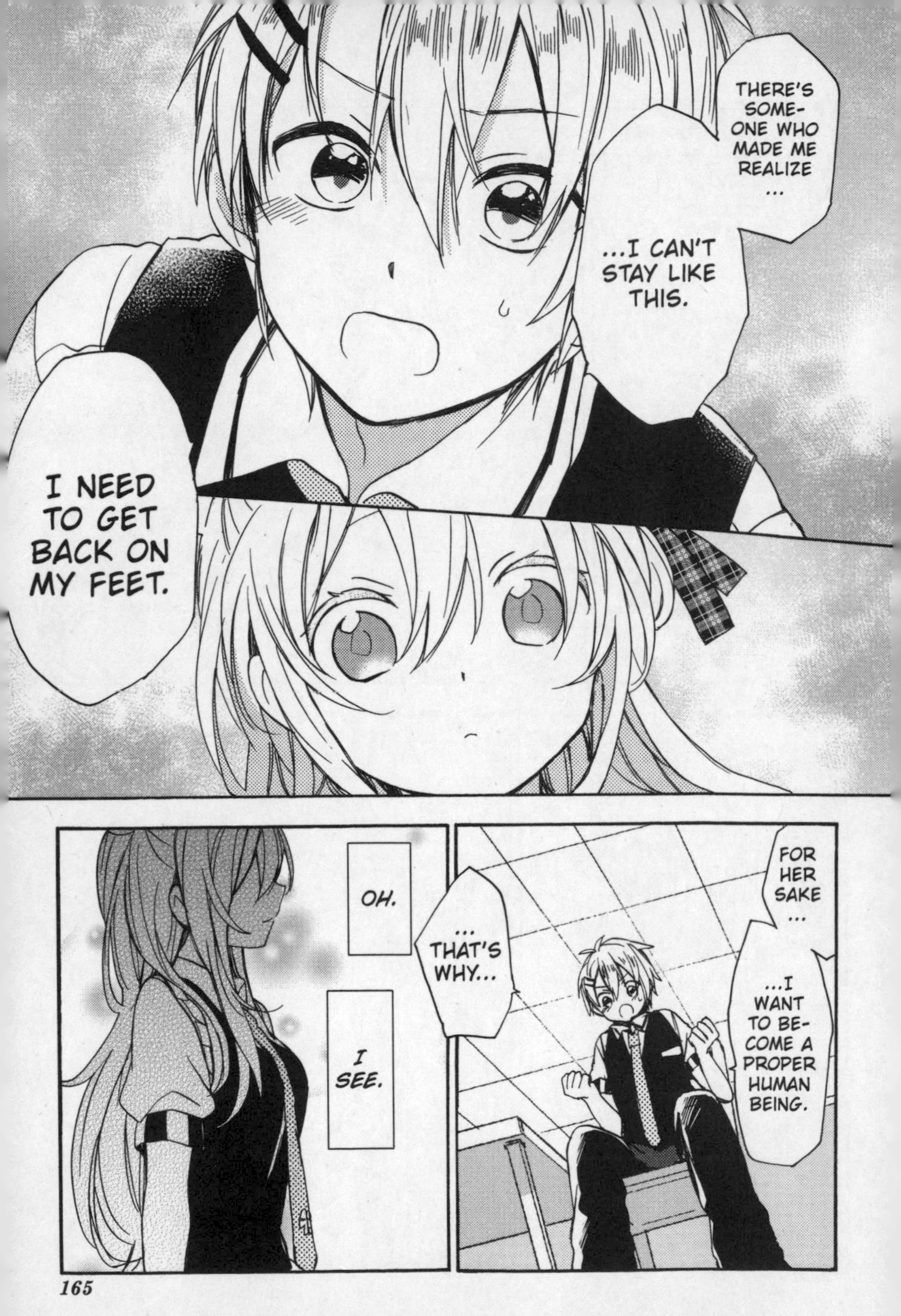
THERE'S SOME-ONE WHO MADE ME REALIZE ...
...I CAN'T STAY LIKE THIS.
I NEED TO GET BACK ON MY FEET.
FOR HER SAKE ...
...I WANT TO BE-COME A PROPER HUMAN BEING.
... THAT'S WHY...
OH.
I SEE.

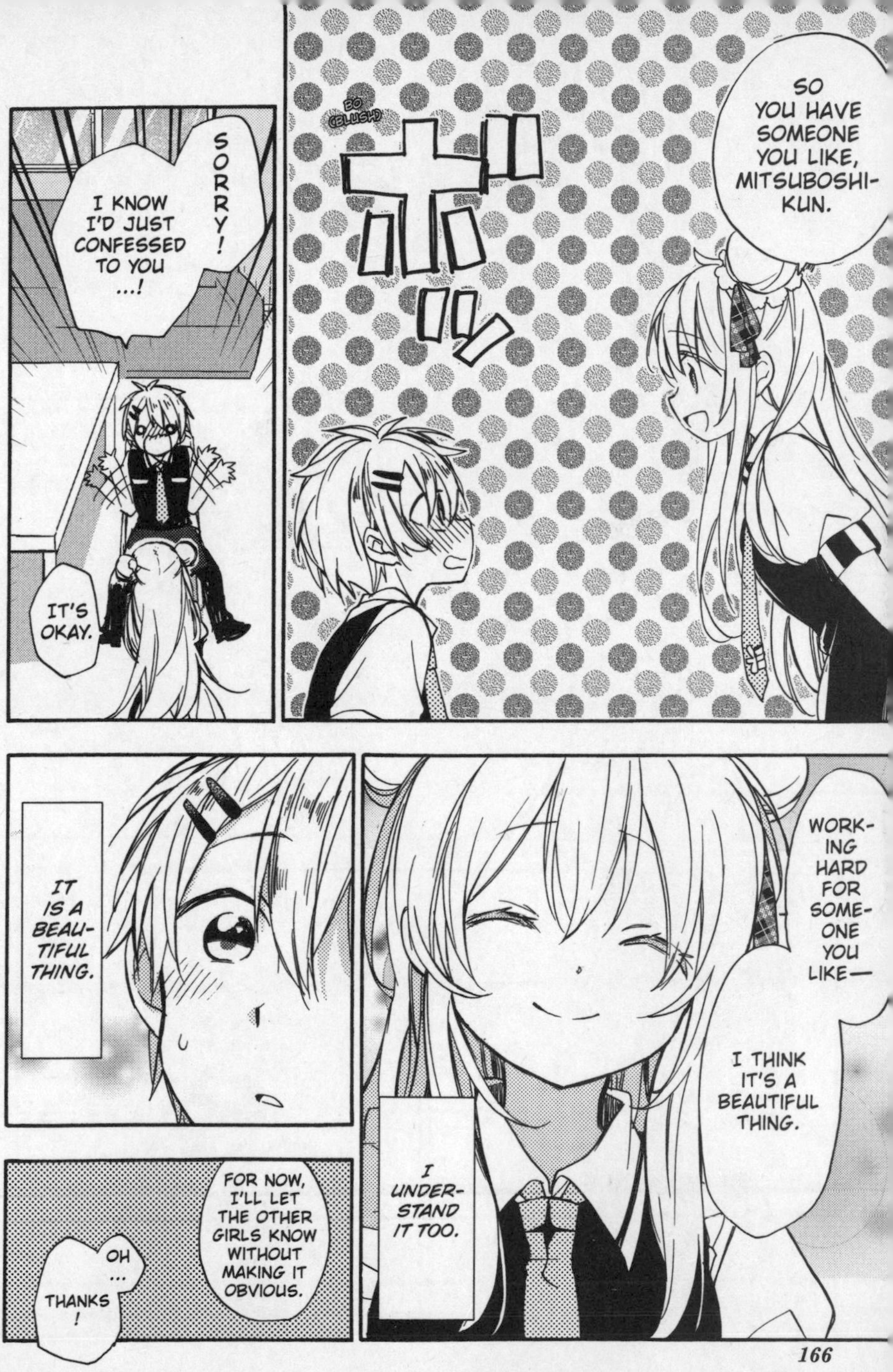
SO YOU HAVE SOMEONE YOU LIKE, MITSUBOSHI-KUN.
BO (BLUSH)
SORRY!
I KNOW I'D JUST CONFESSED TO YOU ...!
IT'S OKAY.
WORKING HARD FOR SOMEONE YOU LIKE—
I THINK IT'S A BEAUTIFUL THING.
I UNDERSTAND IT TOO.
IT IS A BEAUTIFUL THING.
FOR NOW, I'LL LET THE OTHER GIRLS KNOW WITHOUT MAKING IT OBVIOUS.
OH ... THANKS!

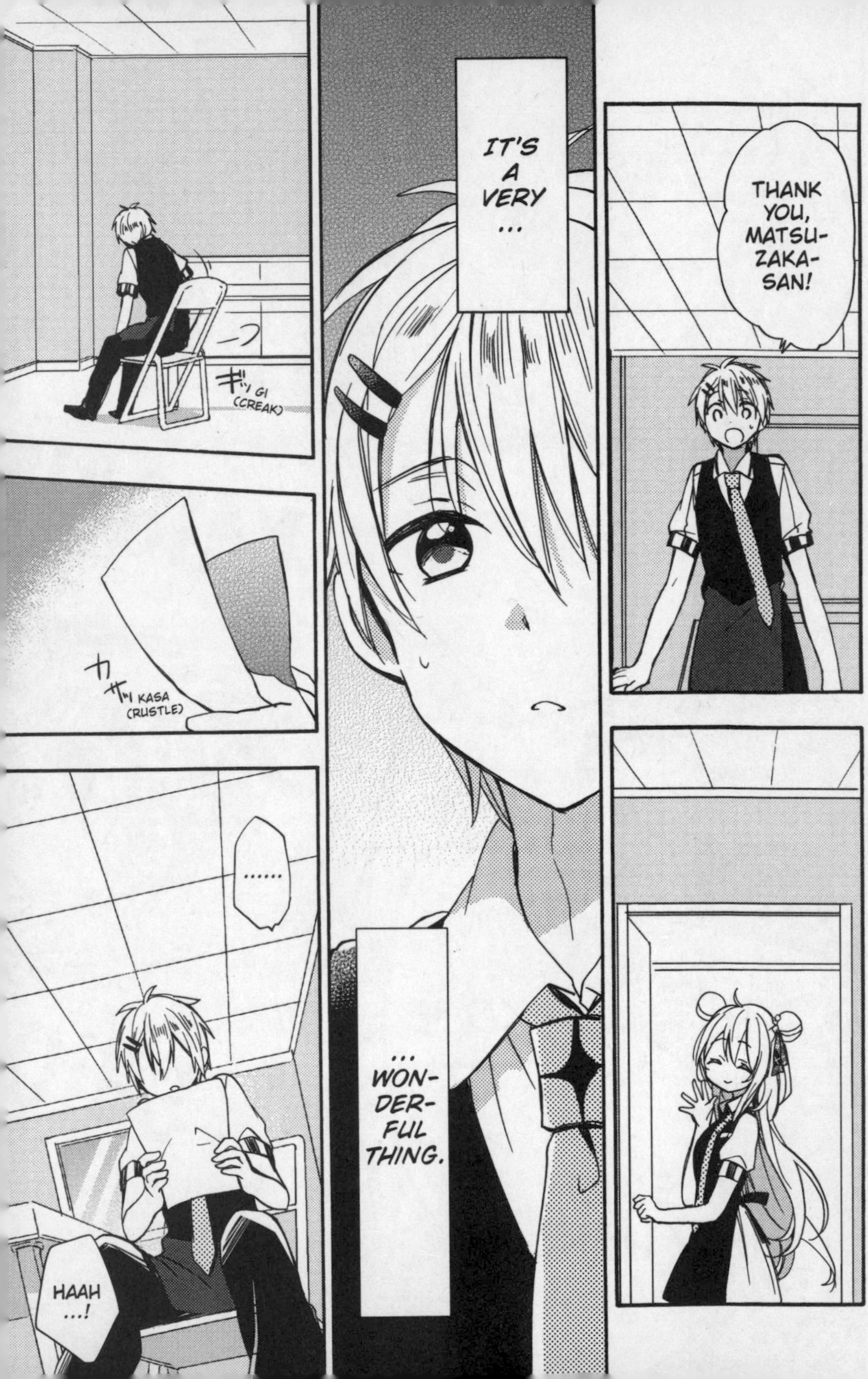
THANK YOU, MATSU-ZAKA-SAN!
IT'S A VERY ...
... WON-DER-FUL THING.
ギッ GI (CREAK)
カサッ KASA (RUSTLE)
......
HAAH ...!

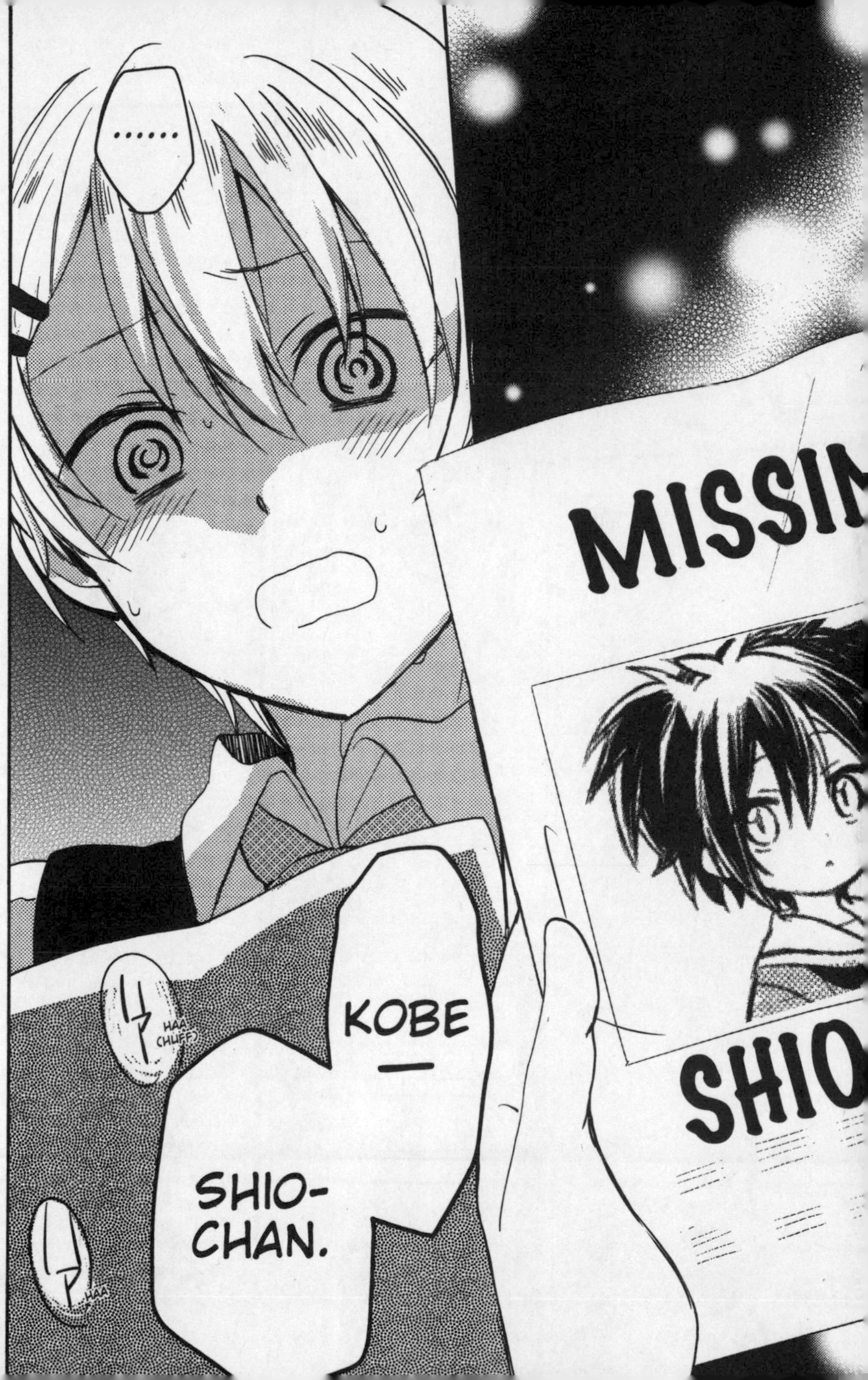
MISSIN
SHIO
......
KOBE —
SHIO-CHAN.
HAA (CHUFF)
HAA

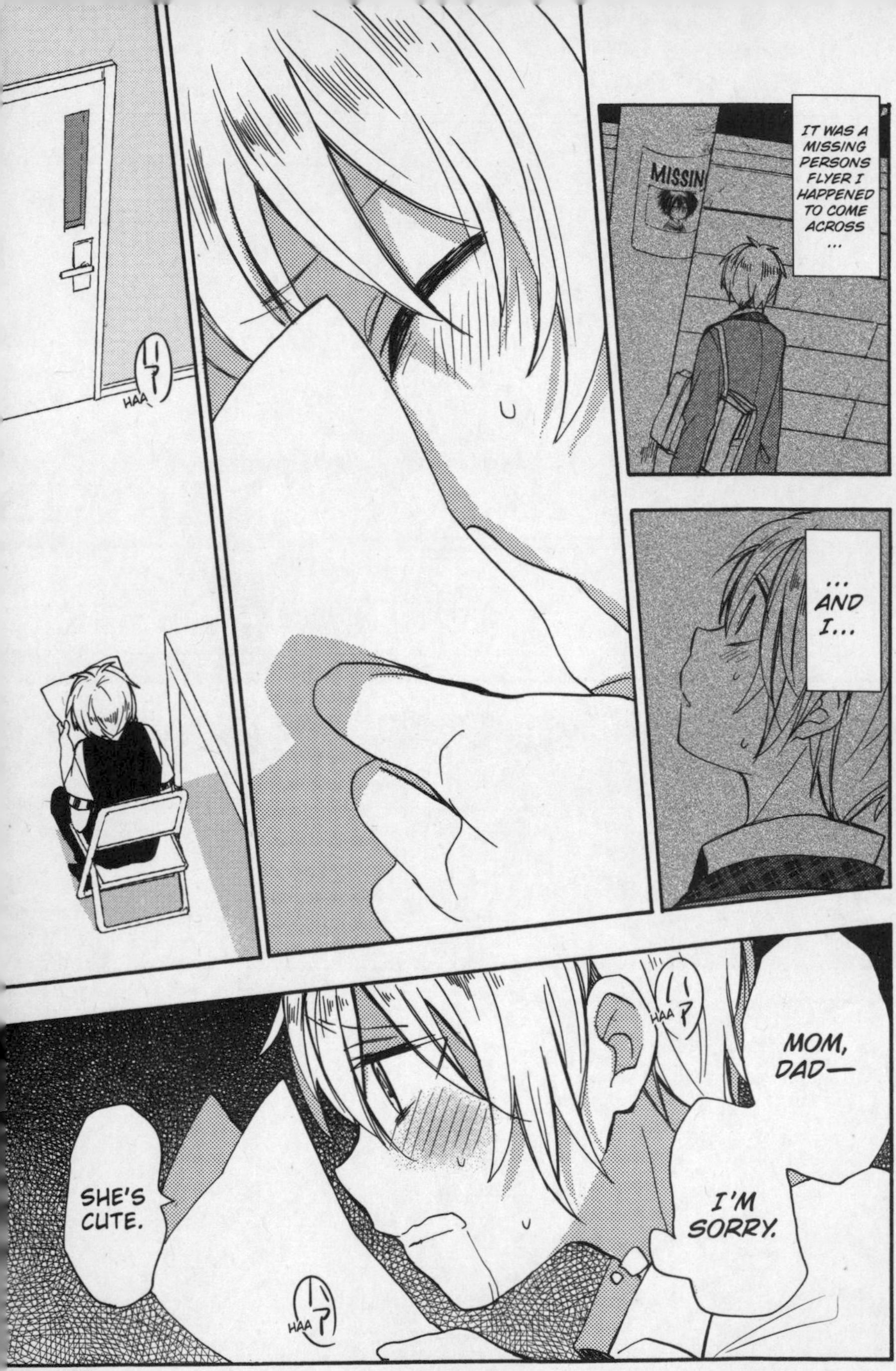
IT WAS A MISSING PERSONS FLYER I HAPPENED TO COME ACROSS ...
MISSIN
... AND I...
HAA
HAA
MOM, DAD—
I'M SORRY.
SHE'S CUTE.
HAA

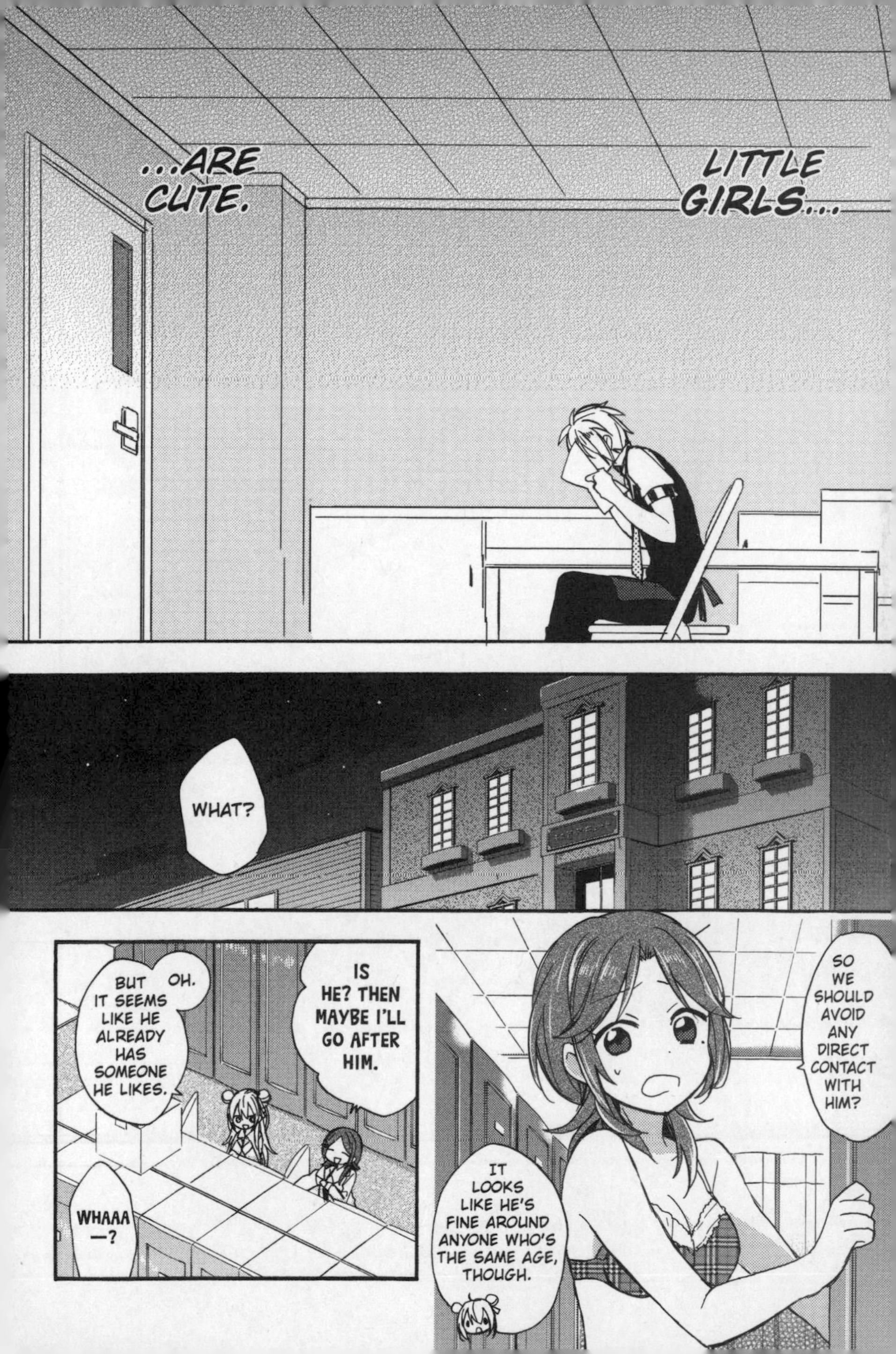
LITTLE GIRLS...
...ARE CUTE.
WHAT?
SO WE SHOULD AVOID ANY DIRECT CONTACT WITH HIM?
IT LOOKS LIKE HE'S FINE AROUND ANYONE WHO'S THE SAME AGE, THOUGH.
IS HE? THEN MAYBE I'LL GO AFTER HIM.
OH.
BUT IT SEEMS LIKE HE ALREADY HAS SOMEONE HE LIKES.
WHAAA—?

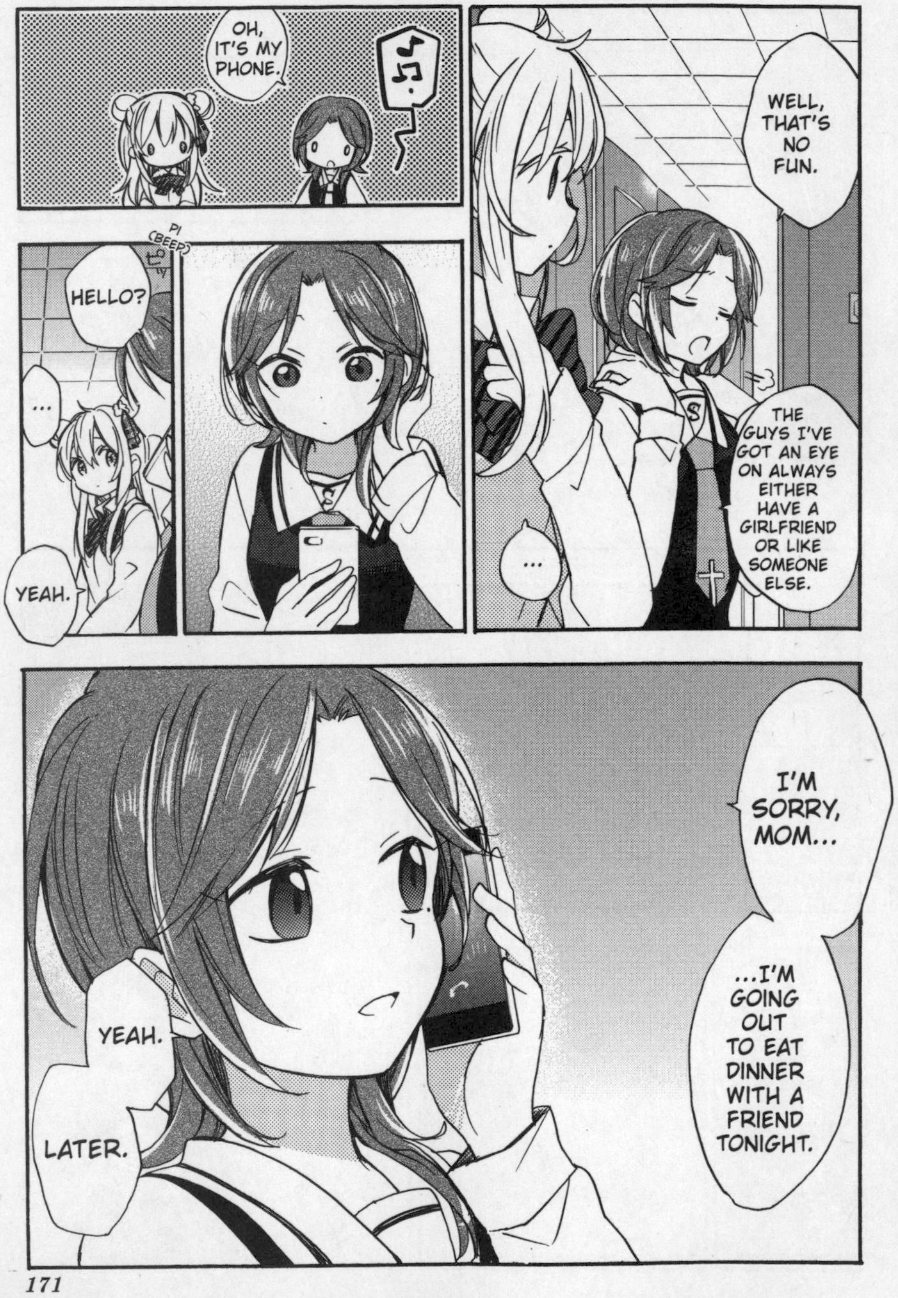
WELL, THAT'S NO FUN.
THE GUYS I'VE GOT AN EYE ON ALWAYS EITHER HAVE A GIRLFRIEND OR LIKE SOMEONE ELSE.
...
♫♫
OH, IT'S MY PHONE.
PI (BEEP)
HELLO?
...
YEAH.
I'M SORRY, MOM...
...I'M GOING OUT TO EAT DINNER WITH A FRIEND TONIGHT.
YEAH.
LATER.

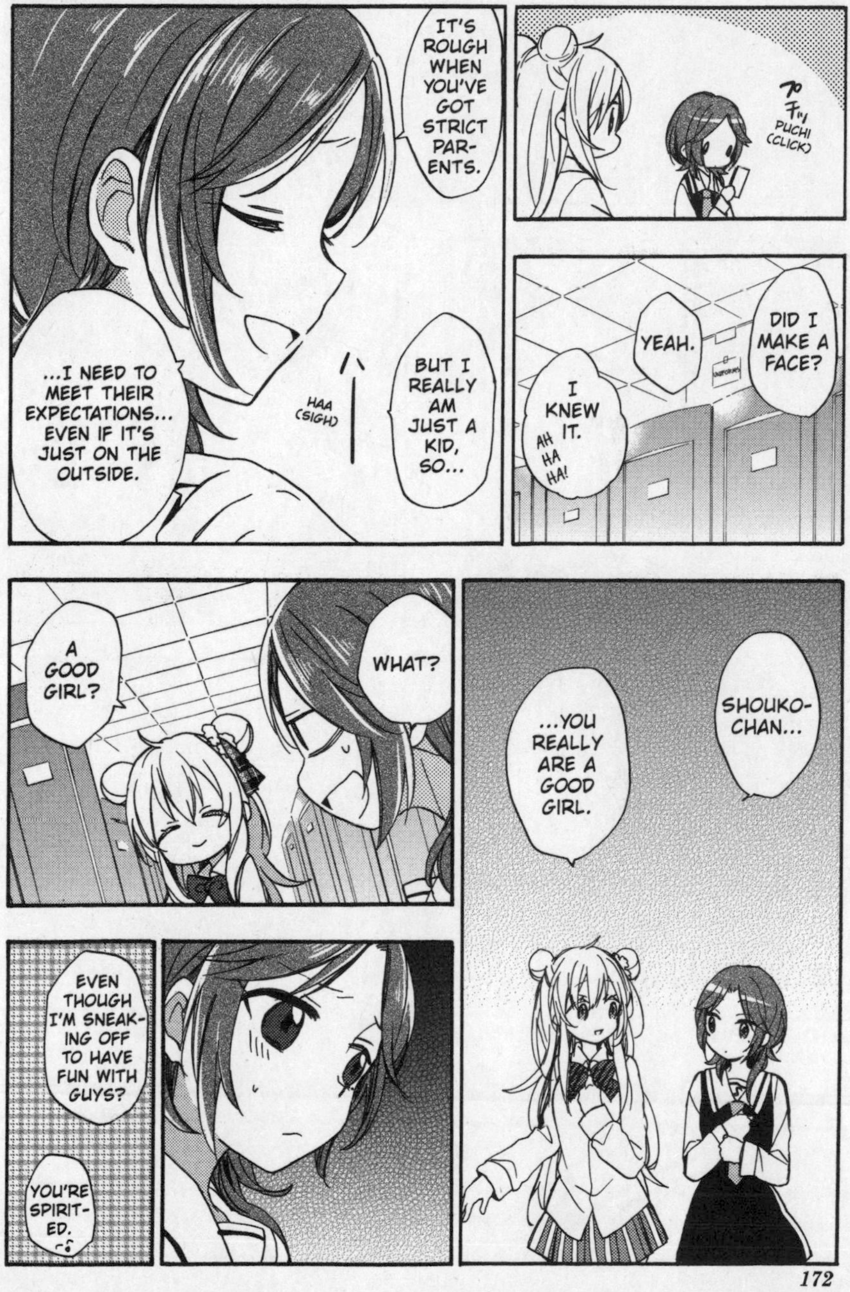
プチッ
PUCHI (CLICK)
DID I MAKE A FACE?
YEAH.
UNIFORMS
I KNEW IT.
AH HA HA!
IT'S ROUGH WHEN YOU'VE GOT STRICT PAR-ENTS.
BUT I REALLY AM JUST A KID, SO...
HAA (SIGH)
...I NEED TO MEET THEIR EXPECTATIONS... EVEN IF IT'S JUST ON THE OUTSIDE.
SHOUKO-CHAN...
...YOU REALLY ARE A GOOD GIRL.
WHAT?
A GOOD GIRL?
EVEN THOUGH I'M SNEAK-ING OFF TO HAVE FUN WITH GUYS?
YOU'RE SPIRIT-ED.

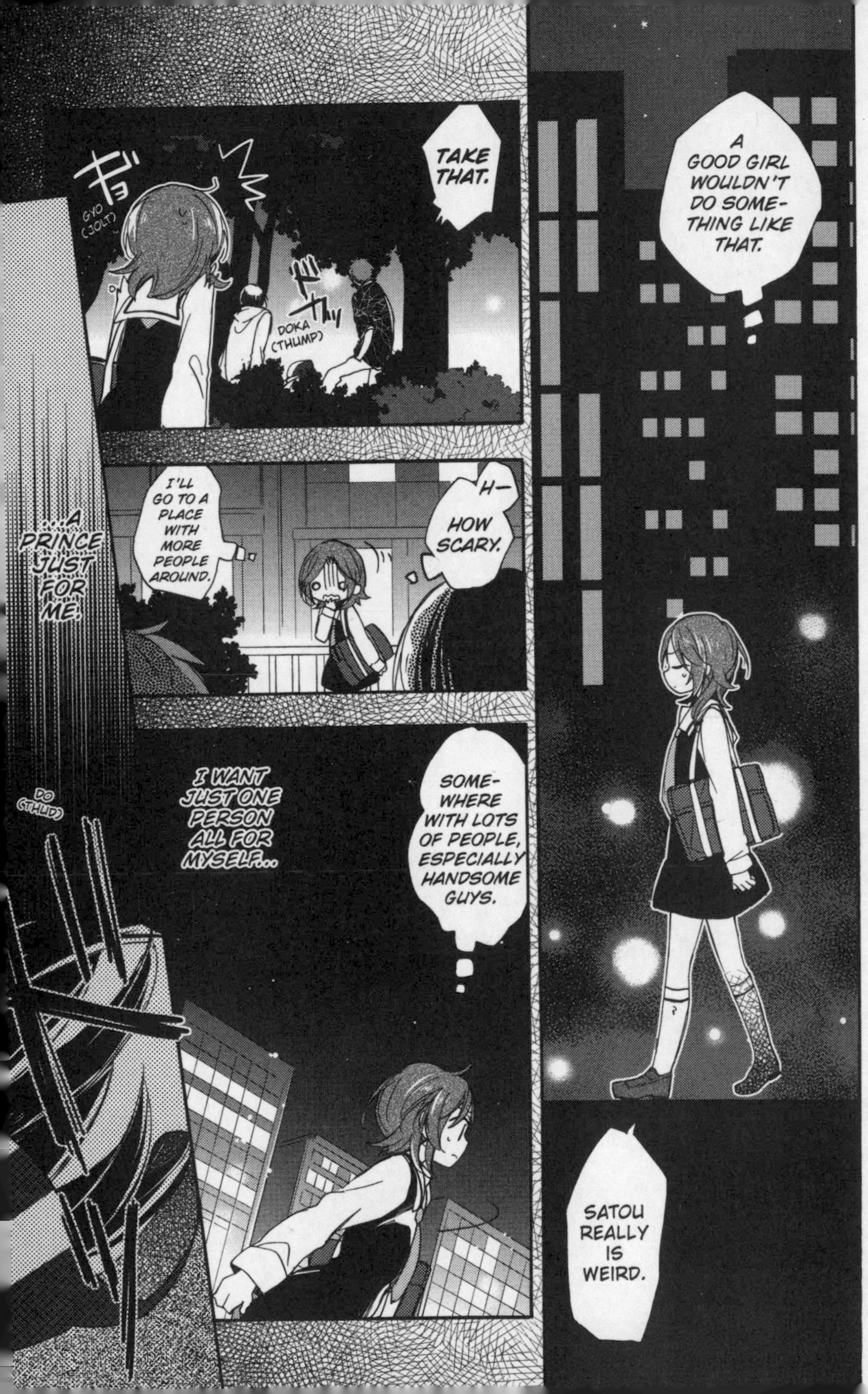
A GOOD GIRL WOULDN'T DO SOMETHING LIKE THAT.
SATOU REALLY IS WEIRD.
TAKE THAT.
DOKA (THUMP)
GYO (JOLT)
H— HOW SCARY.
I'LL GO TO A PLACE WITH MORE PEOPLE AROUND.
SOME-WHERE WITH LOTS OF PEOPLE, ESPECIALLY HANDSOME GUYS.
I WANT JUST ONE PERSON ALL FOR MYSELF...
...A PRINCE JUST FOR ME.
DO (THUD)

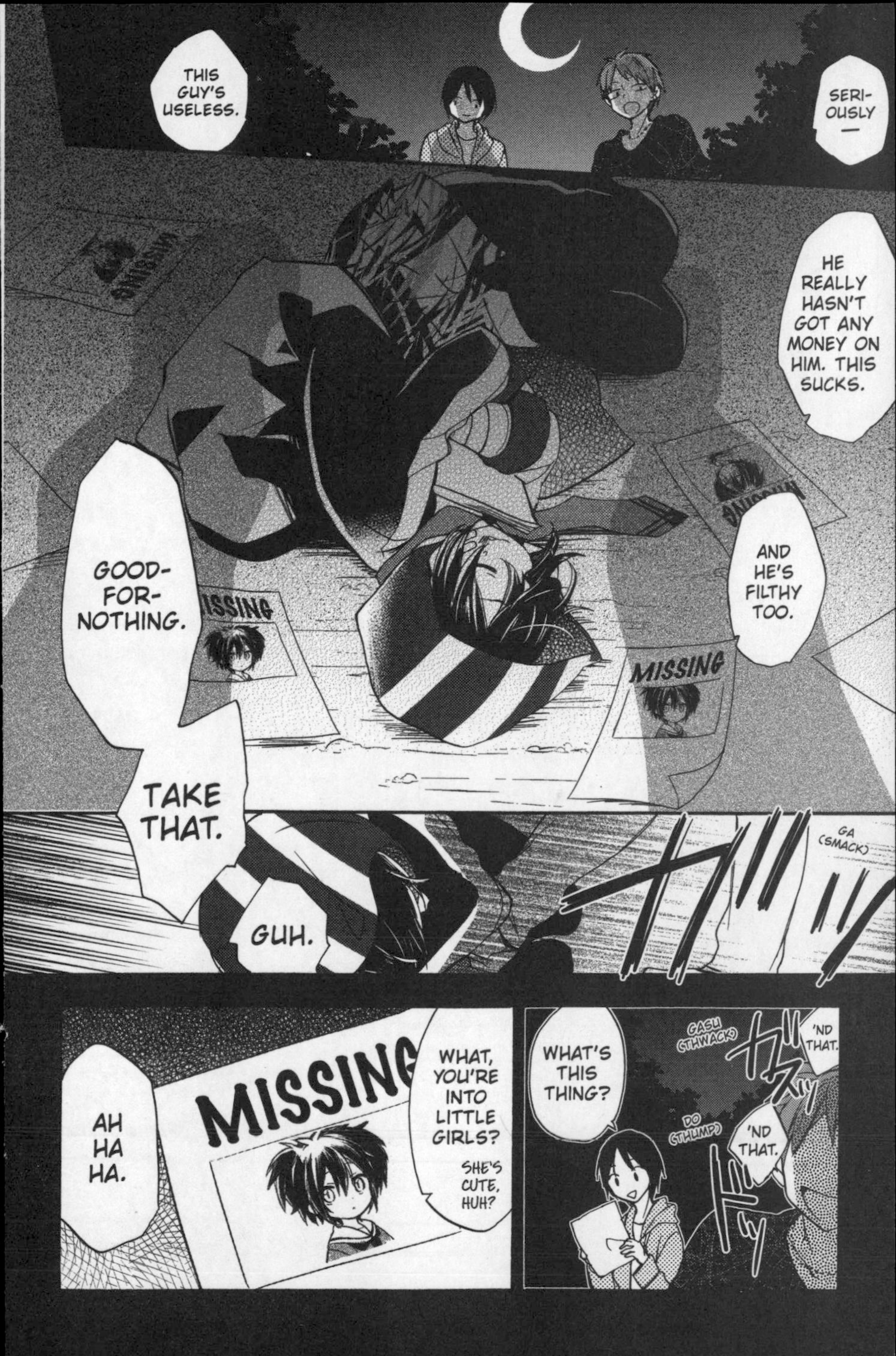
SERI-OUSLY —
THIS GUY'S USELESS.
HE REALLY HASN'T GOT ANY MONEY ON HIM. THIS SUCKS.
MISSING
MISSING
AND HE'S FILTHY TOO.
MISSING
MISSING
GOOD-FOR-NOTHING.
GA (SMACK)
TAKE THAT.
GUH.
GASU (THWACK)
'ND THAT.
DO (THUMP)
'ND THAT.
WHAT'S THIS THING?
WHAT, YOU'RE INTO LITTLE GIRLS?
SHE'S CUTE, HUH?
MISSING
AH HA HA.

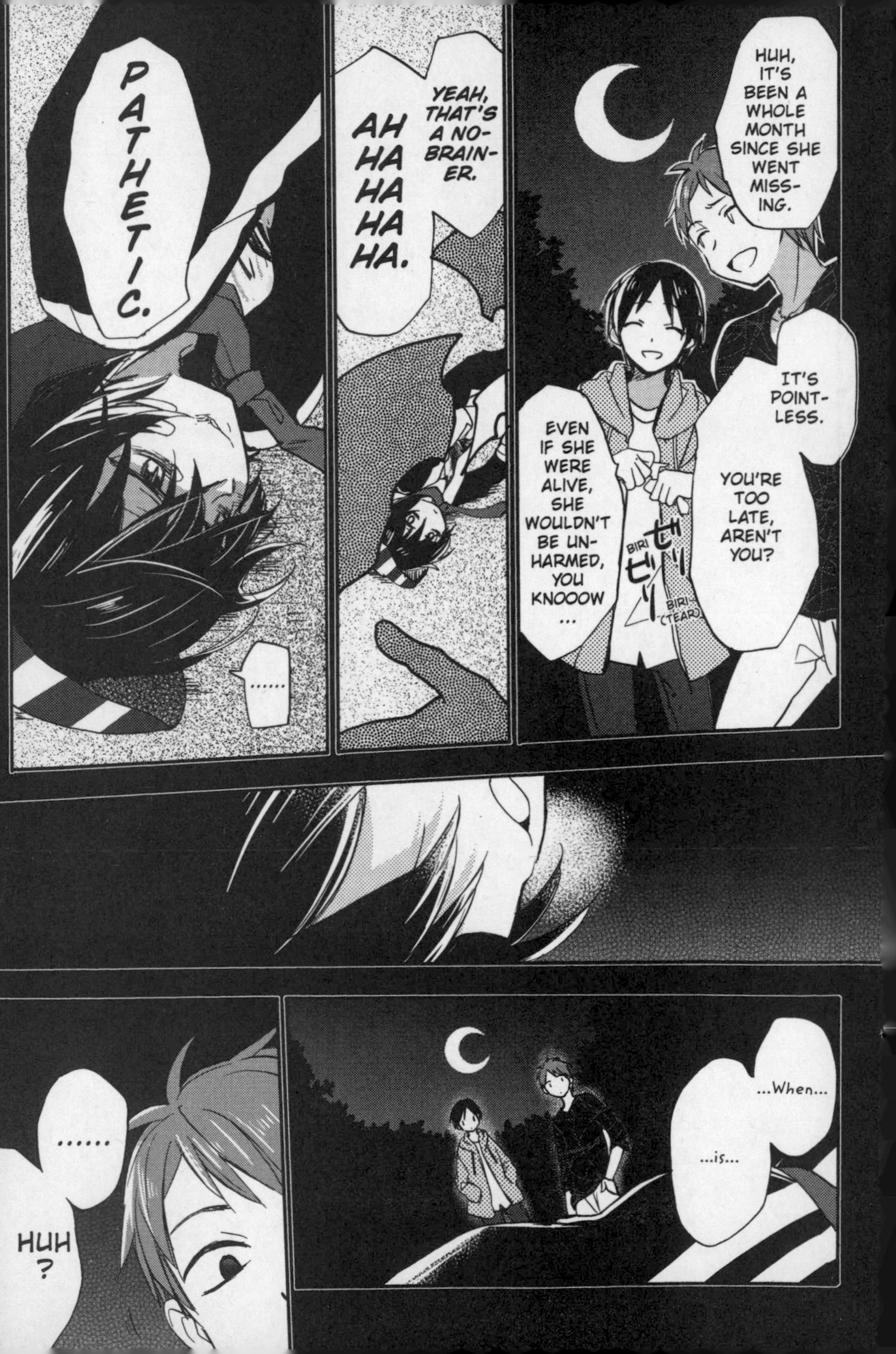
HUH, IT'S BEEN A WHOLE MONTH SINCE SHE WENT MISSING.
IT'S POINTLESS.
YOU'RE TOO LATE, AREN'T YOU?
EVEN IF SHE WERE ALIVE, SHE WOULDN'T BE UNHARMED, YOU KNOOOW...
BIRI BIRI (TEAR)
YEAH, THAT'S A NO-BRAINER.
AH HA HA HA HA HA.
PATHETIC.
......
...When...
...is...
......
HUH?

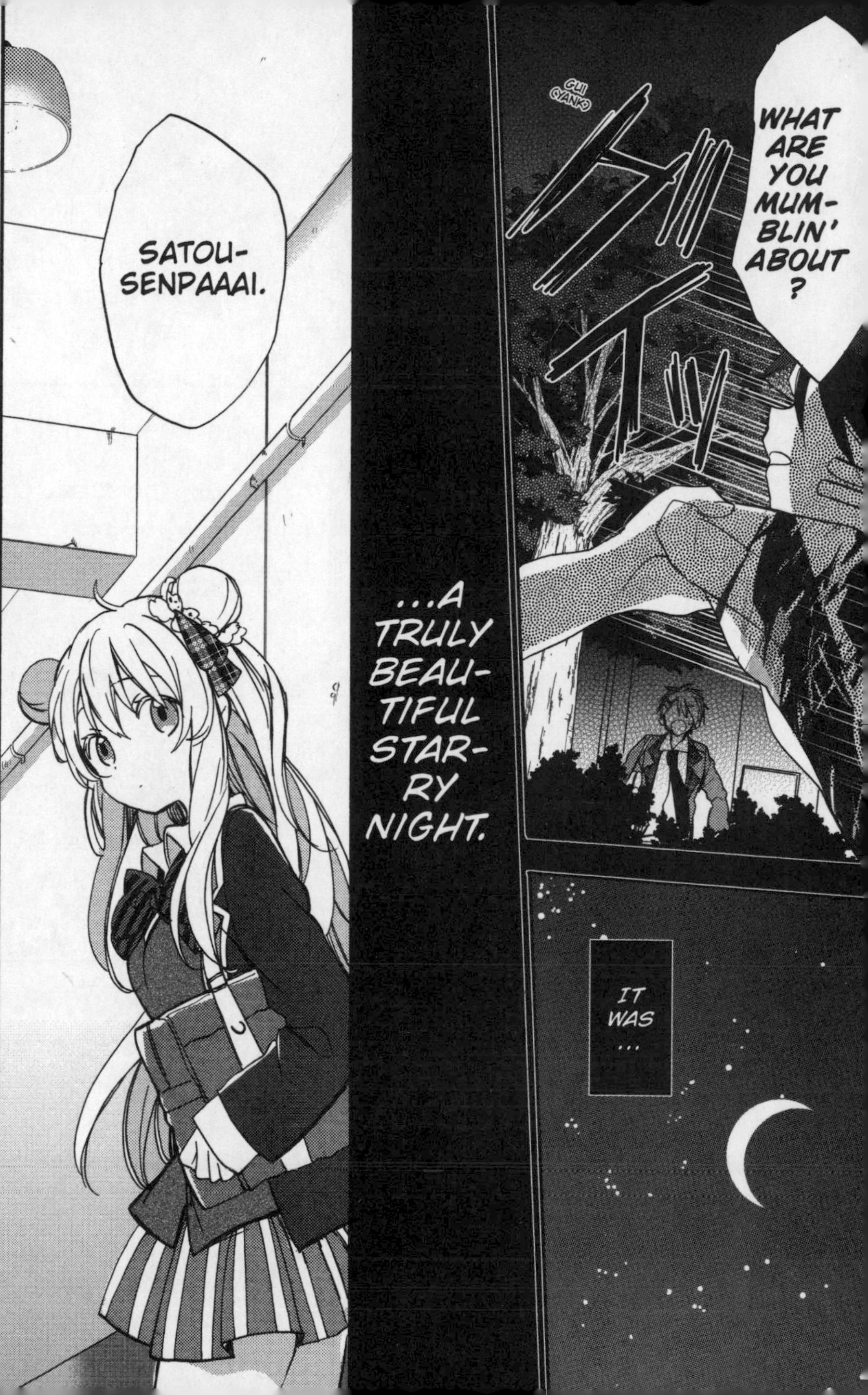
GUI (YANK)
WHAT ARE YOU MUM-BLIN' ABOUT?
IT WAS...
...A TRULY BEAU-TIFUL STAR-RY NIGHT.
SATOU-SENPAAAI.

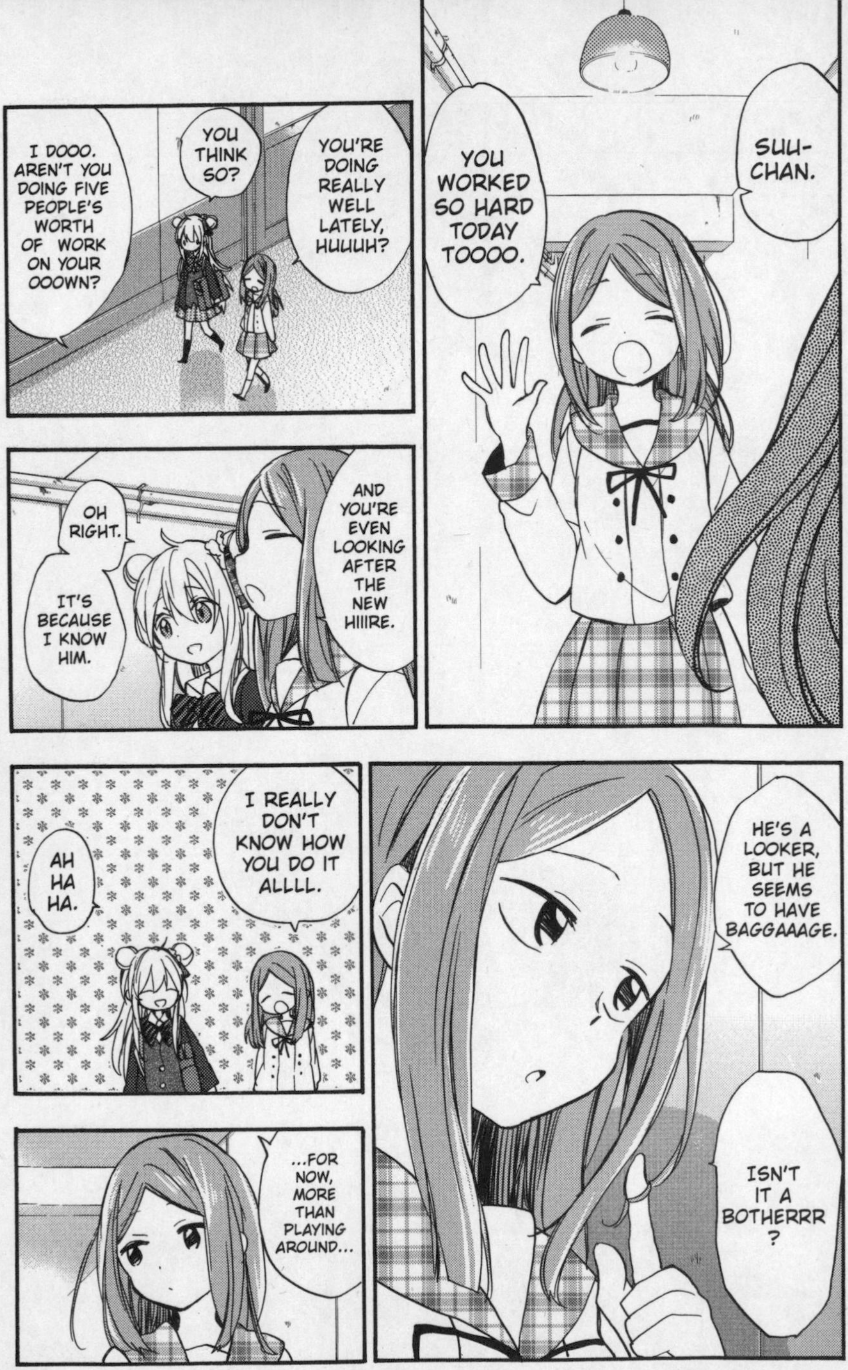
SUU-CHAN.
YOU WORKED SO HARD TODAY TOOOO.
YOU'RE DOING REALLY WELL LATELY, HUUUH?
YOU THINK SO?
I DOOO. AREN'T YOU DOING FIVE PEOPLE'S WORTH OF WORK ON YOUR OOOWN?
AND YOU'RE EVEN LOOKING AFTER THE NEW HIIIRE.
OH RIGHT.
IT'S BECAUSE I KNOW HIM.
HE'S A LOOKER, BUT HE SEEMS TO HAVE BAGGAAAGE.
ISN'T IT A BOTHERRR?
I REALLY DON'T KNOW HOW YOU DO IT ALLLL.
AH HA HA.
...FOR NOW, MORE THAN PLAYING AROUND...

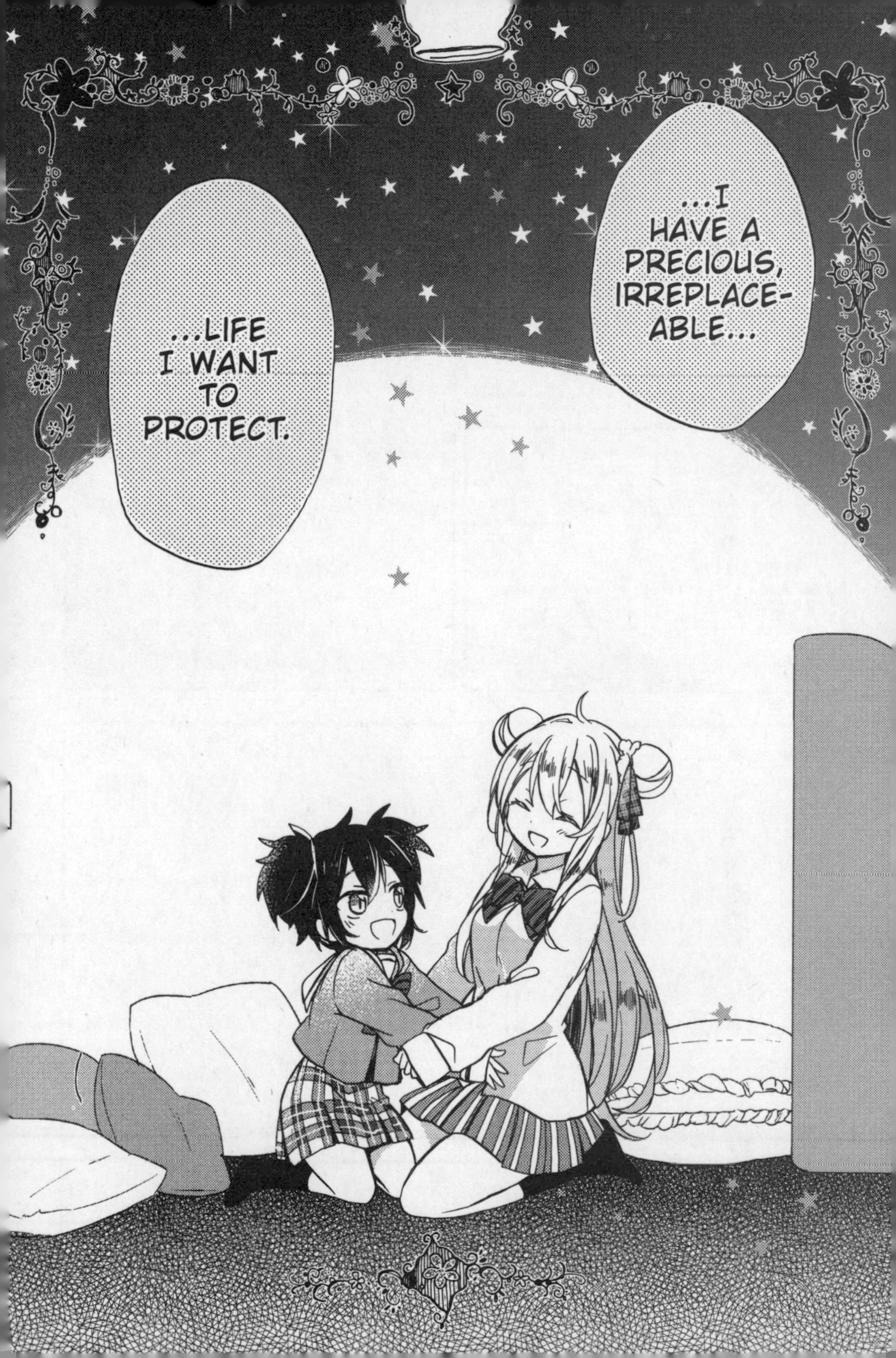
...I HAVE A PRECIOUS, IRREPLACE-ABLE...
...LIFE I WANT TO PROTECT.

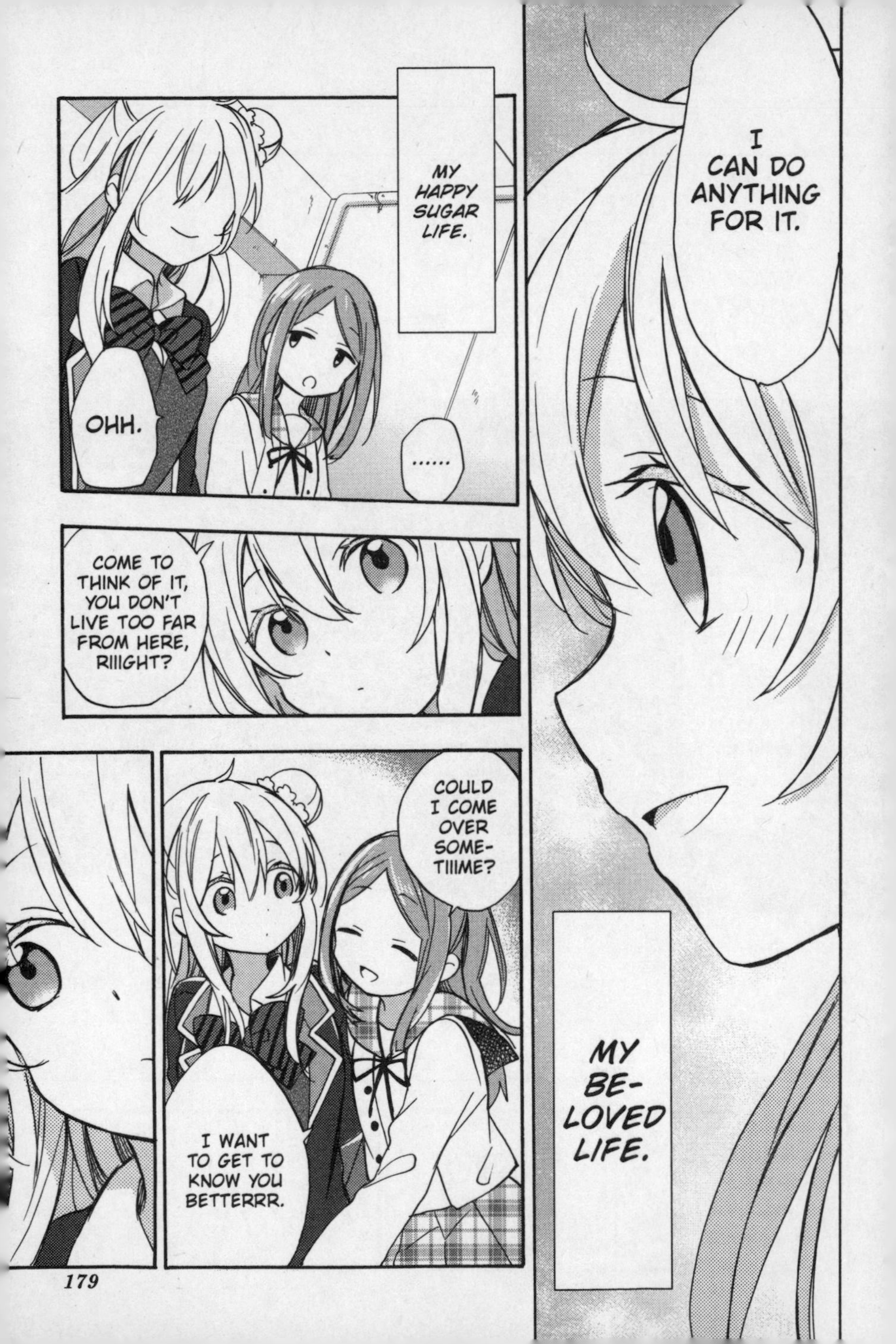
I CAN DO ANYTHING FOR IT.
MY BE-LOVED LIFE.
MY HAPPY SUGAR LIFE.
......
OHH.
COME TO THINK OF IT, YOU DON'T LIVE TOO FAR FROM HERE, RIIIGHT?
COULD I COME OVER SOME-TIIIME?
I WANT TO GET TO KNOW YOU BETTERRR.

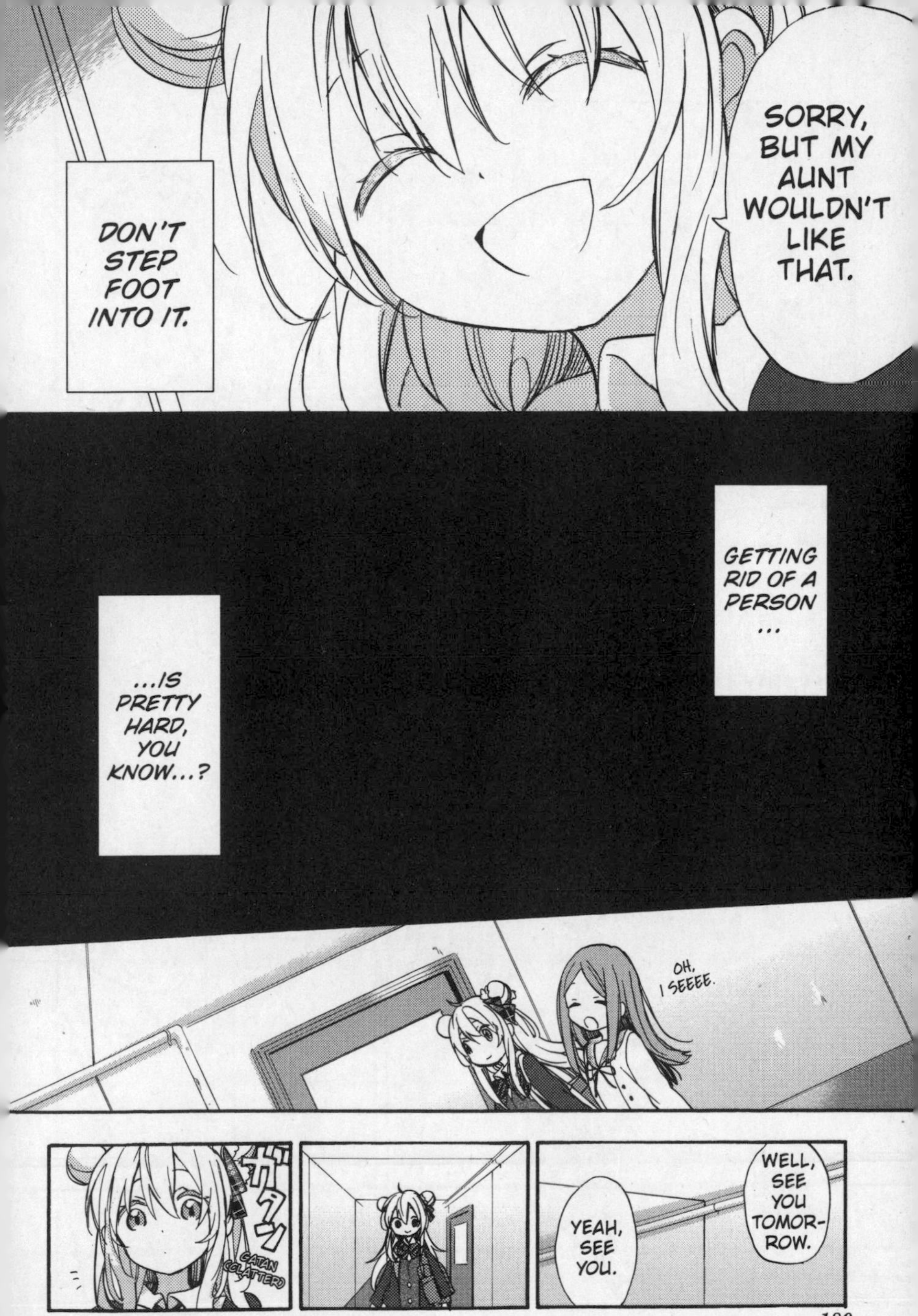
SORRY, BUT MY AUNT WOULDN'T LIKE THAT.
DON'T STEP FOOT INTO IT.
GETTING RID OF A PERSON ...
...IS PRETTY HARD, YOU KNOW...?
OH, I SEEEE.
WELL, SEE YOU TOMOR-ROW.
YEAH, SEE YOU.
GATAN (CLATTER)

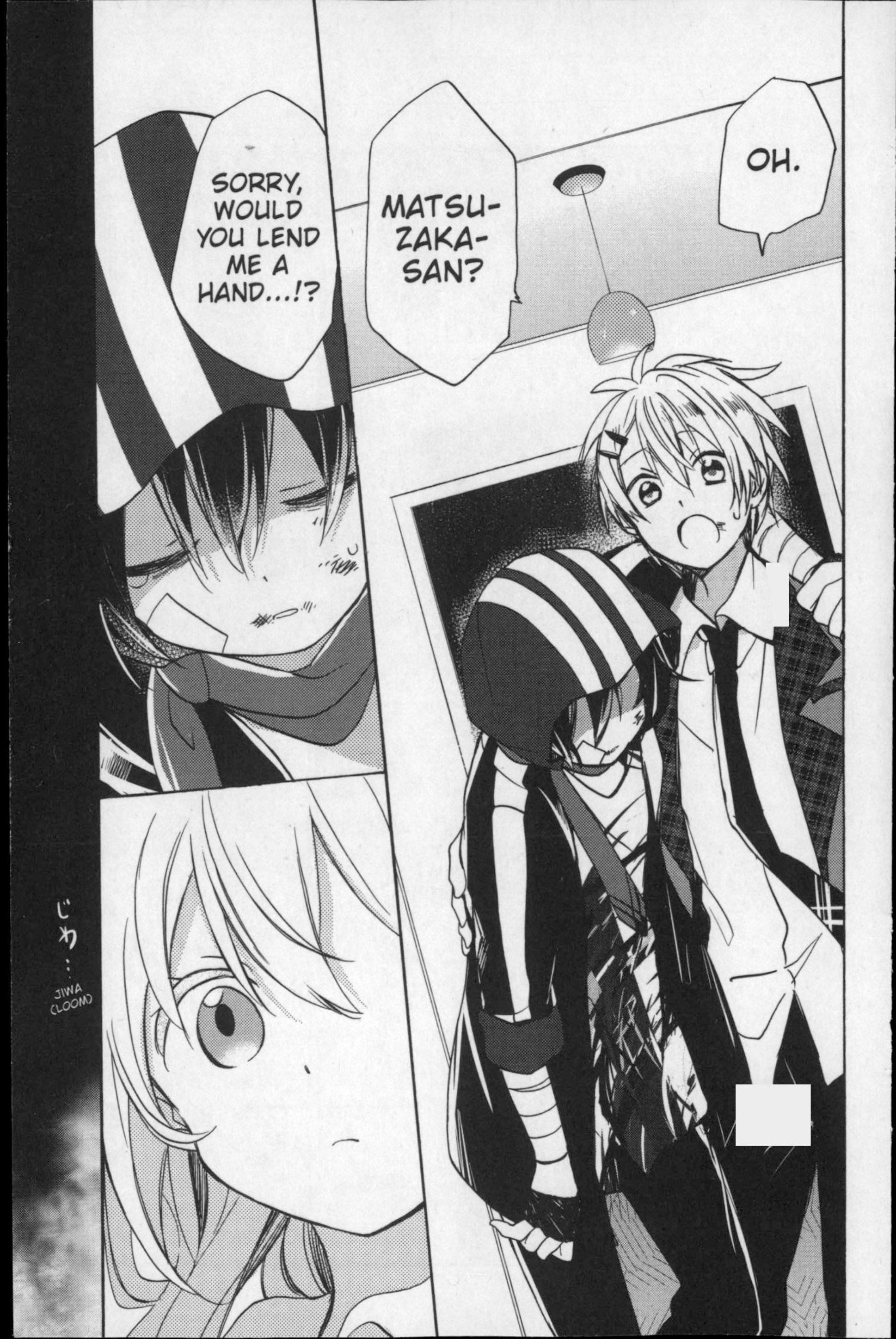
OH.
MATSU-ZAKA-SAN?
SORRY, WOULD YOU LEND ME A HAND...!?
じわ…
JIWA (LOOM)

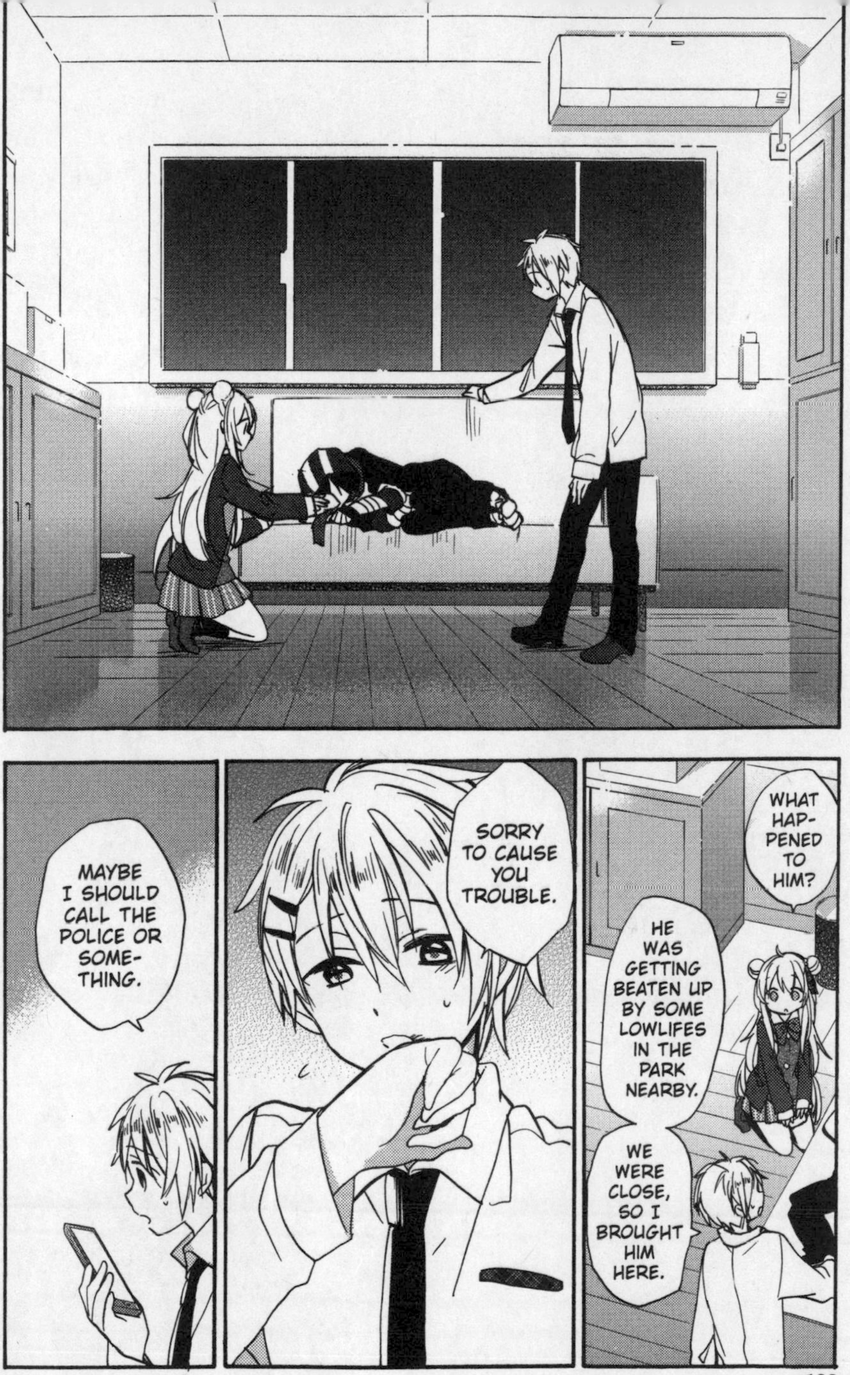
WHAT HAPPENED TO HIM?
HE WAS GETTING BEATEN UP BY SOME LOWLIFES IN THE PARK NEARBY.
WE WERE CLOSE, SO I BROUGHT HIM HERE.
SORRY TO CAUSE YOU TROUBLE.
MAYBE I SHOULD CALL THE POLICE OR SOMETHING.

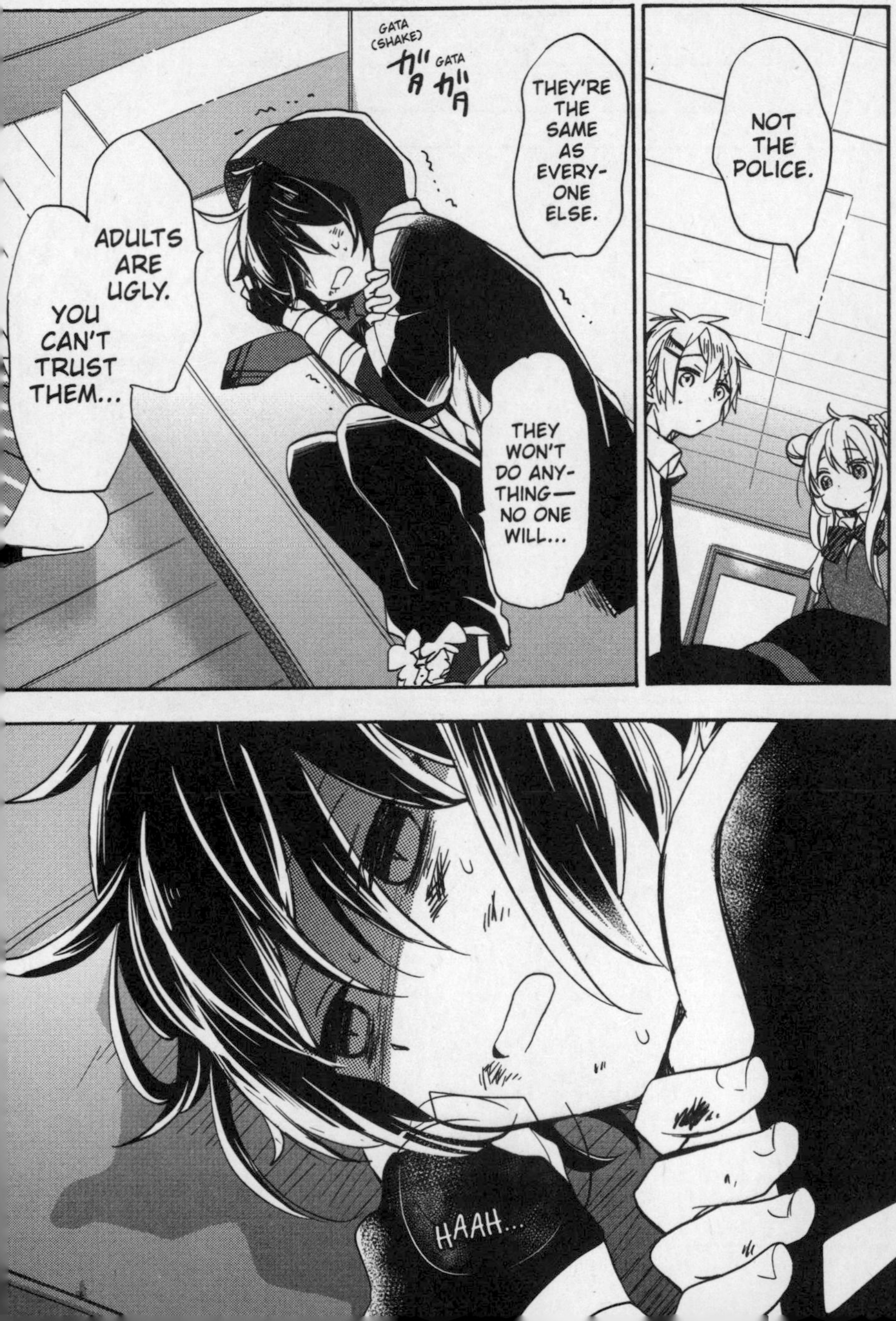
NOT THE POLICE.
GATA (SHAKE)
GATA
THEY'RE THE SAME AS EVERY-ONE ELSE.
ADULTS ARE UGLY.
YOU CAN'T TRUST THEM...
THEY WON'T DO ANY-THING— NO ONE WILL...
HAAH...

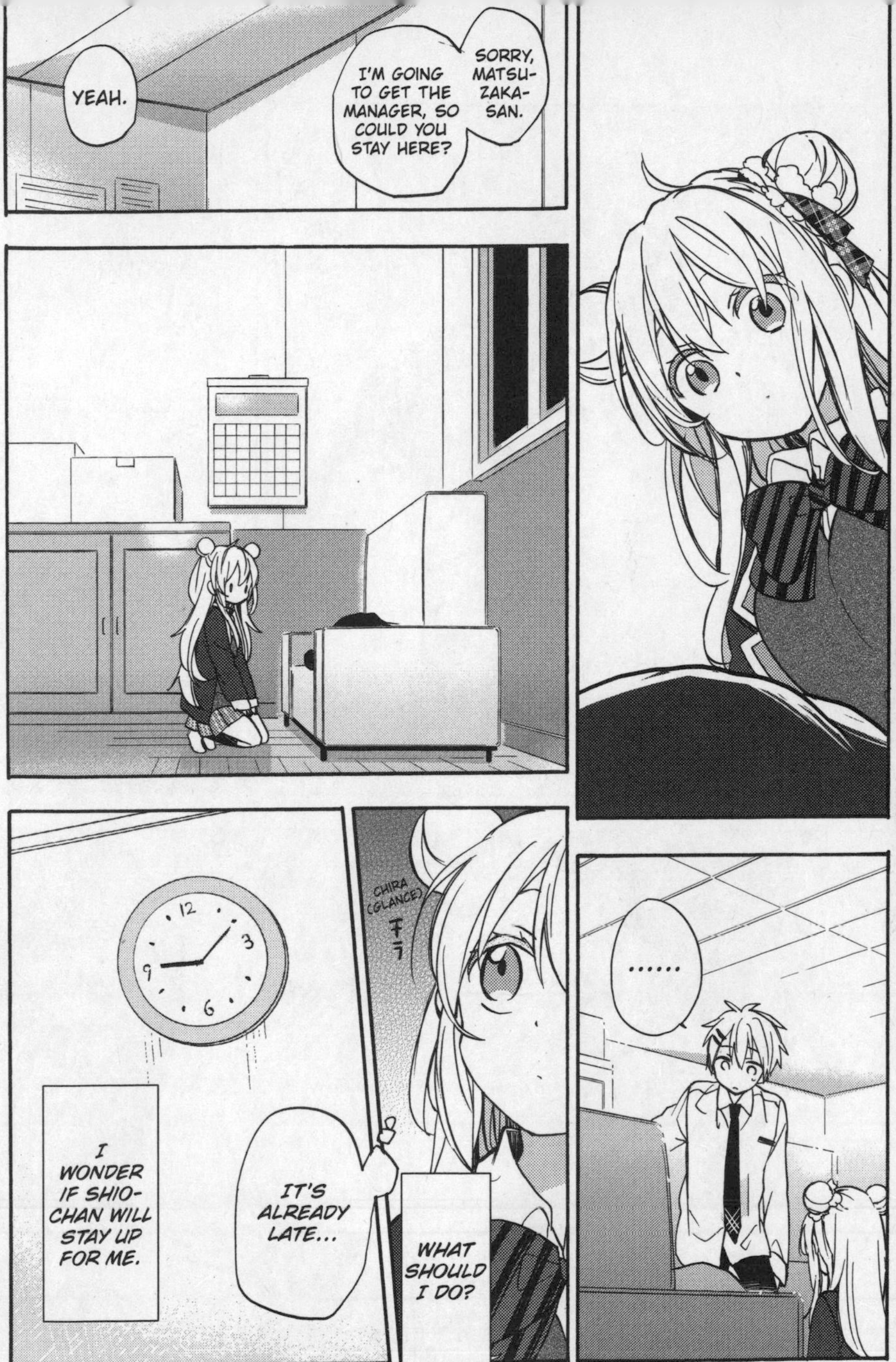
SORRY, MATSU-ZAKA-SAN.
I'M GOING TO GET THE MANAGER, SO COULD YOU STAY HERE?
YEAH.
......
CHIRA (GLANCE)
WHAT SHOULD I DO?
IT'S ALREADY LATE...
I WONDER IF SHIO-CHAN WILL STAY UP FOR ME.

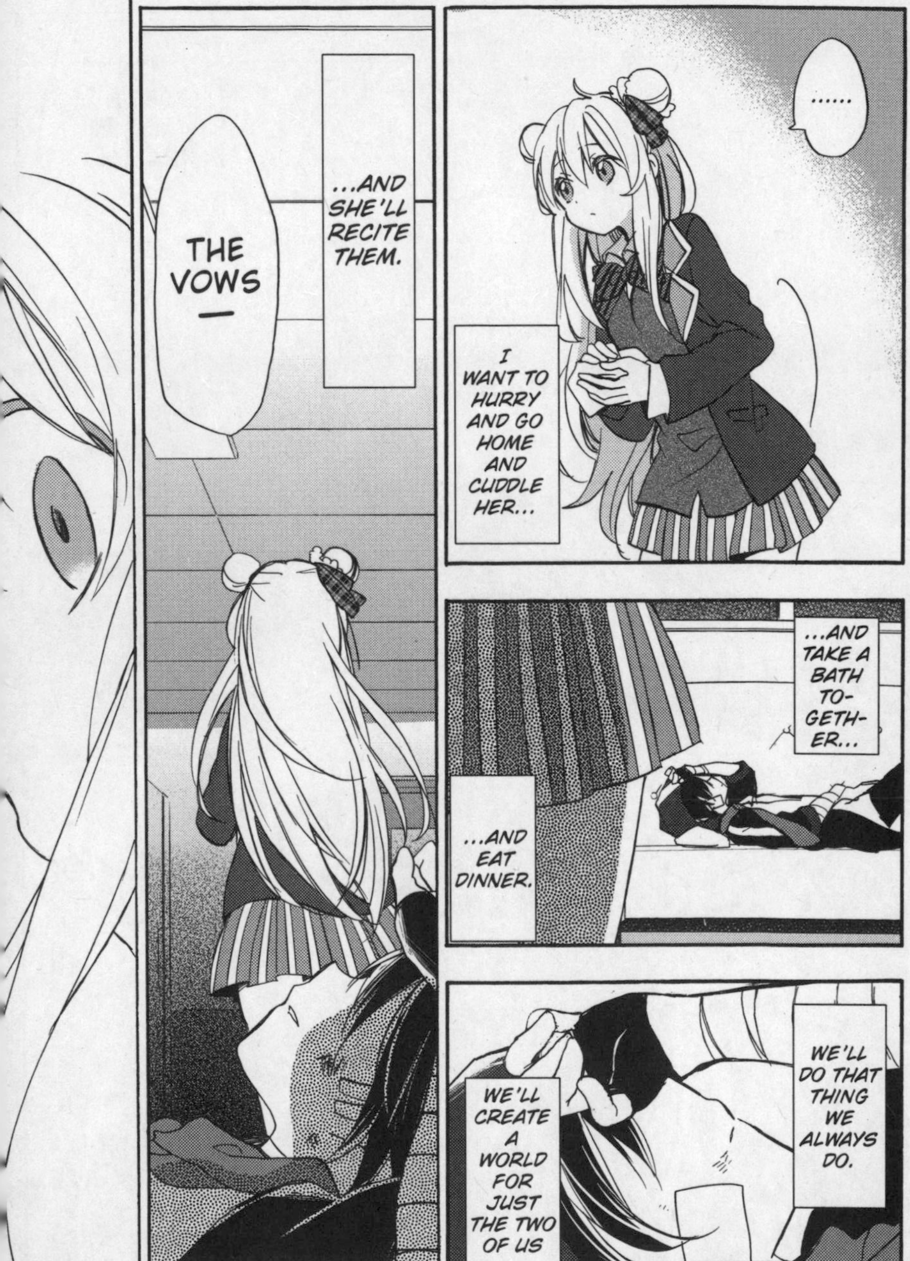
......
I WANT TO HURRY AND GO HOME AND CUDDLE HER...
...AND TAKE A BATH TO-GETH-ER...
...AND EAT DINNER.
WE'LL DO THAT THING WE ALWAYS DO.
WE'LL CREATE A WORLD FOR JUST THE TWO OF US...
...AND SHE'LL RECITE THEM.
THE VOWS—

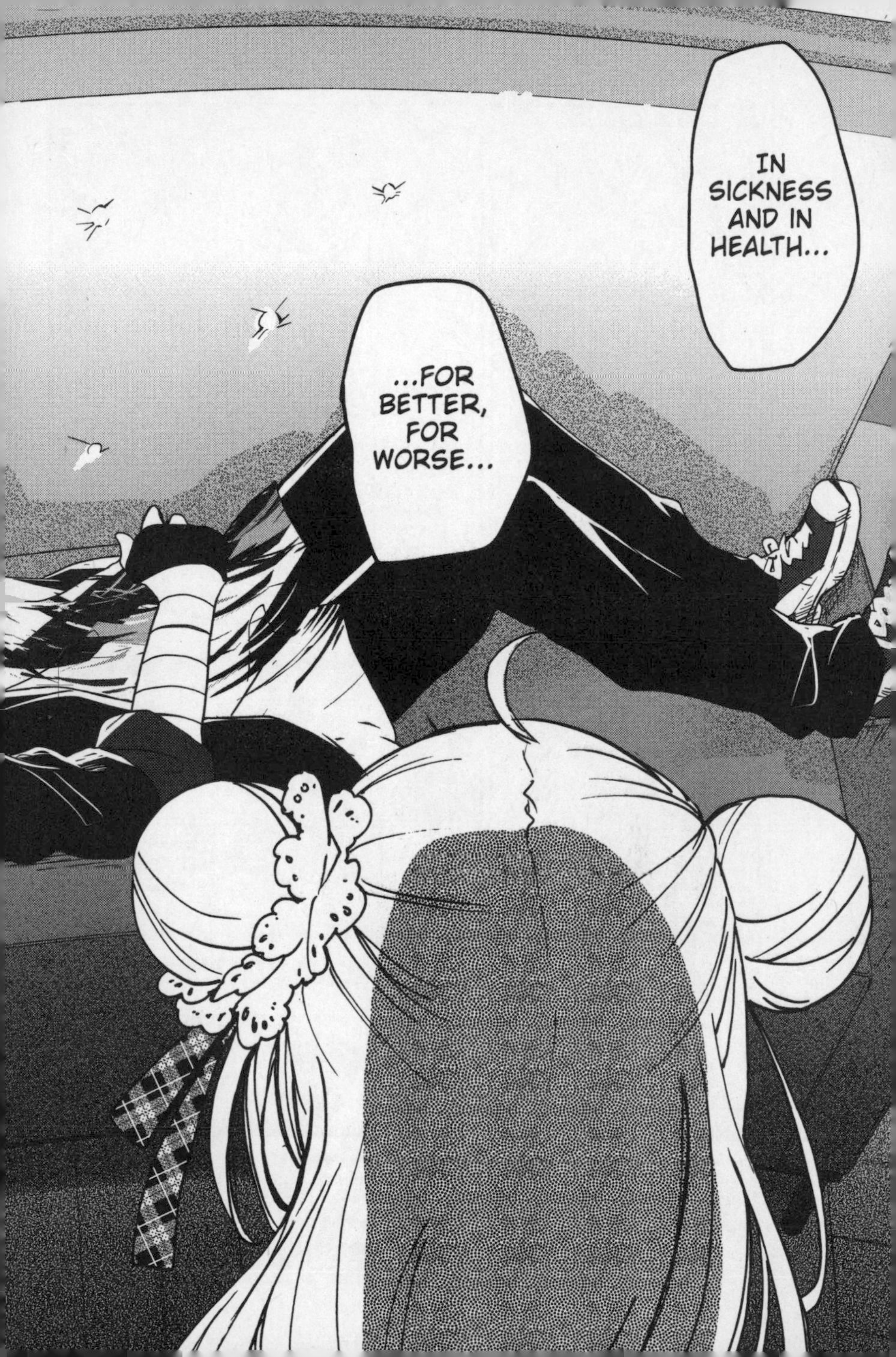
IN SICKNESS AND IN HEALTH...
...FOR BETTER, FOR WORSE...

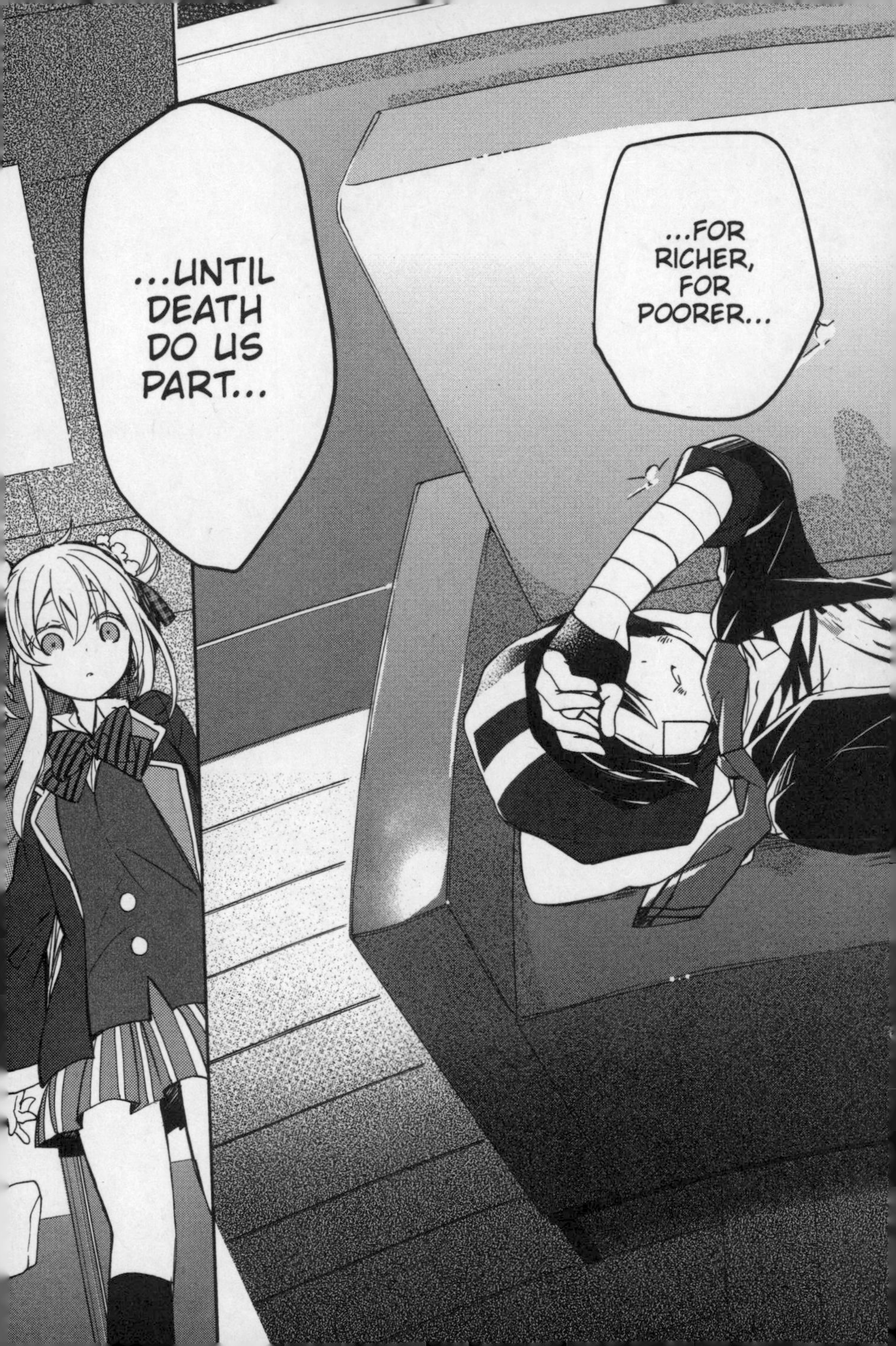
...FOR RICHER, FOR POORER...
...UNTIL DEATH DO US PART...

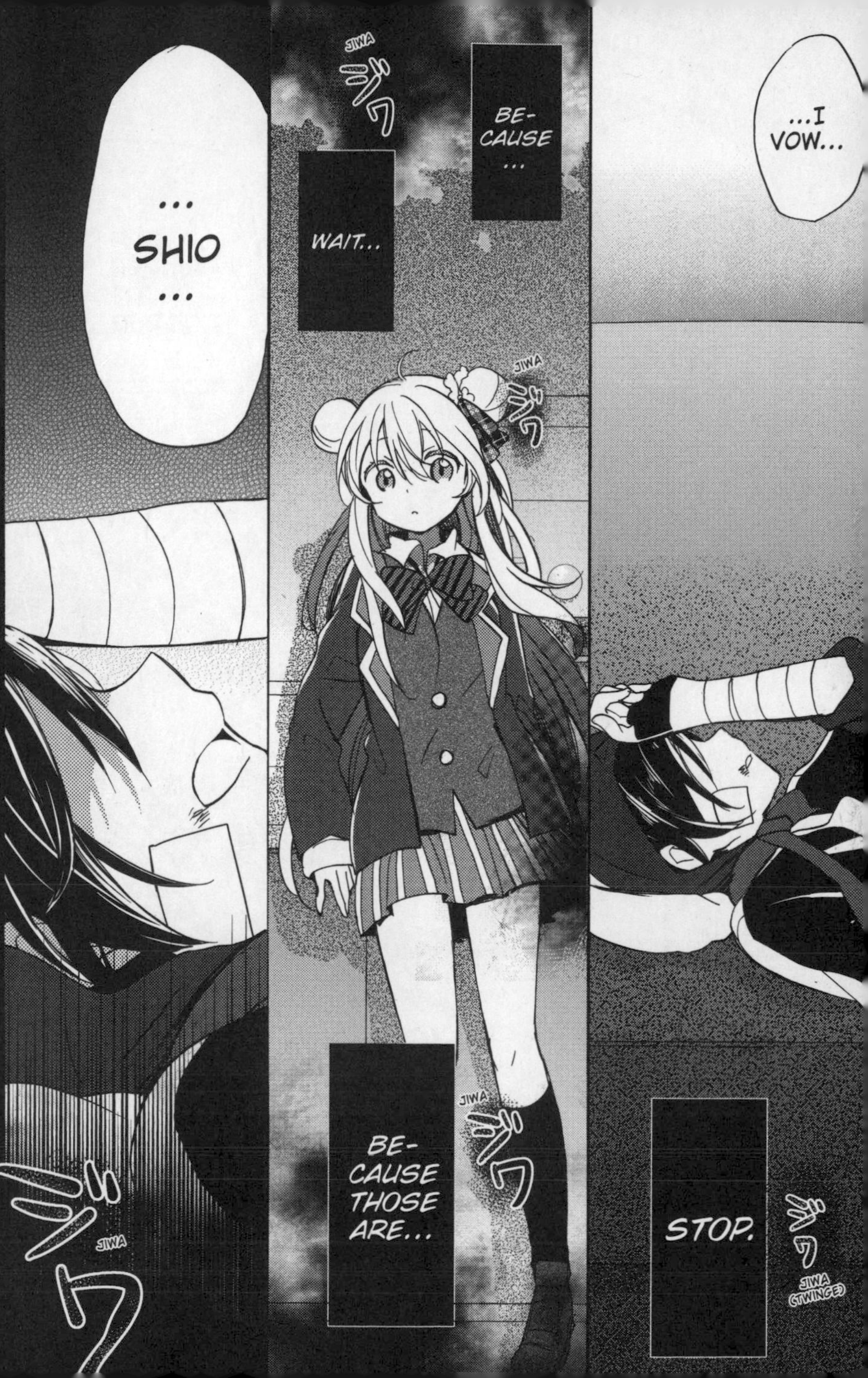
...I VOW...
STOP.
ジワ
JIWA (TWINGE)
BE-CAUSE...
JIWA
ジワ
WAIT...
JIWA
ジワ
BE-CAUSE THOSE ARE...
JIWA
ジワ
... SHIO ...
ジワ
JIWA

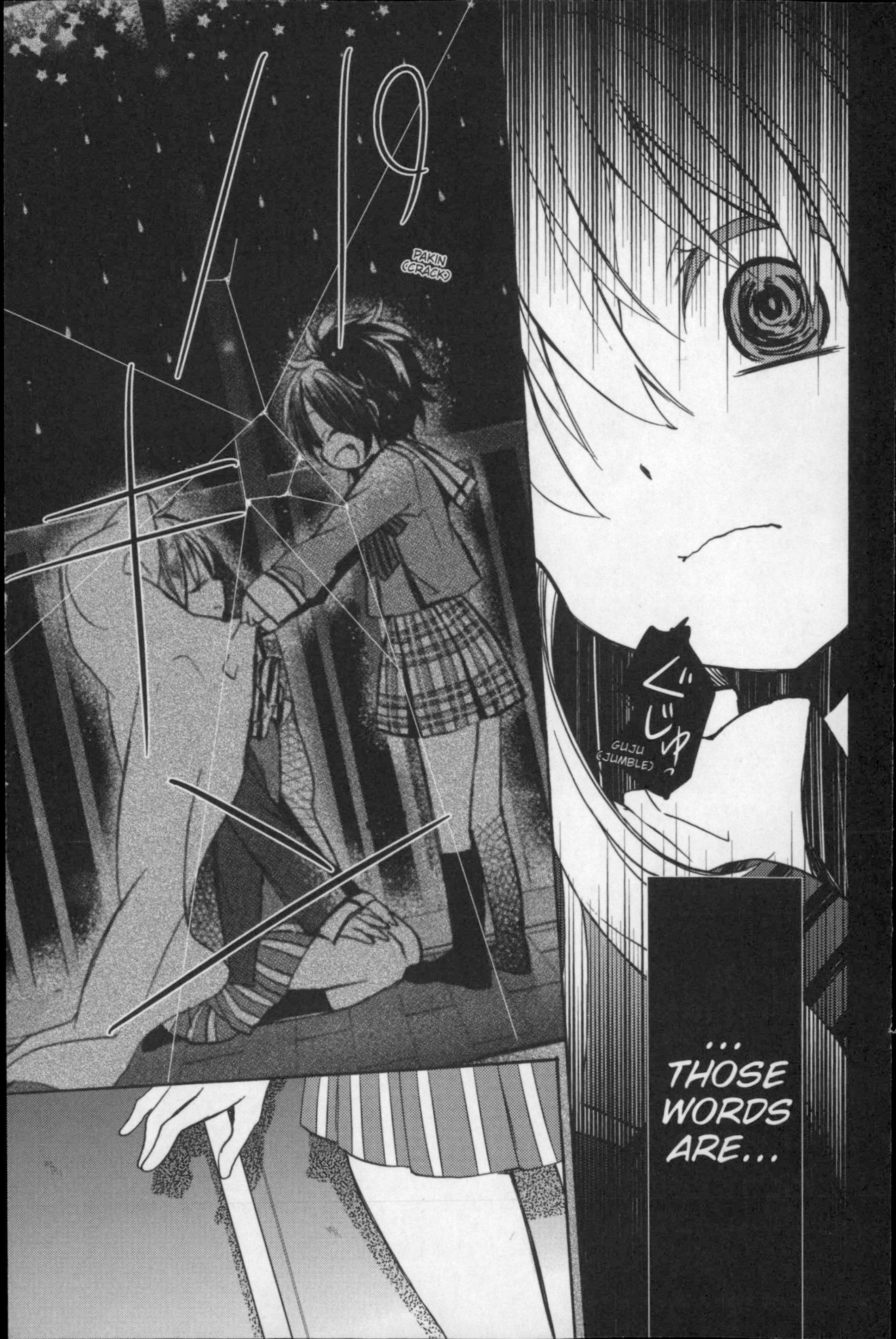
ぐじゅっ
GUJU (JUMBLE)
... THOSE WORDS ARE...
PAKIN (CRACK)

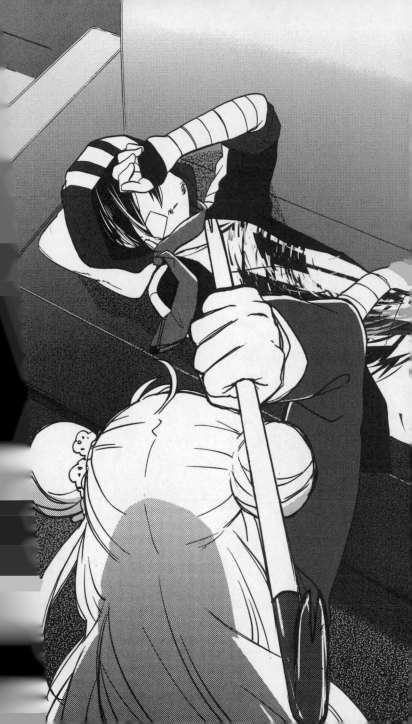

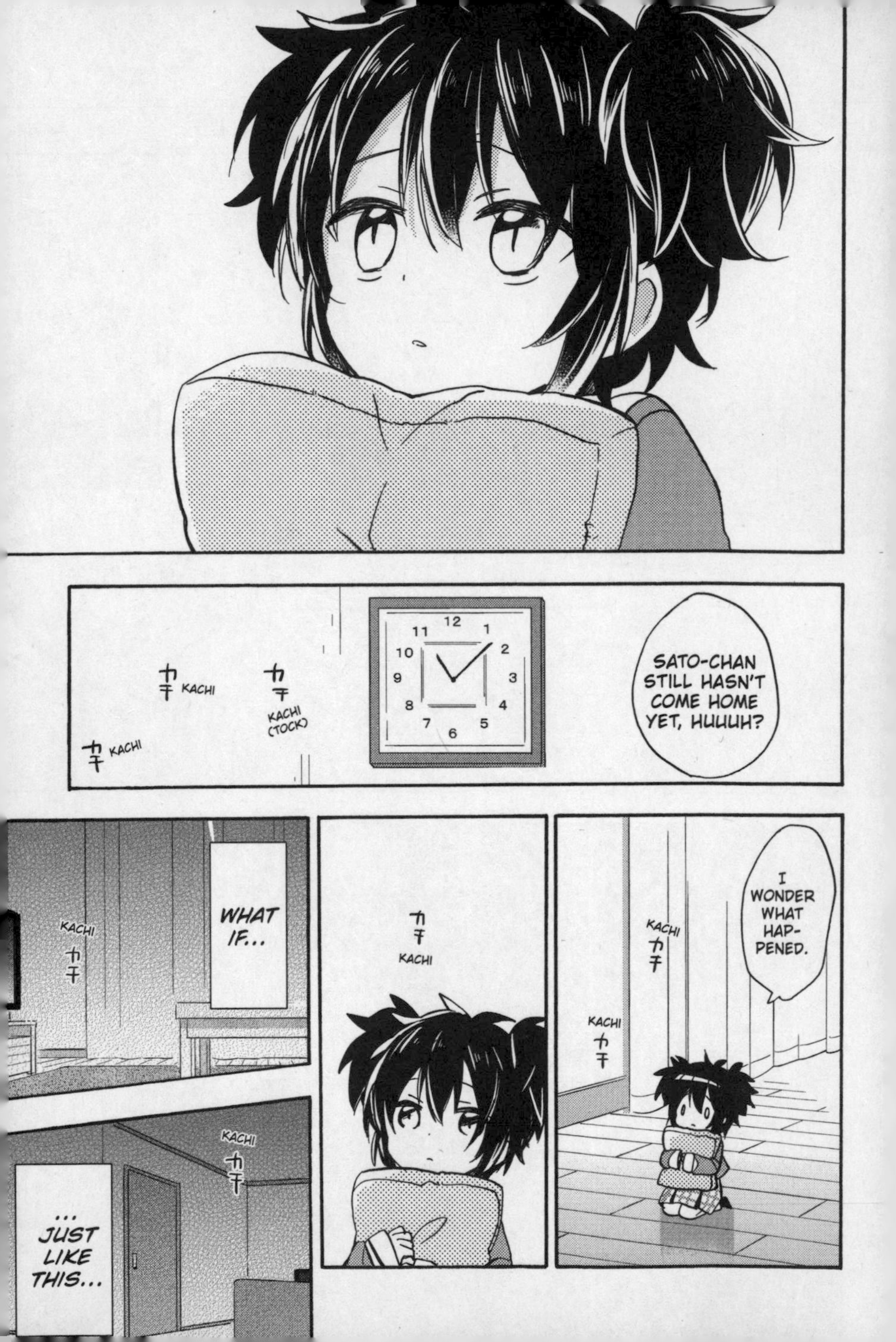
SATO-CHAN STILL HASN'T COME HOME YET, HUUUH?
KACHI (TOCK)
KACHI
KACHI
I WONDER WHAT HAP-PENED.
KACHI
KACHI
KACHI
WHAT IF...
KACHI
KACHI
...JUST LIKE THIS...

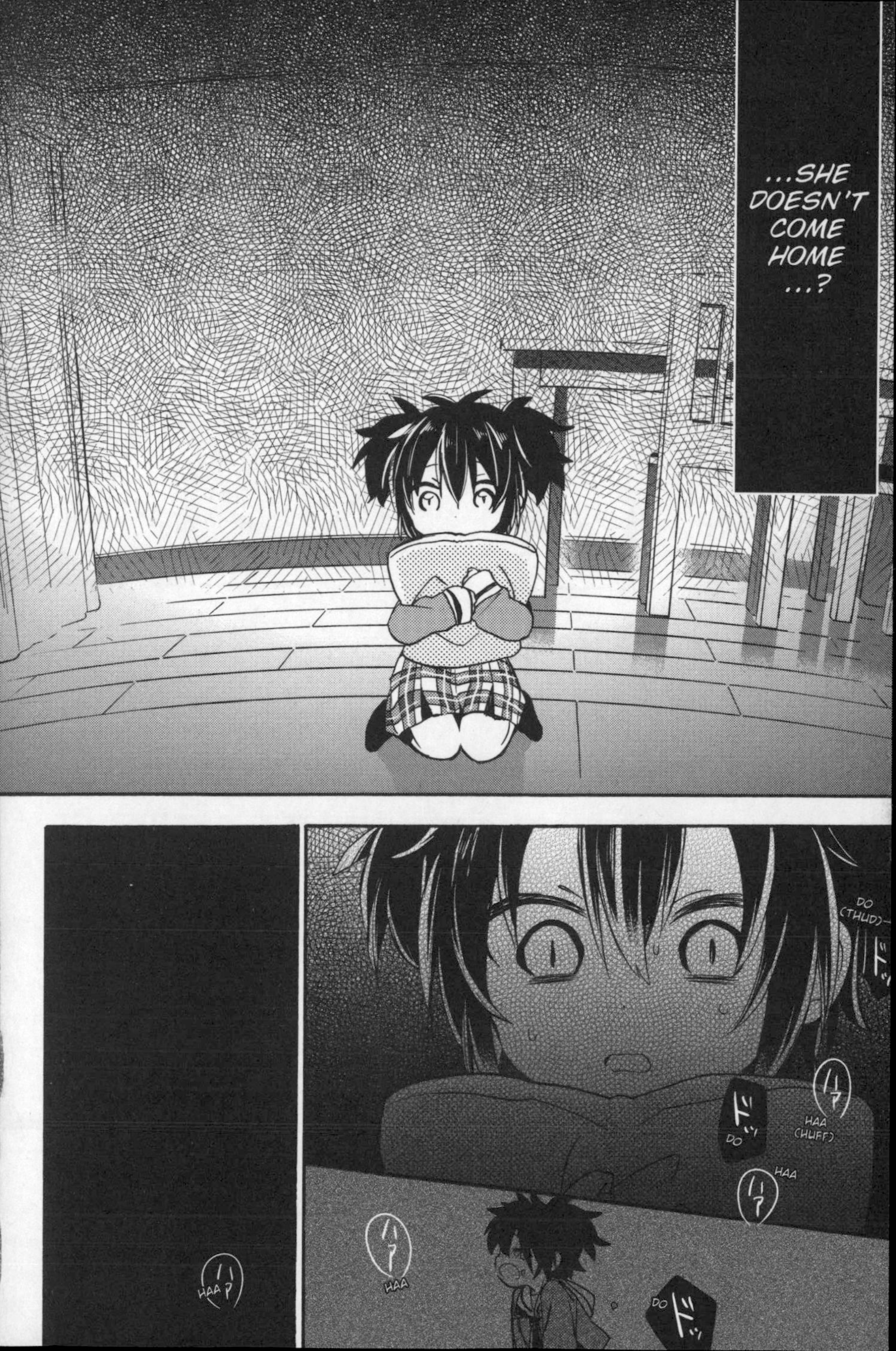
...SHE DOESN'T COME HOME ...?
DO (THUD)— ドッ
ハァ HAA (HUFF)
ドッ DO
ハァ HAA
ハァ HAA
ドッ DO
ハァ HAA

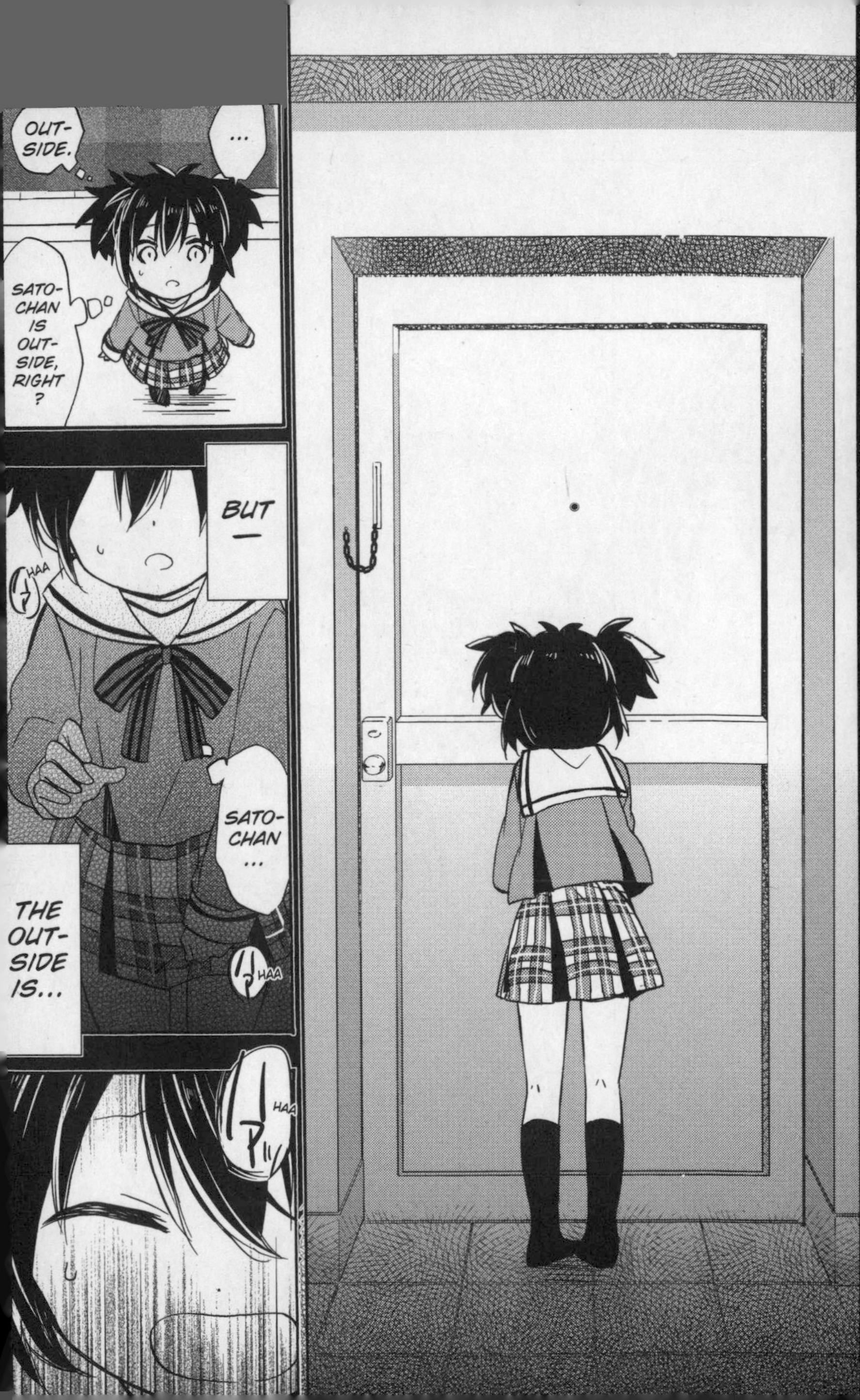
...
OUT-SIDE.
SATO-CHAN IS OUT-SIDE, RIGHT?
BUT —
HAA
SATO-CHAN...
HAA
THE OUT-SIDE IS...
HAA

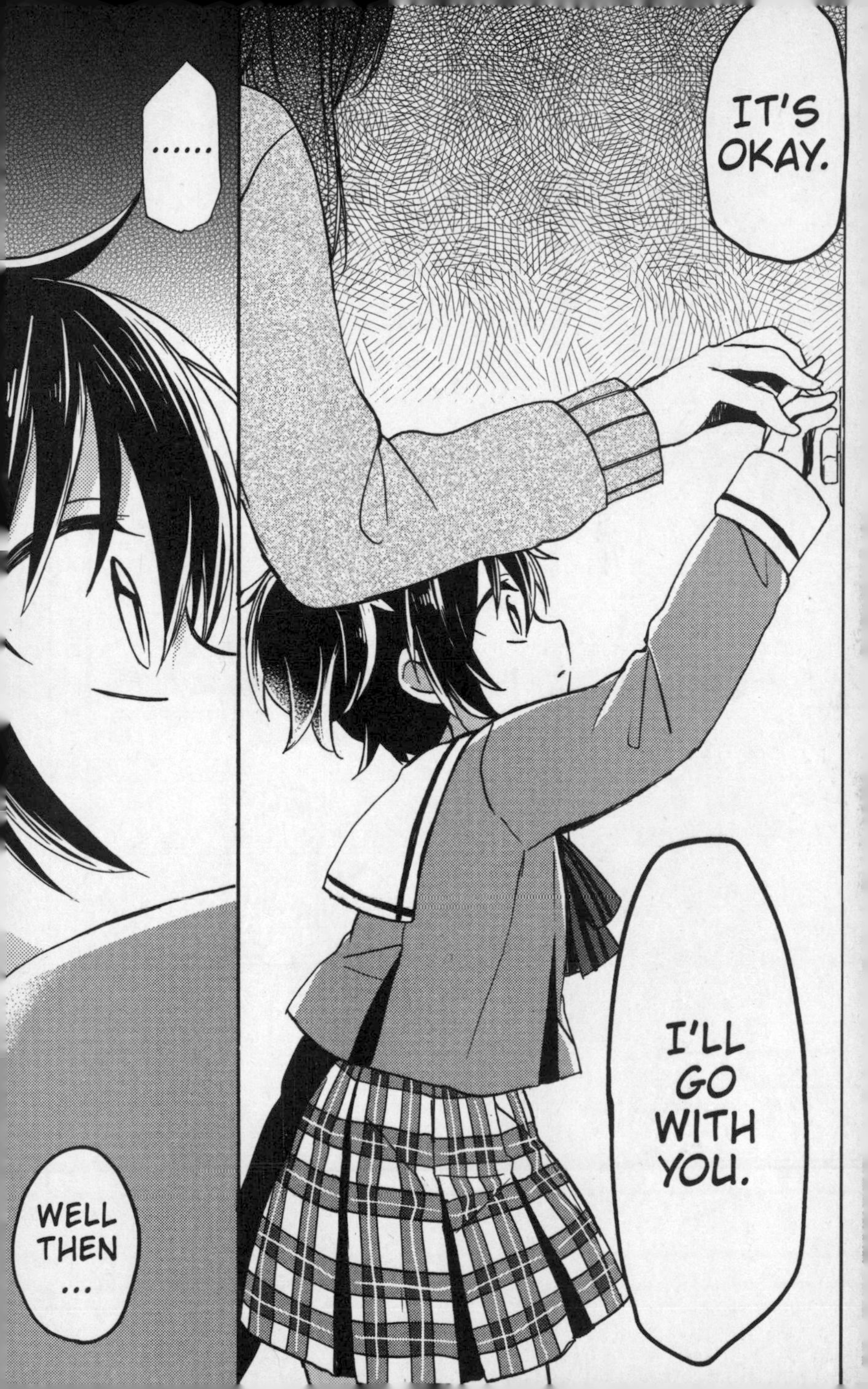
IT'S OKAY.
I'LL GO WITH YOU.
......
WELL THEN ...

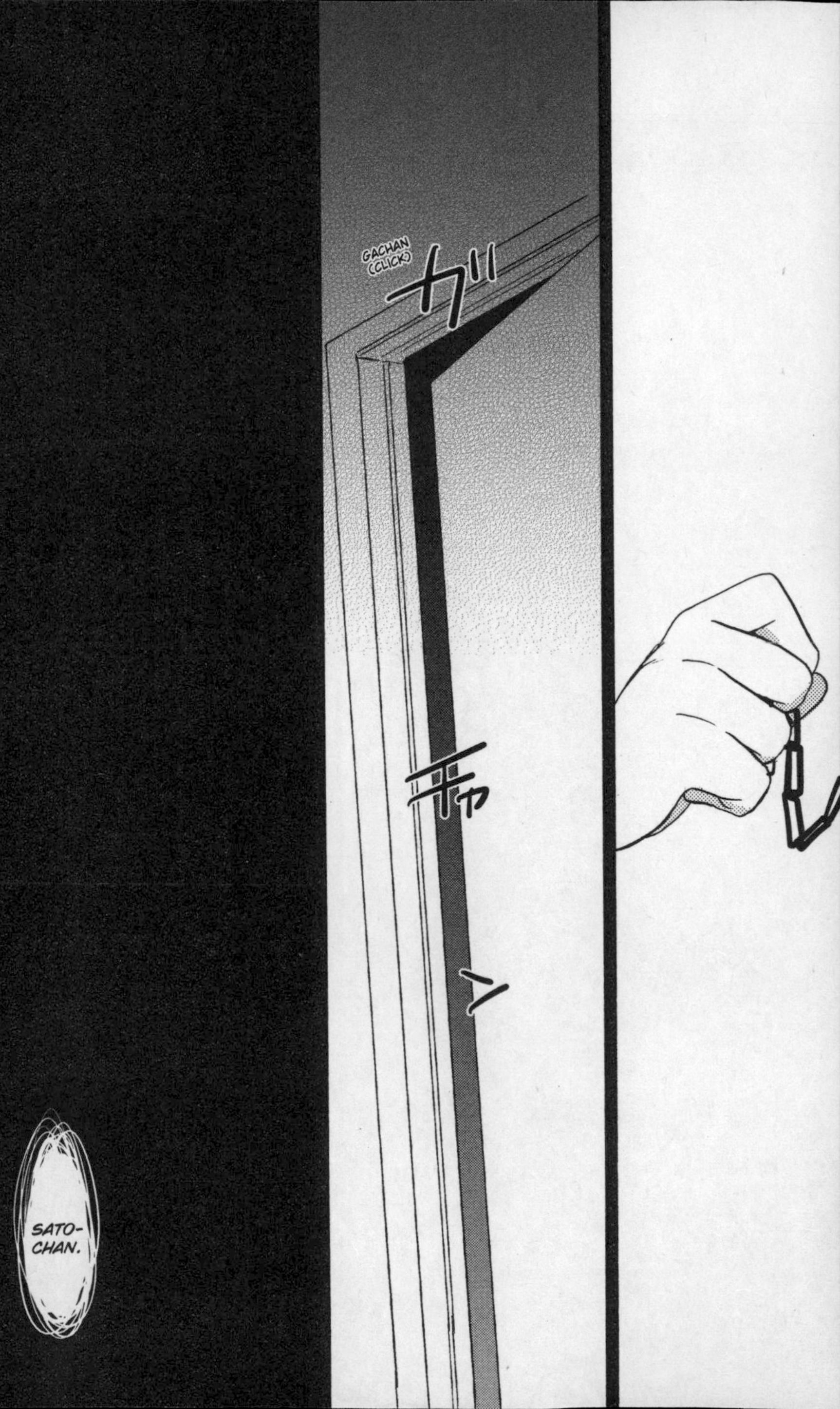
GACHAN (CLICK)
SATO-CHAN.

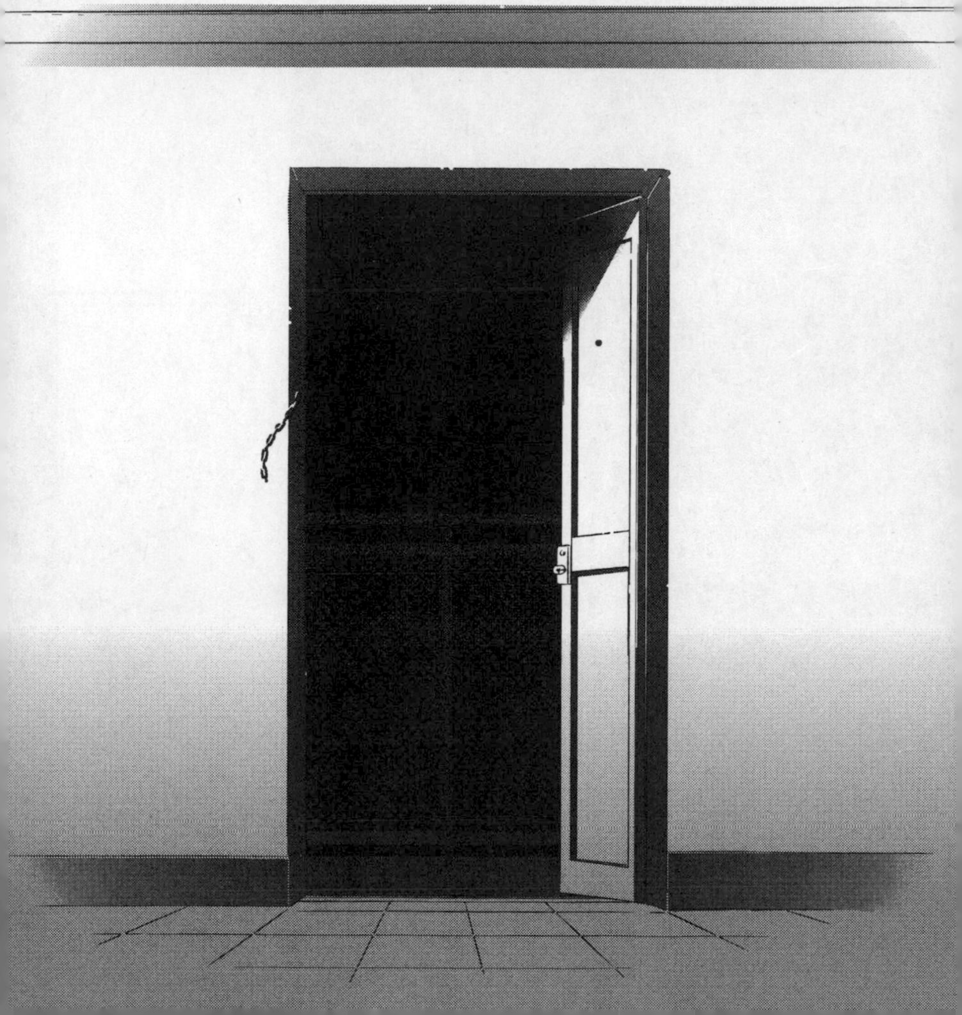

Happy
Sugar
Life

BONUS MANGA

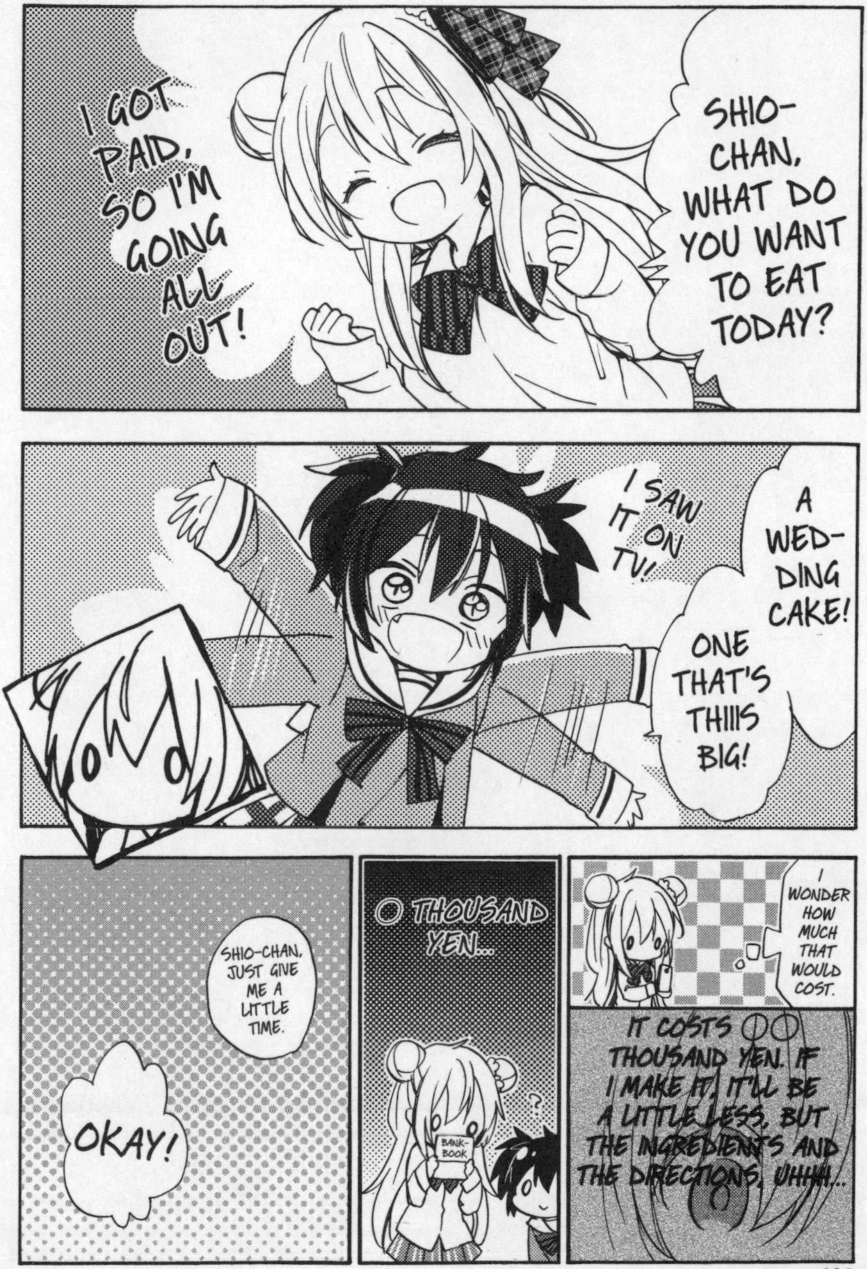
SHIO-CHAN, WHAT DO YOU WANT TO EAT TODAY?
I GOT PAID, SO I'M GOING ALL OUT!
A WED-DING CAKE!
I SAW IT ON TV!
ONE THAT'S THIIIS BIG!
I WONDER HOW MUCH THAT WOULD COST.
IT COSTS ○○ THOUSAND YEN. IF I MAKE IT, IT'LL BE A LITTLE LESS, BUT THE INGREDIENTS AND THE DIRECTIONS, UHHH...
○ THOUSAND YEN...
BANK-BOOK
?
SHIO-CHAN, JUST GIVE ME A LITTLE TIME.
OKAY!

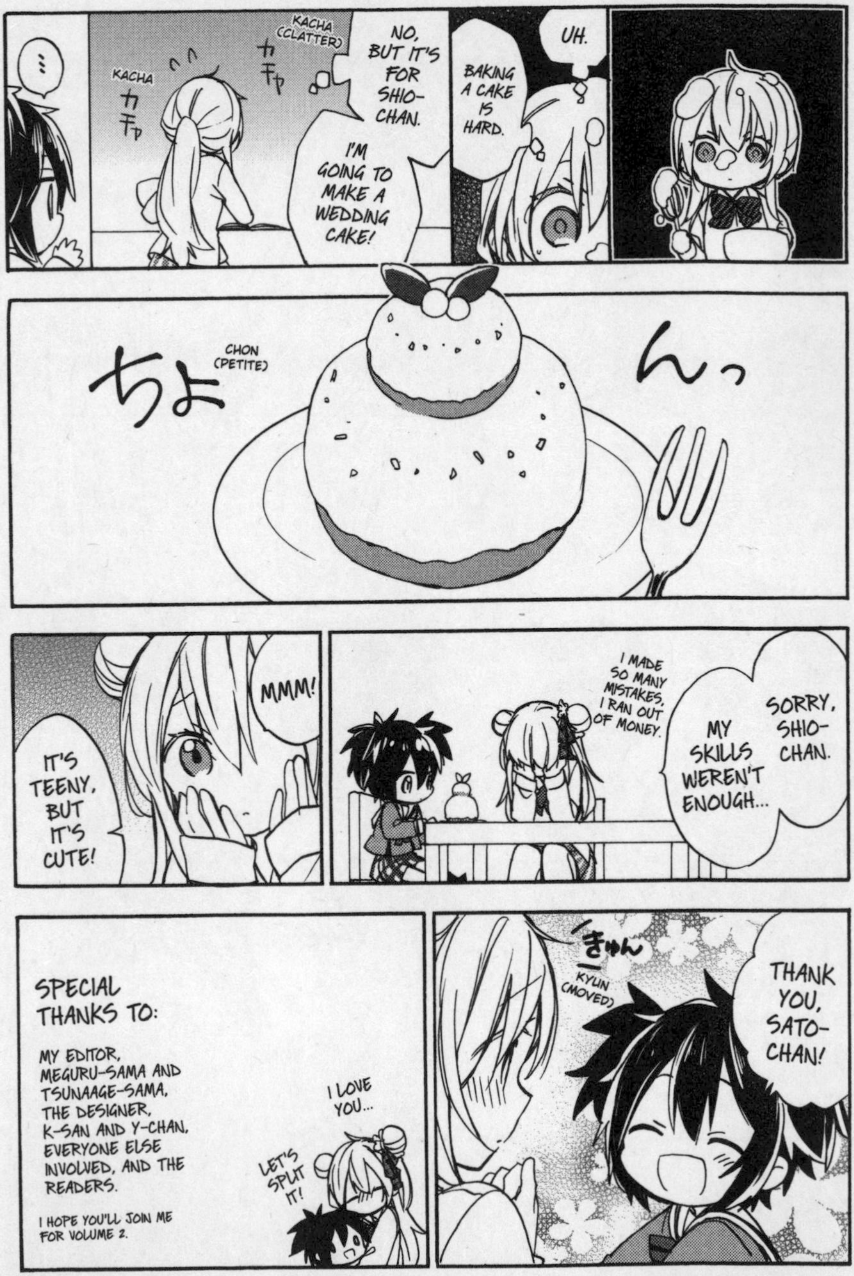
UH.
BAKING A CAKE IS HARD.
NO, BUT IT'S FOR SHIO-CHAN.
I'M GOING TO MAKE A WEDDING CAKE!
カチャ
KACHA (CLATTER)
カチャ
KACHA
...
ちょんっ
CHON (PETITE)
SORRY, SHIO-CHAN.
MY SKILLS WEREN'T ENOUGH...
I MADE SO MANY MISTAKES, I RAN OUT OF MONEY.
MMM!
IT'S TEENY, BUT IT'S CUTE!
THANK YOU, SATO-CHAN!
きゅん
KYUN (MOVED)
SPECIAL THANKS TO:
MY EDITOR, MEGURU-SAMA AND TSUNAAGE-SAMA, THE DESIGNER, K-SAN AND Y-CHAN, EVERYONE ELSE INVOLVED, AND THE READERS.
I HOPE YOU'LL JOIN ME FOR VOLUME 2.
I LOVE YOU...
LET'S SPLIT IT!

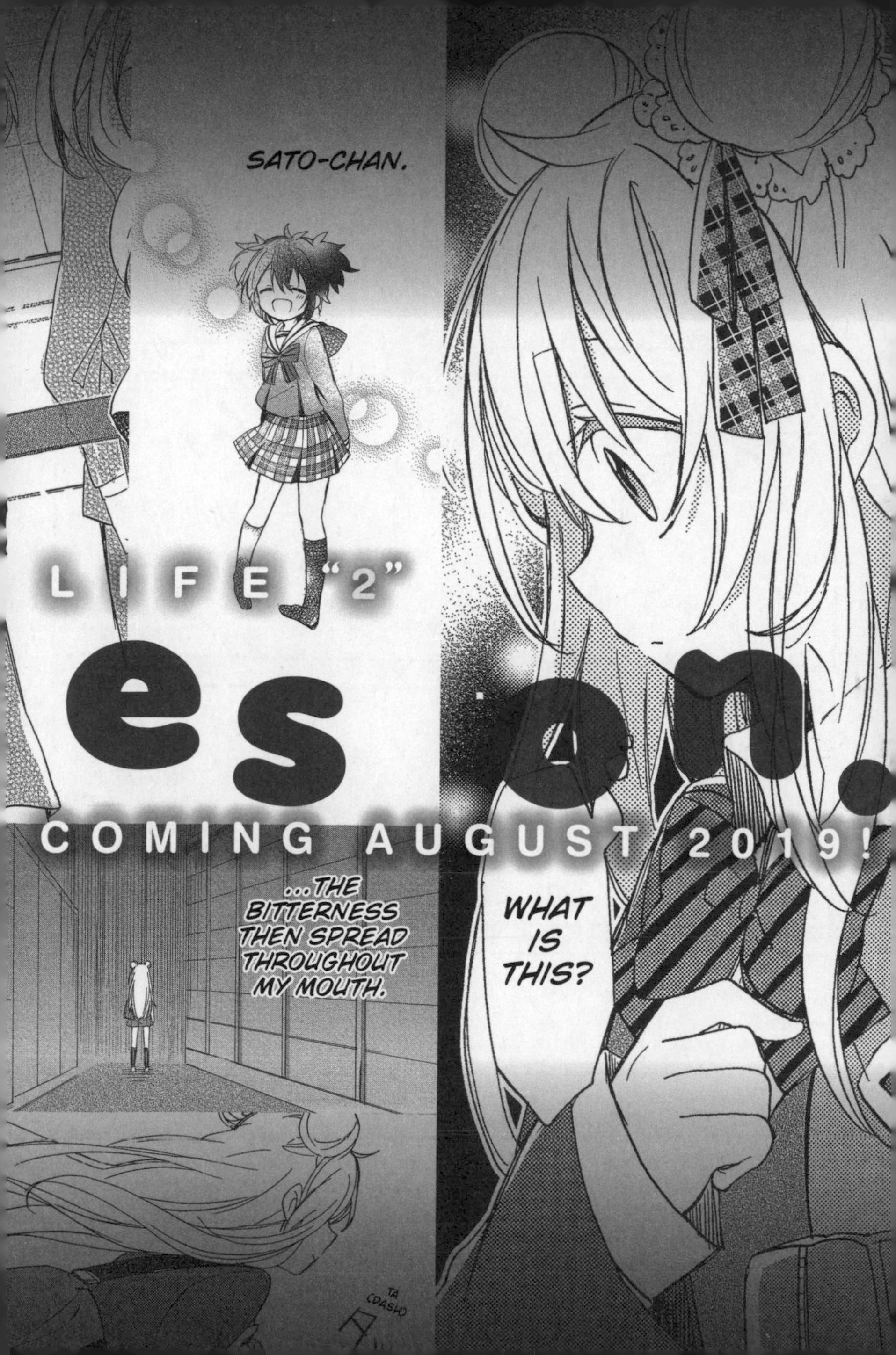
LIFE "2"
es on.
COMING AUGUST 2019!
WHAT IS THIS?
SATO-CHAN.
...THE BITTERNESS THEN SPREAD THROUGHOUT MY MOUTH.
TA (DASH)

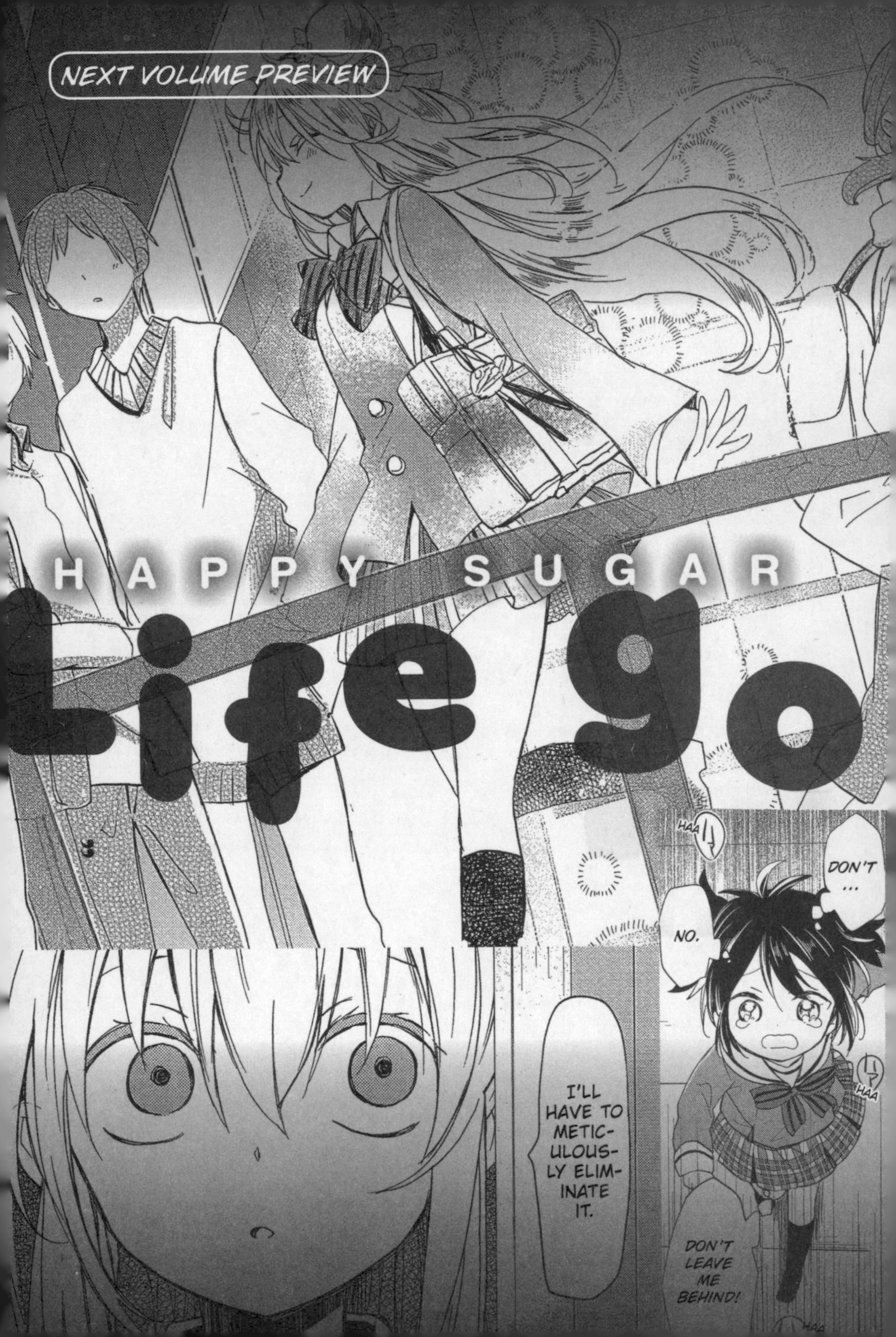
NEXT VOLUME PREVIEW
HAPPY SUGAR
Life go
HAA
DON'T ...
NO.
HAA
DON'T LEAVE ME BEHIND!
I'LL HAVE TO METIC-ULOUS-LY ELIM-INATE IT.

TRANSLATION NOTES

Common Honorifics

no honorific: Indicates familiarity or closeness; if used without permission or reason, addressing someone in this manner would constitute an insult.

-san: The Japanese equivalent of Mr./Mrs./Miss. If a situation calls for politeness, this is the fail-safe honorific.

-sama: Conveys great respect; may also indicate that the social status of the speaker is lower than that of the addressee.

-kun: Used most often when referring to boys, this indicates affection or familiarity. Occasionally used by older men among their peers, but it may also be used by anyone referring to a person of lower standing.

-chan: An affectionate honorific indicating familiarity used mostly in reference to girls; also used in reference to cute persons or animals of either gender.

-senpai: A suffix used to address upperclassmen or more experienced coworkers.

-sensei: A respectful term for teachers, artists, or high-level professionals.

Page 6
Satou is a Japanese girls' name and also the word for "sugar."

Shio is a Japanese girls' name and also the word for "salt."

Page 9
Fifty-four kilos, or kilograms, is the equivalent of about one hundred and nineteen pounds.

Page 10
In Japanese maid cafés, employees customarily refer to male customers as *goshujinsama*, meaning "master." This is why later, on page 89, after Shouko calls a customer "sir" instead, he gets irritated that she has not addressed him as "master."

Page 13
Shio calls Satou **"Sato-chan,"** a shortened version of her name meant as more of a nickname or affectionate way of referring to her.

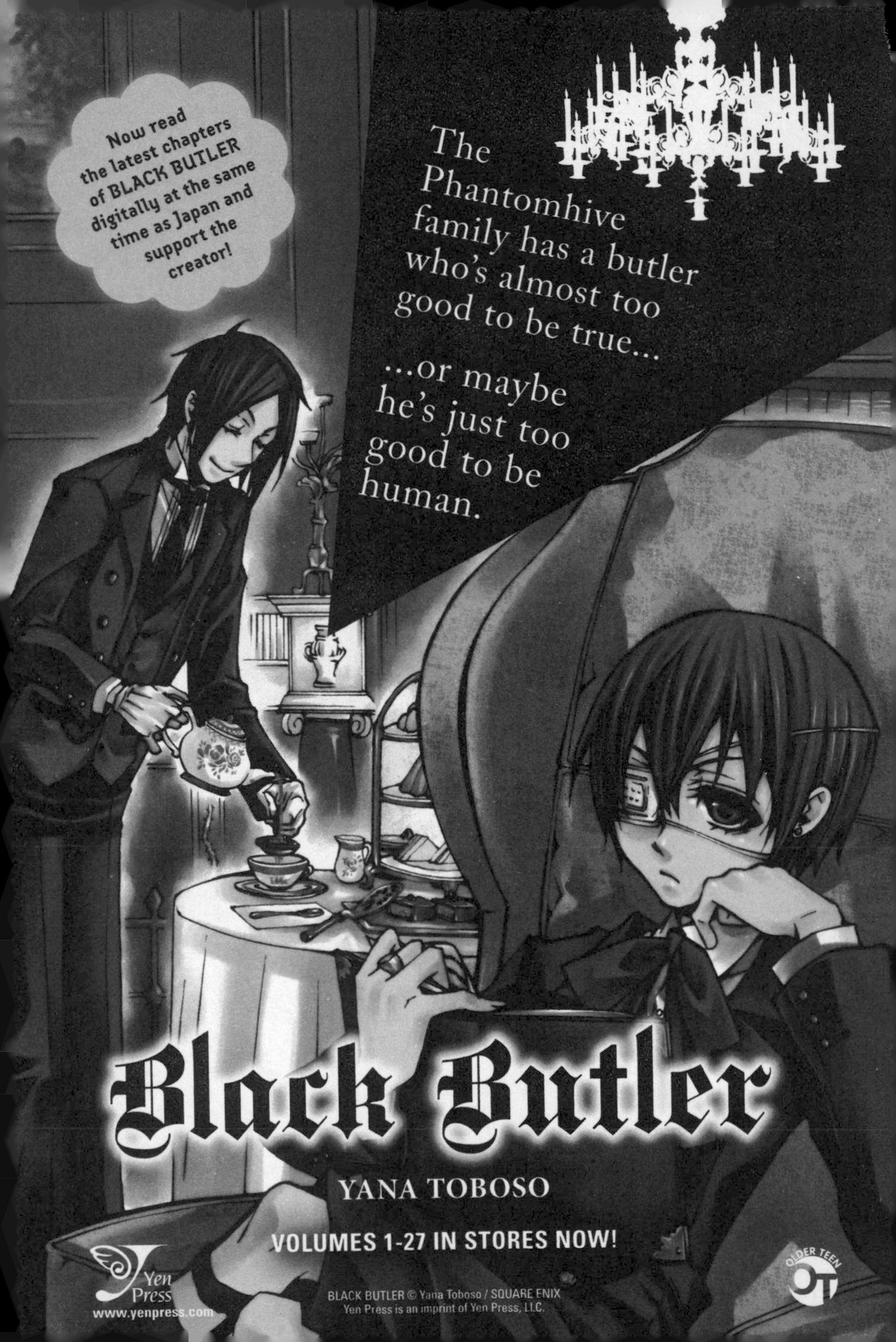

Now read the latest chapters of BLACK BUTLER digitally at the same time as Japan and support the creator!
The Phantomhive family has a butler who's almost too good to be true...
...or maybe he's just too good to be human.
Black Butler
YANA TOBOSO
VOLUMES 1-27 IN STORES NOW!
Yen Press
www.yenpress.com
BLACK BUTLER © Yana Toboso / SQUARE ENIX
Yen Press is an imprint of Yen Press, LLC.
OLDER TEEN
OT

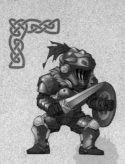

HE DOES NOT LET ANYONE ROLL THE DICE.

A young Priestess joins her first adventuring party, but blind to the dangers, they almost immediately find themselves in trouble. It's Goblin Slayer who comes to their rescue—a man who has dedicated his life to the extermination of all goblins by any means necessary. A dangerous, dirty, and thankless job, but he does it better than anyone. And when rumors of his feats begin to circulate, there's no telling who might come calling next...

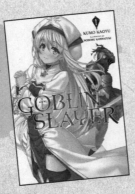

Light Novel V. 1-6 Available Now!

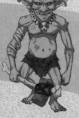

Check out the simul-pub manga chapters every month!

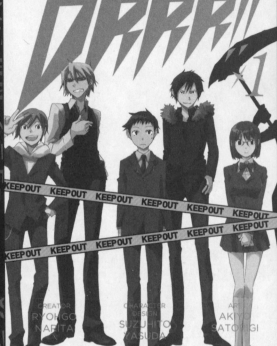

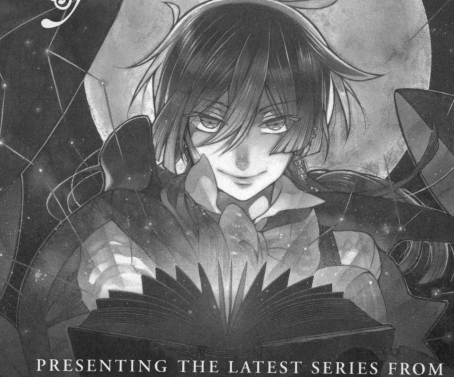
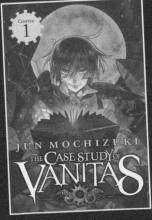

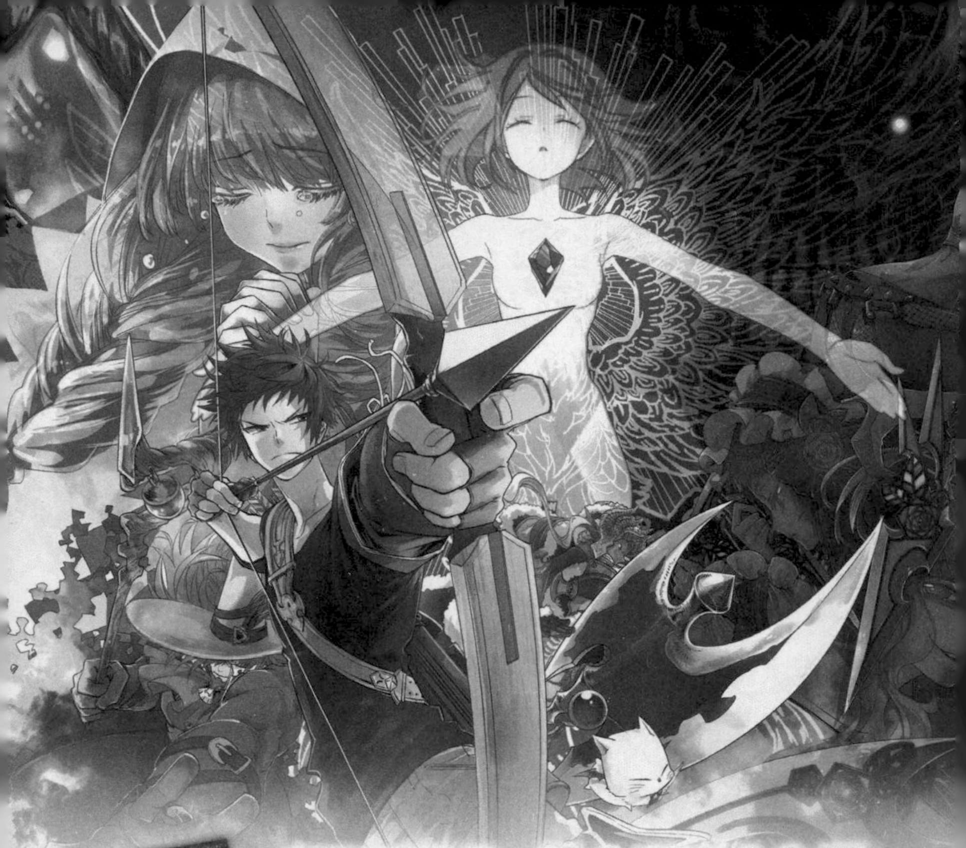

FINAL FANTASY®

ファイナルファンタジー ロスト・ストレンジャー

LOST STRANGER

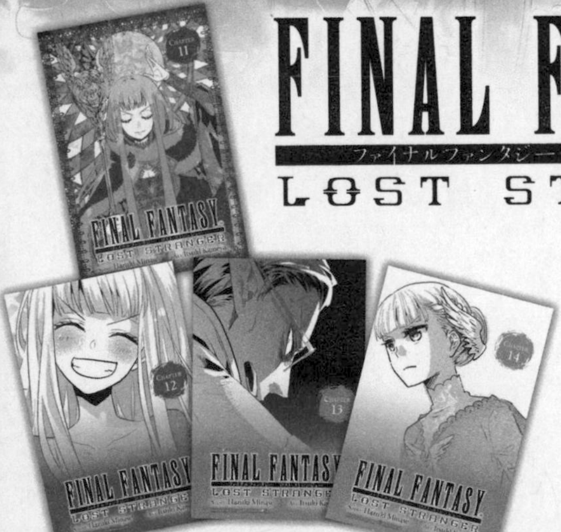

Keep up with the latest chapters in the simul-pub version! Available now worldwide wherever e-books are sold!

For more information, visit www.yenpress.com

Yen Press

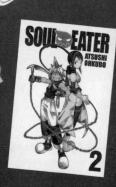

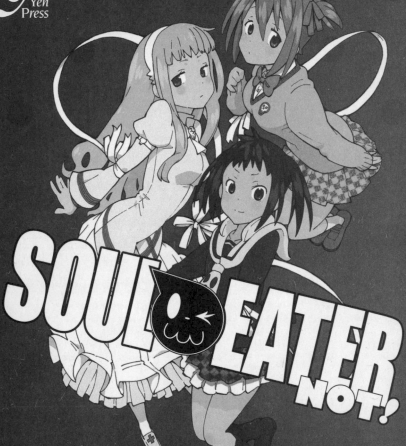
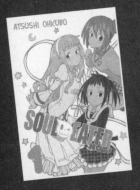

Happy Sugar Life 1

Tomiyaki Kagisora

Translation: **JAN MITSUKO CASH**

Lettering: **NICOLE DOCHYCH**

HAPPY SUGAR LIFE vol. 1 ©2015 Tomiyaki Kagisora / SQUARE ENIX CO., LTD.
First published in Japan in 2015 by SQUARE ENIX CO., LTD. English translation rights arranged with SQUARE ENIX CO., LTD. and Yen Press, LLC through Tuttle-Mori Agency, Inc.

English translation ©2019 by SQUARE ENIX CO., LTD.

Yen Press
1290 Avenue of the Americas
New York, NY 10104

Visit us at yenpress.com
facebook.com/yenpress
twitter.com/yenpress
yenpress.tumblr.com
instagram.com/yenpress

First Yen Press Edition: May 2019

Yen Press is an imprint of Yen Press, LLC.
The Yen Press name and logo are trademarks of Yen Press, LLC.

The publisher is not responsible for websites (or their content) that are not owned by the publisher.

Library of Congress Control Number: 2019932474

ISBN: 978-1-9753-0330-3 (paperback)

10 9 8 7 6 5 4

WOR

Printed in the United States of America

Happy Sugar Life

Tomiyaki Kagisora

Lifelog ★

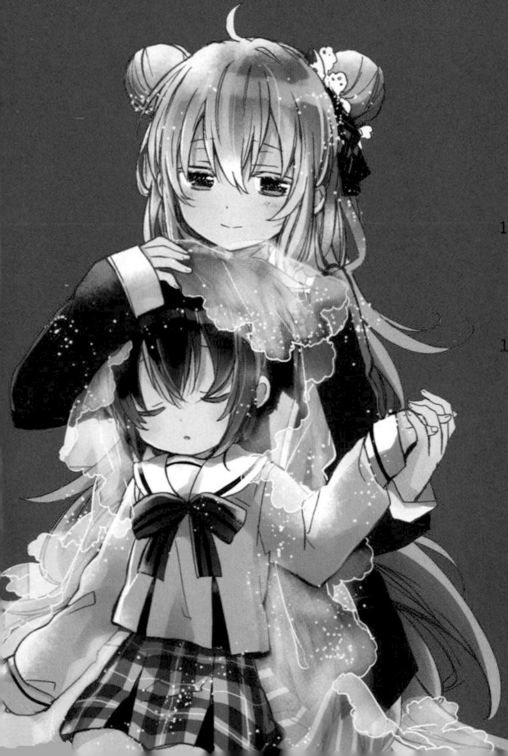

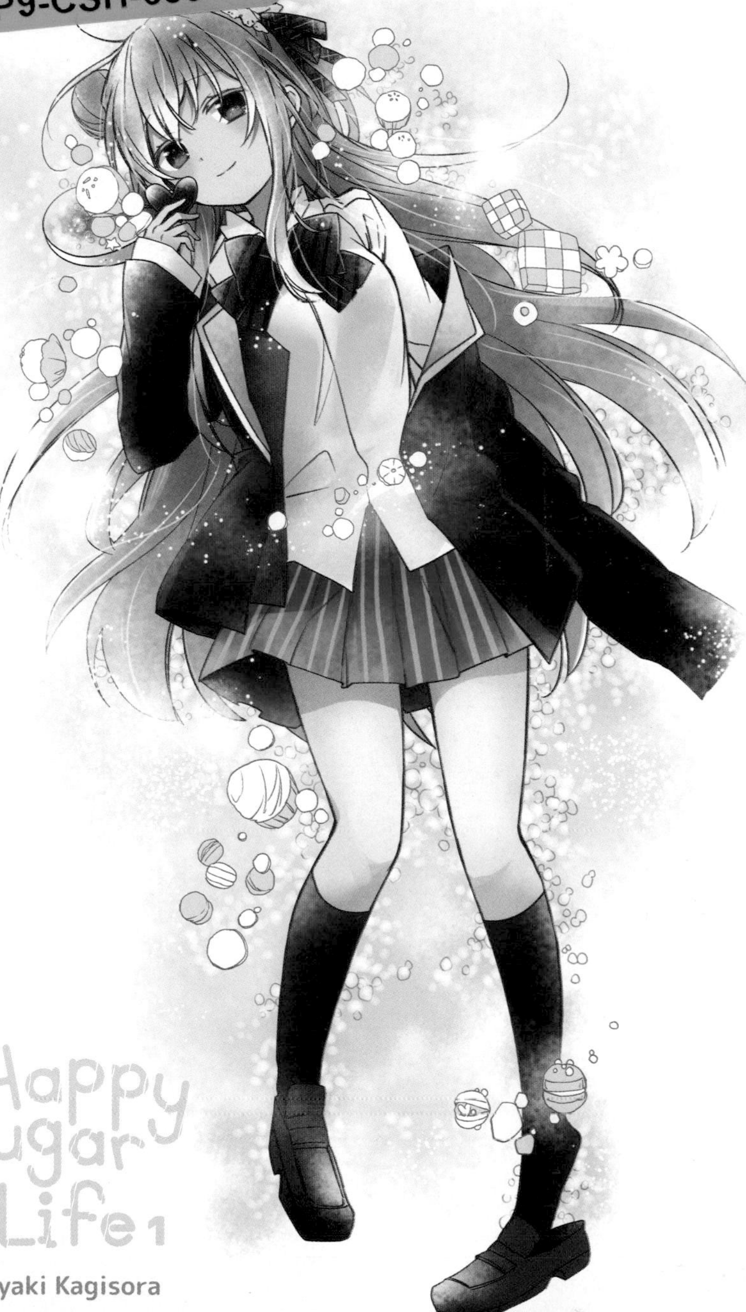

Happy Sugar Life 1

Tomiyaki Kagisora